The Pocket Lawyer for Comic Book Creators

The *Pocket Lawyer* series serves as a legal toolkit for independent producers and artists in creative industries.

The Pocket Lawyer for Comic Book Creators is designed to help emerging artists and veteran professionals in the comic book industry build a solid foundation of business and legal practices for their comic book projects.

Readers will learn to:

- Protect their copyrights and IP,
- Negotiate publishing deals,
- Hire artists so everyone wins,
- Learn the ins and outs of key contracts,
- Understand the risks of AI in comic book creation,
- Explore innovative new distribution methods, and
- Develop strategies they need to thrive in today's ever-changing, uncertain world of indie comics.

Thomas A. Crowell, Esq., is a practicing attorney, law professor, and comic book writer specializing in entertainment law and intellectual property rights issues. He is the editor of the *Pocket Lawyer* series and the author of *The Pocket Lawyer for Filmmakers* (Focal Press, 3rd ed. 2022). For more information, see www.ThomasCrowell.com

The Pocket Lawyer for Comic Book Creators

A Legal Toolkit for Comic Book Artists and Writers

Second Edition

Thomas A. Crowell, Esq.

Illustrated by Alan Norico

CRC Press
Taylor & Francis Group
Boca Raton London New York

CRC Press is an imprint of the
Taylor & Francis Group, an **informa** business

Designed cover image: Jonathan Pennell

Second edition published 2026
by CRC Press
2385 NW Executive Center Drive, Suite 320, Boca Raton FL 33431

and by CRC Press
4 Park Square, Milton Park, Abingdon, Oxon, OX14 4RN

CRC Press is an imprint of Taylor & Francis Group, LLC

First edition published by Focal Press 2015

Library of Congress Cataloging-in-Publication Data
Names: Crowell, Thomas A, author | Norico, Allan illustrator
Title: The pocket lawyer for comic book creators : a legal toolkit for comic book artists and writers / Thomas A Crowell, Esq. ; Illustrated by Alan Norico.
Other titles: Pocket lawyer for comic books
Description: Second Edition. | New York : CRC Press, 2025. | Includes bibliographical references and index.
Identifiers: LCCN 2025032625 (print) | LCCN 2025032626 (ebook) | ISBN 9781032802480 hardback | ISBN 9781032763446 paperback | ISBN 9781003496052 ebook
Subjects: LCSH: Comic books, strips, etc.—Law and legislation—United States
Classification: LCC KF2750 .C76 2025 (print) | LCC KF2750 (ebook) | DDC 343.07/87415—dc23/eng/20250728
LC record available at https://lccn.loc.gov/2025032625
LC ebook record available at https://lccn.loc.gov/2025032626

ISBN: 9781032802480 (hbk)
ISBN: 9781032763446 (pbk)
ISBN: 9781003496052 (ebk)

DOI: 10.1201/9781003496052

Typeset in Bembo
by codeMantra

To my wife, Natali; my sons, Connor and Xander;
my parents, Caleb and Sheila;
and to frustrated comic book creators everywhere.

Contents

DISCLAIMER

Welcome to the thrilling world of legal literature! Authored by a lawyer, this book naturally kicks off with a disclaimer, because what's a law book without a little fine print? So, let's dive in. Firstly, let's address the elephant in the room: despite its sharp corners and undeniable bookish charm, this is indeed a book, not a lawyer. It won't stand up in court, and it certainly won't fit in a suit. If you're seeking legal advice, this stack of bound paper won't suffice. For that, you'll need a real, live attorney—one that talks back and probably charges by the hour.

Remember, laws are as fickle as fashion; what's in today might be out tomorrow. This book might not keep up with the latest legal trends, and it's definitely not accessorized with all the exceptions and footnotes that could apply to your unique situation.

So, while this book contains many words, and some of them are even about laws; there are no promises that these words are accurate, applicable, or able to leap tall buildings in a single bound. Always consult your personal lawyer, who is equipped with the latest legal GPS to navigate the ever-changing landscape of the law. Enjoy the read, and may your legal adventures be many (but not too many)!

Any names I've made up for this book, whether character names or otherwise, are purely fictitious, and any similarity to actual people, living or dead, or actual companies is purely coincidental. I have also used some real trademarked and copyrighted characters, properties, and business names to illustrate certain legal issues. The use of these names and marks does not imply any approval, sponsorship, endorsement by, or affiliation with the owners of these trademarks and copyrights. All views expressed are mine and do not necessarily reflect those of either the publisher or anyone I consulted while writing this book.

I have also included the URLs of websites that you may find useful. They were current to the best of my knowledge at the time of writing but may no longer be current or may refer to different material than that which I have discussed. Furthermore, in the interest of space, I have not gone into detail about all of the contract clauses that may impact your particular situation. In fact, were I to sit down with you as your attorney, there would be numerous places in virtually every contract I've included that warrant further thought on your part as to the potential liability to which you could be exposed.

The point is this: this book may only get you part of the way. I am not providing you with a complete interpretation of the key points of every agreement.

Hopefully, however, I am providing you with the tools you need to be able to read and understand many of the key issues for yourself. And beyond that—you may want to seek the advice of an attorney before entering into any agreement, whether signed in your own hands or clicked through on a website.

And for those who prefer their disclaimers of a more standard flavor:

> **Nothing in this book is intended as legal advice or to substitute for the personalized advice of a lawyer. Only your lawyer can tell you which laws apply to your particular situation. Laws change all the time and may be subject to numerous exceptions that are not covered by this book. There are no guarantees as to the accuracy or applicability of the information presented herein.**

Special Thanks

This book would not have been possible without the gracious participation of so many people. In particular, I would like to thank the editorial staff at Focal Press for once again placing their trust in me and recognizing the need for comic book creators to have their own "The Pocket Lawyer for …" title.

Because this is a new edition, I will start by thanking the crew that helped with the first edition:

My editor, David Bevans, deserves singling out for his ability to be both responsive and analytical without being a micromanager … a truly welcome combination in an editor. In the seven years since I first started writing for Focal Press, I have found it one of the most supportive and writer-friendly publishing companies I've ever worked with.

Allan Norico, this book's most amazing illustrator, has put so much of his heart, soul, and breathtaking talent into this project. It is such a joy to work with an artist as gifted as he is in creating the illustrations and characters that appear herein.

Matthew Tynan, Esq., my former law student and now a talented lawyer in his own right, was invaluable to this project. His help with both case law research and analysis, as well as contract preparation, allowed us to pack this book to the brim with legal resources.

A very special thanks to Sheafe B. Walker, Esq., for helping with the first edition of this book and for his participation over the years in lecturing with me at New York Comic Con.

Peter Tatara, Kimberly Mueller, Mike Armstrong, and the rest of the New York Comic Con team have done so much for the growth of the comic book industry. Their continued support, both in inviting me back time and again to lecture on legal issues for comic book creators, and in giving so freely of their collective wisdom to these pages, is unparalleled.

While so many industry insiders gave so freely of their time to this project, special mention must be made of the following: Alan Robert, whose IDW-published comic titles continue to break new ground in the horror genre; David Gallaher, whose experience with Marvel and DC gave me a unique perspective on writing for the "big boys"; comic book creator Charles Yoakum, who provided insight on the trials and tribulations of indie publishing; and Time Warp Comics and Games, for giving me a peek behind the retailer's perspective on comic book sales.

I greatly appreciate the efforts of the professionals who reviewed early drafts of the manuscript, adding their own insight and helping me shape my thoughts.

Katie Lane Esq., of "Work Made for Hire Consulting," did more than just provide a set of legal eyes; she gave the manuscript a thorough and much-needed edit.

My most loving thanks, of course, go to my wife, Natali B. Crowell, for shouldering much of the parenting burden as I wrote this book, locked away in the Stygian depths of my office—and for transcribing many of the book's interviews.

I will be forever indebted—in ways too numerous to count—to my father, Caleb E. Crowell: A comic book geek since before I was born, he had the foresight to collect and hold onto over a thousand Silver Age Marvel comic books, allowing my childhood to be shaped by the mind-bending tales of Doctor Strange, Silver Surfer, and the rest of the Marvel Menagerie.

The Second Edition, written almost a decade later, was made possible by a phenomenal editing team at Focal Press: Sean Connelly, my editor, and Alyss Barraza, his editorial assistant. I couldn't hope for a happier home for these books.

And since I wrote this book, my NY Comic Con workshop team has expanded to include some of the best colleagues (and friends) I have had the pleasure of working with: Jeff Trexler, Jason Yarn, and Gamal Hennessey. Truly, these are the heavy hitters of the comic book community bar, and I am grateful for their support over the years.

And to my son Connor, who was a kid when the first edition was written, and who helped me behind the scenes putting together this new edition.

And finally, to the countless others who provided their support, in the words of the great Doctor Strange: "By the Hoary Hosts of Hoggoth, may the Vishanti watch over thee!"*

* *Doctor Strange* Vol. 1. #175 and *Marvel Treasury Edition* Vol. 1 #13, 1976 (http://marvel.wikia.com/Category:Stephen_Strange_(Earth-616)/Quotes)

ACTIVATE:
>QUICKSTART
INITIALIZATION
SEQUENCE:
>BEGIN
CHAMBER DOOR:
>UNLOCK
HELLO JD,
>THIS WAY TO
>FAQ

PART 1

Quick Start

DOI: 10.1201/9781003496052-1

FAQS (Frequently Asked Questions)

Start Here

- This book has a lot of material. How do I find it all? *See The Structure of the Book, p. 5*
- This book has unique formatting; how do I use it? *See How to Use This Book, p. 8*
- Who is that comic hero flying through the pages of this book? *See Our Heroes, p. 4*

Copyrights

- How do I register my copyright? See Copyright Registration, *p. 363*
- What is work for hire? *See Work Made For Hire, p. 350*
- What can I protect through my copyright? *See Copyright Rights, p. 338*
- I was inspired by someone else's work. How do I determine whether I can be sued for copyright infringement? *See Copyright Infringement, p. 44*
- I want to use someone else's copyrighted work. How do I do that? *See Licensing and Assigning the Copyright, p. 356*
- How do I find out if someone still has a registered copyright in their work? *See Copyright Searches, p. 383*

Ideas & Concepts

- How do I copyright my idea? **You can't**
- Okay, Mr. Smarty-Pants, how do I protect my idea? *See Protecting Ideas Through Contract, p. 397*
- Where's the line between a concept and something that can be protected by copyright? *See Ideas vs. Expression, p. 392*

Trademarks

- Can I use a company's trademark without its permission? *See Defenses to Trademark Injury, p. 418*
- How do I get a company's permission to use their trademark in my comic? *See Trademark License Letter, on the companion website*: www.routledge.com/9781032763446

Right of Publicity

- Can I base my character on a real-life person? *See The Right of Publicity and Other Privacy Rights, p. 426*

- Don't I have a First Amendment right to draw anybody I want? *See First Amendment and the Right of Publicity, p. 427*

Contracts

- Help—Legal mumbo-jumbo!!! How do I understand my contract? *See Appendix G: Contract Anatomy for Comic Book Creators, p. 447*
- I just got a publishing contract—I don't understand it! *See The Comic Book Publishing Agreement, p. 256*
- I want to make a comic book with another artist; what kind of contract do we need? *See The Collaboration Agreement, p. 119*
- Someone wants to hire me to draw his or her comic book. How do I know if I have a good contract? *See Illustrator Work for Hire Agreement, p. 161*

Making a Comic

- How do I form a company? *See Setting Up Shop, p. 101*
- I'm working solo. *See The Solo Creator, p. 96*
- I'm collaborating with someone. *See Collaboration, p. 116*
- I want to pay someone to work on my comic. *See Hiring Other Artists, p. 150*
- Someone is paying me to work on his or her comic. *See Working for a Publishing Company, p. 250*
- How do I get the word out about my comic? *See Get your Message Out, p. 229*

Exploiting Your Work

- How do I get my comic published? *See Landing a Publisher, p. 240*
- How do I self-publish my comic? *See Self-Publishing, p. 301*
- How do I digitally publish my comic? *See Digital Distribution, p. 313*
- I just got an angry letter from a lawyer; I think I'm being sued! What do I do? *See What Happens When Something Goes Wrong? p. 320*

GETTING STARTED

Introduction

A decade has passed since "The Pocket Lawyer for Comic Book Creators" first set out to be your legal sidekick, and oh, how the comic book universe has expanded! Siegel & Shuster, Joe Simon & Jack Kirby, and the artistic guardians of Batman, Capt. Marvel, and Spawn have all faced their Lex Luthors and Red Skulls in the form of the legal system's kryptonite: precarious contract and copyright laws.

In the years since, battles have only grown more epic. The ink and newsprint heroes of yesteryear now leap from page to screen, commanding the spotlight in a multiverse of media adaptations. This new edition arms you with the legal lassos and shields needed to navigate the complex landscape of comic book IP.

And now, a cutting-edge player has entered the scene: GEN-AI. This revolutionary technology is transforming comic creation by generating visuals and narratives at lightning speed... and threatening the careers of seasoned artists and writers just as fast, while simultaneously raising fresh legal questions about authorship and intellectual property.

Since the last edition, crowdfunding has become the superhero team-up you didn't know you needed. Learn how to harness the power of online platforms and mobile apps to bring your comics to life while safeguarding your rights in the vast digital expanse. The distribution battleground has shifted too, with old players leaving the field and new ones emerging to pick up the slack.

So, whether you're a seasoned creator or a new recruit to the comic book league, this book is your trusty utility belt—packed with everything you need to protect and profit from your work. Let's turn the page on a new chapter of comic book creation, and may your legal adventures be victorious!

Let's Get Started (Again)!

Our Heroes

No tome on comic book law would be complete without its own heroes to help us fight through the tangled web of law that threatens to ensnare our creative efforts.

J.D. Esq.: Hero-at-Law

Mild-mannered hero Superb-Man endured three years of punishing legal education and crushing student debt. Trained in the steely art of the "Socratic method," he emerged as "**J.D. Esq.: Hero-at-Law!**"

J.D. Esq. now fights a tireless battle against legalese and the Byzantine tyranny of copyright laws. He will also help us throughout the book by pointing out tips and tricks and areas that pose the greatest dangers to comic book creators everywhere.

The Action Render Team (A.R.T.)

Crime-fighting is just a day job for these super-powered heroes whose real dream is to become indie comic book creators. In their secret lair in Williamsburg, Brooklyn, the A.R.T. combine their forces to create scintillating works of sequential art. But can they withstand the confusing cantrips of contract and copyright law... And each other? Check out their copyright conundrums in the comic pages of this tome.

THE STRUCTURE OF THE BOOK

Part 1—Quick Start (*p.3*)

Much like the Quick Start guide that comes with a new computer, this section provides you with FAQs, a quick guide on using the book, and an overview of the book's structure.

Part 2—Intellectual Property: The Heart of the Work (p. 13)

This section lays down the first of two critical foundations necessary for understanding how to protect your rights by introducing you to the branches of intellectual property and providing an overview of **copyright** law for comic book creators.

If you only have a vague understanding of copyright law or whether or not ideas are protectable at all, this is the place you should start. Even if you have a solid grasp of copyright law, you still may want to peruse this section. You might be surprised to find out that some of the things you thought you knew are actually common misunderstandings shared by many artists (e.g., just because you paid someone to illustrate your comic book script for you doesn't automatically mean that you own their drawings as a work for hire).

It's also the section with the comic book pages!

Part 3—Contracts: Getting into Gear (p. 75)

Once you've protected your work, you then need to know how to sell it. In fact, making money from your work and your artistic services is what the rest of the book is all about. But in order to do that, we have to lay our second foundation, and that's in **contract law**.

Just as an understanding of human anatomy is critical to drawing awesome heroes, understanding a contract's anatomy is critical to protecting your creative properties. You need to know what makes a contract work and how to recognize its various parts. So if you're new to reading contracts—or are just plain bad at reading contracts—**Part 3** and **Appendix G: Contract Anatomy for Comic Book Creators** (p. 447) are designed for you.

Those of you who are expert negotiators may learn the hidden meanings of some commonly misinterpreted contract clauses. In fact, you may want to bookmark **Appendix G**, as it provides you with definitions for most of the key contract provisions you will encounter in the comic book industry.

IMPORTANT TIP

You will get much more out of the book if you read Parts 2 and 3 and Appendices A and G before attacking the rest of the book.

Part 4—Putting It Together (p. 91)

This section is where we learn to put all of that intellectual property and contract knowledge to good use. Working solo or with a collaborator? Hiring artists? Starting a business? It's all in this section. Registering your copyright? Want to make sure that you have all of the contract and intellectual property permissions you need? This section's got it; it's like a one-stop shop for putting your book together.

Part 5—Getting It Out There (p. 227)

Now your comic book is complete, and you need to get it into the eager hands of your readers. That's where this section comes in: we will learn how to promote our work, meet publishers, make the best of comic book conventions, and negotiate publishing deals. And for those of you who are unable, unwilling, or uninterested in working with a publisher, we will learn how to self-publish and self-distribute your own printed and digital comics.

Part 6—The Law Library (p. 333)

The last section of all—which bookends our overstuffed tome—is the **Law Library**. This section is a book unto itself and contains appendices on copyright, trademark, rights of privacy & publicity, defamation, moral rights, and the Visual Artists Rights Act—it's a veritable Parnassus of IP, yet it is written in a nuts-and-bolts style to give you quick rules at a glance.

This is also where you will find the appendix on contract anatomy.

ONLINE SUPPLEMENT: WWW.ROUTLEDGE.COM/ 9781032763446

Okay, I admit it: I wrote way too much material to be able to include it all in a book that purports to fit in your pocket. However, rather than throw this material out, we've decided to include additional chapters in the special online supplement!

- Go to: www.routledge.com/ 9781032763446 and log in, there you can download chapters on:
  - Famous Comic Book Cases
  - Trademark Registration
  - Online resources

... and more.

GRAPHIC NOVEL OR COMIC BOOK?

Throughout this book, I've used the terms "graphic novel" and "comic book" fairly interchangeably, which, by and large, they are (from a legal perspective).

Of course, there are differences with respect to how publishing companies will treat the two types of property, and we will deal with those later in the book. But I just know that if I talk about copyright applying to a comic book in a certain way, unless I indicate otherwise, it will apply to a graphic novel in the same fashion.

HOW TO USE THIS BOOK

The Linear Approach. This book can be read linearly, cover to cover. As a matter of fact, readers will probably get the most information that way—the information you learn in Chapter 5 builds upon the information you learned in Chapters 1–4, and so on.

However, I also understand full well that sometimes you need a question answered RIGHT NOW, without having to first read through several scintillating chapters of legal exegesis. As a matter of fact, it can be tempting to throw out any book in which the word "exegesis" appears (except this one, of course, and this is the last time I use that word, I promise).

This is why I have designed a book that can be used in several different ways.

- **The Nonlinear Approach**. What's that you say? Do you need information immediately? All right then, here's what you do:
    1. Use the FAQs (p. 2) as a launching pad to find the answer to your question, or
    2. Jump right into a relevant chapter and use the handy-dandy "Static Hyperlinks" (see later) to help refine your search, or
    3. "Kick it old school" and use the table of contents and index to pinpoint your topic.
- **The Serendipity Approach (not recommended)**. Formulate the question in your mind, light some scented candles, and flip the book open to a random page. If the advice is *not* pertinent, you did it wrong. If the advice is applicable to your situation, I take full credit for possessing metaphysical powers of perception granted to me by the "All Seeing Order of the Coif."[1]

The Keys to Power

Throughout the book, you'll see the following icons.

10,000-foot view—it's easy to get bogged down with the details when you're focusing on legal and business issues; to not be able to see the forest for the trees. That's why every chapter opens up with a 10,000-foot view of the subject. Here we will soar above each issue to get the big picture before we dive down into the nitty-gritty. In fact, you may want to take your first pass at the book by reading through all of the 10,000-foot view sections sequentially— surveying all of our legal forests—before choosing which trees to climb.

Caution!—Some legal and business issues are fraught with extra danger. Fortunately, J.D. Esq., Hero-at-Law, is here to let us know when to slow down and take extra care. Skim over these warnings at your peril!

Tips and tricks—It helps to have a "guy on the inside," and J.D. Esq. is just that man. Negotiation strategies, helpful hints, and a host of other insider tips are identified by this icon.

Lex-O-Tron—legal words and concepts can be confusing; they can mean very different things in legalese than they do in ordinary English. J.D. Esq.'s "Lex-O-Tron" gauntlet will help us decipher these tricky phrases.

STATIC HYPERLINKS

Within each chapter, I have made sure to include copious cross-references, like this: *(See Static Hyperlinks, p. 9)*

The static hyperlinks cross-reference to other sections of the book that will help to flesh out core concepts that you may have missed during your peripatetic leapfrog through this book. Years of research and development— and countless cute lab rats—were sacrificed to provide you with this latest innovation in Static Hyperlink Information Technology. Use these static hyperlinks wisely and often—your artistic freedom may depend upon them!

And for you lawyerly types, I've provided a plethora of endnotes to legal statutes, case law, websites, and other esquire-appropriate ephemera.

Note: If you read through this book sequentially, you will find that I reiterate some information. This is for the benefit of those readers who read the book using the nonlinear approach. Some material is simply too important to be missed and bears repeating. Some material is simply too important to be missed and bears repeating.

THE AUDIENCE FOR THIS BOOK

This book is aimed at both comic book creators and graphic novelists who want to make money by selling their work. You, the reader, may be an industry professional, a recent art school graduate, or an amateur who wants to break into "the biz." Regardless of who you are, if you want a chance at selling your comic book property, in addition to artistic passion, you must be prepared to treat your artwork as goods and your services as a business.

The landscape of comic book creation has evolved dramatically in the past ten years, with the onslaught of comic book movies, AI-generated content, and crowdfunding platforms like Kickstarter. These avenues have opened up new opportunities and also introduced complex copyright problems (I'm looking at you, AI).

My core message is this: if you neglect the legal side of comic book creation, you risk losing the rights to your work. But by understanding the copyright issues of ownership, drafting careful contracts, and mastering the art of the sale, you protect yourself and prime your project for commercial success.

What about Newspaper Cartoonists?

I've chosen to concentrate on comic book creators and graphic novelists, as opposed to newspaper cartoonists or animators.

Newspaper cartoon syndication is a different industry from comic book publishing. Yes, both kinds of artists work by illustrating within panels, but from a legal perspective, being picked up by a syndicator is quite different from being picked up by a comic book publisher. Moreover, there are already a few good books on the market that deal with newspaper syndication. (See Bibliography, p. 505.)

Fear not: while this book won't show you how to deal with newspaper syndicators, the other contract and intellectual property legal issues we're unpacking are very much on point.

Note

1 www.orderofthecoif.org

COPYRIGHT
EXPRESSION
AUTHORSHIP
ARTWORK
SCRIPTS
LOGOS
TITLES
SYMBOLS
GOODWILL
TRADEMARK
IDEAS
C
R

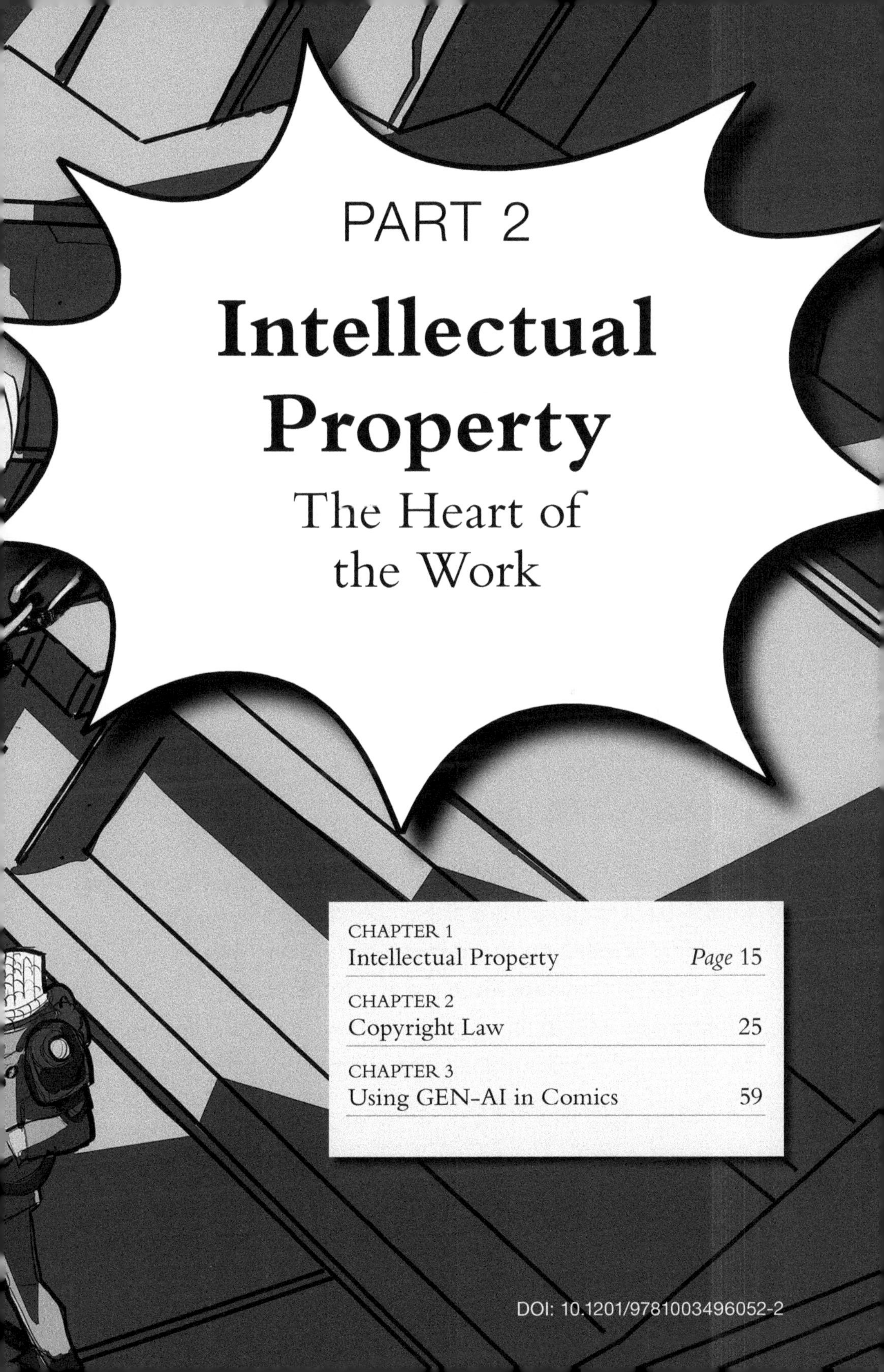

PART 2

Intellectual Property

The Heart of the Work

DOI: 10.1201/9781003496052-2

CAUTION!

INTELLECTUAL PROPERTY: THE SHIELD AND BLUEPRINT OF YOUR CREATION

In today's ever-evolving creative arena, intellectual property law and contracts aren't mere legal formalities—they're the guardian angels of your comic book universe. Think of IP law as your indestructible shield, ensuring your original characters and storylines remain uniquely yours, while rock-solid contracts act as blueprints that secure licensing deals with publishers, toy makers, and Hollywood itself. Together, these building blocks protect your creative vision and empower you to take on the world—with a knowing wink at any copyright villain who dares cross your path.

Even though you can hopscotch through this book, leaping from subject to subject in a single bound, you will need a little bit of preparation: the next two parts, along with **Appendix G: Contract Anatomy for Comic Book Creators (p. 447)** lay the groundwork for understanding the nitty-gritty of contract clauses and IP protections that will fortify your growing creative empire.

CHAPTER 1

Intellectual Property

DOI: 10.1201/9781003496052-3

INTELLECTUAL PROPERTY—THE HEART OF YOUR WORK

The term "intellectual property" (IP) refers to a collection of laws that protect products of the mind or personality, such as

- Copyrights
- Trademarks
- Rights in ideas, and
- Rights of publicity.[1]

The laws that protect patents and trade secrets are also part of intellectual property, but these are generally less important to the comic book creator. Intellectual property is often referred to by its abbreviated label, "IP." When you see "IP" in this book, it means intellectual property, NOT internet protocol (nor Iberian Peninsula, nor Ice Pellets, nor Interstitial Pneumonia, nor Instant Pants ..., etc.).

INTELLECTUAL PROPERTY—THE HEART OF YOUR WORK

All comic book deals are built upon the foundation of IP. When you design a costumed hero, you own more than the drawing in your sketchbook: you own the copyright to your drawing, the potential to trademark that character's name, and the legal rights to control how that character is used in comic books, merchandising, films, and beyond.[2] In other words, even though your copyright registration certificate is not as pretty as the drawing it represents, it may potentially be worth a lot more than even your most valuable signed original sketch!

It may be helpful to think of your IP as the "heart" of your creative rights.

THE COMIC BOOK PROPERTY

When you own any property, you have the exclusive right to sell, license, dispose of, possess, and exploit it. When you sell property, you are really selling these rights. This holds true for all forms of property—whether you're selling your house, your comic book collection, or the copyright to your graphic novel. You may want a publishing company to publish your comic, or you may want to self-publish; either way, you must treat it and protect it as the valuable property it is.

The "comic book property" is the collection of property rights in the graphic novel or comic book. The term usually refers to a collection of rights necessary for publishing, distributing, and otherwise exploiting your comic book.

Among other things, the comic book property rights might include:

EXPLOIT ME, PLEASE!

Nobody wants to be taken advantage of and treated unfairly; when we are, we say we feel "exploited." However, when we talk about IP, like your comic book rights, "exploitation" is a good thing: It means simply "to take full advantage of the IP in the commercial marketplace." So, when you're reviewing your contract with a publishing company, you will be giving that company rights to "exploit your work." Don't worry; they're not looking for express permission to cheat you. Ideally, a publishing company would like to use your property in a way that is, hopefully, profitable to both you and that company. In other words, you don't want to be exploited by a publishing company, but you certainly want your comic book to be.

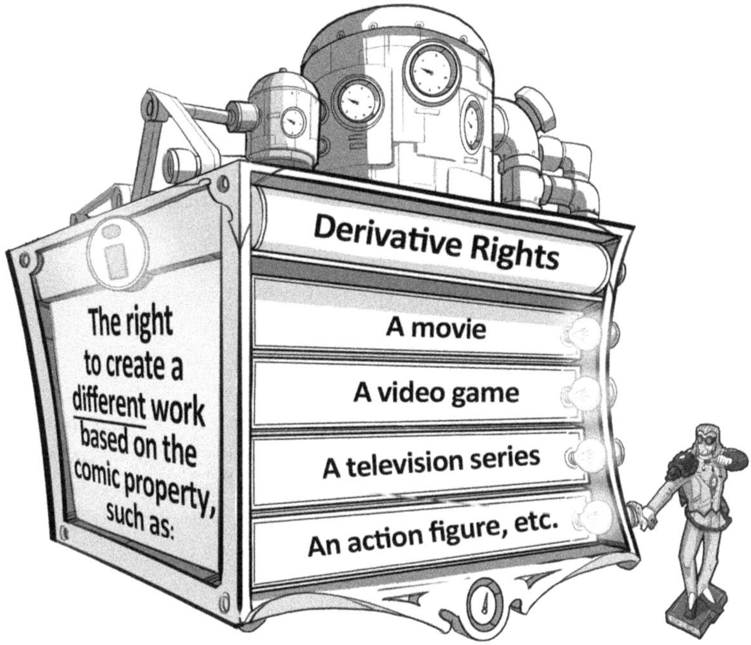
Derivative Rights
The right to create a different work based on the comic property, such as:
A movie
A video game
A television series
An action figure, etc.

Adaptation Rights
A book or movie
A television show
A radio program
A toy
The right to adapt the comic from another work,such as:

SLICE AND DICE YOUR IP

IP rights, especially copyright, can be divided up and licensed in many ways. Typically, rights are granted and divided by the media in which rights are granted (print, digital, or film); the duration of the grant (such as five years or until the end of time); the territory (could be just in the US, worldwide, or even the entire galaxy if aliens are into comics); the exclusivity of the grant (meaning whether you're the only one with the rights or if you're sharing the spotlight); and the scope of the grant (which parts of your work are you letting others use—just the text, the artwork, or everything including your genius character names). As a result, it is possible for a comic book creator to convey the publishing rights in a comic book to a publishing company while retaining the rights to make a movie from the comic. That's like keeping the recipe to your grandma's secret sauce while letting a restaurant sell the sauce under their name. That is why it is critical for comic and graphic novel creators to be aware of exactly which rights they have, what rights they are receiving, and what rights they are granting to others—because nobody wants to accidentally give away their superhero's cape when they only meant to lend it!

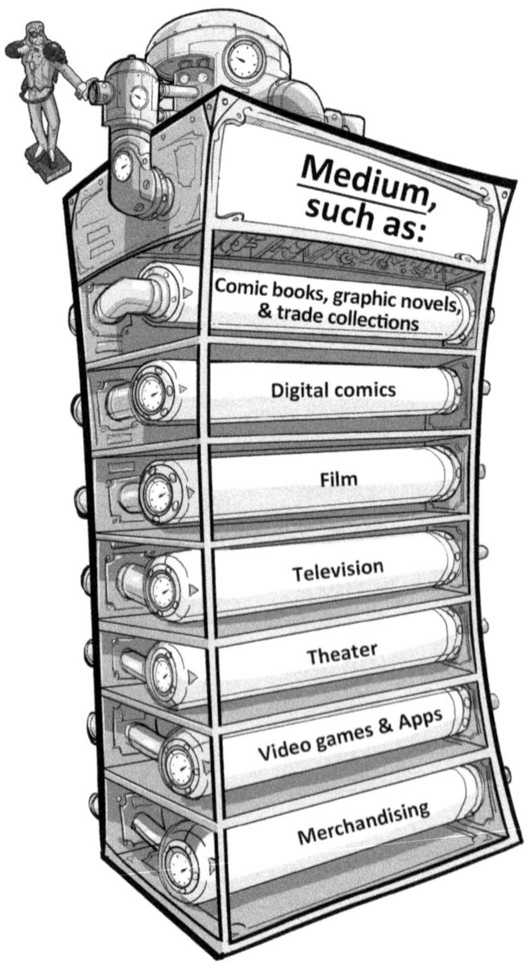

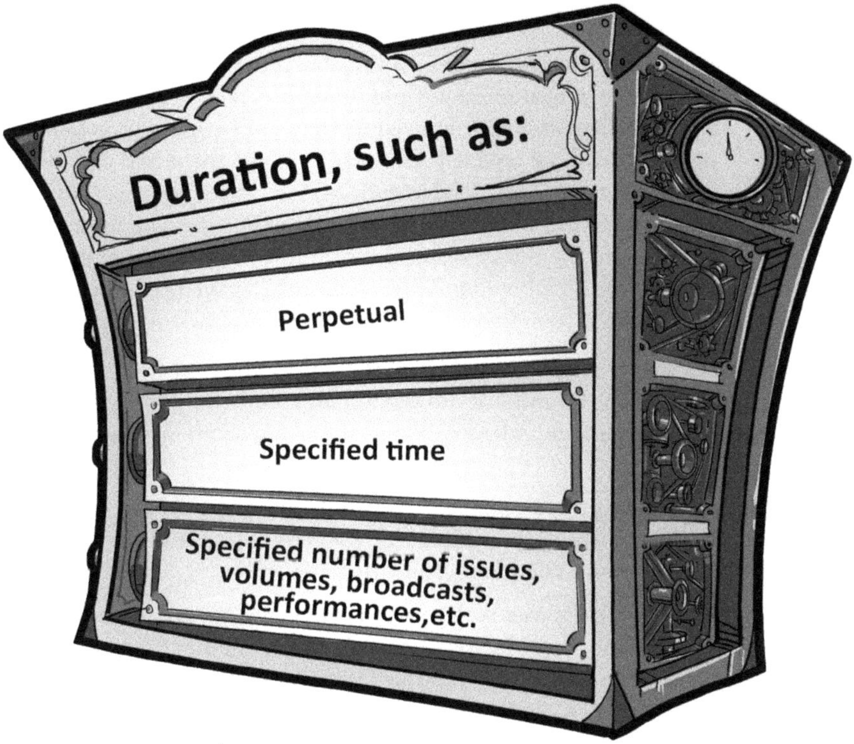
Duration, such as:
Perpetual
Specified time
Specified number of issues, volumes, broadcasts, performances,etc.

Territory, such as:
North America
Europe
The Universe

RULES OF THUMB FOR IP

Hopefully, this book will be a valuable resource to you, one that you will turn to numerous times in your career. However, in order to get the best results, you need to view your copyright as both a superpower to be wielded with precision and the world that you are sworn to protect. To that end, here are the Copyright Commandments you should follow to harness the awesome might of the "Circled C." Some of them may seem counterintuitive or overly cautious; however, if you commit the following "rules of thumb" to memory, they may give you some guidance if you're cornered by a lawyer in a dark alley.

- **Origin of Power.** Your copyright is both your legal sword and your legal shield, granting you the authority to control and monetize your work. Guard it as you would your secret identity. Control the copyright → control the revenue.
- **Flex Your Copyright Muscles.** Actively use your copyright to generate revenue. If you control the copyright, it's yours to sell, license, or assign to a third party for money. You get revenue; they get rights.
- **Copyright Has No Power to Protect Ideas.** Ideas alone cannot be protected; it's the unique manifestation of those ideas, whether on paper, on a computer, or on the screen of a multiplex theater—it's your artistic expression—that's shielded by copyright.
- **Team-Up Rights.** Co-creating with other artists may give both artists joint rights to the copyright—shared equally, with equal rights to the profits—unless a written contract specifies otherwise.
- **Work for Hire Should Always be Paid For.** If you create a work as a WORK FOR HIRE, you don't keep any copyright rights to it—no matter how much work you put into it. If you created something as a "work for hire," you simply have no rights to it whatsoever. In fact, without permission from the person or company that hired you—that is, legally the work's author—you don't even have the right to include it in your online portfolio. Why agree to that for a lowball figure? From my perspective, the less you want to pay my client, the fewer rights you should get to their work.
- **The Fall of the Gavel Decides "Fair Use."** How you used another person's IP is the decisive factor in infringement suits: **context is key.** Did you use another person's IP to create a comic that competes with them? You may believe your use of another person's work in your own wovzrk is **Fair Use**, but it is *up to a court* to tell you whether your use is fair use or not … After you have been sued. And fair use tends to crumble if you use someone's own copyrighted work to compete against them.
- **Register to Supercharge Your Rights.** Register your work with the Copyright Office to enhance your legal protections and potential damages in case of infringement.

- **Exclusivity Requires a Signature.** You want to be the only one with the rights to adapt your buddy's short story into a comic book? You must get those rights in writing and signed by the copyright owner. This also cuts the other way; if someone wants to lock up the exclusive rights to work you've already authored, they must get your signed, written permission.
- **Your copyright and your physical artwork are not the same thing.** The copyright to a work of art is a separate legal property from the physical artwork itself. Just because you own an original Frank Miller pencil drawing doesn't mean you have the right to reproduce it or adapt it into a comic book. The converse is also true: if you work for a publishing company under a work-for-hire agreement, and they let you keep your original pencil sketches, you have no rights to reproduce those pencil sketches or turn them into a comic book.
- **AI Artwork Uncertainty.** Introducing AI into your creative universe can be like opening Pandora's box: the results may not be copyrightable, and many publishers have a "no AI" policy, akin to a superhero code of honor. Always check if your digital sidekick aligns with the publisher's ethos before you join forces.

Remember, heroes that with great copyright comes great responsibility. Use these rules to navigate the galaxy of copyright law and keep your creative universe safe from threats to your most precious power.

NEXT STEPS

Understanding copyright law is critical to protecting your work. In the next chapter, we will run through some copyright law basics.

However, there are a number of other foundational issues that you undoubtedly want to know, such as: How do I protect an idea? How do I register trademarks? Do I need somebody's permission to use their picture in my comic book?

The answers to these and other pertinent IP questions can be found in the **Law Library** section at the back of the book. There, I've even included a much more detailed section on copyright law for those who really want to drill down into the fine points of the all-powerful "**C**-in-a-circle."

In the Law Library, you will find in-depth guides to:

- Copyright law (p. 335)
- Using GEN-AI in Comics
- Protecting ideas (p. 390)
- Trademark law (p. 408)
- Right of Publicity and Other Privacy Rights (p. 426)
- Libel and Defamation (p. 433)
- Moral Rights and The Visual Artists Rights Act (p. 442)
- A Comic Book Creator's Guide to Contract Anatomy (p. ##).

Notes

1 Rights of publicity are often considered "privacy rights," as in N.Y. Civ. Rights Law §§ 50–51 (2021).

2 This is not true if the work has been created as a work for hire. (See Work for Hire, p. 39.)

CHAPTER 2

Copyright Law

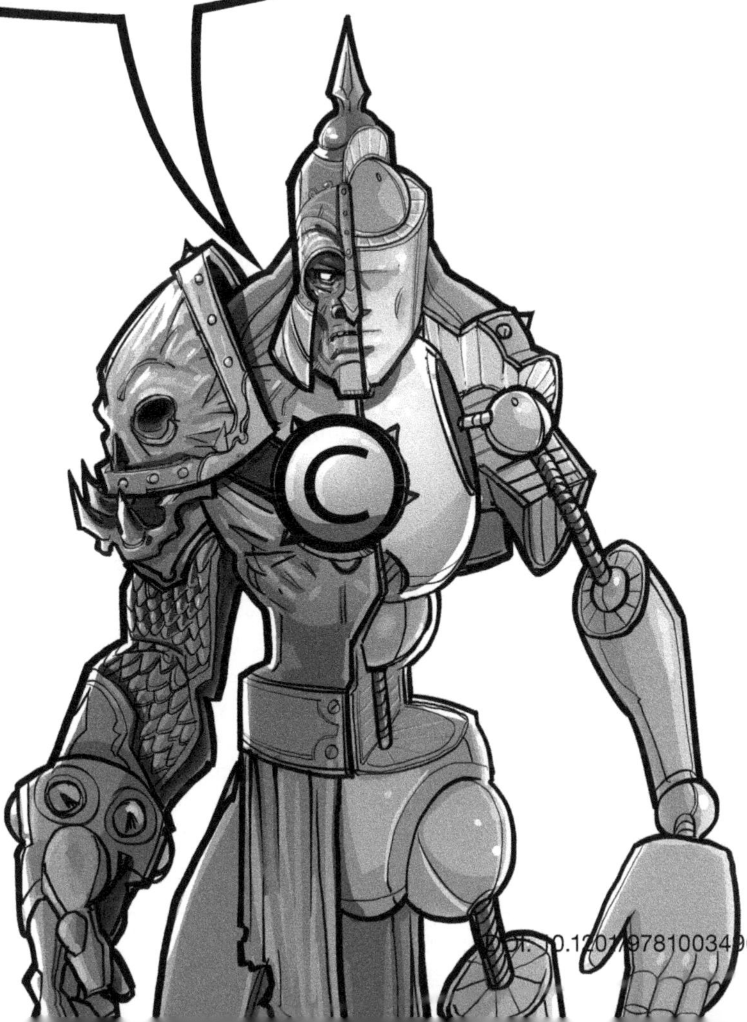

DOI: 10.1201/9781003496052-4

COPYRIGHT LAW—OVERVIEW

Copyright law protects "original works of authorship fixed in any tangible medium of expression"[1] like a comic book page, a script, concept art, and cover art. In fact, each time you draw a comic book page, you actually create two very different kinds of property:

1. **The Physical Artwork:** This is your divinely inspired combination of pencil and ink on paper. While your Bristol board masterpiece may have value when you sell it at a convention, once you sell it, you may no longer have any more rights to the physical copy,[2] but you can still exploit the copyright.
2. **The Copyright to Your Work:** This is the set of legal rights that gives the copyright owner exclusive control over whether the artwork can be copied, distributed, publicly displayed, or performed. Most importantly, the owner of the copyright has the exclusive right to determine whether or not "**derivative works**" can be made from the copyrighted work.

Who Owns it? The initial creator of a copyrighted work is its **author** (unless it's created as a **work for hire**, more on that later). Authors make money by licensing permission to use their copyrights to publishing companies, merchandisers, and Hollywood studios. An author can grant limited rights in her copyright, or sell the entire copyright altogether, retaining no rights for herself. There's an endless variety of ways in which the copyright can be partitioned and licensed to others. In exchange for the right to use the author's copyright, the author often receives **royalties**: A portion of the sales revenue of each comic book, action figure, movie, or video game based upon the author's copyrighted work.

Expired Copyrights. Like milk, copyright does have an expiration date. Once copyright expires, the work becomes part of the **public domain**, and anybody can use it without paying for it. Fortunately, for creators, copyright lasts for a very long time. Any work created today will last for 70 years after the author(s') death (except for **work for hire**, as I said, more on that later).

No © for You! Copyright can protect a vast variety of types of expression. However, there are many things which copyright will **NOT** protect, including: Facts, theories, inventions, short phrases or names, and data. Most importantly, **copyright law will not protect ideas** and concepts. However, it will protect the unique manner in which these ideas are expressed. For example, copyright law will not protect the *idea* of a superhero whose superpowers come from spiders. However, the unique design and storyline of Spider-Man® are protected by copyright.

Keep Control. Keeping control of one's copyright is the key to success as a comic book creator. Two common threats to keeping exclusive control of your copyright are **joint authorship** and **work for hire**. If you work with a partner, copyright law may dictate that you both share the copyright to your joint work as joint authors. It doesn't matter that you came up with the idea and put in the most work—absent a contract between two joint authors, they must still share profits 50/50 with each other. And if you are hired by somebody to create a comic book, either as their employee or as a work-for-hire contractor, you won't even be recognized as the copyright's author and won't have any rights to the copyright in your work. You may be able to avoid both of these scenarios through careful contract drafting.

Don't Step on the Rights of Others. As a comic book creator, you also need to make sure that you do not **infringe** on anybody else's copyright by incorporating their work into yours without permission. While everybody can use some portion of any copyrighted work under the doctrine of "**fair use**," determining what portion and how much of another artist's work may be used is left up to the courts. The better practice may be to get permission by negotiating a **license** to use another copyright owner's work in yours.

Protecting your ©. Protecting your copyright involves:

- **Avoiding** any use of GEN-AI that creates ambiguity of authorship or ownership,
- **Registration** with the United States Copyright Office,
- Placing a **copyright notice** (©) on your work, and
- Making sure that you have **written agreements** with your publishers, merchandisers, and co-authors, which clearly outline the ownership of the copyright in a manner that all parties understand.

Let's explore some of these concepts a bit more.

COPYRIGHT OWNERSHIP

The ownership of the copyright initially resides with its "author." Note: We call the creator of a copyrighted work an "author" even if she is painting a picture, composing a song, writing a comic book script, directing a film, or sculpting a butter bust of Batman.

However, here's the catch: Not all creators are authors, and not all authors are creators. More about this in a few pages when we explore "work for hire" arrangements (spoiler alert: Initially, the copyright in work for hire belongs to ("vests") not the creator, but the hiring party).

Your Copyright Rights

For comic book creators, copyright law gives the copyright owner the *exclusive* right to take their work and:

1. **Make copies of it.**

   Example: Beard-O has just written and illustrated his first graphic novel, "Bearded in Brooklyn," the first volume of his planned series "Hipster Apocalypse." Only Beard-O can authorize the copying of his novel, or any of the drawings or text within it. No publishers are allowed to print copies of his book unless Beard-O gives permission.

2. **Distribute it.**

   Example: Beard-O also gets to control whether or not a distributor may sell his novel to comic book stores. However, once his graphic novel is sold (as opposed to licensed), Beard-O has no more control over to whom that particular physical copy can be sold.

3. **Publicly perform that work.**

   Example: Only Beard-O can authorize the public exhibition or broadcast of a theatrical, motion picture, or broadcast performance based on "Hipster Apocalypse."

4. **Publicly display that work.**

   Example: Beard-O has the exclusive right to authorize a website display of panels from "Hipster Apocalypse."

5. **Make derivative works based upon the original work.**

   Example: If Hollywood wants to make a first-person shooter video game based upon "Hipster Apocalypse," they will need Beard-O's permission. The same goes for anybody making action figures, movies, television shows, and other licensed products based upon his work. And most importantly, this means that no other artist can take Beard-O's copyrighted characters and designs and make new books without getting Beard-O's permission.

Of course, Beard-O can **license** or **sell** any of these rights to a third party. In fact, that's exactly what Beard-O will need to do if he wants to get a publishing, distribution, merchandising, or film deal.

DERIVATIVE WORKS

A derivative work is based on the original copyrighted work, like another issue of your comic, or an animated film based upon your character, or an action figure, or a T-shirt design. As a result of this right to make derivative works, the **copyright** to your work may actually be worth more than the **physical artwork** itself.

Once you create your comic, anything else that's made from that comic, or that copyrighted character, is a derivative work. In fact, if you create by starting with a script, your artwork is a derivative work of that script, as is a motion picture based upon your comic book, digital versions of that comic book, apps based upon your character, lunch boxes emblazoned with your character's picture, T-shirts featuring your character, video games, and Broadway musicals based upon your comic book. As you can see, the right to control derivative works of your copyrighted work is extremely important.

WHAT COPYRIGHT DOESN'T PROTECT

Don't worry—from character design and illustrations to panel sequences, dialogue, plot, and script—copyright law can protect them all!

However, there's also a lot of copyright law that won't protect, and it's important to understand the limits to copyright's protection before sharing or discussing your work with others.

Copyright law will not protect:

- Titles, Names, Short Phrases, and Slogans
- Works That Have Not Been "Fixed in a Tangible Form" of Expression
- Familiar Symbols or Designs; Mere Variations of Typographic Ornamentation, Lettering, or Coloring
- Raw Data
- Historical Facts and Theories
- Procedures, Methods, Systems, Processes, Principles, Discoveries, or Devices
- Works in Which the Copyright Term Has Expired
- Works Created by the U.S. Government

And perhaps, most importantly, **COPYRIGHT LAW WILL NOT** protect:

- Ideas, Themes, or Concepts

For more on these exceptions, see Appendix A: What is not Protectable Under U.S. Copyright Law? (p. 341).

LICENSING TERMS

Licensor: The person granting the license is the **licensor**. Sometimes referred to as the **Grantor**.

Licensee: The person receiving the license is the **licensee**. Sometimes referred to as the **Licensor**.

Non-Exclusive License: A license that may be granted to any number of licensees at the same time.

Exclusive License: A license that gives the licensee a monopoly on certain rights (like the exclusive right to publish a comic book). Once an exclusive right is granted to a licensee, even the original copyright owner can't exploit those same rights until that license terminates.

COPYRIGHT LICENSING

A copyright **license** is the grant of a portion of the copyright (usually limited by time, geography, medium, etc.). One way copyright owners can make money is by licensing or assigning the copyrights to their works to others in exchange for money (e.g., royalties from the sale of comic books and merchandise).

Non-Exclusive Copyright Licenses

A **non-exclusive license** is a license that may be granted to any number of licensees at the same time. A non-exclusive license can be granted in writing, through oral agreement, or may be inferred from the actions of the parties involved. However, the holder of a non-exclusive license may not grant licenses to the work to others without the copyright owner's permission.

> **Example**: Bullpen Publishing Inc., the exclusive rights holder to all of the rights in the "Sgt. Slime Mold" comic books, wants to create a line of branded Sgt. Slime Mold bath toys. As the *licensor*, Bullpen grants a five-year license to make the bath toys to manufacturing company Tubz, LLC, who is now the *licensee* of these rights. Just because Tubz now has the right to manufacture bath toys based on Sgt. Slime Mold, it doesn't mean that it has the right to make comic books based on those bath toys or make anything else based upon Sgt. Slime Mold. Licensing deals are usually very specific and limited in nature.
>
> Furthermore, if Bullpen Publishing only granted Tubz a *non-exclusive license* to make toys, Bullpen could still grant a license to make Sgt. Slime Mold bath toys to another toy company.

Exclusive Copyright Licenses

By contrast, an **exclusive license**, also known as an *assignment*, is a license that gives the licensee the exclusive power to a certain right. It is a transfer of ownership of a copyright or any of the exclusive copyright rights (keep in mind that the transfer may be limited in duration, scope, geography, or pretty much any other way you can think of). Once an exclusive license is granted, the licensor no longer has any power to grant that same right to someone else or to exercise that right herself. However, an exclusive copyright license must be in **writing**, be **signed** by the licensor, and the writing must clearly and unequivocally **transfer** the copyright.[3]

> **Example**: Bullpen Publishing, Inc. wants to bring Sgt. Slime Mold to the big screen. To do this, it negotiates a deal with Big Pictures, Inc., granting the Hollywood movie studio an exclusive license in the motion picture rights to the comic book. Because this is an *exclusive license* to Big Pictures, the movie company may make the Sgt. Slime Mold movie and Bullpen Publishing no longer has these rights to grant to anybody else. Furthermore, even if it wanted to, Bullpen Publishing couldn't make a Sgt. Slime Mold movie itself. If it did, Big Pictures (as the exclusive motion picture rights holder to Sgt. Slime Mold) could sue Bullpen for copyright infringement. However, Bullpen may have retained the right to continue to publish comic books based upon the Sgt. Slime Mold character.

Because Bullpen Publishing is granting an exclusive license (also known as a copyright assignment), the agreement must be in writing and signed by Bullpen Publishing to be effective. An oral agreement—or a handshake—simply won't work here.

PERILOUS COPYRIGHT TRAPS FOR THE UNWARY

We've seen that copyright doesn't protect ideas, but that's not the only trap waiting for the unwary artist. Here's another you may be familiar with: If you are hired by a publishing company to create your comic book under a "work for hire agreement," you will have no rights to the comic book at all—unless you negotiate for them!

But what if you partner up with somebody to create your book—perhaps, an illustrator or writer—and you come up with all of the ideas, and do a majority of the work? You may be surprised to find out that copyright law may see your collaborator as a **Joint Author** and an equal owner of the copyright to your comic book! And as an equal owner of the copyright, this collaborator will have powers you never dreamed of, like the ability to license the work without your permission!

It is precisely this copyright trap that is about to be sprung on the A.C.T. team of Quill, Penciller, and Beard-O-Brush in "**Collaboration Sabotage**!"

J.D. ESQUIRE, HERO-AT-LAW, SOARS HIGH ABOVE WILLIAMSBURG, BROOKLYN, WHEN HE SPIES TROUBLE BELOW!
IT LOOKS LIKE A POSSIBLE CASE OF...
COLLABORATION SABOTAGE!
THE ACTION RENDER TEAM COLLABORATES ON A SCINTILLATING WORK OF SEQUENTIAL ART! A COMIC IS BORN!
JOINT AUTHORS WITHOUT A CONTRACT! ANY ONE OF THEM COULD BE A SABOTEUR!
THIS WILL LOOK GREAT ON MY BUDDY'S BLOG!
SNATCH!!
HE'S GOING TO BUY ME A FEW BEERS IF HE CAN USE THESE CHARACTERS IN HIS NEW BLOG:
TATTOOS & TRASH!
WHAT?! THE COMIC WAS MY IDEA!
YOU CAN'T LET OTHER PEOPLE USE OUR WORK WITHOUT PERMISSION!
...AND FOR ONLY A FEW BEERS!
YOU CAN'T STOP ME! I'M A JOINT AUTHOR! I CAN LICENSE IT TO ANYONE I WANT-- AND I DON'T NEED YOUR PERMISSION! BWA-HA-HA!

AND DON'T WORRY
--I'LL SHARE THE--
BEER!
FOOOMPH!
IF OUR WORK APPEARS IN TATTOOS & TRASH IT WILL KILL OUR BOOK'S CHANCES AS A KID'S TITLE!
TATTOOS AND TRASH BLOG
OPEN ALL NITE
SFFWOOSH!!!
MAYBE I CAN HELP!
FEEL THE FORCE OF MY COLLABORATION AGREEMENT!

WHY WOULD I NEED TO SIGN A COLLABORATION AGREEMENT? COPYRIGHT LAW ALREADY GIVES ME THE RIGHT TO LET ANYONE I WANT USE OUR COMIC...
..WITHOUT ME SIGNING ANY STUPID CONTRACTS!
BECAUSE YOUR FELLOW JOINT AUTHORS DON'T NEED YOUR PERMISSION EITHER! THEY CAN LET ANYONE THEY WANT SHARE YOUR WORK, TOO!!!
STAND DOWN OR WE WILL GRANT A LICENSE TO "NEW JERSEY DOLL HOUSE MAGAZINE"! WHAT WOULD YOUR "TATTOOS & TRASH" FRIENDS SAY ABOUT THAT?
NEW JERSEY DOLL HOUSE
YEAH, THEY MAY NOT WANT TO SHARE THEIR BEERS ANYMORE!
NOT COOL, GUYS! I'LL SIGN!
REMEMBER CITIZENS: ANY JOINT AUTHOR CAN GRANT A NON-EXCLUSIVE LICENSE TO THEIR JOINT WORK...
...AND THEY DON'T NEED APPROVAL OF THEIR FELLOW AUTHORS! ONLY A SIGNED AGREEMENT BETWEEN ALL JOINT AUTHORS CAN STOP...
COLLABORATION SABOTAGE!

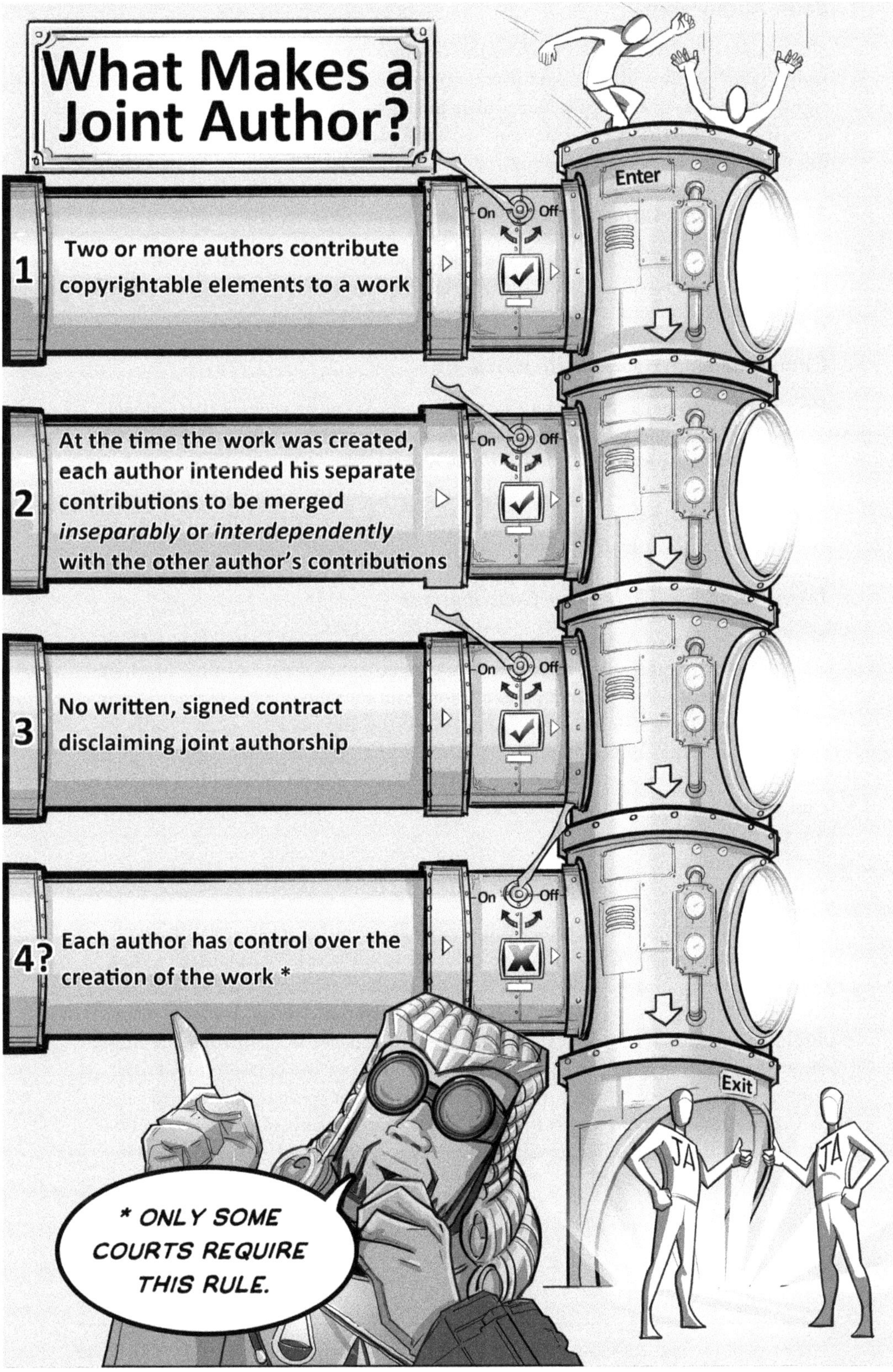
What Makes a Joint Author?
Enter
On
Off
1
Two or more authors contribute copyrightable elements to a work
2
At the time the work was created, each author intended his separate contributions to be merged *inseparably* or *interdependently* with the other author's contributions
3
No written, signed contract disclaiming joint authorship
4?
Each author has control over the creation of the work *
Exit
JA
JA
* ONLY SOME COURTS REQUIRE THIS RULE.

Joint Authorship

The author of a copyrighted work is the original owner (we say that the copyright "vests" in the author). And if you create a comic book with a partner, those rights could vest in both of you, as **joint authors**. Unfortunately, this is true even if you were the one to come up with the idea for the comic, *and* even if you did more work than your collaborator.

Making a Joint Author

When two or more authors work together to create a comic book or graphic novel, copyright law may deem them to be joint authors. Let's take a close look at just what this means.

Contribute Copyrightable Elements

First, in order to be considered a joint author, most courts require that you actually contribute something copyrightable to the collaboration. In other words, you have to create something expressive and tangible—like a script or drawings. Some courts have ruled that if you're merely the "idea person," you're not a joint author (remember, ideas are not copyrightable). Writer/artist collaborations generally pass this test and are copyrightable.

Intend to Merge Their Own Contributions

Second, when you're creating the comic book (or other copyrightable work), you and your collaborator must intend to work together[4] to create a single product, and to "merge your respective contributions" into a whole. This merger of copyrightable expression could be *inseparable*—inking and penciling can't really be separated once they're combined, or *interdependent*—like a comic book script and the artwork that illustrates it. Both the artwork and the script could be shown or exploited separately, but here, they are intended to be merged together to form this particular comic book.

Control

Third, some courts say that joint authorship also requires that a creator have a certain amount of control over the creation of the work.[5] Under this test, a book editor would not be considered a joint author: Although the editor may contribute new phrasing and new structure to a graphic novel, both of which might be independently copyrightable, the editor is not determining the major direction of the manuscript, but rather, responding to the creative input and control of the author. Again, not all courts agree that joint authorship requires this last element of control, so if you're collaborating with someone, it is always better to come to an understanding before you work together as to how the copyright will be owned.

BE MORE THAN THE "IDEA PERSON"

To be on the safe side, if you want to be a joint author, contribute more than just an idea!

Joint Authorship Example

Quill has written a script for a new comic book: "Olm Man: Up from the Stygian Depths." A bit of an artist herself, she creates the first character sketches of "Olm-Man," the world's only superhero with the power of a blind albino cave salamander. She starts a collaboration with Penciller who draws the first issue, based upon Quill's original character design and script. Penciller adds embellishments to the hero and really brings him to life. They decide against writing up a contract; they figure that they'll get to "the legal stuff" later.

With respect to the first issue of Olm Man, and maybe the character of the slimy superhero himself, Quill and Penciller are joint authors.

Quill takes the first issue of Olm Man to a Comic Con to meet with prospective publishers. While she is there, she is inspired by all the zombie-themed titles. She calls up Penciller, who is hard at work at her drawing board at home, and pitches her the following new superhero idea: "Zom-Bee! He was stung to death by bees, and brought back to life with Radioactive Royal Jelly, which he must consume every eight hours or die once more." Since Quill doesn't have time to write anything up, Penciller offers to quickly create a short comic based on Quill's idea so that Quill can take it around the Comic Con to show publishers.

With respect to the "Zom-Bee!" comic Penciller creates, she is the sole author and copyright owner. Even though Quill came up with the idea, she didn't contribute anything copyrightable (like a script; remember, ideas aren't copyrightable). However, since they arguably had some sort of contract or partnership (See Collaborating with a Partner, p. 117), Quill may still have some rights in the project. (See Appendix B: A Comic Creator's Guide to Protecting Ideas, p. 390.)

The Rights of a Joint Author

Okay, so someone is a joint author. So what? Well, joint authors have certain rights under copyright law; if the authors want to change these rights, they need to do so by a signed contract between them, such as a collaboration agreement. (See Collaboration Agreement, p. 119.)

When someone is a joint author, she has the following rights (again, unless a contract says otherwise):

- **Right to Equal Ownership**. Each joint author is entitled to an equal and undivided ownership interest in the copyright with the other joint authors.

Note: The authors' contributions do not have to be equal; ownership will still be shared equally with other joint authors!

- **Right to License.** Joint authors may grant **non-exclusive licenses** to the joint work. But all joint authors must agree to grant an **exclusive** copyright license to the joint work.
- **Right to Payment.** Any joint author who sells or licenses the joint work must pay other joint authors an equal share of the money.
- **Right to Use.** Joint authors are free to make their own derivative works from their joint work. They are not liable to each other for copyright infringement. Joint authors can't grant exclusive licenses, however, unless all agree.

GET IT IN WRITING!

Many courts require a signed contract to change a joint author's rights from those guaranteed by copyright law. (See Collaboration Agreement, p. 119.)

Example: In our example, Quill and Penciller have created "Olm Man" as a joint work, to which they are joint authors. No matter how much creative work either one of them did with respect to the other, they both equally own the copyright to the Olm Man comic book, and maybe even the character himself. Quill is busy negotiating with licensing agents and apparel manufacturers, trying to put Olm Man on T-shirts and posters. Without telling Quill, Penciller creates a Café Press[6] account and begins selling T-shirts to whoever orders online. Because Penciller is a joint author, she can do this without seeking Quill's permission, even though it might ruin the deal between Quill and the licensing agents. This is because either joint author may grant *non-exclusive licenses* in the copyrighted work (the license to Café Press is non-exclusive). This may not be at all what Quill may want, because as of this writing, the Café Press license also grants Café Press the right to "train artificial intelligence" with uploaded designs![7]

Ironically, Quill would need Penciller's permission to grant an *exclusive license* to an apparel manufacturer.

Joint authors also have a duty to share any proceeds they make from the exploitation of the copyrighted work, so Penciller must give Quill half of what she makes from Café Press.

Modifying the Rights of a Joint Author

Ensuring that all joint authors agree on how the property is licensed is essential to sustaining a successful business strategy. The only way to rein in the rights of a joint author is to have a written agreement, signed by all joint authors, in which the rights and duties of each author are clearly spelled out. (See Collaboration Agreement, p. 119.) A handshake, or other unwritten understanding between the parties, simply won't do the job.

If you want to avoid a joint authorship situation altogether, you should have all of your collaborators sign a simple agreement in which they acknowledge that they do not intend to be considered joint authors or copyright owners in the resulting collaboration. And if you're putting up all the money in the creative project, you may even want your collaborators to sign a "work for hire agreement."

Work for Hire

When artwork is created under a "work for hire" arrangement, the copyright to that work is owned by the hiring party, not by the artist who created it.

Normally, the person who creates a work is considered the author and owns the work's copyright as well. Not so here; for, with a work made for hire, the *hiring party* is the work's author and the original owner—with the power to exploit the copyrighted work as that hiring party sees fit. Furthermore, if the artist wants to use the work she created under the work-for-hire relationship, she must get permission from the hiring party.

As you can see, a "work for hire" relationship is great for a hiring party, like a publishing company, but may not be so great for the artist.

Of course, the converse is also true. If you are creating a comic book and want to hire a few people to help you write or illustrate it, the work-for-hire law can really help you out by reducing the transaction costs and business complications that come with sharing a copyright with the artist you hire, if that's what everybody agrees on.

Regardless of whether or not a work-for-hire relationship helps or hinders you, it is important for both sides to realize that work created as a work for hire does not affect an artist's rights to receive royalties from that work. To put it another way, just because an artist gives up copyright ownership and the control that comes with it, doesn't mean she can't still make money from the work—if that's what the parties agree to. As a matter of fact, when an artist is presented with a work-for-hire deal on a royalty-generating property (like a comic book), they may want to negotiate a royalty payment for themselves. (See: Compensation, p. 464.)

There are only two ways a work gets to be a work made for hire, and they differ depending upon whether the creator was an employee or an independent contractor:[8]

OFF
ON
Work made by **employee** during scope of employment.
Work for Hire
Independent contractor must sign a contract.
+
Contract must state that the work is a Work-Made-For-Hire.
+
The contract should be signed before the work starts.
OFF
ON

OFF
ON
Work made by **employee** during scope of employment.
Work for Hire
Independent contractor must sign a contract.
+
Contract must state that the work is a Work-Made-For-Hire.
+
The contract should be signed before the work starts.
OFF
Include a © assignment clause
ON

Work for Hire: Employees

Any copyrighted work created by **employees** within the scope of their employment is considered work made for hire and is automatically owned by the employer.

EXAMPLE

Arlo, the artist, is employed full-time by Bullpen Publishing, Inc., drawing pencil art and occasionally inking comic pages. Anytime Arlo creates a work for his employers, the copyright to that work is automatically owned by Bullpen Publishing. Even if Arlo creates that work at home, if it is for a Bullpen Publishing project, the copyright will vest initially with Bullpen, because it is within the scope of the work that he is employed to do. However, if Arlo works on his own comic book—a project that is separate and distinct from any Bullpen projects—he will initially own the copyright to that comic book. To be on the safe side, Arlo should document the fact that his personal comic book project is not connected with any Bullpen project, nor does it use any unique content or copyrightable elements that he created while working on any Bullpen project.

Before starting any personal project, Arlo needs to carefully review any written employment agreement he may have with Bullpen, as well as its company policies and manuals.[9] Many employers hire their employees/artists to independently generate ideas for comic book properties. If this is the case for Arlo, Bullpen might be able to successfully argue that Arlo's comic book side project falls within the scope of his duties to create independent properties for their company, and that the copyright in Arlo's project is owned by Bullpen by virtue of the work-for-hire relationship between the parties.

Work for Hire: Independent Contractors

For an **independent contractor's** work on a comic book or graphic novel to be considered a work made for hire, he must sign a written agreement explicitly stating that the work is a "work made for hire," a "work for hire," or a "work specially ordered or commissioned." Without *both* the written and signed contract *and* the clause that says the work produced is a "work made for hire," the independent contractor's work is *not a work made for hire*. To make it even harder, an independent contractor's work must fall into one of several categories (as a part of a motion picture or other audiovisual work, as a translation, as a supplementary work, as a compilation, as an instructional text, as a test, as answer material for a test, or as an atlas[10]). It is important to note that an exchange of emails with signature blocks, which collectively establish a binding agreement between the parties, might satisfy the "signed written contract" requirement.[11] For more information on contract construction, see What is a Contract?, p. 78 and Appendix G: Contract Anatomy for Comic Book Creators, p. 447)

EXAMPLE

Arlo, the artist, quits Bullpen Publishing, Inc., and works as an independent contractor for several comic book publishing companies. He picks up a project from Gertie and McCay Publishing, Inc., creating backgrounds for a "Manga-Saurs"—a manga dinosaur series. He does the work at his home studio on his own equipment and, except for the delivery date, on his own schedule. Arlo is clearly an independent contractor. To own Arlo's work product as a work made for hire, Gertie and McCay Publishing must have a written contract with Arlo, which Arlo must sign. The contract must expressly state that any work he produces for them is considered work made for hire.

For more info on the difference between independent contractors and employees, see Employee or Independent Contractor, p. 111.

Work for Hire Clause

If you're an employer, the work you hired your employees to perform is owned by you as work for hire.

If you engage an independent contractor (in other words, a worker who is NOT your employee), and you want the work they create for you to be work for hire, you will need a written agreement with them which:

- Explicitly lists the work the independent contractor is doing for your comic,
- The independent contractor understands and agrees that the work is being created as a "work made for hire,"
- The contract should have an alternate copyright assignment clause, and
- It should be signed by the independent contractor *before* they start working on your comic book project.

Tip!: To be doubly sure that the copyright is effectively transferred from the creator to the hiring party, most work-made-for-hire agreements provide for an **alternative copyright assignment**. That way, if, for some reason, the work is not considered a work made for hire, the hiring party gets the copyright anyway by virtue of the alternate copyright assignment clause.

WORK FOR HIRE: "Artist acknowledges and agrees that all of his contributions to the Comic Book, including, but not limited to writing, layout, pencil art, inking, coloring, and any other result of the Artist's services provided under this contract, or any part thereof, (the 'Results and Proceeds'), are created as 'Works Made For Hire,'[12] with all copyright and other rights thereto vesting initially in the Publishing Company. Accordingly, the Publishing Company shall be considered the sole and exclusive author and copyright owner of the Results and Proceeds and of the Comic Book. To the extent, if any, that ownership of the Comic Book produced hereunder or the Results and Proceeds of Artist's services do not immediately vest in Publishing Company by virtue of this Agreement, Artist hereby assigns to Publishing Company all rights (including all rights of copyright)[13] of every kind and character in and to the Comic Book and the results and proceeds of Artist's services. Artist hereby waives all 'moral rights,' 'droit moral,'[14] and similar rights. All rights hereunder assigned shall be assigned in perpetuity, and such an assignment shall be irrevocable. The effect of this clause shall survive any termination of this Agreement."

COPYRIGHT DURATION

Your copyright has an expiration date; when and how a copyrighted work was created determines how long its copyright lasts. Any work that you author today will be protected by copyright for the rest of your life and then for another 70 years. In other words, your copyright expires 70 years after you do.

While "**Life+70**" is a good rule of thumb to determine the duration (or **term**) of the lifespan of copyright in a new work, factors like when the work was created, whether it is a work made for hire, or a jointly authored work, whether the copyright needed to be "renewed," and other circumstances will affect how long the copyright lasts.

Once the copyright term has run, the work you authored falls into the *public domain*, and anybody can use your creation for any purpose whatsoever.

As an artist, you may feel that it is unfair that your great-grandchildren may be denied the ability to receive royalties on your work, but the law sees "an overriding interest in the 'release to the public of the products of the author's creative genius.'"[15] In short, a strong public domain means that there's a wealth of new expression to use as ingredients for new works.

LIFESPAN OF A COPYRIGHT

Copyright duration in works created today:

Non-Work for Hire: 70 years after the author's death (or the last surviving author's death, in the case of works of joint authorship).

Work for Hire Duration: 120 years from the date of creation or 95 years from when it was first published, whichever comes first.

Note: Works created prior to January 1, 1978, had different terms, depending upon when they were created. (See Copyright Duration, p. 361.)

Now, if you've been following along, you may be thinking "Whaaaa? If a work for hire could expire sooner than a copyright created by an artist and then assigned to a publishing company, why would any company want to put a work-for-hire clause in a contract? Everybody seems to benefit if the copyright to that work was just assigned instead!"

Well, that might be true, except for one little thing: Copyright law's "termination of transfer."

Termination of Transfer

One seemingly odd wrinkle in copyright law is the **termination of transfer provision**,[16] which allows a valid and otherwise irrevocable copyright assignment or license to be revoked after 35 years by the copyrighted work's author or the author's heirs. That's right, the copyright can be yanked back by the owner, no matter how many iron-clad "no backsies"[17] clauses are in the contract that originally assigned the copyright. Unlike *assigned* copyrights, the copyright created as a work for hire is *not* subject to the termination-of-transfer provisions.

Superman, Captain America, Fantastic Four, X-Men, Iron Man, Spider-Man, The Incredible Hulk, Thor, The Avengers, Nick Fury, and Ant-Man[18] have all seen the inside of a courtroom as their creators and owners battled over copyright's termination of transfer provisions.

To learn more about termination of transfer provisions, see Termination of Transfer, p. 357.

COPYRIGHT INFRINGEMENT

The power to grant *exclusive* use or ownership of the copyright to your work in a specified medium and territory is a requirement in virtually all comic book publishing, motion picture, and television deals. But what happens when someone uses your copyright, such as by copying it, distributing it, or using it to make derivative works without your permission?

Anyone who violates any of the exclusive rights of a copyright owner may be liable for **copyright infringement**. A key aspect here is that what is copied *must be protectable by copyright law.* A court will find copyright infringement if the work being challenged is "**substantially similar**" to the copyrighted work—unless there is an exception, such as fair use. (See "Fair Use," this chapter.)

In the landscape of copyright law, ideas roam the streets as common citizens, free and unshielded. They are the public domain, the shared thoughts upon which all creativity is built. Yet, it is not these citizens themselves that the law enshrines; it is only when they don the distinctive garb of penciling and illustration, when they speak through the crafted voice of dramatic scripts, that they gain the superpower of copyright protection. It's this transformation from idea to expression that copyright law stands guard over, ensuring that only creative expression, not the idea itself, ever wears the cape of legal defense.

How Similar Is Too Similar?

A court compares not the basic plot *ideas* for stories, but "the actual concrete elements that make up the total sequence of events and the relationships between the major characters."[19] One such test for substantial similarity focuses on "articulable similarities between the plot, themes, dialogue, mood, setting, pace, characters, and sequence of events" in the two works.

EXAMPLE

Beard-O is a big fan of Spider-Man. He decides he wants to create his own comic book hero. Inspired by "ol' web-head," Beard-O creates a hero called "Fireleg," named after the Mexican "fireleg" tarantula.[20] The character is a former Mexican wrestler. He received his powers from an old Brujo medicine man after saving his life. Fireleg's costume is yellow and blue and patterned like that of a Mexican wrestler, and his superpowers largely involve his ability to shoot irritating bristles from his hairy red legs.

If Marvel Comics sues Beard-O for copyright infringement over "Fireleg," claiming that he's too close to Spider-Man, Beard-O can defend by saying that, while he may have been inspired by Spider-Man, the similarity between the two superheroes is merely that they both draw their powers from spiders. A spider-themed superhero is merely an idea, or concept and ideas or concepts are not protected by copyright law. Beard-O can point out that Spider-Man and Fireleg have different costumes, powers, and backstories. Because the only similarity between the two characters is something that is not protected by copyright law, Marvel Comics will likely lose the lawsuit, notwithstanding the 50 crates of Spider-Man comics in Beard-O's apartment.

Anyone found liable for copyright infringement may be required to pay damages and profits, costs and attorney's fees, and other criminal and civil penalties. (See Penalties for Infringement, p. 374.)

Plagiarism Is Not the Same Thing as Copyright Infringement

It's important to keep in mind that plagiarism is not the same thing as copyright infringement. Plagiarism is an ethical violation, not a legal cause of action. It is possible for an artist to be guilty of plagiarizing another artist's work without being legally guilty of copyright infringement. For instance, plagiarism can occur when ideas are taken from a source without correct attribution. As indicated earlier, copyright law does not protect ideas.

Plagiarism can be a very fuzzy concept. It can often be hard to draw the line between inspiration (ethical and legal), plagiarism (unethical, but legal), and infringement (unethical and illegal).

Fair Use of a Copyright

If there's one thing that most people have heard about copyright, it is that one of the copyright rights is "fair use." **Fair use** allows you to take a portion of somebody else's copyrighted work and use it in your own without having to ask permission from the original creator! Wait—it gets stranger—even if the original creator objects to your use of his work, if your use is "fair use," he can't stop you!

FAIR USE

Fair use[21] of copyright allows the taking of part of a copyrighted work without the need to secure the author's permission. Examples of fair use include news reporting, criticism, comment, teaching (including multiple copies for classroom use), parody, scholarship, or research.

In general, a court is more likely to find fair use when the use has been **transformative**. The court will ask, "Does this new work add anything to the original, or recast it in a different light?" (more likely to be fair use) Or, instead, "does it merely copy and compete in the same marketplace as the original?" (less likely to be fair use).

The "Myth" of Fair Use

Everyone knows that you can use another author's work in yours. Common wisdom is that artists can take up to 500 words when quoting from a book, use up to 10% of an image, and use 8 bars of a song without having to seek the writer's, artist's, or composer's permission. These things are protected under our right to fair use, right? It's cut-and-dry!

Unfortunately, Virtually All of the Above "Common Sense" Beliefs about Fair Use Are Wrong!

Believe me, I wish it were that simple. To begin with, fair use is a *defense* to copyright infringement. Unlike the affirmative rights we discussed (the right to copy, the right to distribute, etc.), when you're relying on fair use, you're essentially saying, "Sure, I copied your work, but it's excused because of fair use." And because it's a defense, not a right, the one who usually determines whether your use was permissible is the guy or girl wearing the black robe and sitting behind the judge's bench.

And as to whether it's permissible to take 500 words, 10%, or 8 bars of music, there are simply no absolute measurements to how much you can take.

Maybe you can take 500 words from somebody else's novel and include them in your comic book without permission. But maybe you can't. There's simply no "Great Big Book of Fair Use Weights and Measures," which a judge consults to see whether you took more than your share. Although it certainly would be easier if we could turn to such a book and say, "Let's take a look, you want your comic book hero to sing a Green Day song as he's fighting bad guys... This table says you can use one complete verse without seeking permission..."

Nope. Permissible use is not based upon word count, but on a much more nuanced analysis of not just how much you took, but also the content of what you took, as well as the purpose for which you used it.

Okay, how do you calculate fair use?

Unfortunately, for the artist, it is up to the court to decide—after the fact—whether the taking was excused because of the fair use doctrine. This means that the artist has already been dragged into court by the copyright holder, something clearances are designed to avoid altogether. (See Chapter 9, Clearances and Licensing the Rights of Others, p. 198.)

§17 U.S.C. 107 – HOW COURTS DECIDE IF A USE IS FAIR USE –

The federal copyright statute[22] says that courts must give weight to the following four factors in determining fair use under copyright law:

1. "The purpose and character of the use, including whether such use is of a commercial nature or is for nonprofit educational purposes;
2. The nature of the copyrighted work;
3. The amount and substantiality of the portion used in relation to the copyrighted work as a whole; and
4. The effect of the use upon the potential market for or value of the copyrighted work."

As you can see, the doctrine of fair use is not always so straightforward. Let's take a look at how the **A**ction **R**ender **T**eam handles the issue.

QUILL—A DARING LINGUA-MANCER—WIELDS CALLIOPE'S PEN, CONJURING HERETOFORE UNSEEN WORLDS FROM THE VOID.
LIKE GRAPHITE SCALPELS, THE PENCILLER'S №2H CLAWS CARVE THE BLANK BRISTOL BOARD OF REALITY, LEAVING BEHIND LINE, FORM, AND COMPOSITION.
BUT IT IS VIVID COLOR THAT BREATHES THE SPARK OF LIFE INTO THE TEAM'S ART, WITH EACH STROKE OF BEARD-O-BRUSH'S PREHENSILE SIDEBURNS.
TODAY, THESE MIGHTY TALENTS WILL BE TESTED IN THE CRUCIBLE OF COPYRIGHT LAW IN---
FAIR USE OR FOAL?
IN HER SECRET BROOKLYN H.Q., PENCILLER IS FINISHING UP THE LAST FEW TOUCHES ON THE "PROSPECT PONY" KIDS' COMIC SHE'S CREATING WITH HER ACTION RENDER TEAMMATES.
DESIGN SKETCH #21
GLASSES? SADDLE?
DESIGN SKETCH #50
PROSPECT PONY
FINAL VERSION!
GOSSAMER PONY
NOTE: USE GOSSAMER PONY'S MANE 1.FLIP IT! 2.ADD RIPPLES.
TITLE? THE PONY OF PROSPECT PARK
LIKE MANY ARTISTS, SHE DRAWS INSPIRATION FROM ANOTHER SOURCE...

BUT THE LINE BETWEEN INSPIRATION AND INFRINGEMENT CAN BE PERILOUSLY THIN, AS THE PENCILLER IS ABOUT TO FIND OUT...
POUND!
POUND!
INCOMING LAWSUIT! BATTLE STATIONS EVERYBODY!
BOOM
INFRINGE MY COMIC? OH YOU SILLY-BILLIES! NOW I'M GOING TO SUE YOUR SORRY A$$ES!
IT'S GOSSAMER PONY AND HER ATTORNEY MINIONS!
BACK OFF YOU BELLICOSE BARRISTERS!
KICK!

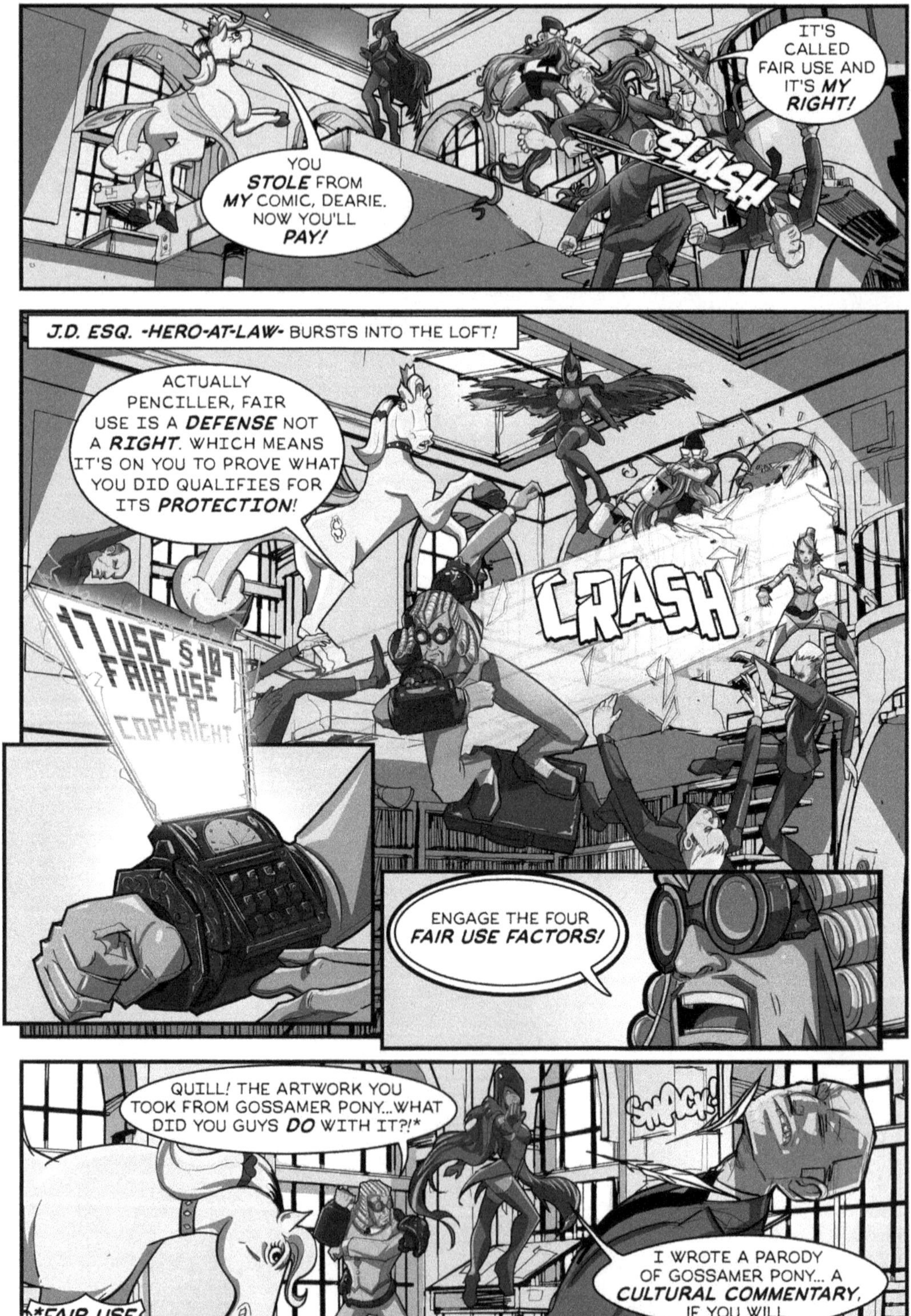
YOU STOLE FROM MY COMIC, DEARIE. NOW YOU'LL PAY!
IT'S CALLED FAIR USE AND IT'S MY RIGHT!
SLASH!
J.D. ESQ. -HERO-AT-LAW- BURSTS INTO THE LOFT!
ACTUALLY PENCILLER, FAIR USE IS A DEFENSE NOT A RIGHT. WHICH MEANS IT'S ON YOU TO PROVE WHAT YOU DID QUALIFIES FOR ITS PROTECTION!
CRASH
17 USC § 107 FAIR USE OF A COPYRIGHT
ENGAGE THE FOUR FAIR USE FACTORS!
QUILL! THE ARTWORK YOU TOOK FROM GOSSAMER PONY...WHAT DID YOU GUYS DO WITH IT?!*
SMACK!
I WROTE A PARODY OF GOSSAMER PONY... A CULTURAL COMMENTARY, IF YOU WILL.
*FAIR USE FACTOR 1
"THE PURPOSE AND CHARACTER OF THE USE, INCLUDING WHETHER SUCH USE IS OF A COMMERCIAL NATURE OR IS FOR NONPROFIT EDUCATIONAL PURPOSES."

REALLY? I JUST THOUGHT GOSSAMER PONY'S MANE WOULD LOOK FIERCE IF I FLIPPED IT AND ADDED SOME RIPPLES!
XOXO —GP

GREAT JOB! PENCILLER, YOU MODIFIED GOSSAMER'S ARTWORK. QUILL, YOU PARODIED IT.
YOUR WORK IS TRANSFORMATIVE--THAT'S ONE HUGE ELEMENT IN YOUR FAVOR!

NOBODY MESSES WITH MY HAIR!
WHAT KIND OF WORK IS GOSSAMER PONY?*
GOSSAMER PONY IS JUST ANOTHER COMIC. A STUPID ONE!
SLASH
SLASH
DOESN'T MATTER IF IT'S A STUPID COMIC. YOU TOOK MATERIAL FROM A WORK OF CREATIVE FICTION. YOU'VE JUST LOST THIS ELEMENT!
*FAIR USE FACTOR 2
"THE NATURE OF THE COPYRIGHTED WORK." 17 USC §107(2):

SEIZING THE INITIATIVE, GOSSAMER PONY CREATES A DAINTY VORTEX OF DOOM!
I WON THIS ROUND!
SHOVE!
LITIGATION IS MAGIC!
BEARD-O IS SUCKED OUT INTO THIN AIR, HIS HANDLEBARS FLAILING FOR A HANDHOLD!

QUILL ATTACK!
SMACK!
LISTEN YOU LITIGIOUS LIPIZZANER! INSPIRATION IS NOT INFRINGEMENT! WE STILL HAVE TWO MORE ELEMENTS TO PROVE.
PENCILLER - THIS IS CRITICAL! HOW MUCH OF GOSSAMER PONY'S WORK DID YOU TAKE?
AND DID YOU TAKE THE IMPORTANT PARTS OF THE WORK?*
*FAIR USE FACTOR 3
"THE AMOUNT AND SUBSTANTIALITY OF THE PORTION USED IN RELATION TO THE COPYRIGHTED WORK AS A WHOLE."

DISPLAY MODE:PROJECTION
STATUS:COMPARING
TARGET 1: PROSPECT PONY
TARGET 2: GOSSAMER PONY
NOT REALLY. I CREATED MY OWN PONY. I ONLY COPIED A SMALL PART OF GOSSAMER PONY'S MANE.
GOOD. YOU ONLY TOOK A LITTLE BIT - NOT THE "HEART" OF THE WORK. THAT'S IN YOUR FAVOR!

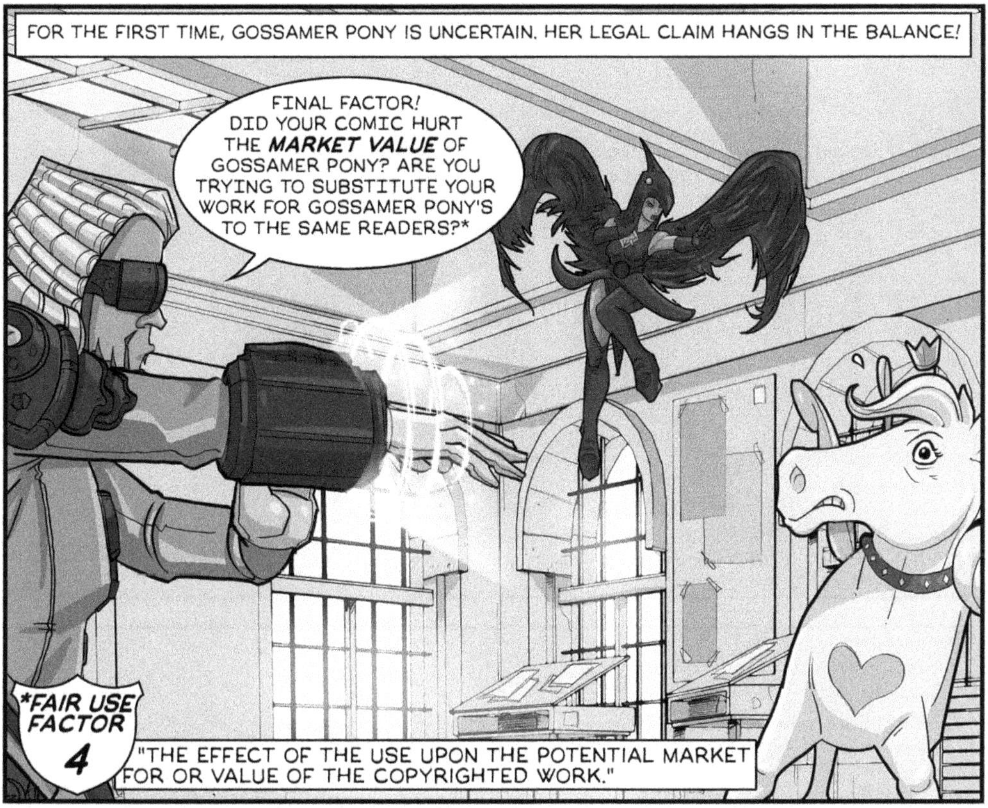
FOR THE FIRST TIME, GOSSAMER PONY IS UNCERTAIN. HER LEGAL CLAIM HANGS IN THE BALANCE!
FINAL FACTOR! DID YOUR COMIC HURT THE MARKET VALUE OF GOSSAMER PONY? ARE YOU TRYING TO SUBSTITUTE YOUR WORK FOR GOSSAMER PONY'S TO THE SAME READERS?*
*FAIR USE FACTOR 4
"THE EFFECT OF THE USE UPON THE POTENTIAL MARKET FOR OR VALUE OF THE COPYRIGHTED WORK."

J.D. ESQ. SENDS GOSSAMER PONY THROUGH THE VORTEX WITH A SWIFT MOTION TO DISMISS!
NO WAY! WE DIDN'T HURT THEIR SALES AT ALL!
ZAAA-DOOSH!

OUTSIDE, BEARD-O CATCHES THE ANGRY PONY IN A WEB OF WHISKERS!
WE HAVE A VERY DIFFERENT READERSHIP. OUR PROSPECT PONY COMICS ARE READ BY KIDS, WHILE GOSSAMER PONY...
SNATCH!!
...HAS MORE OF A MIDDLE AGED DEMOGRAPHIC.
GOSSAMER PONY POWER
DRINK THE RAINBOW
ON THE STREETS BELOW, GOSSAMER PONY'S FANBOYS ARE AGHAST AT THE DEFEAT OF THEIR OAT-EATING IDOL!
HEY, THAT'S THREE OUT OF FOUR FAIR USE FACTORS IN OUR FAVOR, WE WIN!

BUT THE HEROES' HAPPINESS SHATTERS LIKE THE TIP OF AN OVER-SHARPENED PENCIL-
-AS THE HAND OF JUDGE-ZILLA YANKS THE WARRING PARTIES HIGH INTO THE AIR!
CEASE THY PREMATURE UTTERANCES! NOTHING IS FAIR USE UNTIL I SO RULE IT THUS!

REMEMBER CITIZENS: FAIR USE IS NOT A RIGHT, YOU HAVE TO PROVE IT EACH TIME. AND WHETHER YOU SUCCEED IS ULTIMATELY UP TO THE PERSON WITH THE GAVEL AND BLACK ROBE.
DON'T MISS NEXT ISSUE'S EXCITING CONCLUSION -- UNLESS THERE'S AN APPEAL--IN "SHARPLY FALLS THE GAVEL"

We will examine copyright fair use a lot more closely—and walk through several fair use hypotheticals—in Fair Use, p. 375.

COPYRIGHT PRE-FLIGHT CHECKLIST

Because copyright is such a tricky subject, it is easy to get into trouble either by (1) failing to protect your work adequately or (2) inadvertently infringing somebody else's copyright.

Keep in mind that you don't have to intend to infringe a copyright to be held liable for copyright infringement.

Now that you have some copyright law under your utility belt, you may want to flesh out your knowledge of IP by reading the IP for Comic Book Creators sections in the Law Library.

- The United States Copyright Office also has a very helpful website. Its FAQ page can help answer some basic questions about copyright law: www.copyright.gov/help/faq/
- Are you planning to include any text or images created by artificial intelligence in your comic? Be careful you don't destroy your copyright! (See Using GEN-AI in your Comic, p. 59)
- Remember to keep in mind those joint authorship issues! If you're about to collaborate with a partner or another artist, you should read through the section on collaboration agreements. (See Collaboration Agreements, p. 119.)
- Does somebody want to hire you to work on his or her project? Do you want to hire somebody else? Remember the importance of work for hire! (See Hiring Artists, p. 150.)
- Have you created a comic book script or illustrations? You should register them with the United States Copyright Office. (See Copyright Registration, p. 363.)
- Are you about to publish your comic? Make sure you control all of the IP that has gone into it; if not, get permission from any third-party owners (or determine that permission is not needed, for instance, if the material is in the public domain). (See Clearances and Licensing the Rights of Others, p. 198.)

<u>NEXT STEPS</u>

If you're planning on using artificial intelligence to create your comic, you need to read Chapter 3 on GEN-AI in Comics before you go any further. If not, you can skip it and dive into the basics of contract law–where every clause packs a plot twist and your rights are the unsung heroes of your narrative (p. 77).

Notes

1 17 USC §102 (2016).

2 However, see Visual Artists Rights Act (p. 443): with respect to some rights, you may have in limited editions of your work.

3 Weinstein Co. v. Smokewood Entertainment Group, LLC, 664 F.Supp.2d 332, 341 (S.D.N.Y., 2009). ("The intention of a copyright owner seeking to transfer an ownership interest must be clear and unequivocal").

4 "With respect to the first element, we explained that the intent prong does not have to do with the collaborators' intent to recognize each other as co-authors for purposes of copyright law; the focus is on the parties' intent to work together in the creation of a single product, not on the legal consequences of that collaboration" Janky v. Lake County Convention And Visitors Bureau, 576 F.3d 356, 362 (7th Cir. 2009).

5 Berman v. Johnson, 518 F.Supp.2d 791, 796–797 (E.D. Va. 2007) aff'd, 315 F. App'x 461 (4th Cir. 2009) ("a circuit split regarding the requirements for joint authorship. Defendants cite to the Ninth Circuit's decision in Aalmuhammed v. Lee, which held that joint authorship requires a party (i) to make an independently copyrightable contribution and (ii) to establish 'authorship' by demonstrating (a) control over the creation of the work, (b) 'objective manifestations of a shared intent to be coauthors,' and (c) audience appeal based on each contributor's contribution. 202 F.3d 1227, 1232 (9th Cir.2000). By contrast, the Second and Seventh Circuits hold that authorship of a joint work is established merely by 'establishing that each of the putative co-authors (1) made independently copyrightable contributions to the work; and (2) fully intended to be co-authors.'").

6 www.cafepress.com.

7 "By submitting Your Designs to us, you grant us a nonexclusive, worldwide, royalty- or commission-bearing, transferable, sublicensable right and license to reproduce, distribute copies of, prepare derivative works based upon, publicly perform, publicly display, train artificial intelligence on, and otherwise use and exploit Your Designs in all media and sales channels, existing now or created in the future, as we deem appropriate to provide the Services including, without limitation [...]" CafePress, Terms of Use for Sellers, https://www.cafepress.com/p/seller-terms (last visited May 10, 2025).

8 17 USC §101 (2024).

9 "One significant factor is the employee's job description, either as individually drafted, contained in company policies or manuals, or practiced" 2 Patry on Copyright §5:69.

10 17 U.S.C. §101 (2024).

11 "If an e-mail is to form the basis for a work for hire arrangement, there must be an agreement, determined by ordinary principles of contract construction, and that agreement must be signed by both parties." 2 Patry on Copyright §5:77.50.

12 Note the special "Work for Hire" phrase. It would also work if it said: "Work Made for Hire," or "Work Specially Ordered and Commissioned."

13 Note the alternate assignment language. This gives the hiring party the copyright, even if the "work for hire" provision fails for some reason.

14 These rights don't really exist under United States law, but they do exist in other countries like France and Germany. We have something called the Visual Artist Rights Act (§17 USC 106A), but its extremely limited compared to its EU cousins, and doesn't apply to comic books. (See Moral Rights, p. 443.)

15 Eldred v. Ashcroft, 537 U.S. 186, 227, 123 S. Ct. 769, 793, 154 L. Ed. 2d 683 (2003) (internal citations omitted).

16 17 USC §203.

17 "No backsies" is an ancient legal doctrine that originated in the Code of Hammura-backsies.

18 Eriq Gardner, Marvel Jack Kirby Estate Settlement, The Hollywood Reporter (Sept. 26, 2014), https://www.hollywoodreporter.com/business/business-news/marvel-jack-kirby-estate-settlement-735921 (last visited May 1, 2025).

19 Funky Films, Inc. v. Time Warner Entm't Co., L.P., 462 F.3d 1072, 1077 (9th Cir. 2006).

20 Brachypelma boehmei.

21 17 USC §107.

22 17 USC §107.

CHAPTER 3

Using GEN-AI in Comics

DOI: 10.1201/9781003496052-5

The advent of generative artificial intelligence—GEN-AI—is the most disruptive development the comic book community has seen since the censorship measures suggested by Frederick Wertham in the 1950s.

Hang on. Let me start again, this time in a tone more befitting the hyperbole with which the issue of AI in comics is usually discussed—because at the heart of this debate lies a true existential crisis. Let's see. Some Silver Age purple prose should do the trick:

There is a lot of passion and rage surrounding the use of GEN-AI in the comic book industry. Artists, writers, and editors are losing jobs or competing with the perception that they can be automated away as companies fall for the false promise that software alone can replace years of hard-earned skill, learning how to build tension in a story, draw a compelling figure, or structure a proper page composition.

And as if automation weren't troubling enough, many AI models were trained on massive datasets scraped from the Internet, with no permission sought from the original artists and copyright owners of the works ingested. One well-known illustrator didn't mince words when he told me: "*AI is a firing squad aimed at my career—and they stole my art to make the bullets.*"

So, should you use GEN-AI in comics? Right now, the industry's stance walks a tightrope between skepticism and outright hostility. Legal risks loom large, with copyright disputes around AI-generated work and the questionable ethics of its training methods. But my job isn't to make your creative decisions—it's to help you make them legally. While I will make a case *against* using GEN-AI for comics, I'll also lay out what's allowed and how to stay on the right side of the law. In this chapter, we will cover

1. Understanding GEN-AI Technology
2. The History of the Human Authorship Rule in Copyright Law
3. How to Use GEN-AI in your Work
4. How to Register GEN-AI Works
5. How to Avoid Using GEN-AI in your Comic.

UNDERSTANDING GEN-AI TECHNOLOGY

Generative AI (GEN-AI) systems are trained on extensive datasets composed of human-authored works, allowing them to recognize patterns and produce expressive content across various media formats, such as text, graphics, audio, and video. These systems generate outputs dynamically in response to user-provided inputs, or 'prompts,' which may include texts, visuals, audios, or videos. However, questions remain regarding the copyrightability of GEN-AI outputs, particularly when they lack the required element of human authorship. (See below, US Copyright Office Current Rules for AI and Non-Human Authorship, p. 65.)

ESSENTIAL GEN-AI TERMS FOR COMIC BOOK ARTISTS

- **Attention Mechanism:** The AI's way of deciding what elements are important when generating an image or scene. Picture an editor working on a splash page—choosing

ESSENTIAL GEN-AI—*continued*

which details pop while toning down the clutter. Sometimes it nails the balance, and sometimes it gives you Batman with three elbows.

- **Diffusion Model:** The process behind most AI-generated images, where the model starts with noisy, abstract shapes and refines them into coherent artwork—like an invisible penciler sketching rough outlines and then progressively tightening the composition with each pass.
- **GEN-AI (Generative AI):** AI models trained on vast collections of human-created works, learning patterns to generate new content.
- **Prompt:** The user's instruction to the AI. A precise prompt determines whether you get something you asked for or *hyper-muscular nightmare fuel*. If you're vague or confusing in your prompts, instead of getting a picture of your superhero eating lunch in a diner, you might get a pic of a super-sized hero sandwich being eaten by a diner for lunch.
- **Tokens:** The fundamental units of text (or even image elements) that the AI uses to understand and generate content.
- **Training Data Set:** The collection of works that AI learns from, often pulled from the Internet—sometimes ethically, sometimes like a villain swiping secrets from a rival's lair. This raises big questions about *who* the AI is really learning from and *whether* it should be.
- **Transformer Architecture:** The neural network framework that helps AI process complex relationships between characters, backgrounds, and details.

Step 1: Understanding the Prompt: When you type "create a picture of a monkey taking a selfie at the beach," the AI first changes your words into numbers. It does this in two steps:

- **Tokenization:** The AI splits the sentence into small pieces (tokens), which might be whole words or parts of words. This helps the system understand even unusual words by breaking them down into known bits.
- **Embeddings:** Each token is turned into a list of numbers that represent its meaning. For example, words like "monkey" and "ape" are turned into similar numbers because they share similar meanings.

Step 2: Mapping to Latent Space: Instead of pulling a ready-made picture from storage, the AI uses a "latent space"—a kind of mathematical map of visual features. In this space:

- Every point represents a mix of visual details like color, shape, and texture.
- The ideas from your text ("selfie," "beach," etc.) are aligned with these visual elements, so the AI knows how they might fit together in an image.

Step 3: Generating the Image: The AI then creates the image using one of several methods:

- **Diffusion Models:** They start with random noise (like TV static) and slowly refine it to reveal a clear image.
- **GANs (Generative Adversarial Networks):** Here, one system creates the image while another checks if it looks realistic, pushing the generator to improve its output.
- **VAEs (Variational Autoencoders):** These compress the information into a simple form and then rebuild the image from that data.

Step 4: Refining Details: Once the main image emerges, the AI fine-tunes the details—from the texture of the monkey's fur to the reflections on the phone—making sure the final picture looks polished and realistic.

But as impressive as this tech may be, beneath the shiny surface lies a sobering truth: the AI's creativity is entirely reliant on patterns from human-created works, and it often ends up as a brilliant mimic rather than a genuine originator. This fact raises serious questions about originality and authorship, and it highlights the ethical conundrums of using creative material without clear permission.

Many of the datasets used for training these models include copyrighted works sourced online—often without the creators' or copyright owners' consent—which brings up thorny legal issues over whether incorporating unlicensed works constitutes copyright infringement. As of this writing, we find ourselves navigating uncertain legal waters where the ownership of GEN-AI creations remains a murky gray area, much like a superhero's origin story that never quite gets resolved, despite the cheerful "kittens polka-dancing" outputs the AI might churn out.

CAUTION!!! While these models replicate many aspects of human authorship, they lack the unique originality and intellectual authorial mind that define human creativity. As a result, AI-generated content often fails to meet the requirements for copyright protection, sparking critical legal questions of ownership of the GEN-AI artwork and writing.

THE HISTORY OF THE HUMAN AUTHORSHIP RULE IN COPYRIGHT LAW

Since 1884, U.S. Copyright law has explicitly protected only the work of human authors. The term "author" in the Constitution and the Copyright Act excludes nonhumans. The Supreme Court's decision in Burrow-Giles Lithographic Co. v. Sarony[1] established that copyright protection requires human creativity. In this case, the Court held that a photograph could be subject to copyright as long as it represented the original intellectual conceptions of the human author.

Federal appellate courts have reached similar conclusions, holding that works must be the product of human authorship to qualify for copyright protection. The U.S. Copyright Office's policies reflect this requirement, stating that works must be created by humans to qualify for copyright protection.

WILDE RIDE: THE 19TH CENTURY CASE SHAPING AI TODAY

Burrow-Giles Lithographic Co. v. Sarony, 111 U.S. 53 (1884)

Picture this: It's the late 19th century, and Napoleon Sarony, a flamboyant photographer with a knack for capturing the essence of his subjects, snaps a photo of the ever-dapper Oscar Wilde. Wilde, known for his razor-sharp wit and flamboyant style, strikes a pose that only he could pull off. Sarony, seeing the brilliance of his work, registers the photo for copyright protection.

Enter Burrow-Giles Lithographic Company, which decides to make unauthorized lithographs of Sarony's masterpiece. Naturally, Sarony isn't thrilled and takes them to court for copyright infringement. The legal battle that ensued answered the question of whether photographs can be considered "writings" under the U.S. Constitution and thus eligible for copyright protection. But more than that, it was the first case to try to understand where human authorship can be found for works of expression produced entirely through mechanical means.

In 1884, the U.S. Supreme Court stepped in and delivered a landmark decision, ruling that photographs can indeed be protected under copyright law, to the extent that they represent the photographer's original intellectual conceptions. The Court emphasizes that "writings" should include all forms of expression that give ideas visible form, recognizing the creative choices made by photographers. The Court noted that Sarony's photograph was a product of his "original mental conception," brought to life through his selection, coordination, and arrangement of the subject, costume, and lighting. So, Sarony's dramatic flair pays off, and his photograph of Wilde is protected.

The Court's reasoning about the selection, coordination, and arrangement of elements in a photograph is still a cornerstone of contemporary copyright jurisprudence. This principle underscores that the creative process involves more than just mechanical reproduction; it requires intellectual effort and artistic judgment. This reasoning is crucial in determining the copyrightability of works, ensuring that the creator's mental conceptions and creative choices are protected.

Now, fast forward to the age of GEN-AI. The Burrow-Giles case is crucial because it underscores the need for *human* creativity in copyright protection. AI-generated content, while impressive, lacks this human element, raising questions about authorship, ownership, and protection of works that mix human and AI-generated elements.

As AI technology evolves, balancing innovation with respect for intellectual property rights is increasingly crucial. So, while AI might be able to whip up a masterpiece, it still needs a human touch to make it copyrightable and keep it out of the infringement zone.

US Copyright Office Current Rules for AI and Nonhuman Authorship

The landmark Burrow-Giles decision hammered home that copyright protection isn't for robots—it's all about human creativity. This principle still rules the roost in our GEN-AI era, even as clever algorithms try to steal the spotlight. Today, the U.S. Copyright Office takes a case-by-case approach when it comes to works with AI-generated content: If a machine produces the very elements that define authorship—like the dialogue, creative order of events, and other expression typically originated by human creators—the work is deemed to lack human authorship and, therefore, cannot be registered for copyright protection. However, if a human creatively selects or arranges AI-generated material, or significantly modifies it, the human-authored aspects may be protected by copyright. The copyright law only protects "the fruits of intellectual labor" that "are founded in the creative powers of the mind."[2]

The U.S. Copyright Office reinforces the **human authorship principle** in its Compendium of U.S. Copyright Office Practices, stating: "**To qualify as a work of 'authorship' a work must be created by a human being. See Burrow-Giles Lithographic Co., 111 U.S. at 58. Works that do not satisfy this requirement are not copyrightable**" (Compendium § 313.2). Real-world examples include:

- A photograph taken by a monkey.
- A mural painted by an elephant.
- A claim based on the appearance of actual animal skin.
- An application for a song naming the Holy Spirit as the author of the work."[3]

And as of this writing, in addition to questions of authorship, there are other ethical issues involved in the construction of many GEN-AI systems that are trained on vast amounts of data sourced from the Internet without explicit permission from copyright holders. This raises a gray legal area about whether using unlicensed works in training datasets constitutes copyright infringement.

USING GEN-AI IN YOUR WORK

I'm an art school alumnus myself and spent a decade making my living in film, TV, and publishing before heading to law school. As an artist, I'm deeply troubled by AI's impact on the arts and artists' careers. The way this tech has been rolled out is like a bad sequel—unlicensed copyrighted materials, buggy tech, and a lack of clear guidelines on what can be protected. It's a full-frontal assault on creativity, and I'm heartsick over the loss of unique art styles and artists' livelihoods. In short, I'm personally not really a fan of GEN-AI.

And I'm not the only one. As of this writing, professional comic creators and publishers are largely opposed to GEN-AI-designed characters, panels, and scripts.[4] For example, *DC Comics* faced significant backlash when it was discovered that some of its comic covers were generated by AI. This led to the company pulling and replacing those covers. In Europe, the comic book industry has seen a complete rejection of AI-generated art,[5] with publishers like Le Lombard, known for *Tintin*, taking a strong stance against it.[6]

But here's the twist: I'm also a lawyer and an educator. That means I must advise clients on strategies I might personally disagree with and teach laws I find problematic—all without turning into a soapbox preacher. It's a necessary part of the gig, especially for you readers trying to understand whether the law protects GEN-AI-created comic books, and if so, how.

So, while I hope to give you a legal roadmap for using GEN-AI in your works, it's not a journey I recommend you take. Think of it as a treasure map with a big "Here Be Dragons" warning. Given the current and understandable antipathy in the comic book industry, diving headfirst into the world of GEN-AI might not be the wisest move. Proceed with caution and remember: even the most brilliant AI needs a human touch to keep it on the right side of the law.

Avoiding Infringement When Using GEN-AI

Using GEN-AI tools to create comic book content can be a double-edged sword. While these tools can enhance creativity and productivity, they also pose significant risks of copyright infringement. Here are some guidelines to avoid infringement:

- **Understand the Terms of Service for the GEN-AI Ap:** It's critical to understand how your data is used, who owns the work created with the app, and to watch out for any hidden clauses in the platform's Terms of Service (ToS). Neglecting this review could mean losing control of your creation or getting entangled in other legal issues.
- **Use Licensed or Public Domain Content:** Ensure that the data used to train the AI model is either licensed or in the public domain. Using copyrighted material without permission is like inviting a legal storm over your digital doorstep—you might soon find yourself starring in a copyright infringement lawsuit.
- **Document Your Process:** Keep detailed records of how the AI tool was used in the creation process. This documentation can help demonstrate to the Copyright Office which elements are generated by GEN-AI and which are the human-authored elements.
- **Review and Edit AI Outputs:** Before including AI-generated content in your comic, thoroughly inspect every element—this covers narrative text, dialogues, scene descriptions, and any textual excerpts—to ensure that none

of it inadvertently replicates copyrighted material. You should verify that the AI output does not reproduce recognizable phrases, passages, or stylistic elements from copyrighted sources. If you identify any potentially problematic content, make significant and material modifications such as rephrasing, restructuring the dialogue, or altering the narrative details to clearly establish that the final work bears your human creative input. This rigorous review and editing process helps demonstrate that the work is an original creation rather than a derivative of pre-existing copyrighted materials. For detailed guidelines on the required degree of transformation and acceptable modifications, please refer to the Clearances guidelines. (See Chapter 9 —Clearances and Licensing the Rights of Others,, p. 198.)

- **Consult Legal Experts:** When in doubt, consult with legal experts who specialize in intellectual property law to ensure compliance with copyright regulations.

What to Look for in Terms of Service

Reviewing the Terms of Service (ToS) of AI generation apps is like reading the fine print before signing a deal with a mischievous genie. You need to know how your data is used, who owns the content, and what sneaky clauses might come back to bite you. Skipping this step could mean handing over your masterpiece or getting caught in a legal quagmire. So, grab a magnifying glass and dive into that ToS to protect your GEN-AI results. When reviewing the Terms of Service (ToS) of GEN-AI platforms, look for:

1. **Data Collection and Usage:** Assess how the platform collects, uses, and shares user data. Ensure the ToS includes mechanisms for obtaining user consent and aligns with privacy commitments. For example, an AI tool sharing your data with advertisers without consent could lead to unwanted ads and privacy breaches.
2. **Content Ownership:** Verify who owns the AI-generated content. Ensure the creator retains ownership or understands the platform's usage rights. E.g., creating a comic with an AI tool only to find the platform claims ownership could limit your ability to monetize or distribute your work.
3. **Usage Restrictions:** Verify any restrictions on AI usage, ensuring they align with the creator's intended use. Identify any prohibited uses that could impact the creator's projects. E.g., if the ToS prohibits commercial use of the AI, it could hinder your ability to sell or license your AI-generated comic.
4. **User Rights and Appeals:** Look for clear processes for users to challenge or appeal decisions made by AI systems. Ensure users can request corrections or deletions of their data. For example, if the AI system makes an unfavorable decision about your content, having a clear process to appeal or correct that decision is essential.
5. **Compliance with Laws:** Confirm that the ToS complies with local and international laws governing AI and data privacy. Check how the platform handles updates to the ToS and notifies users of significant changes.

E.g., frequent ToS updates without user notification could introduce new terms that negatively impact your rights.

6. **Underlying Model Transparency:** Examine how the platform's underlying AI models were built. Investigate whether the training data was ethically and legally obtained, and check if the platform discloses details about its data sourcing and ingestion practices. For example, ensure that the models weren't trained via unauthorized data scraping, as this could expose you to legal and ethical issues.

Registering the Copyright to the Work with GEN-AI Components

When registering the copyright to a work that includes GEN-AI components, it is crucial to understand the nuances of copyright law. The U.S. Copyright Office has made it clear that *only human-authored elements* of a work are eligible for copyright protection. Therefore, when registering a comic book that includes AI-generated images, the registration will cover only the human-authored text and the creative arrangement of the AI-generated images within the comic. **The AI-generated images themselves will not be protected by copyright**:

> If a work's traditional elements of authorship were produced by a machine, the work lacks human authorship and the Office will not register it. For example, when an AI technology receives solely a prompt from a human and produces complex written, visual, or musical works in response, the 'traditional elements of authorship' are determined and executed by the technology—not the human user.[7]
>
> *Copyright Registration Guidance: Works Containing Material Generated by Artificial Intelligence*, U.S. Copyright Office. (2023)

Zarya of the Dawn *and "A Single Piece of American Cheese"*

The U.S. Copyright Office's decision on *Zarya of the Dawn* delves into the intricacies of copyright protection for works involving AI-generated content.[8] The graphic novel, created by Kristina Kashtanova, utilized the AI tool Mid-Journey to generate images, while Kashtanova authored the text and arranged the images. Initially, the Copyright Office granted copyright protection for the entire work. However, upon discovering the use of AI, the Office re-evaluated the registration.

The Office concluded that only the human-authored elements of the work, such as the text *and the creative arrangement of the images*, are eligible for copyright protection. The AI-generated images themselves do not qualify for copyright because they lack human authorship. However, the **compilation work**,[9] which includes both human-authored and AI-generated elements, can still be protectable. (A compilation work is a compilation of individual contributions brought together into a cohesive whole, such as a magazine, anthology, or, in this case, a graphic novel; *the unified whole may be eligible for copyright protection.*)

This decision is grounded in key legal precedents, including Burrow-Giles Lithographic Co. v. Sarony[10] and Feist Publications, Inc. v. Rural Telephone Service Co.,[11] which together provide a framework for understanding how collective works can be protected even when individual components are not eligible for copyright. Burrow-Giles Lithographic Co. v. Sarony (1884) established that photographs could be protected by copyright because they are "representatives of original intellectual conceptions of the author". The Supreme Court emphasized that copyright protection extends to works that are the product of human creativity and intellectual effort. This case set a precedent that human authorship is a fundamental requirement for copyright protection.

Feist Publications, Inc. v. Rural Telephone Service Co. (1991) further clarified the concept of originality in copyright law. The Supreme Court ruled that a work must possess "a modicum of creativity" to be eligible for copyright protection.[12] In this case, the Court held that the white pages of a telephone directory, which merely listed names and phone numbers in alphabetical order, did not meet the originality requirement because they lacked creative expression. However, the Court also noted that the selection, coordination, and arrangement of otherwise public domain materials can be copyrighted as a compilation work if they reflect the author's creative choices. But be careful, "the copyright in a compilation **does not** extend to the preexisting material employed in the work.[13]"

By applying the principles from Burrow-Giles and Feist, the Copyright Office ensures that the collective work, which reflects the author's original and creative input, is protected, thereby preserving the integrity of copyright law while adapting to technological advancements.

The recent approval of a copyright registration for an AI-generated image—aptly titled "A Single Piece of American Cheese"—signals a nuanced yet significant evolution in the application of copyright law in the era of generative AI. In this case, Invoke's CEO, Kent Keirsey, harnessed an AI platform to produce visual elements that he then meticulously curated, edited, and collaged into a composite work. The Copyright Office ultimately ruled that while the individual AI-generated components are not eligible for copyright due to the lack of human authorship, the final assembled image was sufficiently shaped by human creativity in its selection, arrangement, and coordination.[14] This decision underscores the continuing importance of the human authorship rule, illustrating that even when AI plays a significant role, it is the human "touch" that confers copyright protection.

Both cases reaffirm that while AI can serve as a powerful tool in the creative process, only the material contributed through original and creative human selection, coordination, and arrangement meets the threshold for copyright.

Registering Hybrid GEN-AI Works

To register a hybrid work that incorporates both human-authored and AI-generated elements, follow these updated steps in light of recent rulings:

1. **Prepare Your Application:** Clearly delineate all human-authored components—such as the text, creative arrangement, and editorial decisions—and distinctly identify any AI-generated material. In your application, explicitly state that your copyright claim is confined to the human-created aspects and the selection, arrangement, and coordination of the AI outputs, not the underlying AI-generated images themselves. For example, include a disclaimer such as:

   "This claim is limited solely to the human-authored text and the creative arrangement—including the selection, coordination, and integration—of the AI-generated images. The underlying AI-generated images are not claimed as original creative expression."

   For a work following the "American Cheese" model—where the final composite image is produced through extensive human intervention that directs the iterative creation of wholly AI-generated elements and then selects, edits, arranges, and the results—include a disclaimer such as:

   "This copyright registration is confined solely to the original creative process, namely the human-directed iterative creation, selection, editing, and arrangement of the AI-generated images into a composite work. The registration expressly excludes all non-iteratively created individual AI-generated images, or any fragments thereof, which in their unaltered state are not claimed as original creative expression."

   These tailored disclaimers emphasize that while the AI tools provide raw material, it is solely the human creativity in collaging and reconfiguring these elements that is being protected, thereby conforming with current Copyright Office guidance for such hybrid works.
2. **Submit Your Work:** Provide a complete copy of your work, ensuring that both the human-authored portions and the AI-generated material are clearly identifiable, with an emphasis on the sections where your creative intervention transformed the AI outputs into something new.
3. **Pay the Fee:** Submit the appropriate registration fee as required by the U.S. Copyright Office.
4. **Receive Your Certificate:** Once processed, the Copyright Office will issue a certificate covering the human-authored elements and the overall composite work, while expressly excluding the AI-generated components.
5. **Supplemental Documentation:** Consider including an explanatory letter with your application. This letter should detail your creative process, explain how you curated and arranged the AI-generated elements alongside your own original contributions, and clarify the distinct role of human creativity in the final work. Such supplemental documentation can bolster your claim by providing additional evidence of human authorship that forms the basis of your claim to copyright protection.

For more information on copyright registration, see Protecting and Registering your Copyright.

KEEPING YOUR COMICS GEN-AI FREE

As of this writing, AI is not widely accepted in the professional comic book community. Many find GEN-AI's initial data set training unethical and see it as the Grim Reaper of jobs or feel it undermines the artistic process; some simply dislike the look of GEN-AI. Whatever the reason for your decision to "REJECT THE TECH," there are several stages in your comic book creation, publishing, marketing, and distribution where you need to be vigilant. Here are some key areas to watch out for:

First, be cautious when working with collaborators who are enthusiastic about using AI. Make sure to include clear "No AI" language in your contracts to ensure that your work remains untouched by AI-generated content. This will help you avoid any legal ambiguities and maintain the integrity of your creative vision. (See Chapter 7, Trust, AI, and Protecting Your Creative Collaboration, p. 148.)

Second, it's crucial to negotiate "No AI" clauses in your contracts with publishers. For example, you might negotiate language prohibiting any use of your work to train datasets or to be used in prompts, or to prevent GEN-AI elements from being added to your comic, like a variant cover or in associated marketing. And make sure the contract specifies that the publisher will not use your work in AI-powered tools to generate new published works in the style of your comic. (See, Prohibition on GEN-AI, p. 240, p. 265.)

Key Legal Issues to Consider

- **Collaborators Using AI:** Clearly define the prohibition of AI in collaboration agreements to prevent disputes. (See Trust, AI, and Protecting Your Creative Collaboration, p. 148.)
- **No AI Clauses with Publishers:** Negotiate terms that explicitly prohibit the use of AI in your comic, its advertising, or on its website. (See Chapter 13, Prohibition on GEN-AI, p. 265.)
- **Avoiding AI-Driven Apps:** Steer clear of apps that might use your artwork to create training data sets, as this could compromise your creative control and intellectual property. (See Get Your Message Out, p. 229.)
- **Fans Using Your Work as AI Prompts:** Establish guidelines and communicate them to your audience to protect your intellectual property.

Other GEN-AI Legal Pitfalls to Avoid

Using GEN-AI in your comic can stir up more than just copyright issues. Imagine your AI creates a superhero who looks suspiciously like a famous actor. Suddenly, you're not just dealing with copyright law but also facing a lawsuit for unauthorized use of someone's likeness. Oops!

And let's not forget about trademarks. If your GEN-AI generates a logo that looks a lot like a famous sports brand, you could be in for a trademark infringement battle. Picture this: your comic book villain has a logo that's a dead ringer for a well-known brand. Not only could this confuse your readers, but it could also land you in a legal mess.

- **Example: Right of Publicity.** Imagine you're creating a new superhero and decide to use GEN-AI to generate a character based on a famous celebrity. You prompt the AI with "Create a superhero that looks like Dwayne 'The Rock' Johnson but with a cape and laser eyes." The AI generates a spitting image of The Rock, now with superpowers. You think it's a great idea to mass-produce T-shirts featuring this new superhero. If you start selling these T-shirts, you could be violating The Rock's right of publicity, which protects against unauthorized commercial use of a person's likeness. The Rock might not appreciate his new laser-eyed alter ego gracing your merchandise and could sue for damages. (See Appendix D, What is the Right of Publicity?, p. 427.)
- **Example: Trademark Law and Tarnishment.** Let's say you're a big fan of a popular soda brand and decide to use GEN-AI to create a villain named "Dr. Pepperoni," who has a logo suspiciously similar to the Dr. Pepper brand. You prompt the AI with "Create a villain with a logo like Dr. Pepper but with a pizza twist." The AI obliges, and you end up with a character that could easily be mistaken for an official Dr. Pepper mascot. This could lead to a trademark infringement lawsuit under the Lanham Act, as it creates confusion about the source of the product and could tarnish the brand's reputation by associating it with something unsavory or inappropriate. (See Appendix C, Injuries to a Trademark, p. 413.)
- **Example: Defamation.** You decide to use GEN-AI to create a fake photo of your old art school teacher burning a student's portfolio. You prompt the AI with "Create a hyperrealistic photo of [Teacher's Name] burning a student's portfolio." The AI generates a realistic image that is clearly identifiable as your teacher. If you publish this photo, you could be facing a defamation lawsuit, as it could harm your teacher's reputation and career. (See Appendix E, Defamation Defined, p. 434.)

NEXT STEPS

Alright, creative crusader, you've unlocked the secrets of IP law and learned about the dangers of GEN-AI. Now it's time to meet your new best friend: Contract Law. Far from being the dastardly villain of our saga, contracts are the sturdy engine that propels your creative journey. If your IP is the heart pumping life into your comic, then your contract is the engine—carefully engineering every clause to safeguard your rights and map out royalty payouts, ensuring that the rewards of your masterpiece flow just as perfectly as your adventures unfold. Turn the page, and let's dive in!

Notes

1 *Burrow-Giles Lithographic Co. v. Sarony*, 111 U.S. 53 (1884).

2 *Trade-Mark Cases*, 100 U.S. 82, 94 (1879).

3 Compendium of U.S. Copyright Office Practices, Third Edition, § 313.2: U.S. Copyright Office, Compendium of U.S. Copyright Office Practices § 313.2 (3d ed. 2021), https://www.copyright.gov/comp3/chap300/ch300-copyrightable-authorship.pdf.

4 Epps, J. (2024, November 29). As AI grows, the comic industry is fighting back against the encroaching tech. Screen Rant. Retrieved from https://screenrant.com/comics-industry-ai-fears-future-plans-op-ed/.

5 Thomson Reuters Foundation. (2024, June 28). AI for creating comics? Europe's industry completely rejects it, Tintin executive says. South China Morning Post. Retrieved from https://www.scmp.com/lifestyle/arts-culture/article/3268398/ai-creating-comics-europes-industry-completely-rejects-it-tintin-executive-says.

6 Agency. (2024, July 2). European cartoon artists now face a new, faceless adversary: AI. *The Star.* Retrieved from https://www.thestar.com.my/lifestyle/culture/2024/07/02/european-cartoon-artists-now-face-a-new faceless-adversary-ai (Additionally, the European Union's upcoming Artificial Intelligence Act is expected to enforce transparency in AI training models and open them up to copyright lawsuits, a move supported by many European comic creators.).

7 U.S. Copyright Office. (2023). *Copyright Registration Guidance: Works Containing Material Generated by Artificial Intelligence* (p. 4). Retrieved from https://www.copyright.gov/ai/ai_policy_guidance.pdf.

8 U.S. Copyright Office. (2023). *Zarya of the Dawn: Registration Decision*. Retrieved from https://www.copyright.gov/docs/zarya-of-the-dawn.pdf.

9 17 U.S.C. §101.

10 Burrow-Giles Lithographic Co. v. Sarony, 111 U.S. 53 (1884). Retrieved from https://supreme.justia.com/cases/federal/us/111/53/.

11 Feist Publications, Inc. v. Rural Tel. Serv. Co., 499 U.S. 340 (1991). Retrieved from https://supreme.justia.com/cases/federal/us/499/340/.

12 Feist Publications, Inc. v. Rural Tel. Serv. Co., 499 U.S. 340, 362 (1991). Retrieved from https://supreme.justia.com/cases/federal/us/499/340/.

13 Feist Publications, Inc. v. Rural Tel. Serv. Co., 499 U.S. 340, 362 (1991). Retrieved from https://supreme.justia.com/cases/federal/us/499/340/.

14 Katelyn Chedraoui, "This Company Got a Copyright for an Image Made Entirely With AI. Here's How," *CNET* (Feb. 10, 2025, 6:00 a.m. PT), https://www.cnet.com/tech/services-and-software/this-company-got-a-copyright-for-an-image-made-entirely-with-ai-heres-how/.

JOINT AUTHORSHIP
INDEPENDENT CONTRACTORS
LICENSES & OPTIONS
SOLO AUTHORSHIP
PLOYEES
IN
CREATOR AGREEMENTS
WARRANTIES
REPRESENTATIONS
IDEAS
COPYRIGHT
EXPRESSION
AUTHORSHIP
ARTWORK
SCRIPTS
INDEMNITY
NOTICE & CURE
LICENSING AGREEMENTS
OUT
PUBLISHING
MERCHANDISING
MOVIES & TV
ANCILLARY
ROYALTY

PART 3

Contracts

The Engine Which Drives the Deal

DOI: 10.1201/9781003496052-6

GETTING INTO GEAR

While intellectual property forms the vibrant heart of your comic universe, contracts are the engine that propels your work forward—ensuring that your IP, payment, and other essential rights remain secure. A well-drafted contract clearly delineates each party's roles and responsibilities, preventing your creative collaboration from veering into a maze of legal complications. Just as a pilot must understand the controls of the aircraft before taking flight, you must understand your contracts to keep your project aloft and your rights safely on course.

CHAPTER 4

Contracts

The Engine Which Drives the Deal

DOI: 10.1201/9781003496052-7

WHAT IS A CONTRACT?

IP may be the heart of your work, but a **contract** is the engine that drives the deal. Without a contract to define the duties and obligations of each party, a collaboration can quickly spiral out of control, ending up in a thicket of thorny legal problems. And like an engine, unless you understand how one works, you're not going to be able to build or fix one when a working relationship starts to sputter and seize up.

My goal throughout this book is to give you the tools to help you navigate your agreements so that you can understand your contractual obligations well enough to steer clear of those scary areas that would put you in breach of contract. Hopefully, you'll find that the better you are able to read a contract, the less boring it will appear. I don't want to oversell it—you're not going to find reading a license agreement as adrenaline-spiking as the latest Marvel/DC/Archie crossover, but you will find that when you know what each clause in your agreement means and how it functions, you'll be able to see exactly how it applies to *you*. It will become personal … and *that* will make it interesting.

THE COMPREHENSIBLE CONTRACT

Understanding legal mumbo-jumbo can be tricky, but it really helps if you imagine how you would be affected by each clause. So, if you feel your eyes glazing over, think: "What does this clause stop *me* from doing? What does it require *me* to do? What does it make *me* responsible for?" As they say in Hollywood trailers, "This time it's personal!"

A contract is a legally enforceable agreement that determines the rights and obligations of each contracting party. In the United States, every valid contract needs:

- An offer that is accepted.
- Terms that are definite and specific, not vague, or ambiguous (although sometimes these terms can be implied).
- Consideration—something that each party gives or gets for entering into the contract.
- Legal capacity—each party must be competent to enter into a contract.
- Legal purpose—a contract to do something illegal is automatically void.

An **express contract** is one where all of the material terms are stated, as are the contract formation steps of **offer**, **acceptance**, and **consideration**.

An **implied contract** is one that is formed through the behavior of the parties or assumed by the circumstances. When certain key terms are not discussed in an implied contract, a court may fill them in with "reasonable" terms. For the most part, you want to be very careful to avoid creating implied contracts, since, by definition, their terms are uncertain. However, if you're pitching an idea to a publishing company, you may want there to be at least an implied contract for its protection.

Breach of Contract: When one party does not perform their duties or fulfill their obligations under a contract, they are in default or have breached the contract. We will deal with contract breach more fully in Breach of Contract, p. 322.

READ IT OR WEEP!

The fact that you didn't read your contract or that you didn't understand what you read is no defense to the enforcement of the contract. As the Supreme Court of Montana pointed out:

> One who executes a written contract is presumed to know the contents of the contract and to assent to those specified terms, in the absence of fraud, misrepresentation, or other wrongful act by the other contracting party. Absent incapacity to contract, **ignorance of the contents of a written contract is not a ground for relief from liability**.

Quinn v. Briggs, 172 Mont 468, 476, 565 P2d 297, 301 [1977]

THINGS THAT LOOK LIKE CONTRACTS, BUT MAY NOT BE CONTRACTS

A Proposal

A proposal, by contrast, is merely an offer to enter into a contract. If someone sends you a proposal, they are essentially saying, "Here are the terms which, should you accept them, will form our contract." Many artists submit proposals with a signature block at the end with a statement like "sign below to indicate your intent to be bound by the above." If the person to whom the proposal is submitted signs, then the proposal may in fact be transformed into a contract. In fact, even **if it isn't signed**, if the person to whom a proposal has been submitted acts as if there is a contract in place (e.g., using the artist's work after receiving a proposal), then a court may find that a contract was formed between the parties. The downside to a proposal is that it's often extremely cursory and doesn't contain many important clauses that a more fully expressed contract would. As a result, if this is the only contract in place, the parties may soon find themselves fighting over what exactly their agreement is. Furthermore, if the proposal doesn't address key deal points and is too vague, a court might find that it's not a contract at all.

A Deal Memo

A deal memo is a short memorandum outlining the major deal points of a contract. It is often a more complete agreement than a proposal. Signed by both parties, the deal memo is often (but not always) a binding contract. It is often used as a quick agreement to get the parties working together until a more complete agreement (a "long-form" agreement) can be drafted and signed by the parties.

Memorandum of Understanding

A Memorandum of Understanding (MOU),[1] by contrast, is "an agreement to agree" and is usually **not** legally binding. Keep in mind that people, unfortunately, use the terms MOU and Deal Memo interchangeably. Whether or not a document is binding is controlled by its terms, not its title.

Deal Points

Deal points are those terms that everyone must agree on before negotiating the rest of a contract. These are the terms that would appear on a deal memo or short-form contract. Major deal points are usually the points that are negotiated first between the parties; as a result, these are the clauses on which this book will spend the most time.[2]

Promises Are Not Always Contracts

In your professional career, you should have at least a rough idea of what constitutes a contract: A contract is an agreement that a court will enforce. Not all agreements are contracts, and not all agreements are enforceable. Here are some examples:

- A publishing company executive says to you at Comic Con, "Your comic looks good. I think we may try to publish it." You would have a hard time claiming there is a contract at this point. There are no terms and no definite obligation on the publishing company's part.
- Imagine your dear ol' granny, with a twinkle in her eye, pulls you aside and whispers, "Darling, I'm going to give you a cool $10,000 so you can print those snazzy comic books of yours. No strings attached!" You're over the moon, already dreaming in CMYK. But hold the press! A few days later, after Granny's hot streak turned ice cold at the Vegas slots, she backpedaled faster than a superhero in reverse. Suddenly, that promise of cash is deader than Bruce Wayne's mom. If you think you can legally strong-arm her into paying up, think again. Promises to make a gift aren't worth the paper they're not printed on. And besides, Granny's now penniless, ducking and weaving from a bookie named "Big Tony" who doesn't take IOUs. So, unless you can draw a comic that pays, you might want to start brainstorming Plan B!
- Even if the parties agree on the key terms, if they are still negotiating the agreement, there is likely no contract.[3]

THE CONTRACT "THEMES"

Just as comic books tackle big dramatic themes betwixt their two glossy covers, contracts confront important business themes in the paragraphs between the introduction and signature block.

Most contract clauses deal with one or more of the following themes:

- Who are the parties?
- What are you getting?
- What are you giving in exchange for what you are getting?
- Who owns the IP? What specific rights are owned by which parties, and is that ownership exclusive?
- What promises are being made about the IP?
- What protections do you have?
- What rules govern the business relationship between the parties?
- What happens when something goes wrong?

As you'll see, these concepts are interdependent. Any given contract clause may deal with several concepts, each one affecting the other. Once you learn to view each paragraph of an agreement through one of these thematic "windows," the parts of the contract should start to appear more integrated in your mind. Let's look at each of these themes in greater depth from a creator's point of view.

Who Are the Parties?

This is not as simple as it may seem; the inker you're hiring may, in fact, want their loan-out company to be party to the contract (See Loan-Out Companies p. 109), or the script that you're acquiring may be based on a novel written by someone other than the author of the script, and that original author may have rights to receive money from your comic. Furthermore, a contract may have more than two parties, each of whom may have a different set of duties and obligations toward the others.

What Are the Parties Getting?

What you're getting depends on the kind of deal you're negotiating. From a comic book creator's perspective, you will generally be acquiring the following:

- **Rights**. Contract clauses that deal with intellectual property rights are often the most critical part of your contract. And as we saw in the last section, controlling IP rights is the key to maintaining control of your property. (See Part 6, The Law Library, p. 333.)
  - If you hire an artist or writer to work on your book, you will need contract clauses that deal with:
    - The copyright in that artist's illustrations or writing. (See Appendix A A Comic Creator's Guide to Copyright Law, p. 335.)
    - Any idea rights that the artist may have in your project. (See Appendix B A Comic Creator's Guide to Protecting Ideas, p. 390.)
    - The right to use any character designs they own and have used on your project

- If your comic book features third-party intellectual property rights, you will need to license those rights from their owners (See Chapter 9—Clearances and Licensing the Rights of Others, p. 198), including:
    - The right to use third-party copyrighted characters, scripts, and song lyrics
    - The right to use third-party trademarked logos, catchphrases, and costume designs
    - The right to use a real person's likeness in your work. (See Appendix D A Comic Creator's Guide to the Right of Publicity and Other Privacy Rights, p. 426.)

In addition to IP rights, a contract can grant you rights to:

- **Services**. Virtually anybody whom you or your company hires is performing services for you. You'll be getting the right to direct their creative input and require them to deliver certain creative assets to you (such as sketches, completed pages, scripts, etc.).
- **Property**. The lease of equipment, the purchase of materials to create your book, and the physical hand-drawn comic book pages are all physical property that you may acquire under the contract.
- **Money**. Money to fund your comic book run, or your services as an artist, or the royalties from your publishing company, or your merchandiser are situations in which one of the parties receives monetary compensation.

What Are the Parties Giving in Exchange for What They're Getting?

This is the flip side of the above:

- **Services**. If you're an artist working for a comic book company, you're trading your services as an illustrator in exchange for a fee. You're also trading away the right to use the work you produce.
- **Property**. Whether or not you are obligated to let the publishing company keep your physical artwork is also subject to contract. Make no mistake about it: if you sign a work-for-hire agreement, your right to keep your physical artwork must also be in writing, or you may end up with a paycheck and little more.
- **Intellectual Property Rights**. Artists trade a portion (or all) of their IP rights to publishers. As we've seen, these rights could be nonexclusive, exclusive, or work for hire.
- **Money or the right to money** is usually what a publishing company gives an artist when it hires them or publishes the artist's book (in exchange for the Artist's IP rights, services, and property). Obviously, compensation comes in many forms: royalties, kill fees, salaries, deferred compensation, profit participation, bonuses, licensing fees, buyouts, option prices, and so on. (See Appendix G Compensation, p. ##.)

Who Owns the IP? What Specific Rights Are Owned by Which Parties, and Is That Ownership Exclusive?

For a comic book creator, grasping the concept of IP ownership isn't just smart, it's their superpower. Why? Because knowing who owns the IP and what specific rights and ownership exclusivity entail is like having the ultimate defense against the kryptonite of legal woes. It's the shield that guards the realms of creativity and the hammer that forges the path to commercial success. When a creator understands to what extent they own or control all the rights to reproduce, distribute, and transform their work, they can strategically navigate the galaxy of publishing deals. But if their work is conjured under the spell of a publisher's work-for-hire contract, then, faster than a speeding bullet, the publisher swoops in to claim all the IP rights. And when creators band together like a league of extraordinary artists, they must ensure their joint ownership agreement is as solid as adamantium, clearly defining who can wield what powers. So, dear creators, don your capes of diligence and arm yourselves with the knowledge of IP rights—because in the comic book industry, it's your origin story that defines your future adventures.

HIRING AN ARTIST? PUT THE IP IN THE CONTRACT!

If you're hiring another artist to work on your book, your contract with them MUST address their IP rights in the project. Do you own the IP rights to their work, or are they just licensing them to you? And regardless of which of you owns the work, you also must have the right to license and assign all the IP rights in your comic to publishers, merchandisers, and other third parties ... or you'll never be able to exploit your comic. As you can see, IP clauses can be both tricky and critical. Tread carefully. (See Hiring Other Artists, p. 150.)

What Promises Are Being Made about the IP?

In addition to the exchange of services or property for money, what other promises are being made by the parties about the IP (and other critical areas)? For instance, you might be promising:

- That you have the right to enter into the contract with the other party and that you have all the IP rights to the comic. (See Contract Anatomy, "Representations and Warranties," p. 470.)
- That you agree to the publishing company's restrictions on your ability to publicize your work. (See Contract Anatomy, "Publicity," p. 468.)
- That your comic book or graphic novel will not defame anybody or infringe on anybody's copyrights or trademarks. (See Appendix E: A Comic Creator's Guide to Libel and Defamation, p. 433.)

What Protections Do the Parties Have?

Smooth business relationships require more than promises between the parties; they require each party to be able to protect his or her valuable assets. For example:

- How often can you check the other party's accounting to make sure that you have been paid what you were promised? (See Contract Anatomy, "Audit and Accounting," p. 447.)
- Who has approval over a creative or business decision? (See Contract Anatomy, "Approvals," p. 462.)
- Who pays the legal bill if you are sued for somebody else's mistake or breach? (See Contract Anatomy, "Indemnification," p. 473.)

What Rules Govern the Business Relationship between the Parties?

In a sense, the entire contract is a rulebook for the relationship between the parties. Many provisions determine important housekeeping functions that are separate and apart from the quid pro quo issues at the heart of the contract.

For example:

- How do you communicate with the other parties? (See Contract Anatomy, "Notice and Cure," p. 475.)
- Can you assign your rights or duties under the contract to other people? (See Contract Anatomy, "Assignment and Delegation," p. 473.)
- How long is the contract in effect? (See Contract Anatomy, "Engagement," p. 453.)

What Happens When Something Goes Wrong?

If something goes wrong, you can always sue, right? Perhaps not. It is quite common for contracts to contain clauses limiting a person's right to sue in court, requiring that person to arbitrate instead. Several kinds of clauses govern how the parties must solve their disagreements. The following questions might be addressed, for example:

- Can the parties sue, or must they arbitrate disputes? (See Contract Anatomy, "Remedies," p. 476.)
- Do the parties have time to cure problems before they are in breach of contract? (See Contract Anatomy, "Notice and Cure," p. 475.)
- What happens if something goes wrong and it's nobody's fault (e.g., an earthquake, flood, or fire)? (See Contract Anatomy, "*Force Majeure*," p. 469.)
- Where must a lawsuit or arbitration be initiated? (See Contract Anatomy, "Choice of Law," p. 477.)

CLARITY, CLARITY, CLARITY!

You should always draft your contracts so that they can be read and understood by somebody who was not part of the negotiations. Contracts are very often assigned to third parties who were not present during the initial deal-making. As a result, if the language of the contract is not clear, these third parties may not understand how to interpret the contract. For instance, if you land a publisher for your comic, and your publishing agreement says only that you "**must deliver the 'Comic Book' to the publisher**," you may think that's straightforward.

But pause for a moment—what does that term "comic book" mean in this instance? Does it mean: All the physical artwork required to publish the comic? Just the digital files? The physical artwork, digital files, and legal deliverables required in the making of the comic (contracts with writers and artists, etc.)? A fully printed comic book? You could think it means one thing; the publisher could think it means another.

You want to make sure that there are no hidden assumptions as to what each party was supposed to do. The best contract is like a roadmap for a business transaction—it shouldn't require a legal specialist to help you understand it.

RULES OF THUMB FOR CONTRACTS

1. **Some kinds of contracts must be in writing**. Sometimes a handshake just won't do. It doesn't matter that the layout artist whom you hired as an independent contractor to design your website promised that she is creating her website design as a work for hire, unless she signed the contract with you that *says* it's a work for hire, it's just not a work for hire. In fact, she may still have some rights to use her design on other sites, and in other media, because she owns the copyright and has—at best—only granted you a license to use the site.
2. **Some kinds of contracts don't need to be in writing**. Contracts for the protection of an idea, for instance, don't need to be in writing. Neither do many contracts to perform services for a certain amount of money. What this means is that you need to be very careful when brainstorming with somebody about working on their concept or negotiating with somebody about the possibility of their working with you. You need to understand when you're forming a contract and when you're not. Which is why, for clarity's sake, the best practice is to get all contracts in writing.
3. **Especially when you're working with your friends, you need a contract**. When you're working with your friends, feelings can get easily hurt; it's best to have a written contract to which everyone can refer in order to determine what duties each friend owes to the other. It's just human nature; people remember their obligations toward others in a way that's most favorable to themselves. Written contracts can preserve friendships.

4. **A contract should be clear**. A good contract should be so clear and understandable that even people who were not involved in its negotiation should be able to follow it. It's true that there's a lot of bad contract drafting out there, many lawyers are sesquipedalian when they should be plainspoken (see what I did there?). As a matter of fact, there are very few "magic legal words" needed in a contract. If you can state each party's duties and obligations to each other in plain language, you will have a more effective contract.
5. **Watch out for "Defined Terms."** Words don't always mean what you think they do, especially if a contract defines them very differently from the dictionary meaning. So, if a contract defines the term "comic book," to mean "*that work of sequential art prepared by the creator, as well as any audio-visual work defined therefrom* ..." Well then, guess what? For the purpose of the contract, the term Comic Book could also include *any movie based upon your comic*! Not something you want to suddenly find out when Hollywood comes to you for the rights, only to have your publisher step forward, clear its throat, point to the contract, and tell Tinseltown that studios should be dealing directly with the publisher and not you.
6. **Know what you're representing, warranting, and indemnifying**. Every publishing agreement has both "representations and warranties" and "indemnification" provisions. Among other things, the representations and warranties are promises that you are making to the publisher about the ownership of the artwork that you are letting them publish. If you don't own everything free and clear, and the publisher gets sued, the indemnification clause may stipulate that you must pay all of their legal bills.
7. **Hiring a lawyer to negotiate and draft a contract is cheaper than hiring a lawyer to litigate a breach of contract**. I know lawyers can be expensive. Still, they can save you a lot more money than they cost. And while it might cost a couple of grand to negotiate a potentially lucrative publishing agreement, it would cost you tens of thousands of dollars to litigate the same agreement. Publishers have lawyers; shouldn't you?
8. **A "click-wrap" agreement is binding**. Yes, I hate it too. But the fact remains that when you click "I Agree" before you register with a website or load a piece of software, you have likely formed a binding agreement. Yes, I know there was no negotiation. Yes, I know you don't have time to read the darn thing. Yes, I know you don't have any choice if you want to use the service. Bottom line: a click can consummate a contract.
9. **When negotiating with somebody, don't take his or her word for what the contract says**. Publishers use contracts that they are very familiar with, and it may be tempting to have the well-meaning acquisitions editor explain her contract to you. But the fact is, she is not your attorney, and she may not be an attorney at all. In short, she may think the contract means one thing for you when in fact it doesn't. Furthermore, there will be language in that contract that says, in effect, that the only legally binding agreement is what's on the page and not what has been explained to you.

I sincerely hope this book will help you interpret your contracts, but as I said before, nothing can replace the advice of an experienced lawyer who has read your agreement.

10. **You will be bound by a contract even if you didn't understand it, and even if you didn't read it**. Saying you didn't understand your contract when you signed it is not a defense. And saying that you didn't even *read* your contract before you signed it is not a defense to anything … Except the allegation that you treat your work as a professional.

Now that you have an overview of some of the issues involved in contract law, how about a crash course in the particulars?

THE ANATOMY OF A CONTRACT

You will get more out of the rest of the book if you flip to the back and work your way through "**Appendix G Contract Anatomy for Comic Book Creators**," p. 447. There, we will place a contract on our lab table, and like a first-year medical student, dissect it clause-by-clause and peer into all its gory anatomy.

Just as the tendons and muscles define and power a body, a contract's clauses determine its shape. When you understand how clauses work—what each one of them means—you can better negotiate your contractual obligations, rights, and compensation. In our contract anatomy class, we'll learn the key phrases that get us money and the critical paragraphs that transfer our rights.

There, you will learn how to read the kinds of clauses that we will be referring to throughout the rest of this book. We will look at sample contract language and how these clauses fit into the contract as a whole. It's a great place to start if you need to get familiar with the function and definition of typical clauses. So, if you're uncertain as to the difference between an "Indemnification" and an "Inducement" provision or need to know how to troubleshoot "Defined Terms," this is the place to go. In fact, it's a good idea to bookmark this section as a handy guide to understanding the clauses you will see in the contracts in the rest of the book.

If you're already familiar with contract anatomy, feel free to jump to the next section and flip back to **Appendix G Contract Anatomy for Comic Book Creators, p. 447** as a refresher.

NEXT STEPS

Now that we have an IP heart and our contract engine, we're ready to build the chassis of our Comic Book Property. Turn the page and pick up your rivet gun; it's time to build a "Com-MECH!"

Or, if you need some specific jumping-off points:

- I just got a publishing contract—I don't understand it! (See The Comic Book Publishing Agreement, p. 256.)
- I want to make a comic book with another artist; what kind of contract do we need? (See The Collaboration Agreement, p. 119.)
- Someone wants to hire me to draw a comic book (or I want to hire an artist to work on my book). What should the contract say? (See Illustrator Work for Hire Agreement, p. 161.)
- I'm ready for my anatomy class! (See Appendix G Contract Anatomy for Comic Book Creators, p. 447.)

Notes

1 For a cogent description of MOUs, see Memorandum of Understanding (MOU): Definition, Contents, Pros/Cons, vs. MOA, Investopedia (06/26/2024), https://www.investopedia.com/terms/m/mou.asp.

2 I realize that a more exact phrase might be "these are the clauses on which this book will spend the most *space*," but given the fact that a sequential art narrative like a comic book creates the illusion of time, I'm just keeping with the theme.

3 *Weinstein Co. v. Smokewood Entertainment Group, LLC*, 664 F.Supp.2d 332, 346 (S.D.N.Y., 2009). ("It is fundamental to contract law that mere participation in negotiations and discussions does not create binding obligation, even if agreement is reached on all disputed terms.") However, a court can find that parties have entered a preliminary agreement to negotiate in good faith based on the following factors: "(1) the language of the agreement; (2) the context of the negotiations; (3) the existence of open terms; (4) any partial performance; and (5) the necessity of putting the agreement in final form, as indicated by the customary form of such transactions." Weinstein at 356, internal citations omitted.

LLABORATION
BOTAGE!
COMPANY
FORMATION
REGISTRATION
CLEARANCES
COLLABORATION
AGREEMENTS
LICENSE
AGREEMENTS
SERVICE
AGREEMENTS

PART 4

Putting It Together

DOI: 10.1201/9781003496052-8

SECTION OVERVIEW

Now that you have a background in intellectual property and contracts, let's start to build on that foundation by constructing a solid comic book property. Whether you're working solo, with a partner, or hiring a few extra artists to get the job done, this is the section for you. You will learn how to surf the perilous waters of service agreements, traverse the pitfalls of partnerships, and forge mighty links in your copyright's chain of title. You'll even learn how to make a legal person—parthenogenetically—through the blessed miracle of corporate formation.

Yes, righteous reader, in this section you will sew all the legal pieces of your comic book property together, raise it up to receive that Promethean spark of copyright, and shout: "IT'S ALIVE!"

This section will help you:

- Identify key issues for solo creators (See *The Solo Creator*, p. 96.)
- Understand GEN-AI and its effect on the ownership of your work (See, Using GEN-AI in Comics, p. 59.)
- Register and protect your copyright (See Copyright Registration, p. 363.)
- Setup a company, like an LLC or corporation (See Setting Up Shop, p. 102.)
- Hire attorneys and accountants (See Accountants and Attorneys, p. 110.)
- Identify legal issues with potential partners and negotiate a collaboration agreement (See Collaboration, p. 116.)
- Hire illustrators and writers to help you make your comic book (See Hiring Other Artists, p. 150.)
- Identify potential legal issues with comic book intellectual property and clearances (See Clearances and Licensing the Rights of Others, p. 198.)

CREATIVE ROLES

It takes a lot of creative input to make a comic book or graphic novel. And while it is true that a number of comic creators do it all by themselves, other creators prefer to hire specialists, such as:

- **Writer**. Writing comic books is a very specific craft. In fact, it's more similar to writing screenplays than it is to writing short stories, which is why the literary component of a comic book is called the script. The emphasis is on visual storytelling: the interplay between what is seen in the panel and what is described in the captions or spoken by the characters. While most comic book writers produce the comic book script themselves, some comic book writers specialize in certain aspects of script creation:

- **The Plotter** shapes the overall narrative, designs the character arcs, and provides the theme of the work. In short, the events and characters that appear in the comic book are generated by the plotter. If the comic book is based on a short story, the short story's author may receive credit for creating the plot.
- **The Scripter,** by contrast, is largely responsible for creating the text in the dialogue and captions. A good scripter must have an ear for language and the ability to convey character using a minimum amount of words.
- **Penciller**. This is the first visual artist to put her stamp on the work. The penciller sketches out the action in each panel (traditionally in pencil on Bristol board, but now often on the computer tablet) and designs the layout of the panels. In many respects, the penciller is like a combination of a film director and a cinematographer: she decides where to put the metaphorical "camera" through which each panel is "shot."
- **Inker**. Once the penciller has finished laying out the panels, the inker commits the frequently wispy, sketchy, penciller's lines to their final form. The inker outlines the Penciller's work in bold strokes, adding detail, shading, and omitting extraneous visual noise.
- **Colorist**. From the inker, the panels go to the Colorist, who colors each panel, adds highlights, and adds visual special effects (lens flares, sunbursts, etc.). Key aspects of the job are providing appropriate colors to help tell a compelling visual story and maintaining consistency of color from panel to panel.

- **Letterer**. All text in the comic is laid down by the letterer. More than just a typesetter, a good letterer adds emotional color and inflection to the words through typeface selection, font choice, and sound effect design.
- **Editor:** The editor is the guardian of precision and cohesion in the final product. They review and refine both text and visuals—spotting discrepancies, ensuring clarity, and polishing the work so that every element aligns perfectly with the intended vision.

CATEGORIES OF COMIC PROPERTY

There are typically three ways in which you might get your comic book published, each with its own form of comic book property:

- **Publisher-Owned Work**. You are hired by a comic book publishing company and create the comic book, often using their characters and their brands. This arrangement is usually done as a work for hire, with the publishing company owning the comic property. (See Chapter 12, Working for a Publishing Company, p. 250.)
- **Creator-Driven Work**. You pitch your concept to a publisher, which agrees to publish it upon completion. You put your creative team together and create the comic book. You license certain publishing and other rights to the publisher. (See Chapter 13, The Comic Book Publishing Agreement, p. 256.)
- **Creator-Owned Work**. You create a comic book and publish the comic yourself. You own the comic property. (See "The Solo Creator," p. 97.)

Whether you're self-publishing or hope to have your comic released by a publishing company, the concerns are the same: make sure that you own or control all of the rights to the comic. Remember, publishing involves the exercise of copyrights to the work. If your comic contains work by other artists, authors, or owners, *you must have their written permission use their work in your comic, as well as their permission allowing you to grant these rights to any publishing company*. Unfortunately, this is one instance where a handshake just won't do. You need it in writing. We will explore how to do this in the next few chapters.

INTERVIEW

Advice for Newbie Writers

"In this current era, when you're just starting out, the most prominent way to own a comic property is to be **creator-owned**. For instance, most webcomics are creator-owned. However, there is no upfront money when you're producing a creator-owned property. With a **work for hire**, however, you get paid up front. With **creator-driven**, the publisher says, 'I owe you,' and pays you when it sells the book."

If you want to be a comic book writer, here's what you need to know:

- Be professional
- Be brief
- Be courteous
- Be polite
- Be engaging

- Be exciting
- **Don't be** that guy that everybody tells stories about later.
- **Don't be** the guy who chases down the editor-in-chief of the publishing company just to find out what hotel room he is staying at San Diego Comic Con.
- Write anything. Writing anything is better than writing nothing.

A writer writes. Don't just talk: 'Oh, I can write a better story than so-and-so.' Don't talk. Write. Don't 'wait for the writing to percolate.' We all have stories we can write about. A writer writes.

Once you've written your story, get it published. Even if it is self-publishing. Publish it.

Don't be a user—be a creator. There's a line in *Glengarry Glen Ross*, when Alec Baldwin says: 'ABC: Always Be Closing.' That's a good mantra for the comic book creator: 'ABC: Always Be comic-ing.'"

DAVID GALLAHER *is the Harvey Award-winning comic book author of the DC Comics' series High Moon.*

CHAPTER 5

The Solo Creator

DOI: 10.1201/9781003496052-9

THE SOLO CREATOR

From a legal perspective, creating a comic book by yourself is the easiest route... if you don't consider the countless hours of writing, drawing, inking, coloring, lettering, proofreading, and coffee-fueled soul-searching.

But once all the hard work is done, all you really have to do is register the copyright to your work and try to get it published. Couldn't be simpler, right?

Almost.

Believe it or not, the toughest legal aspect to creating a comic book solo may be ensuring that you really did, in fact, create all the work that went into your book. Because the minute you work with another illustrator, base a part of your work on somebody else's story, include somebody else's trademark, or even develop your comic book plot and characters in the context of a writing support group, well then... you may have legal issues.

Let me be clear: it doesn't mean that any of the above is impermissible; in fact there are straightforward contractual methods for dealing with all the above scenarios. Furthermore, some of those situations—like developing your concept in a writer support group—may not even require any contract drafting at all.

What it does mean, however, is that as you're developing your solo opus, you must periodically analyze how you're creating your work to ensure that your final creation will not be derailed by unexpected third parties demanding a seat at the bargaining table with your publisher. In other words, even if you are working alone, *you must take time to think of the impact of your creative relationships as well as the sources of all of your material.*

THE SOLO CREATOR'S KEY TASKS

As a solo creator, you have several key legal tasks when creating your book:

1. Making sure that your comic property doesn't include the IP rights of unidentified third parties, and
2. Making sure the IP rights to the comic book property are protected by:
   a. **Contacting** for and **recording** with the Copyright Office any third-party IP rights you've used in your comic, and
   b. **Registering** your copyright in the comic.

What Kind of Solo Are You?

Super-Solo: The purist form of solo creator creates everything in his comic book: from story to script, from pencils to inking and lettering. If you're tackling a project like that, your primary legal concern in the creation stage is to make sure your copyright is registered with the U.S. Copyright Office. (See Copyright Registration, p. 363.)

Semi-Solo: You may be writing the script and drawing the book, but you've gotten the story from someone else. Or perhaps you've included snippets from song lyrics or newspaper advertisements. Maybe you've designed a character based on your boyfriend (minus the video game controller surgically attached to his hand).

Point being, your book contains some elements that didn't originate with you (let's call them "third-party elements"). Unlike the "super-solo," you now have several tasks:

1. Analyze those third-party elements to see if you need to get permission to use them, and if you do need permission, either get that permission or cut out those elements. (See Clearances and Licensing the Rights of Others, p. 198.)
2. Register the copyright to your work. (See Copyright Registration, p. 363.)
3. Record any licenses from those third parties. (See Copyright Recordation, Assignments, and Transfers, p. 368.)

LESS THAN $100 COULD GET YOU $150,000

Don't "blow off" copyright registration! It's less than $100, and you can potentially get a lot more money winning a lawsuit against a copyright infringer if someone infringes your work *after* you've registered it—up to $150,000 for willful infringement of your copyright (these are called "statutory damages"). But you lose this right to statutory damages if you don't register on time. (See Copyright Infringement, p. 44.)

For a step-by-step guided walk-through on how to register your copyright. (See Copyright Registration, p. 363.)

PROTECTING THE CHAIN OF TITLE

To protect the rights in your work you need to maintain a strong **chain of title**, by registering your copyright with the U.S. Copyright Office, recording any copyright transfers (to you or from you), always displaying the proper copyright notice on all copies of the book (and any derivative works, like action figures, posters, movies, etc.), and getting contractual permission to use any third-party-owned copyrights you've included in your book.

What Is a Chain of Title?

The **chain of title** is the (hopefully) unbroken record of ownership and conveyance of the copyright and other legal rights to the comic book property. If there are any breaks in this chain, you have a "**Color-of-title**": a document that appears to be evidence of copyright ownership, but due to the broken link, it is not actually evidence—but can be, if that link is repaired.

You will need to prove your **chain of title** to potential partners, publishers, distributors, merchandisers, Hollywood producers, and a variety of other third parties during the life of a comic book property.

> **Example**: Jules registers the copyright to his comic book, "Captain Cuttlefish vs. the Parakeet Patrol," and e-mails his pitch deck into Klortho Comics, with the hopes of striking a publishing deal with them. His illustrator, Quinn, uploads some of the designs onto a T-Shirt design website but fails to read the fine print which lets the T-Shirt company mass produce any design and sell it, even without letting the account holder know. Klortho Comics is interested in the comic book and wants to acquire the broadest possible exclusive rights. However, as long as the T-Shirt company has the right to make and sell Captain Cuttlefish T-Shirts, those rights cannot be exclusive to the Klortho Comics. And Klortho might wonder, if that is a break in the chain and there is a color-of-title, are there other problems as well?

Any document related to copyright ownership should be a link in your chain of title, including elements like:

- Copyright registrations
- Certificates of authorship
- Work for Hire and other contracts dealing with the creation of copyright interests
- Copyright licenses
- Copyright assignments

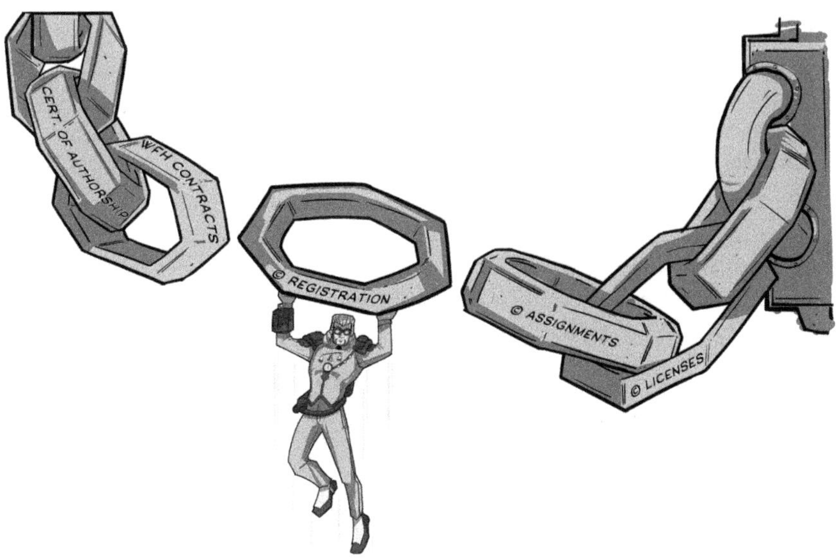

GEN-AI: A WORD OF CAUTION

If you want to use GEN-AI writing and artwork in your comic, you need to be aware of the potential impact that has on your chain of title. When a generative AI system ingests your comic book artwork, it effectively "blurs the clear chain of your legal title" by interpolating your creative content with thousands, if not millions, of other copyrighted works. It can inadvertently produce material that is substantially similar to the copyrighted work of others, raising potential infringement claims and muddying the market by introducing near duplicates that challenge both the originality and the economic value of your creations.[1] Comic book publishers are understandably cautious when accepting works with AI components. And before you can whisper, "Who's to know?" you should know that: AI checkers are getting better, and any publishing contract you sign will require you to pay the legal bill for you and the publishing company if your work is the subject of a copyright infringement lawsuit.

For more on using GEN-AI in your work, see Chapter 3: Using GEN-AI in Comics, p. 59.

SOLE CREATION—STEP BY STEP

1. If you're planning on working with other artists or licensing any IP, you may want to form your own company, preferably one that will limit your personal legal liability for lawsuits. You need to have this in place before you enter into any agreements, because it will be your company that will be executing the contracts, not you in your individual capacity. (See Setting Up Shop, p. 102.)
2. Avoid using GEN-AI; if you do decide to use it, make sure you understand the implications for your ability to sell and protect your work. (See Using GEN-AI in Comics, p. 59.)
3. Make sure your work has been cleared and is free from intellectual property issues. If necessary, negotiate and draft agreements with any third parties whose work you have used. (See Clearances and Licensing the Rights of Others, p. 198.)
4. If you are planning to incorporate third-party, copyright-free work into your comic (old paintings, early 20th-century short stories, etc.), make sure to perform a copyright search to ensure that it actually is in the public domain. (See Clearances and Licensing the Rights of Others, p. 198.)
5. Negotiate and execute agreements with any artists and writers:
   a) With whom have you collaborated. (See The Collaboration Agreement—Key Issues, p. 119.)
   b) ... And those whom you have hired or otherwise engaged to work for you. (See Hiring Other Artists, p. 150)
   c) Make sure all collaborators sign a "certificate of authorship." (See Certificate of Authorship, p. 370.)

6. Register the copyright in your comic. (See Copyright Registration, p. 363.)
7. Record any copyright assignments necessary to perfect your chain of title. (See Copyright Recordation, Assignments, and Transfers, p. 368.)
8. Promote your work like a pro. (See Get your Message Out, p. 229.)
9. Prepare to launch your comic.
10. Get your work into the hands of publishers, printers, and readers! (See Part 5: Getting It out There, p. 227.)

Note

1 See U.S. Copyright Office, *Copyright and Artificial Intelligence, Part 3: Generative AI Training Report—Pre-Publication Version* (May 2025), available at <https://copyright.gov/ai/Copyright-and-Artificial-Intelligence-Part-3-Generative-AI-Training-Report-Pre-Publication-Version.pdf>.

CHAPTER 6

Setting Up Shop

DOI: 10.1201/9781003496052-10

GETTING DOWN TO BUSINESS

Many comic artists form a creative services company for the sole purpose of offering their artistic services to a publisher. Other comic creators form their own publishing companies to hold all the IP rights in their works (don't worry, you can still call yourself a publishing company even if you are ultimately trying to interest a bigger publishing company in acquiring your book). Heck, you might want to think even bigger and form an entertainment company for the purpose of exploiting your comic books properties in print, games, and movies. No matter the purpose of your company, the first step is often to create a *business entity*, such as a **limited liability company** (LLC) or **corporation**. There are many advantages to setting up a business entity:

1. You can divide the financial risk among several people. The members, partners, or shareholders of a business share in the company's profits and losses.
2. Your company is considered a *legal person* and as such can enter into contracts, bring lawsuits, and hold intellectual property rights (such as the copyright to a comic book).
3. You can separate your personal finances from the company's finances.
4. You may die someday, but your company doesn't have to. Some kinds of businesses can last forever, and ownership of those companies, such as shares or membership interests, can be passed down from generation to generation.

And perhaps, most importantly:

5. **You can avoid personal lawsuits!** If your company breaches a contract or infringes a copyright, it will be the company that pays the damages, *not* the company's officers or individual members. However, this **limited liability** protection is only offered with certain kinds of business entities (see the information that follows).

Obviously, forming a company doesn't guarantee profits—or even steady work—but it can shield your personal assets if your company is sued, and creating a company is crucial if you are hiring other artists to work for you.

- This chapter covers many of the key issues involved in setting up and running a creative services company:
  - How to choose and create the right type of company.
  - How to contract with loan-out companies commonly used by artists. (See Loan-Out Companies, p. 109.)
  - How to select and hire professionals such as lawyers and accountants. (See Getting Professional Help: Accountants and Attorneys, p. 110.)
  - What to do if someone threatens to sue your company. (See Chapter. 15, "Cease-and-Desist Letters," p. 328.)

A FEW KEY BUSINESS CONCEPTS

Limitation of Liability

Some business entities, such as LLCs and corporations, allow their members to limit their liability to the amount that they have invested in the company. The members of such companies are not personally liable for the debts or other legal claims against the company.

So, for example, if an LLC or corporation is sued for breach of contract, the most that each member or shareholder can lose is the amount of his or her investment in that company. If the company is bankrupt and has no more assets, the company's creditors cannot collect the company's unpaid debts from the personal assets of its members.

It is important to note, however, that the limitation of liability a company's owners (its members, shareholders, or partners) might enjoy is not ironclad. There are situations in which a court will allow creditors to "pierce the corporate veil" (a term used for LLCs as well as corporations) and hold the company's owners personally liable for the debts of the company. Courts may "pierce the corporate veil," and allow you to be sued personally if:

- If the company's members or shareholders have used the company to commit fraud.
- If the company's members or shareholders have treated the company as their "alter egos"—in other words, if the members fail to keep proper company records, mix their personal finances in with the assets of the company, or undercapitalize the company, leaving it without sufficient assets to perform normal business functions.

Respondeat Superior

Keep in mind that an employer, such as a publishing company, is generally legally responsible for the actions of its employees and agents performed during the scope of their duties.[1] This is the *respondeat superior* doctrine.

This means that if your employee gets into a car accident while picking up art supplies, your company is responsible for paying the damages from any lawsuit that may arise. Similarly, if your penciller infringes somebody's copyright in creating a splash page, your company is responsible. Furthermore, if your employee or agent enters into a contract with a third party on your company's behalf, your company may be bound by that contract. Here the employee vs. independent contractor distinction really matters. (See "Employee or Independent Contractors," p. 111.) Liability for the actions of independent contractors, unlike employees, often doesn't transfer to the contracting party except for:

- Inherently dangerous activities
- Activities that can't be delegated
- Where the contracting party exercises control over the manner in which the independent contractor performs the work.[2]

If you have a limited liability entity (such as an LLC or corporation) and your company hires an employee, your *company*, and *not you personally*, will be responsible for paying the legal damages that result from your employee's actions. On the other hand, if the employee was hired by you rather than by your limited liability business, *you personally* will be responsible for paying all claims, legal costs, and damages.

It is extra work and money to set up and run a limited liability business, but it may save you from having to sell your house to pay for a lawsuit caused by an employee's actions.

Keep in mind that it's not always clear just who is an employee and who is an independent contractor; and in some states, like California or New Jersey, the default status for a worker is that they are employees, unless you can establish otherwise. You may think you are working only with independent contractors, but you could in fact be managing employees. (See Hiring Other Artists, p. 150.)

TYPES OF BUSINESS ENTITIES

The first step in establishing your business is selecting the type of company you will establish. Comic creators typically do business as one of the following kinds of companies:

- Sole proprietorship
- General partnership
- Limited partnership
- S corporation (S corp.)
- LLC

Some business entities, such as the sole proprietorship or the general partnership, do not require any legal formalities to start up. Other kinds of businesses, such as the LLC or the corporation (S or C corp.), can only be created by filing and registering with the state government.

Details on how to set up all of these entities are beyond the scope of this book, so we are only going to concentrate on three kinds of businesses:

- Sole proprietorships
- General partnerships
- Limited Liability Companies (LLC)

INFO BEYOND THIS BOOK

TIP: This book cannot cover all the legal requirements for creating a business; there are entire books devoted to that subject alone. Nolo Press (www.nolo.com) has a series of easy-to-read books on business entity formation. Before you take any money, sign any contracts, or hire anyone, you are encouraged to seek an attorney who is experienced in setting up business organizations.

Sole Proprietorship

The *sole proprietorship* is the default form of business. You are a sole proprietor—automatically—the moment you start doing business by yourself, without having formed another kind of company.

There are some advantages to being a sole proprietor:

- Virtually no legal paperwork is involved.
- Decision-making is easy because there is only one member of the company—you.
- However, there is one *huge* disadvantage to sole proprietorships:
- **There is no limitation of liability**. If your business is sued, you are sued. If the business defaults on its debts, you personally must pay the debts.

WHAT'S IN A NAME? THE D.B.A. CERTIFICATE

The law begins with the presumption that sole proprietors do business under their own name (e.g., "Nora Aron"). However, if you want to operate your sole proprietorship under a name that is different from your own (e.g., "Broken Bristol Board Publishing"), depending on where you live, you will need to file a fictitious name statement with either the city government where your business is located or with the county clerk's office or the Secretary of State's Office. These are also known as D.B.A. certificates (which stands for "doing business as"). Additionally, you should also perform business name and trademark searches to make sure that your proposed name is not currently being used by another company.

General Partnership

A general partnership may be formed when two or more people work together to own and operate a business for profit. There is usually no government filing required to create a general partnership, although it is recommended that partners have a *partnership agreement* or other contract which lays out the partners' respective rights and duties. Two or more people who work together in a common business enterprise are often surprised when the court determines that they are in fact partners in a general partnership.

A partnership carries with it certain legal implications, such as

- *Fiduciary duty*. Each partner has a heightened legal duty of loyalty and good faith toward his or her partners.
- *Unlimited personal liability*. Generally, each partner is **personally** liable for the debts and obligations his partners incur within the scope of the partnership business.
- *Partnership property*. Unless there is a partnership agreement that says otherwise, the partnership—and not the individual partners—will own all

property acquired by partnership funds, brought into the partnership, or contributed to the partnership.

- *Partnership proceeds.* Unless there is a partnership agreement that says otherwise, all partners will share equally in the income and losses of the partnership, regardless of the amount of work they actually do in the management of the business.

KNOW YOUR GENERAL PARTNERS

Be very careful when deciding to do business as a general partnership or joint venture! Because general partners must answer for the debts of the other partners incurred during the scope of the business, choosing the wrong partner can get you into personal financial trouble.

For example, Quill, Penciller, and Beard-O-Brush are general partners in A.C.T. Publishing, a startup publishing company hoping to create its first graphic novel, *Beer Bottle Baby,* a gritty story of an alcoholic anthropomorphic beer bottle and the bartender who loves him.

For the book, Beard-O decides that he needs to do extensive research on the effects of drinking and depression. Over a two-month period, he lives in a neighborhood bar, pounding back expensive imported beer and videotaping himself with the latest high-definition camera, purchased with an eye toward using it to capture images he will later rotoscope for the comic. Needless to say, he runs up quite a bar tab and electronics bill. When his creditors come a-knockin', they can attempt to collect the debt from Beard-O and from the other general partners (Quill and Penciller) as well!

This could be avoided if they formed a limited partnership or an LLC.

Joint Venture

A joint venture is a special type of general partnership; one formed for a particular and limited purpose. Artists and writers often use joint ventures to combine their two skill sets for a particular project, such as creating a comic, graphic novel, or app.

To have a joint venture, the joint venture partners must have (1) a common business purpose, such as the creation and exploitation of a comic book; (2) shared profits and losses; (3) an express or implied contract to work together; and (4) an equal hand in controlling the relationship.

Limited Liability Company (LLC)

The limited liability company, also known as an LLC, has become the business entity of choice for most small companies. This is because it has the limited liability advantages of the corporation with the flexibility of a partnership. Its features include:

- The LLC is owned by its "members."
- The LLC may be managed directly by the members (in the case of a "member-managed" LLC) or by managers whom the members appoint (in the case of a "manager-managed" LLC).
- Like the shareholders of a corporation, the members and managers enjoy limited liability status.
- State filing, called the **articles of organization**, is required to form an LLC.
- Taxation is on the individual member level, similar to the S Corp., the partnership, or the sole proprietorship.
- The rules dictating how the business is run are driven by the **operating agreement**, which is a very flexible and highly customizable contract between the members of the LLC.
- In addition to contributing cash, members may also agree to contribute services to the company, such as drawing the artwork, writing the script, or to contribute property, such as the copyright to the art, or the ownership of the drawing tablet, or the use of the computer system.

Forming an LLC

LLCs are typically formed by filing articles of organization with the secretary of state in the state in which your business is located. At this point, you will need to elect whether your LLC is a member-managed or manager-managed LLC.

- An **operating agreement** should be negotiated, agreed upon, drafted by a lawyer, and signed by the LLC's members. The operating agreement usually governs the company's structure, the duties and obligations of each of the company's members, the amount and manner of the members' contributions to the LLC, the way finances are handled, and the way voting is determined. Many states require the operating agreement to be signed within a certain time after the articles of organization have been filed.
- If you are planning on raising money with your LLC (usually done by offering LLC membership interests to investors), you should have your securities attorney carefully review, and preferably draft, your operating agreement. If you are merely soliciting donations (i.e., Kickstarter) and not offering a return on an investment, you may not need a securities attorney.
- Some states have additional formation requirements. New York, for instance, requires LLCs to publish their formation in two local newspapers within 120 days of formation, designated by the county clerk. Failure to do so results in a suspension of your ability to do business in New York![3]

THE COMPANY AS OWNER OF THE PROJECT

Regardless of which business entity you ultimately form, you must conduct all business related to the making of the comic in the name of your company. This means that:

- Everything should be paid for out of a company bank account, not a personal bank account.
- The copyright and other comic book property assets should be transferred to and owned by the company.
- The company, and not the individuals who own the company, should rent, own, or purchase all the equipment.
- The company should hire all artists and writers.
- Records of membership, partnership, or shareholder interests must be meticulously kept. Each owner's percentage of ownership must be tracked, and records adjusted as new owners join the company. Ownership interest increases and decreases each time owners invest more capital in the company.

Failure to adhere to these and other critical rules could erase the limited liability protections that the company enjoys!

COMPANY AS CONTRACTING PARTY

When engaging artists to work on the comic, it is the *company* that should enter into contracts for their services, not you personally. It is critical that you first form your LLC and execute your operating agreement *before* entering into contracts on behalf of the company! Make sure to sign all contracts in your capacity as company owner, partner, member, manager, shareholder, and so forth. Do not sign them without indicating your company status.

Example: When signing, use "Don Simmons, Managing Member, Pustulant Pimple Publishing, LLC" not "Don Simmons."

Loan-Out Companies

Loan-out companies are often used by artists, writers, and other creative types.

A loan-out company is a company formed for the sole purpose of providing the services of an artist to another company. Loan-out companies are typically either LLCs or subchapter S Corps.

When a publishing company is hiring an artist who has his or her own loan-out company, the publishing company is actually hiring the loan-out company, which in turn is providing the services of the artist.

Any contract with that artist must be drafted so that the contracting party is, in fact, the loan-out company. It is the loan-out company that provides the services of the artist to the contracting party (usually abbreviated as "f/s/o," which means "for the services of").

Example: "Publishing Company, Inc., agrees to employ Lender, Artist's Loan-Out, LLC, f/s/o The Penciller."

Additionally, all contracts with loan-outs should include an *inducement clause* at the end of the contract. (See Appendix G, "Inducement," p. 483.)

Keep in mind that loan-out companies should still be required to transfer or license copyrights and other intellectual property to your publishing company when you engage them under services contracts, just as individuals are required to do. (See Work Made for Hire, p. 350.)

Loan-out company terminology:

- *f/s/o* is a common abbreviation for the term "for services of."
- *Lender* is typically the defined term that refers to the loan-out company.
- *Inducement* is a promise by the artist that she will perform the services required by the publishing company as though she were hired directly by the company rather than through her loan-out company.

GETTING PROFESSIONAL HELP: ACCOUNTANTS AND ATTORNEYS

We can't do everything ourselves and, in some areas, we shouldn't even try. A little help from your friends is great, but sometimes you just need a professional's help. For somebody running a business, as you are, issues that deal with money or the law need a degree of professional oversight.

When Do You Need an Accountant?

You may be able to balance your checkbook, but can you effectively amortize your new drawing tablet? Do you know when to charge sales tax and what expenses can be deducted? Can you set up the payroll and employee deductions required to hire an artist?

If the answer is "no" to these questions (or "what's a balanced checkbook?"), you should sit down with an accountant before you start selling, hiring, or purchasing for your business.

Working with an accountant to help you set up a business is just as important as working with them come tax time in April. An accountant can help you:

- **Set up an EIN Number**. If you are setting up a business entity, like a corporation, LLC, or a partnership, you will need to obtain an employer identification number (EIN).[4] Also known as a Federal Tax Identification Number, the EIN is used to identify a business entity to the IRS. You can think of it like the Social Security number for a business. In fact, for some businesses, the IRS looks to the entity's owner's Social Security number as the business's Taxpayer Identification Number.

- **Set up employee payroll**. If you are hiring or engaging other artists to work on your project, you may need to treat them as employees for tax purposes. (See Federal and State Labor and Employment Laws: An Overview, p. 151.) Employers must withhold federal and state income taxes, Medicare, and Social Security from an employee's paycheck. Employers must also contribute to Social Security and Medicare for each employee. The employer must keep track of the employee's annual gross earnings and withholdings, reflected in a W-2, which must be sent to the employee.
- **Secure worker's compensation insurance**. Although most accountants are not insurance brokers, those accountants who work regularly with small businesses can often provide you with a referral and advice on how to obtain workers' compensation insurance in your state.
- **Help with unemployment fund requirements**. Employers must make contributions to the state's unemployment insurance fund and pay federal unemployment taxes.

EMPLOYEE OR INDEPENDENT CONTRACTOR? MAKE SURE!

The artist you're engaging to work on your comic book, is she an employee or an independent contractor? Make sure to get the answer right, because if you misclassify the employee, you could face legal penalties.

"Employee misclassification occurs when an employer either (1) fails to report its employees to the state and pays them 'off-the-books' or (2) improperly classifies its workers as independent contractors when they meet the legal standards for classification as employees."[5]

If someone is an employee, they *must* be covered under your unemployment insurance policy. However, if they are independent contractors, you don't have to cover them.

For more, See Hiring Artists, p. 150.

Working with an Accountant

Accountants are usually paid hourly; however, they may have a flat fee for certain routine procedures, such as filing certain forms or preparing certain kinds of returns and financial statements. You can keep down hourly costs by making sure that you deliver your financial records to your accountant in as organized a fashion as you can; if you are disorganized, your accountant will spend more billable time having to figure out your finances. You can think of it this way: giving your accountant your receipts in a shoebox will end up costing you more than the pair of shoes that came in the box. It's as if you bought a nice pair of shoes and said: "This is a great box for keeping my receipts!" while tossing the new shoes in the garbage.

A great way to keep organized is by getting on the same software system as your accountant. If she uses Microsoft Excel, deliver your information in Excel files. As a matter of fact during your initial consultation, discuss and establish a plan for:

- What you will deliver them,
- At what time, and
- In what format.

Lawyering Up

When Do You Need an Attorney?

One of the first things you should do is establish a relationship with a good entertainment attorney, preferably one with experience in the comic book, publishing, licensing, and motion picture industries.

It is important to bring in your attorney early in the process of establishing your company. Although forming a company is not brain surgery, creating the company's internal documents can be tricky and is a task better left for your lawyer. In fact, having both your attorney and your accountant help you form your company is advisable, especially if your company will be hiring other people, engaging independent contractors, or taking on additional partners or members. You should be worrying about developing a great comic, not how to draft the operating agreement provision on IP transfers. No, I'm not shilling for lawyers here. You will actually save money on legal fees by making sure that everything is done right from the beginning, rather than bringing in a lawyer after the fact to clean up problems.

Furthermore, an attorney can help with both the negotiation and drafting phase of any deal. In this respect, an attorney possesses a skill set that you may not have; you can let your attorney play hardball with the other side's attorney while you maintain a good interpersonal relationship with the parties with whom you're working. Without an attorney negotiating on your behalf, it can be very difficult to dispassionately discuss deal points with people to whom you're creatively engaged.

INTERVIEW

Advocating for Advocates

If I were to give anybody really good, solid advice, it would be getting a good lawyer.

Keep in mind, nobody has your best interests in mind more than you do. You see, if the publisher is interested in your work, they know it means something to them: it means a return on their investment. They are interested in what that means for them; they are not as interested in what it means for you. So, you need somebody in your corner: you need a lawyer who will protect your interests; someone who understands the intricacies of contract and copyright law. The history of comic book publishing is filled with hundreds of creators who signed bad contracts, if they signed contracts at all. Get a lawyer.

It's like an investment: they will save you thousands of dollars in heartache, and headache, and your own personal time. When my time is not spent creating, I'm losing money. If I'm not making comics, I'm losing money. Don't be that guy who is losing money because he decided to advocate on his own behalf. Every creator I know who comes into a meeting with a lawyer, ends up with a better deal. I know people who have negotiated without lawyers who have come out with really bad deals and made a lot less money.

***AUTHOR DAVID GALLAHER** has received multiple Harvey Award nominations and won The Best Online Comic Award for his work on High Moon for DC Comics.*

In particular, your attorneys can:

- Negotiate or help in the negotiation of key artist and publishing agreements
- Form your business with the state
- Prepare internal company documents (e.g., operating agreements, bylaws, partnership agreements, etc.)
- Help you protect comic book ideas when they are still in the "concept" phase (maybe)
- Advise you regarding employees and independent contractors
- Prepare a comic property clearance report, alerting you to potential legal issues contained in the script
- Register your copyrights and trademarks
- Protect your chain of title.

Engaging an Attorney

Don't be afraid to look around for the right attorney. Someone who handles real estate transactions or criminal law may be fantastic at what they do but may not possess the experience and skill set to negotiate a comic book deal. Entertainment attorneys with comic book experience tend to cluster around Los Angeles and New York City. If you live outside these areas, you may want to call your state Bar Association and ask for referrals.

Once you've located your potential attorney, sit down with him or her and discuss your project. Don't be afraid to interview the attorney before you retain him or her. Make sure that he or she is a good fit for you by asking such questions as:

- How much experience do you have representing comic book creators?
- How much of your practice is devoted to representing artists?
- What experience do you have litigating copyright/trademark/breach of contract cases?
- How long have you been practicing law? What law school did you graduate from?
- Have you ever been sued for malpractice or brought up on disciplinary charges?
- Do you have any relationships with comic book publishers?
- Can you estimate my legal fees, given the nature of my legal matter?

Engagement Letter

Representation typically starts when an attorney sends you an **engagement letter** or **retainer agreement**, which is essentially the contract between you and the law firm which details:

- How much the attorney charges, and the time increments for which you will be charged (e.g., does the attorney bill in quarter hour increments or tenths of an hour?)
- The scope of what the attorney will do for you
- Your rights with respect to terminating the representation

Most entertainment attorneys charge by the hour, or portion thereof, and fees can range from $200 on the low end to $600 an hour on the high end. As you might expect, attorneys in New York and Los Angeles tend to charge more than attorneys in other parts of the country. Some attorneys offer flat fees for certain services like copyright registration or the preparation of simple documents. However, for any deal that requires a significant amount of negotiation, most attorneys prefer to bill in hourly increments. Additionally, many attorneys require new clients to put money into an attorney trust account, to be worked off as they perform services on your behalf. While this may feel like "paying in advance," you're actually putting your money into a special state regulated account, from which the attorney can only withdraw money for legal services as they are performed. Furthermore, most state bars allow clients to discharge attorneys at any time (unless in active litigation), and should you discharge your attorney, he or she is required to immediately refund to you any unearned fees on deposit in the trust account.

ERRORS AND OMISSIONS INSURANCE (E&O)

If you are utilizing the work of other artists or are unsure if the public domain work upon which you based your comic is *really* public domain (hint: establish this first! But hey, sometimes things just slip through the cracks), you may need Errors and Omissions insurance, also called "E&O."

This policy pays claims arising from intellectual property disputes, such as copyright infringement, defamation, trademark tarnishment, idea misappropriation, invasion of privacy, or the like. Although E&O is costly, if you are dealing with risky IP assets, your publishing company may require you to have an E&O policy in place prior to distributing your comic. Securing an E&O policy takes a little bit of work and can cost several thousand dollars. To get insurance, comic creators are required to provide a chain of title to the script, copies of artist agreements, proof of intellectual property licensing, and a title clearance report. Your attorney or accountant can help you locate E&O providers.

NEXT STEPS

- If you are planning on collaborating with other artists and letting them share in the ownership and profits from your project, see Collaboration, p. 116.
- If you are hiring artists or engaging independent contractors to help you with your book, see Hiring Other Artists, p. 150.
- If you're ready to give your comic book an IP "pre-flight check" before you start to promote and publish it, see Clearances and Licensing the Rights of Others, p. 198.

Notes

1 *Texas Integrated Conveyor Systems, Inc. v. Innovative Conveyor Concepts, Inc.*, 300 S.W.3d 348, 368 (Tex.App.-Dallas, 2009) ("Under the doctrine of *respondeat superior*, a principal or employer may be vicariously liable for the tortious acts of an agent or employee if the acts are within the course and scope of employment").
2 *Celia Hendricks v. Pepperidge Farm, Inc., Holiday Supermarkets, Hellendale Distributors, Inc., and Gale Grunigen*, 16 Phila.Co.Rptr. 164, 167 (Pa.Com.Pl. 1987) ("in order to hold a master vicariously liable for the negligence of a servant, it must be shown that the master has the right to control not only the results of the servant's work but also the very manner in which the work is to be done").
3 N.Y. LLC. LAW §206.
4 Internal Revenue Service, How to Apply for an EIN, U.S. Dep't of the Treasury, https://www.irs.gov/Businesses/Small-Businesses-&-Self-Employed/How-to-Apply-for-an-EIN.
5 "Employer's Guide to Unemployment Insurance, Wage Reporting, and Withholding Tax," NY State Dept. of Taxation and Finance Website, (https://www.tax.ny.gov/forms/publications/wt/nys50.htm) Accessed July 15, 2024.

CHAPTER 7
Collaboration

DOI: 10.1201/9781003496052-11

WORKING WITH A PARTNER

What if you're not working solo? Perhaps you're working with a buddy: you're writing the script, and she's illustrating the book. Maybe you're both writing and illustrating the book with several other artists. Either way, you are creating the comic with collaborators before you bring it to a publishing company (or publish it yourself).

Working with somebody is a wonderful way to reduce the workload, get a fresh perspective on creative issues, and open up new artistic vistas by combining divergent talents.

It can also be a recipe for disaster if the relationship is not carefully outlined in a written Collaboration Agreement or a Services Agreement before the work starts. Without the right agreements in place, you could be on the hook for debts your fellow artist incurred while making the comic book or liable for any copyright infringement committed by your partner in the course of making the book. ***You could even lose control over the exclusive copyright to your comic book.***

- If you plan to work with other artists, it is critical that you have a written, signed agreement in place with all collaborators *before* they start working with you.
- Is the idea or concept for your comic valuable in and of itself? If so, before you decide on working with another artist or writer, you may want to have them sign a non-disclosure agreement (NDA), in which they agree that the idea is your property. (See Safeguard Your Ideas with an NDA, p. 401.)
- If you want a partner who shares in the profits and losses of the comic book project, someone who is willing to put in "sweat equity" (in other words, work for free and get paid only if the comic sells), then you should have a **Collaboration Agreement** of some kind. (See Collaboration Agreement, p. 119.) Understand that if they contribute creatively to the project, they may become a joint author with you, with all of the rights we discussed back in Chapter 2: Joint Authorship.
- If instead of a partner, you're looking to engage an artist to perform specific services, like penciling, inking, lettering, etc., in exchange for money, while you keep the copyright, you will need them to sign an **Artist Services Agreement**. (See Hiring Other Artists, p. 150.)

Collaborating with a Partner

Collaboration is exciting, with each partner wanting to put his or her best foot forward while viewing the relationship in only the most positive light. That's why so many artists start working with just a handshake agreement between them (and perhaps a couple of emails vaguely outlining who will do what). However, things can fall apart pretty quickly and messily if one partner is not living up to the expectations of the other.

Without a written agreement, it can be hard to gauge whether the project is on track and whether the partners are doing what they said they would do, when they said they would do it. And if the relationship falls apart, it can be difficult to determine who owns the project. As you can imagine, it's easier to decide ownership issues when both parties are enthusiastic and just starting out, rather than when the relationship is soured. Think of a collaboration contract as both a roadmap and a prenuptial agreement.

I HAVE AN IDEA: HOW ABOUT AN NDA?

If you haven't worked with your potential collaborator before, you may want to try to safeguard your ideas before you pitch them. (See APPENDIX B: A Comic Creator's Guide to Protecting Ideas, p. 390.)

To do this, you may want to have them sign an NDA. This is a contract in which your potential collaborator should agree that:

- Your idea is unique and valuable.
- Your idea is your proprietary information.
- They will keep this idea confidential.

CAUTION

NDAs ARE NOT IRONCLAD!

Keep in mind, NDAs are not ironclad, and a party that signs one may have a number of defenses available to them, such as the fact that they developed a similar idea independently of yours or that your idea is simply too generic to be worthy of protection, which is a matter of law. Furthermore, most publishing companies simply won't sign an NDA, and presenting them with one may just end your negotiations right there and then.

THE COLLABORATION AGREEMENT—KEY ISSUES

Even if you have an NDA in place, it's absolutely critical to secure a written **Collaboration Agreement** before embarking on any joint creative venture. An NDA only binds you to confidentiality—it doesn't address the myriad complex issues that arise in a working relationship. A solid Collaboration Agreement expressly modifies the default rules governing joint authorship under copyright law and ensures that each party clearly understands their respective obligations, contributions, and rights.

Without such an agreement, any collaborative effort automatically falls under the legal doctrine of joint authorship. This means that even if one collaborator contributes just 10% of the work while the other provides 90%, the law will still regard both as equal partners, sharing ownership equally by default. A detailed Collaboration Agreement provides a tailored framework that can allocate rights and responsibilities in a way that reflects the actual distribution of work and investment, thereby avoiding unintended legal repercussions.

By documenting each party's roles, expectations, and entitlements, a Collaboration Agreement not only protects your creative output but also fortifies the business and legal relationship between you and your partner. This is your essential tool to ensure that both the creative and business aspects of your collaboration are governed by mutually agreed-upon terms rather than the inflexible defaults of copyright law. (See Joint Authorship, p. 36.)

Collaboration and Ownership of Rights

Right out of the gate, this needs to be addressed as cleanly and straightforwardly as possible: All collaborators need to understand who owns both the copyright and the other intellectual property rights to the artwork and the script (each can be owned by different people) and who owns the physical artwork. After all, the copyright in a work of art is not automatically owned by the person who owns the physical work. (See Copyright Ownership, p. 347.) And just because you wrote the script for your comic, you may still end up sharing the copyright to your comic with a co-writer or illustrator if you both work relatively independently and then integrate your works together to make the comic without the benefit of having a contract in place. (See Joint Authorship, p. 36.)

From a legal perspective, the easiest solution is for all collaborators to share ownership of the copyright in the comic book property. However, there may be significant reasons not to do that. Perhaps you have drawn a new character and have approached a writer to help you develop a graphic novel, without being obligated to include the writer in future projects concerning that character. In other words, whereas you and the writer might share co-ownership of your premier comic, you may want to wholly retain the copyright in the character for yourself. (See Copyrighting Characters, p. 336.)

In a collaboration agreement, the co-creators should specify clearly whether they intend to be joint authors of the entire comic book (See Joint Authorship, p. 36) infringement or other lawsuit caused by their own individual contributions? (See Indemnification, p. 471.)

Example: Wanda the writer creates an anti-hero character called "Neutral Spirit," whose superpowers involve a psychic mind blast that incapacitates villains as if they were blind drunk. Agamemnon the artist draws the character like a lantern-jawed film noir detective: he sports a blue suit and a Fedora, driving gloves, a red tie, and a black domino mask. In short, "Neutral Spirit" looks a little too much like Will Eisner's famous creation "The Spirit," a fact that does not go unnoticed by Will Eisner Studios, Inc., which promptly sues for copyright infringement. If Agamemnon indemnified Wanda, and she is sued, Agamemnon would have to pay for her legal damages (after all, he represented and warranted that he was creating a character that originated with him and was not copied from any other character).

The Financial Relationship

In addition to figuring out how the rights are allocated, collaborators must decide how to split the proceeds from the exploitation of the comic property.

- What monies are each collaborator expected to contribute *before* the project starts to make money?
  - For instance, art supplies, software, website upkeep, and marketing materials all require money to be shelled out by the collaborators *before* a publishing company picks up the project.
- How are the profits shared?
  - Does each collaborator share equally in all revenue streams?
  - Do individual collaborators receive more money than their partners for certain revenue streams?

  Example: The artist might receive 60% of the profits from a poster, and the writer might receive 60% of the profits from a novel.
- How are profits computed and debts repaid?
  - When the money starts to come in, typically expenses are recouped before people start receiving a share of the profits.
  - But is every expense recouped at the same time, or are the earliest loans by the collaborators repaid first?

  Example: While creating their comic book, Andrea Artist will first spend $500 on art supplies. After the comic book is finished, Waldo Writer will spend $800 building a website to promote the comic book. When creating their collaboration agreement, Andrea and Waldo need to decide how they will recoup their expenses. Do the first monies coming in from the sale of the comic book go to repay Andrea her $500 before Waldo sees a penny from $800? Or do Andrea and Waldo each recoup their loans at the same time, even though Andrea put in her money first?

The Working Relationship

Once you've figured out how to deal with the copyright and financial issues, you need to figure out how the actual working relationship will be handled. Resolve such issues as:

- **Term**. How long does the agreement last?
  - Make sure you distinguish between how long the agreement lasts with respect to the copyright and the right to receive monies and how long the parties have to work together to complete the project.
  - Typically, collaborators find a certain period of time within which they must work together to create a comic book. Once it is created, the right to receive monies from the exploitation of that comic book lasts for the duration of the copyright in the comic book.
- **Schedule**
  - What is the work schedule?
  - When will each collaborator's work be delivered?
  - What happens if the comic book is not completed at all? Who retains the copyright in the collaboration?
  - Believe it or not, going off schedule is one of the most common reasons collaborations fail. Make sure to put in a delivery date for the final project, as well as key dates for project stages. Without a defined schedule, it is all too easy for a project to go off track.
  - Make sure to put in a provision that details what happens when one of the collaborators fails to meet a deadline. An amicably worded notice and cure provision is best here. (See Notice and Cure, p. 475.) It works like this: a missed deadline is only considered a problem if the non-defaulting collaborator points it out in writing within a specific time period after the deadline is missed (this is considered giving notice). Once the notice has been given, the defaulting collaborator has another specific period of time within which to meet the deadline. If this second deadline is then not met, the non-defaulting author has the option to consider the contract breached. (See Breach of Contract, p. 322.)
- **Deliverables**
  - What does each collaborator deliver?
  - Is the artist responsible for delivering pencil roughs, inked drawings, or fully colored panels?
  - In what format must the writer deliver her script?
  - What page layout programs are being used?
- **Non-Artistic Duties**
  - Who will handle marketing and promotion of the project?
  - Who will handle tax and financial issues?
  - Contracts and other legal issues?

- **Dealmaking**
  - Will one collaborator be responsible for negotiation and other business issues, or will this role be spread among several collaborators?—It is critical that negotiation strategies are coordinated between all the collaborators. The last thing you want is for two collaborators to be negotiating separate deals with separate third parties.
  - Does one collaborator have the right to enter into a deal regarding the comic property without the approval of the others?
  - If not, must collaborator approval be unanimous or a majority vote?
  - It is also possible to give collaborators different voting rights depending upon what media are being licensed. For instance, an artist might have one vote in the decision to license the comic property as a novel, but the artist may have two votes on a decision as to whether the comic character may be licensed for posters or other primarily graphic media.
- **Breach**. What happens when collaborators can no longer work together?
  - Is arbitration mandatory, or does a lawsuit need to be filed with a court?
  - Is nonbinding mediation a mandatory preliminary step before any lawsuit is filed?
- **Withdrawal from the Collaboration**
  - Can collaborators unilaterally withdraw from the collaboration before the term of the agreement expires?
  - If collaborators can withdraw, how does that affect their individual ownership of the copyright in the work?
  - Is the withdrawing collaborator's copyright interest abandoned entirely? Is it reduced to a defined percentage?
  - Is the withdrawing collaborator's ownership shared with any new collaborators that need to be brought in to fill the gap left behind by the withdrawing collaborator?
  - Usually, withdrawal requires a *termination agreement*, which may redefine the rights of both the remaining and the withdrawing collaborators. However, the more this contingency can be planned for in the collaboration agreement, the easier it is for all parties when a member withdraws.

KNOW YOUR OWN DEAL BREAKERS

Before you negotiate a contract with another person, you should make your own list of deal points that are *vital* to you. This step is a real time-saver; after all, why start drafting a contract if there's a fundamental disagreement on those deal points that matter most to each of the parties?

KNOW YOUR OWN—*continued*

For collaboration agreements, you *must* know where you stand with respect to these basic issues:

- Sharing the IP rights with your collaborator
- Sharing the profits with your collaborator
- Letting your collaborator have any approvals over the work
- Letting your collaborator have a hand in managing the business end of the collaboration
- Sharing expenses with your collaborator
- Integrating your and your collaborator's work schedules and methods

Quite literally, establish **walk-away points** (e.g., "I must have approval over the script or the collaboration is not worth it to me.")

You need to be very honest with yourself here: for instance, if you are flat broke and know that you won't be able to pay any expenses on the project, you need to bring that issue up before you go to contract. If you don't, the working relationship will quickly become derailed when you're asked to chip in to pay for the printing costs of your comic book... and you'll find yourself in breach of contract.

EXAMPLE: THE WRITER/ILLUSTRATOR COLLABORATION AGREEMENT

Okay, with all of those issues in mind, let's take a look and see how they play out in an actual writer/illustrator collaboration agreement. Here's the background: Waldo Writer came up with the character "Maggot Man—Carrion Eater of Justice" in a short story he wrote in college. Having now graduated and rapidly growing sick of his barista career, Waldo now wants to take his wormy superhero and feature him in his own comic, drawn by his fellow coffee-slinger, Izzy Illustrator. Waldo will write an entirely new story, and Izzy will do the pencils, inks, and other illustration work. With foresight and wisdom that belie their meager years, the two decide to draw up a contract.

Before they start to write the contract, they each make their own list of deal points that are important to them.

Waldo knows going into the collaboration that he wants to keep the literary rights to the Maggot Man character. He likes the short stories he wrote in college, and regardless of whether the comic book collaboration proves fruitful, he wants to be able to write other short stories featuring his character without coordinating with a collaborator.

Izzy really wants to design the book his own way. He values Walden's opinion, but Izzy is only willing to put in time and hard work into such a speculative project if he can have carte blanche with respect to character design.

They're in luck! Waldo and Izzy are comfortable with each other's main deal points, so it's time to start negotiating the collaboration agreement...

CONTRACT ANATOMY

As this is the first contract you may be reading through, to help you walk through it, make sure to bookmark **APPENDIX G: Contract Anatomy for Comic Book Creators**, p. 447.

Read through the contract slowly; take your time. I wish I could make it snarky and illustrated like other sections of the book, but that wouldn't help you learn how to read actual contract language.

What I have done to help you is to provide comment bubbles alerting you to key negotiation points. Hey, bubbles are a *kind* of illustration, I suppose....

[PAGE INTENTIONALLY LEFT BLANK]

WRITER/ILLUSTRATOR COLLABORATION AGREEMENT—EXAMPLE

This agreement dated _______________, 20___ between Waldo Writer★1 residing at ____________________ (hereinafter, "**Writer**"), and Izzy Illustrator, residing at ____________________ (hereinafter, "**Illustrator**"). Collectively, the parties shall be called the "parties," "they," or the "Co-Creators."

Witnesseth:

Whereas, the parties desire to collaborate in the creation of the comic book, tentatively titled "The Adventures of Maggot Man," based on the character "Maggot Man," created by Writer,★2 and consisting of the combination of both text and illustrations (hereinafter, the "Work"★3), on the terms hereinafter set forth.

Now, Therefore, in consideration of the promises and of the mutual undertakings herein contained, and for other good and valuable considerations, the parties agree as follows:

1. Duties and Obligations★4

1.1. Writer shall be solely responsible for writing an original comic book script for the Work (hereinafter, the "Script"★5). Illustrator shall have the right to meaningfully consult with Writer with respect to creative aspects of the Script; however, final approval over creative aspects of the Script shall vest with Writer.★6

1.2. Illustrator shall be solely responsible for producing penciled pages, inking those pages, coloring those pages, and lettering those pages for the Work (hereinafter, the "Illustrations"★7). Writer shall have the right to meaningfully consult with the Illustrator with respect to creative aspects of the Illustrations; however, final approval over creative aspects of the Illustrations shall vest with the Illustrator.★8

1.3. The parties shall make their best efforts to meet the requirements of a third-party comic book publishing agreement, if any. Such requirements may include, but are not limited to, the delivery of the Script and Illustrations on or before any deadline set by a comic book publisher.★9

--------COMMENTS--------

1 If Waldo had a loan-out company, that company would be the party to this agreement "providing the services of Writer." (See Loan-Out Companies, p. 109.)

2 If any of the parties have created their own intellectual property that they are bringing into the collaboration, it should be clearly identified so as to avoid confusion of ownership. Here, Waldo Writer created the character "Maggot Man" in a short story before he started working with Izzy. He's identifying this fact now because, as we'll see in paragraph 2.1, he wants to reserve the copyright in that character for himself.

3 Defined term time. Some contracts define terms as they come along, rather than include them in a separate paragraph in the beginning of the contract. In this contract, "Work" means the initial comic book collaboration.

4 Here we're starting to lay out the duties that each party requires of the other.

5 From now on, whenever we see the word Script with a capital S, it means only the comic book script that Waldo will be creating for this project (e.g., as opposed to a movie script made from the comic).

6 Although Waldo is responsible for creating the Script, he must give Izzy "meaningful consultation" over his literary work. This means that Waldo must listen to Izzy and seriously entertain Izzy's suggestions about his manuscript. However, because Izzy does not have any approval rights over the Script, when it comes to creative decisions on the literary aspect of their collaboration, Waldo has final say.

7 "Illustrations" is defined here to include lettering and coloring, as well as pencils and inks. Unless you read this definition, you might erroneously think that illustrations only meant pencils, and possibly inks.

If you're working with your collaborator for the first time, you may want to also include details as to the file format with which Illustrations will be created.

8 Turnabout is fair play, now Waldo only has a "meaningful consultation" right over Izzy's illustrations. It is important to note that this does not have to be the case. Waldo might argue that he is the initiator of the project, and thus should have final approval over both illustrations and script.

Or Izzy might argue that since he is doing the work of several artists, he should have greater approval rights. Perhaps the Script must be mutually approved, and with respect to the Illustrations, Waldo only has the right to meaningful consultation.

1.4. The parties contemplate that they will complete a first draft of the Work by ________ and a final draft ("Final Draft" or "Completed Work") by ________.**★10**

1.4.1. These completion dates may be extended by mutual agreement. However, in the absence of any such extension, in the event that the parties fail to complete a Final Draft of the Work, as outlined in paragraph 1.4, the parties shall make their best efforts to fix by negotiation their respective rights in any material assembled, written, and/or illustrated, if any, in preparation of the Work, and any rights in the Work itself. The understanding as to these matters shall thereupon be embodied in a settlement agreement. If they are unable to agree, the parties' respective rights and the terms pertaining thereto shall be fixed by neutral third-party arbitration. In either event, this agreement shall cease when the rights of the parties have been fixed as aforesaid, and thereafter they shall have only such rights and obligations as will be set forth in the settlement agreement or the arbitration award, as the case may be.**★11**

1.4.2. Notwithstanding the foregoing, failure to deliver the first or final draft of the Work by the agreed-upon completion dates shall not constitute a breach of this Agreement on the part of either party.

1.4.3 Once the Final Draft has been completed, all rights to each party's individual contribution shall be considered vested in the parties collectively, as joint authors**★12** (with the exception of the literary rights to the Maggot Man character, as outlined in paragraph 2.1.1).**★13**

1.5. After the completion of the Work, no change or alteration shall be made therein by either party to the Script or Illustrations without the other's written consent. However, such consent shall not be unreasonably withheld. No written consent to make a particular revision shall be deemed authority for a general revision.

9 Sometimes publishers require schedule changes or other requirements that may contradict the terms of a collaboration agreement. The parties agree to try and accommodate these publishing company demands.

10 One of the most important aspects to any collaboration agreement is the scheduling of how the parties will work together. The sentence in this agreement is fairly cursory (Waldo and Izzy know each other well and will be working closely with each other). However, it is not uncommon to put in specific delivery dates for drafts of the Script, pencil roughs, and other milestones in the creation of a comic book.

11 Sometimes working relationships don't work out. What happens if the parties can't complete a final draft of the comic? How do the parties own the components they each created on the unfinished project (e.g., unfinished artwork or script)? In this agreement, should the project fail before the Final Draft of the Work is completed, the parties have to negotiate how these components will be owned, and if they can't come to an agreement, they must seek arbitration to decide how the rights to the components are divvied up.

Other variations include
– All rights to the components are jointly owned, even though the Work is not completed.
– The person who came up with the idea for the comic (in this case the Writer) owns all of the component rights, subject to paying the other collaborator a flat fee and/or royalty.

12 Once the Work is finished, both parties will now own the Work—and its parts—as Joint Authors.

13 As we'll see later on in the agreement, the ownership of literary rights in the Maggot Man character will continue to be carved out of this agreement.

1.6. After the completion of the Work, the parties shall endeavor to secure a publishing agreement with a third-party comic book publisher. Each party shall have the right to negotiate for this purpose, but only after they have first come to a mutual agreement with the other party as to (1) the persons with whom they may negotiate and (2) the scope of the negotiations. Both parties have a duty to keep each other fully informed with reference thereto.**★14** No agreement for the publication of the Work or for the disposition of any of the publishing subsidiary or other rights therein shall be valid without the signature of both parties.**★15** However, either party may grant a written power of attorney to the other setting forth the specific conditions under which the power may be exercised. For services rendered under such power of attorney, no agency fee or extra compensation shall be paid to the attorney-in-fact.

2. Ownership of Rights in the Completed Work★16

2.1. Once the Final Draft has been completed,**★17** with the sole exception of the literary rights in the "Maggot Man" character, which copyright and other rights shall be held by Writer alone,**★18** all copyrights and other rights in the Completed Work and its constituent parts shall be obtained in the names of both parties and shall vest jointly in Writer and Illustrator (as joint authors).**★19**

2.1.1. Notwithstanding anything herein to the contrary, Writer shall retain all literary rights, title, and interest to the character, "Maggot Man," in the form that was developed and conceived prior to, and independent of, the Work and this Agreement, and such rights shall not be considered part of the work.**★20** Once the Final Draft has been completed, the Writer's literary rights in the "Maggot Man" character shall only include the right to utilize the character in a primarily textual medium (such as a short story or novel) and do not include the right to create graphic novels, comic books, or other works of sequential art without the prior written approval of the Illustrator.**★21**

<u>14</u> One of the main reasons Waldo and Izzy have collaborated is to create a comic book that will be published. To that end, they need to make sure that any negotiation with publishing companies is done by their mutual consent. Few things kill the project faster than joint authors independently negotiating deals without the knowledge and consent of their co-authors.

<u>15</u> As we saw when we learned about joint authors, unless there is "an agreement to the contrary," each joint author can grant a non-exclusive right to the work without having to seek the permission of the joint authors. (See Joint Authors and Joint Works, p. 347). Well, this is the "agreement to the contrary." Here both joint authors are promising that they will not license the work without the permission of the other.

<u>16</u> This section deals with the copyright and other IP rights in the Work.

<u>17</u> This section details how the rights to the Work are treated AFTER the parties have finished a Final Draft. Remember, under this agreement, until they had completed the comic, the ownership of rights to their individual contributions was subject to negotiation. However, now that the Final Draft is done, these rights now vest in each collaborator as joint authors. The sole exception being, the literary rights to the "Maggot Man" character, as we see below.

<u>18</u> Here's an example of a variation on a shared 50–50 ownership of all the rights. Because Waldo created "Maggot Man" before the collaboration, he wants to keep the literary copyright to that character. In other words, he wants to be able to write novels based upon that character without having to include Izzy in the collaboration (and without having to pay Izzy any of the proceeds from such a purely literary novel). However, the rights in the pictorial/literary Work—that is the comic book and any merchandise, video games, movies, graphic novels, etc. that are derived from the comic book—are owned jointly by the co-creators.

<u>19</u> An express affirmation of joint authorship... once the work is completed.

<u>20</u> With famous properties, this clause would be the subject of much negotiation. When authors' collaboration involves pre-existing characters, ownership issues can get very murky unless they are expressly dealt with in the contract. For an example of how not to handle this issue, see the "Spawn" case in the decade-long legal battle which ensued between Neil Gaiman and Todd McFarlane. (See *Gaiman v. McFarlane*, p. 496.)

2.2. Neither party may sell, transfer, or otherwise voluntarily dispose of the Work★22 or his/her share of the Work or the rights thereof (with the exception of the Writer's literary rights, as outlined in paragraph 2.1.1, hereto, and any parties' right to receive money from the exploitation of the Work, as outlined in paragraph 12, hereto), including rights under the Visual Artists Rights Act,★23 to any third party without the prior written permission of the other party, which consent, however, shall not be unreasonably withheld. Furthermore, if either party desires to transfer his/her rights to a third person, he/she shall give the other party written notice of his/her intention to do so.

2.3. Subject to 2.1 and 2.1.1 herein, neither party may create a derivative work based on the Work or otherwise incorporate the Work, the Script, Illustrations, or any part thereof in any other work without the written consent of the other party.★24

2.4. This Agreement, unless otherwise terminated under the terms hereof, shall continue for the life of the copyright in the Work.

3. Financial Participation★25

3.1. All revenue received from the sale, licensing, or other disposition of the Work and from the sale, licensing, or other disposition of any publishing, subsidiary, or other rights therein shall be divided equally between the parties. Both parties shall make best efforts to ensure that all agreements for the sale, licensing, or other disposition of the Work and for the sale of subsidiary rights therein shall provide that each party's one-half share shall be paid directly to him/her.

3.2. If the parties mutually agree to select an agent to handle any of the rights in the Work or the disposition of the subsidiary rights therein, and if the agent is authorized to make collections for the parties' account, such agent shall remit each party's one-half share directly to him/her after the deduction of agency fees, if applicable.

3.3. Each party agrees to keep complete and accurate books and records relating to the production, licensing, and exploitation of the Work. Each party shall have the right, upon ten days

21 Because the Writer is keeping some rights to the character (the rights to make novels or short stories), the Illustrator wants some protections. Here the Writer must promise that once the Final Draft is complete, the Writer won't use these literary rights to make another comic.

22 It is a good idea for joint authors to restrict the transfer of the copyright in the Work. After all, you don't want somebody you haven't worked to be given the right to create derivative works were to share control of the copyright without your permission. Keep in mind that even though the copyright assignment should be restricted without mutual consent, collaborators almost always allow the assignment of the right to receive money from the exploitation of the Work

23 The Visual Artists Rights Act 17 USC §106A gives visual artists certain additional rights to their artwork. Although it doesn't apply to artwork made for books or periodicals (like a comic), it does apply to individual fine art drawings. Make sure that neither Joint Author can give up these rights without all authors agreeing to it. (See Visual Artists Rights Act, p. 443.)

24 Neither collaborator can create a derivative work without the permission of the other. Without this clause, copyright law would permit either collaborator to create a derivative work (e.g., another comic, film, t-shirt, etc. based on the joint work) without fear of being sued for copyright infringement by their co-authors. The sole exception for this particular deal is the literary rights in the Maggot Man character, which Waldo may exploit independently of Izzy.

25 This lays out how the collaborators will share any monies that come from the exploitation of their Work. 50–50 in this case. (Although, because they are joint authors, the split would be 50–50 even without this agreement.)

advance written notice, to inspect the other party's relevant books and records with respect to the subject matter of this Agreement.**★26**

4. **Representations and Warranties**

4.1. Writer warrants, represents, and agrees that Writer shall create the Script by his/her own efforts and shall not engage third parties to assist with creating the Script without the prior written approval of Illustrator.

4.2. Illustrator warrants, represents, and agrees that Illustrator shall create the Illustrations by his/her own efforts and shall not engage third parties to assist with creating the Illustrations without the prior written approval of Writer.**★27**

4.3. Each Co-Creator warrants, represents, and agrees that he/she has the legal right, power, and authority to enter into this Agreement and grant all rights granted herein, and no rights of any third parties are or will be violated by either Co-Creator entering into or performing this Agreement.**★28**

4.4. Each Co-Creator warrants, represents, and agrees that all of the Work shall be wholly original with each Co-Creator and none of the Work has been or will be copied from or based upon any other work.

4.5. To the best of each Co-Creator's knowledge, the creation, reproduction, exhibition, or any other use of the Work shall not defame any person or entity, infringe any copyright or other intellectual property right, or violate the right of privacy or publicity or any other right of any person or entity.**★29**

4.6. Both parties agree and acknowledge that each party retains any and all rights that are not expressly granted in this Agreement.

26 Any time somebody else may be responsible for keeping track of money that you're owed, it's a good idea to have a right to audit their books.

27 Here both parties agree that they are going to create the work themselves and not subcontract it to others.

28 Here the parties promise that they have the right to enter into this agreement in the first place. This seems like a "no-brainer," but this issue gets artists into trouble more times than you might think. For instance, the illustrator might be employed by a graphic design company under a contract that states that all design work they perform is a work for hire, with the graphic design company as the author. At best, this will cloud the chain of title in the illustrations while the writer and the illustrator's graphic design company argue over who owns illustrations.

29 These warranties should appear in every contract in which intellectual property is created. Each Co-Creator must promise that everything is original with him or her, and that their contribution will not infringe any third party's rights.

5. Withdrawal, Termination★30

5.1. Either party may withdraw from the collaboration by sending written notice of termination to the other. In the event that either Co-Creator gives written notice of his/her withdrawal from the collaboration, dies or suffers a disability which prevents such Co-Creator from performing his/her obligations under this Agreement, the remaining Co-Creator shall have the right to complete the Work alone★31 or in conjunction with one or more new collaborators and unilaterally (or in conjunction with such new collaborators) make any and all decisions with respect to the Work, including the right to sell, assign, license or otherwise dispose of any rights to the Work including without limitation the copyright therein, provided, however, that such remaining Co-Creator shall account and pay to the withdrawn, deceased, or disabled Co-Creator or his/her estate a proportionate share ("Former Co-Creator's Share")★32 of any net revenue obtained in connection with the exploitation of the Work that is directly proportional to the amount of the completed Work originating with such withdrawn, deceased, or disabled Co-Creator. The percentage of the Former Co-Creator's Share shall be based on the percentage of the completed Work that originates from the efforts of such withdrawn, deceased, or disabled Co-Creator, as determined by a neutral arbitrator. Notwithstanding the foregoing, no Former Co-Creator's Share shall exceed their pro rata share of the net revenue of the Work.★33

5.1.1. *For purposes of illustration only:*★34 if there are two Co-Creators, and one withdraws, the Former Co-Creator's Share can never exceed 50%, despite the fact that the withdrawing Co-Creator may have contributed more than 50% of the material to the Work. If there were three Co-Creators, and one withdraws, that Former Co-Creator's Share can never exceed 33%.

5.2. Additionally, in the event that a Co-Creator dies, the remaining Co-Creator shall (1) furnish true copies of all contracts to the decedent's estate and (2) make best efforts to ensure that decedent shall receive credit as provided in Section 6.1 of this Agreement.

<u>30</u> This addresses what happens when one party withdraws or dies prior to completing the collaboration.

<u>31</u> In this contract, if someone withdraws or dies, the remaining Co-Creator can finish up the work and make all decisions regarding copyright of the work. The remaining collaborator may also bring in a new collaborator, and this new creative team may make decisions regarding the Work.

<u>32</u> Of course, even if the Co-Creator withdraws or dies, they still have a right to receive money from the exploitation of the Work. However, the way this particular agreement is drafted, the amount of money they receive is based upon the portion of their contribution to the finished Work (as determined by a neutral third party).

<u>33</u> In other words, no matter how much of the Work originated with the withdrawing Co-Creator, if he was one of three co-creators, the maximum share of the revenue for the work he could receive would be 33%.

<u>34</u> Sometimes it helps the contract to provide an example of how such a complex formula could work. Make sure to clearly mark your illustrations as such. The phrases "For purpose of illustration only …" or "For the purposes of clarity only…" let the reader know that this is not a contract clause, but an illustration of how a clause might operate.

5.3. If prior to the completion of the Work, a dispute arises between the parties with respect to the Work, then this Agreement may be terminated by either party upon written notice to the other party.

5.4. The Agreement may be suspended immediately for the duration of the event in question in case of *Force Majeure*<u>***35**</u> like earthquakes, floods, labor controversies, acts of God, and similar unforeseeable events.

6. Credit<u>*36</u>

6.1. Contingent upon the final draft of the Work being delivered and accepted by a third-party comic book publisher ("Publisher"), and no other writer or illustrator having been utilized in the Work's creation, and neither party being in breach of this Agreement, the parties shall negotiate with such Publisher the right to receive equal authorship credit on the same line and in type of equal size, in substantially the following manner: "**Writer: Waldo Writer, Illustrator: Izzy Illustrator**."<u>***37**</u> It is understood and agreed that the final design and type size of the credit on the front cover and splash page, if any, of the comic book shall be determined by the comic book publisher in consultation with both parties.

6.2. Notwithstanding the foregoing, either party may submit the Work to third parties solely as a portfolio writing or illustration sample without acknowledging the other party as a co-author.<u>***38**</u>

6.3. Notwithstanding anything to the contrary contained in this Agreement, in no event shall either party seek from the other party hereto, or be entitled to, damages of any kind from the other party<u>***39**</u> hereto by reason of any breach or threatened breach of any of the credit requirements, nor shall either party be entitled to seek to enjoin or restrain the exhibition, distribution, advertising, exploitation, or marketing of the comic book, all such equitable remedies being hereby expressly waived by both parties with respect to each other. No casual or inadvertent failure to comply with credit requirements shall be deemed a breach of this Agreement.

__35__ This clause may determine how long the contract is put on hold when a *force majeure* event, like a fire or earthquake, or other event beyond the parties' control stops production.

__36__ Giving credit where credit is due is critical.

__37__ Agreeing on each Co-Creator's credit early on helps eliminate ambiguity in the future.

__38__ Any Co-Creator can use the work in their portfolio.

__39__ The parties are not liable to each other for any breach of the credit provision. Keep in mind, however, this doesn't stop the co-creators from suing third parties (e.g., a manufacturer) for breach of these credit provisions.

7. Approval

7.1. Any and all decisions affecting the marketing, promotion, exploitation, and financial well-being of the Work shall be made by the Co-Creators jointly.★40

8. Expenses

8.1. All reasonable expenses incurred in connection with the Work, or this Agreement shall be subject to mutual agreement in advance and shall be shared equally by both parties and repaid in *pari passu*.★41

9. Notice and Cure★42

9.1. Except as described below, neither party shall be in breach of this Agreement unless the breaching party fails to cure any curable breach or alleged breach within thirty (30) days of receipt of reasonable detailed written notice from the non-breaching party. If the breach is not cured in a timely fashion, the non-breaching party may terminate this Agreement immediately. All notices shall be written and specify with particularity the defaulting party's default. Notices shall be delivered in the form of a certified letter, overnight courier, or personal delivery.

10. No Partnership★43

10.1. Nothing in this Agreement shall be construed to create a partnership or joint venture between the parties or constitute either of the parties as an agent of the other. The relationship between the parties shall be one of collaboration on a single project, namely the creation of the Work.

11. Indemnification★44

11.1. Each Co-Creator shall indemnify and hold the other Co-Creator and his/her successors, licensees, assigns, agents, employees, and/or representatives harmless from any damage, loss, liability, cost, penalty, or expense of any kind (including reasonable attorneys' fees and costs) arising from any claim, demand, or action inconsistent with any agreement, warranty, representation, or grant

40 With the exception of creative contributions, the co-creators need to mutually approve all other decisions relating to the financial promotion, and exploitation of the Work.

41 Each Co-Creator is sharing debts incurred in furtherance of exploiting the Work, and they will get paid back at the same time.

42 If something goes wrong, the injured party must let the breaching party know in writing, and the breaching party has 30 days to correct the damage before it becomes a breach that can spawn a lawsuit.

43 Despite the fact that the parties are working together and have agreed to assume certain debts on the project, they are not in a partnership (and thus will not remain liable for all debts of their partners).

44 Don't worry, I have your back! If one party injures the other, the injuring party will pay for the damage to their Co-Creator (and their co-creator's licenses and assigns, don't forget that!).

made by either Co-Creator in this Agreement. The Co-Creator receiving notice of such claim, demand, or action shall promptly notify the other Co-Creator thereof.

12. No Assignment

12.1. Neither party may delegate his/her duties under this Agreement or sell, license, assign, or otherwise dispose of any rights in and to the Work, including, without limitation, the copyright therein, without the written consent of the other party. Notwithstanding the foregoing, either party may assign his right to receive money from the exploitation of the Work.**★45** Any license or assignment of the Work in violation of this clause shall be void *ab initio*.**★46**

13. Remedies, Choice of Law

13.1. In the event of breach of this Agreement, the parties waive any rights to injunctive or equitable relief,**★47** and agree not to seek the same. In the event of such a breach, the sole remedy available to the non-breaching party is limited to an action at law to recover monetary damages.

13.2. This Agreement shall be construed and enforced in accordance with the laws of the State of New York. Any litigation in connection with this Agreement shall be conducted exclusively before a federal or state court of competent jurisdiction located in the State of New York, County of New York, and both parties each hereby waive any objection and submit to the *in personam* jurisdiction and venue of such court.**★48**

13.3. Both parties have been given ample opportunity to consult an attorney of their choosing and have either done so or have chosen voluntarily not to do so.

14. Further Documents

14.1. The parties agree to execute all additional documents that might be necessary to further the intent of this Agreement. Such documents may include, but are not limited to, certificates of authorship, short-form assignments, etc.**★49**

45 Neither party can license the Work, but either party can license the right to receive money from the Work.

46 "*Ab initio*" is a Latin phrase meaning "from the beginning." When a contract is "*void ab initio*," that means it's as if the contract was never entered into in the first place.

47 If either party breaches this agreement, they can only sue for money damages, and will not attempt to stop the other party from exploiting the Work. You may think carefully about this: if your Co-Creator has breached the contract by attempting to license the work, an injunction is just the thing to stop her from proceeding.

48 Here the parties have chosen to take all legal disputes to court. Alternately, they could have chosen arbitration or mediation and drafted the paragraph like this: "The parties shall attempt in good faith to resolve any and all disputes, differences, and disagreements arising between them through mediation, with each party covering its own costs. If the parties fail to resolve the matter in question through such mediation, they shall thereupon have it settled by arbitration in New York, NY, under the rules of the American Arbitration Association, and judgment may be entered thereon in any court of competent jurisdiction."

15. No Third-Party Beneficiaries

15.1. This Agreement does not create any rights of enforcement in any third-party beneficiary or other person who is not a signatory to this Agreement.

16. Entire Agreement

16.1. This Agreement constitutes the entire agreement between the parties and supersedes all previous and contemporaneous agreements and understandings related to the subject matter hereof.**★50** Both parties hereby warrant that the execution of this Agreement has not been induced by, nor have the parties relied upon or regarded as material, any representations or writings whatsoever not incorporated herein and made a part hereof. Only a written amendment, signed by both parties, shall modify the duties and obligations herein.

17. Severability

17.1. If any provision of this Agreement is adjudged unlawful, void, or unenforceable, in whole or in part, by a court of competent jurisdiction, the remaining provisions shall continue in full force and effect.

18. Survival

18.1. The following clauses shall survive the termination of this Agreement, whether by breach or otherwise: "OWNERSHIP OF RIGHTS," "REPRESENTATIONS AND WARRANTIES," "REMEDIES, CHOICE OF LAW," "INDEMNIFICATION," "ASSIGNMENT," "SEVERABILITY," and "SURVIVAL." If any provision of this Agreement is adjudged unlawful, void, or unenforceable, in whole or in part, the remaining provisions shall continue in full force and effect.

49 It's not always possible to determine every additional document you both need to sign (there might be certificates of authorship, copyright registrations, etc.). It's often easier just to say that you'll each agree to sign any document necessary to effectuate the purpose of the agreement. (See Further Documents, p. 479.)

50 Keep in mind that once this language is in the agreement, any understanding that the parties may have had as to their deal is irrelevant if those terms are not contained in this contract or any signed written amendment to this agreement. (See "Merger," "Integration," or "Entire Agreement" Clause, p. 480.)

19. Counterparts

19.1. This Agreement may be executed in counterparts, each of which shall be deemed an original, and all such counterparts shall constitute only one agreement. Facsimile and scanned copies shall be deemed originals for all purposes. If the agreement is signed in counterparts, it shall only be effective upon delivery of one executed counterpart from each party to the other parties.

In Witness Whereof, the parties hereto have duly executed this Agreement as of the date _______________. Any individual executing this Agreement on behalf of any party hereto does hereby represent and warrant that such execution is made with full authority and that such party is bound by the terms hereof.

Writer:

Waldo Writer, Izzy Illustrator

By: ___________________________ By: ___________________________

TRUST, AI, AND PROTECTING YOUR CREATIVE COLLABORATION

In comic book collaborations, trust is everything. You pour your heart into a project, expecting your partners to respect your creative vision—but without clear agreements, even well-intentioned collaborators can open the door to AI meddling. Generative AI (GEN-AI) poses real risks: automated rewrites, AI systems quietly absorbing your work for training, or AI-generated marketing materials misrepresenting your creation. If your partners aren't on the same page, your work could be altered or exploited in ways you never agreed to. Remember, you can't sue a joint author for copyright infringement unless you are the exclusive owner of the rights.

The solution? Set firm GEN-AI boundaries from the start.

A clause like the following can be added to the collaboration agreement to ensure that, as between your team, (1) no AI interferes with the writing or artwork, (2) your work isn't fed into AI models for training, and (3) marketing remains human-made unless you explicitly approve otherwise.

And most importantly, these rules apply to everyone involved—subcontractors, third parties, and anyone with access to your work. Collaboration thrives on trust, but trust works best when backed by strong agreements that protect your creative vision.

Example Clause: Prohibition on GEN-AI Use

The following provisions are incorporated into this Agreement to safeguard the integrity of the Joint Work by strictly prohibiting the use of Generative Artificial Intelligence ("GEN-AI") in connection with the results and proceeds of the collaboration or the preparation thereof.

a. **Prohibition on GEN-AI Use in Creative Development**. The Writer and Illustrator (the "Parties") mutually agree that neither shall use GEN-AI in creating, drafting, illustrating, or designing any element of the Work. This prohibition covers, without limitation: (a) The generation of text, dialogue, scripts, or storylines; (b) the creation, rendering, or modification of character designs, backgrounds, or any visual components; and (c) the use of AI-generated tools or software to refine, enhance, or complete creative elements initially produced by the other Party. Furthermore, Each Party shall ensure that any employees, contractors, or agents under their control comply with these restrictions.
b. **Prohibition on Training GEN-AI Systems with Work Contributions**. The Parties agree not to submit, upload, cause to be ingested, or use any portion of the Work—or any drafts, sketches, or derivative components thereof—to train, develop, or enhance any GEN-AI system. Any breach of this provision shall, at the non-breaching Party's discretion, trigger the remedies provided elsewhere in this Agreement.
c. **Prohibition on GEN-AI Use in Marketing and Advertising**. The Parties further agree that no GEN-AI-generated content or materials shall be used for marketing, advertising, or promoting the Work. Should any third party be engaged for such marketing activities, they must be contractually bound to these same restrictions. Each Party retains the right to review and approve all marketing materials related to the Work prior to publication."

What if you're not planning on bringing a partner on board, but you'd rather on board an employee or independent contractor? That's what Chapter 8 is all about. Allons-y!

CHAPTER 8

Hiring Other Artists

DOI: 10.1201/9781003496052-12

ENGAGING THE SERVICES OF OTHER ARTISTS

Perhaps you don't need a partner: you've done most of the work yourself and just need a letterer, or perhaps you're a script writer and want to pay an artist to draw your comic book for you. Or perhaps you're a skilled artist but really need a writer to help you hone your plot.

Either way, you've decided to engage an artist to help you with your comic book, and you want to own the results. You don't need a collaborator to work *with* you, you need an artist (or writer) to work *for* you... which means you may have to start thinking like a publishing company.

The contract you need here is an Artist Services Agreement. Again, because of copyright law, this is another instance where a handshake just won't do. If you want to own the artist's work product at the outset, *it is critical that your artist sign a written agreement before they start on your project.*

DON'T LOSE CONTROL

It can be easy to lose control of your exclusive copyright in the comic book when working with other artists—even if you're paying them. It is a myth that merely paying for an artist's services automatically gives you the copyright to their work. Unless the artist is your employee (and given the nature of how these sorts of engagements work, they will usually be independent contractors), you need a signed, written agreement that specifies your copyright rights in the artist's creation. Just as we saw with collaborators, if you don't have a signed written agreement, the artist whom you engaged may be considered a joint author under copyright law. (See Joint Authorship, p. 36.)

But before you can even get to the contract part of working with the contractor, you need to establish whether the law will view your worker as an **independent contractor** or an **employee**. If it turns out that your worker is an employee, you need to make sure that you are complying with federal and state labor laws.

FEDERAL AND STATE LABOR AND EMPLOYMENT LAWS: AN OVERVIEW

Federal and state employment and labor laws govern discrimination, wages, workplace safety, child labor, and workers' compensation/disability/unemployment insurance. Under these laws, an employee may be treated differently from an independent contractor. An employer/contracting party must comply with these laws or show exemption from them, but he or she may not ignore them. These issues and more must be addressed before you engage the services of another artist or you may face fines or state and private legal actions.

Each state has its own set of laws and requirements, which can differ quite radically from one jurisdiction to another—even within the same state. For example, the determination of whether a comic book writer, artist, or any creative contributor should be classified as an independent contractor in California is largely controlled by A.B. 5. Meanwhile, New York not only imposes state requirements but also enforces different classification standards depending on the county (with Nassau County, New York City, Suffolk County, and Westchester County, each having its own system). This patchwork of regulations can be quite confusing for a comic book publisher or production company that just wants to create and distribute groundbreaking stories while simultaneously managing talent across multiple states.

At the federal level, U.S. law demands that employers in the comic book industry comply with regulations concerning wages, health and safety, family leave, and other key aspects of the employer–employee relationship. Although some of these rules only apply when employing more than 50 people, many sizable comic book projects or in-house production teams find these federal laws in play. Here's a brief selection of worker protections under federal law that may affect comic book publishers and production companies:

- **Wages:**
  - The Fair Labor Standards Act (FLSA) is administered by the Wage and Hour Division, establishing standards for minimum wages, overtime pay, recordkeeping, and child labor.[1]
  - Provisions on wage garnishment.[2]
  - Child labor laws.[3]
  - Protections for disabled workers.[4]
- **Safety and Health:**
  - Occupational Safety and Health Administration (OSHA) regulations.[5]
  - Family and medical leave requirements.[6]
- **Work Authorization for Non-U.S. Citizens:**
  - The Immigration and Nationality Act of 1952, as amended.
  - Specialized visas such as the O-1B for individuals with extraordinary ability in the arts or those who have achieved exceptional feats in the comic book industry and O-2 visas for individuals who accompany an O-1 talent to assist on specific projects.[7]

If you're a comic book publisher hiring creative talent as employees, there is also a significant amount of paperwork that the law requires. Just a few of the documents you may need include:

- **IRS Form SS-4:** Used by the publishing company to apply for an employer identification number, enabling it to hire staff.
- **Form I-9:** An immigration status form required by the U.S. Citizenship and Immigration Services.
- **IRS Form W-4/State W-4:** Federal and state tax withholding forms.
- **W-2 Forms:** Must be provided for employees each year.
- **New-Hire Reporting Forms:** Vary based on state requirements.
- **Workers' Compensation Insurance Forms**

In many areas of labor and employment law, state-specific regulations may demand more from comic book publishers than the minimum federal protections and requirements dictate.

WHEN IN DOUBT, SEEK PROFESSIONAL HELP

Before you pay an artist to work for you, bring in your attorney and accountant to advise you as to that worker's status and your responsibilities as a contractor or an employer.

Independent Contractor or Employee?

This distinction between an independent contractor and an employee is found at both the state and federal levels. Independent contractors, for example, do not have the same federal benefits as employees. However, the distinction between the two types of workers is not always clear, and courts and state agencies consider many factors in classifying an individual as an employee or an independent contractor.

To determine a worker's status under federal law, the Internal Revenue Service (IRS) looks at three primary factors to determine whether a worker is an independent contractor or an employee:

- Behavioral control. If the comic book creator or publisher has the right to direct and control how the worker accomplishes their job, the worker is most likely an employee. The more instructions a worker is given on how the work should be done, what steps the worker must perform, and what tools they must use, the more likely it is that the worker is an employee.

- Financial control. The more a worker has a financial stake in the business, shares in its profits and losses, or pays for supplies and materials without reimbursement, the more likely it is that a worker is an independent contractor.
- Relationship between the parties. How the worker and the employer perceive their relationship is also taken into account. Does a written contract specify that the worker is an independent contractor? If so, that tips the scales in favor of independent contractor status. Does the employer pay employee benefits? In that case, the worker is more likely to be an employee.

In addition to the federal test for whether a worker is an independent contractor or an employee, the comic book creator or publisher should also double-check the working relationship under the appropriate state law. Because, yes, it is possible to have a worker classified as an independent contractor under federal law but as an employee under state law.

Determining Worker Status under California Law

If you're publishing comic books in California, the presumption is that any worker is an employee, and it's up to the hiring party—the creator or publisher—to prove otherwise. In fact, even if you don't own a publishing company, you may be subject to this legislation.

Treating a worker as an employee may be the simplest approach, but not necessarily what a creator or a publisher wants to hear. Furthermore, for a worker with their own business—like an illustrator with a loan-out company—it may not be preferable either. In California, legislation has attempted to clarify this relationship by introducing a complex and not easily understood series of exceptions to this "presumed employee" rule. Seriously, as of this writing, lawyers are still trying to parse the law on this one in California. In California, certain workers (illustrators, writers, colorists, letterers, and several other creative professions) might be better classified as an independent contractor, rather than an employee, if all of the following are true:

- The worker has their own place of business.
- The worker has the required business license or business tax registration.
- The worker has the right to set or negotiate their own rates for the services performed.
- Outside of project completion dates and reasonable business hours, the worker has the right to set their own hours.
- The worker routinely carries out the same type of work under contract with another hiring entity or presents themselves as available to offer similar services to other prospective clients.
- The individual consistently demonstrates discretion and independent judgment in carrying out their services.

And even if your publishing company or you as a creator satisfy this test, as well as all of the exceptions, the worker may still be found to be an employee if your company retains the right to control the manner and means by which the work is performed, not just the scope of the work itself.

And if that isn't complex enough, under California law, any time you sign someone to a work-for-hire agreement, they are considered an employee, and you must provide them with workers' compensation insurance. Even issuing a worker an IRS Form 1099 rather than a W-2 does not automatically change an employee into an independent contractor.

Unfortunately, simply writing the words "independent contractor" in your contracts will not change somebody from employee to independent contractor. As the NY Dept. of Labor points out: "The real distinction between the employer–employee relationship and the independent contractor relationship depends primarily on the level of supervision, direction and control exercised by the person engaging the services. It is not defined by what the relationship is called by the participants."[8]

Moreover, the category into which a worker falls is affected by federal law and the laws of the state of their employment as well. For instance, under California law, any time you sign a worker to a work-for-hire agreement, they are considered an employee, and you must provide them with workers' compensation insurance.[9] Failure to insure them subjects your company to serious fines and possible criminal misdemeanor charges.[10] This simply isn't the case in New York, where a worker's classification is dependent on a multifactor test.

Multifactor tests look at a number of aspects of the working relationship to determine how independent the worker is. The worker who has more control over his own hours and manner in which the job is performed is more likely to be classified as an independent contractor.

Even if you are clearly working with an independent contractor, and not an employee, you may still have compliance issues. For instance, if you pay an independent contractor more than $600 in a year, you or your accountant will have to file a 1099-MISC form.[11]

NEW YORK INDEPENDENT CONTRACTOR TEST

In New York,[12] the following are just a few of the factors that may be evidence that the artist you're engaging should be treated as an independent contractor and not an employee.

Signs of independent contractor status include a person who:

- Has an established business
- Advertises in the electronic and/or print media

NEW YORK INDEPENDENT—*continued*

- Buys an ad in the Yellow Pages
- Uses business cards, stationery, and billheads
- Carries insurance
- Keeps a place of business and invests in facilities, equipment, and supplies
- Pays their own expenses
- Assumes risk for profit or loss
- Sets their own schedule
- Sets or negotiates their own pay rate
- Offers services to other businesses (competitive or noncompetitive)
- Is free to refuse work offers
- May choose to hire help.

THE ARTIST SERVICES AGREEMENT

Imagine you're crafting the next iconic comic book masterpiece and decide to bring on board an artist with that extra spark. Even if you're a solo creative genius, once you hire someone else, you must think like a full-scale publisher. A properly drafted services agreement becomes your creative safety net—it lays out every expectation, protecting both your vision and the service provider's rights. Not only does it define who does what, but it also spells out key details such as payment terms, copyright ownership, and termination rights—ensuring that neither party is left in the dark when the creative sparks fly. At a minimum, your agreement should clearly establish:

- The scope of the work he or she will be performing
- The format in which he or she will be delivering that work
- The copyright ownership of that work
- How much and when you will be paying him or her—often both a page rate and a royalty
- Whether or not that artist is exclusive to you during the engagement
- How and when they can be suspended or their engagement terminated by you
- Artist's likeness and biography approvals
- Confidentiality and publicity restrictions
- Representations and warranties that artist is free to enter into the contract and will not infringe any third-party IP rights
- Restriction on the artist's ability to hire others

Key Deal Points: Artist's Services Agreement

Parties

Whenever you are contracting with somebody else to do a job for you, you may want to consider forming a company. (See Setting Up Shop, p. 102.) If you already have a company, that company will be one party, and the artist will be the other. You also want to find out whether the artist you are engaging has a loan-out company. (See Loan-Out Companies, p. 109.). If so, the contract will actually be between both companies.

Services

In our contract example, this paragraph lays out the particular job(s) that will be performed by the illustrator. Be as specific as possible as to what you expect, how many drafts should be done, the period within which the work should take, and the file format in which you expect to receive the illustrator's work. As you can see, this is a critical paragraph, and you need to draft it very carefully.

Compensation

Illustrators may receive both a **page rate**, for each completed and approved page, and a **royalty rate** for their work. How much that royalty rate is, when it's computed, and how frequently it is paid are all subject to negotiation. For details on types of compensation, see Appendix G: Compensation, p. 464.

Page Rate

As is true for most of the arts and entertainment industries, compensation varies widely depending on the worker's experience. For instance, professional pencillers can receive up to $250 per page, whereas an artist straight out of school and looking to build up a portfolio might receive as little as $25 per page.

RESEARCHING PAGE RATES

Rates vary, depending on the artist's experience. The rate for artwork featured on a comic book's cover can be upward of 20% more than artwork featured in the interior of the book.

Furthermore, the rates above may reflect only the top earners in the business, from leading publishing companies. Rates for smaller publishing companies are likely to be much lower than the figures shown above... by some accounts, even 90% less!

The 16th edition of the *Graphic Artists Guild Handbook: Pricing and Ethical Guidelines*[13] lists the following *page rates*:

RESEARCHING PAGE— *continued*

Scripts: $25–$125

Line Art: $20–$225

Inking: $20–$160

Cover: $150-$800

Coloring: $18–$135

Lettering: $04–$45

Additionally, a constantly changing list of page rates can be found at the Creator Resource website: Page Rate Finder—Comic Book Publishers website: https://www.creatorresource.com/page-rate-finder-comic-book-publishers/.[14]

Another factor that might increase the amount of money an artist receives is whether the artist is designing the character "from scratch"—as opposed to continuing to draw an already established character. Artists who originate characters are often paid more, especially when they create **Special Characters**. (See later in this chapter.)

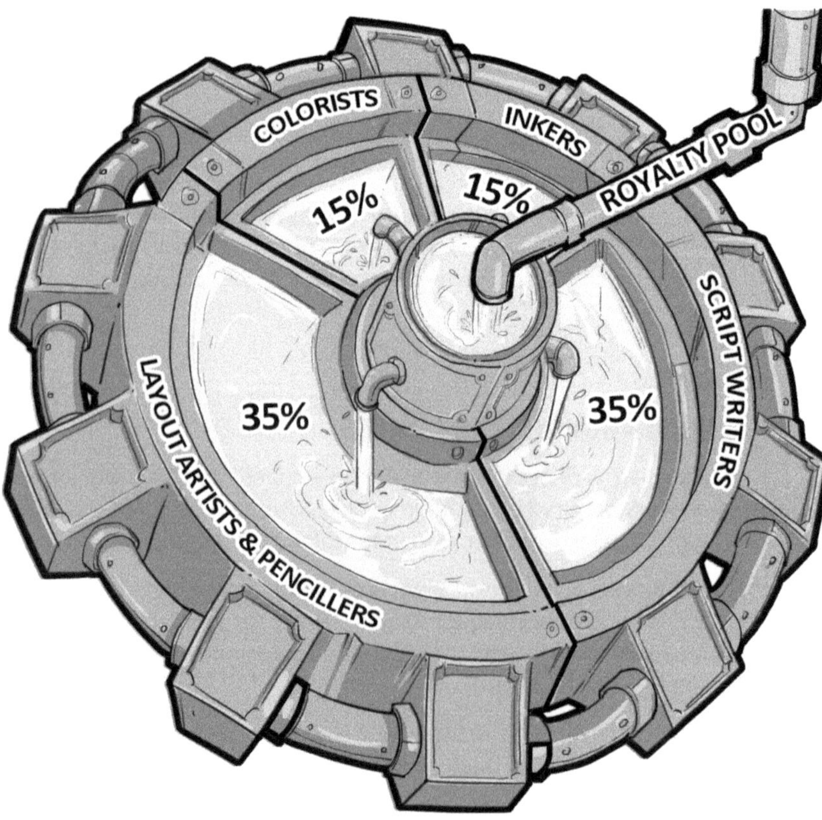

Compensation: Royalties and Royalty Pools

Illustrators frequently receive a **royalty rate**, which may be something like 3% of the cover price, from a shared **royalty pool**. The concept of a royalty pool is somewhat tricky. Since it involves money, let's slow down a moment and take this next part slowly. Don't worry, I'll do the math for you.

In a publisher-owned comic book services agreement like the one that follows, royalty payments to the artist kick in only when the comic book has sold a certain number of copies, often referred to as the "minimum threshold." This is the minimum number that needs to be sold before the illustrator starts receiving any royalties at all.

But does the illustrator start receiving a 3% royalty of the cover price the moment that minimum threshold is exceeded?

No. Because the royalty is often derived from a "Royalty Pool," from which all of the other artists on the book share. To make matters even more confusing, each of those various artists will share that 3% of the cover price in differing proportions.

For example:

- **Plotters and Scriptwriters**: 35% of the royalty pool, **Layout artists and Pencillers**: 35% of the royalty pool
- **Inkers**: 15% of the royalty pool
- **Colorists**: 15% of the royalty pool
- **Letterers**: Unfortunately, letterers usually don't share in royalties despite the tremendous work they do in comic books.

Confused yet? Let's actually plug in some dollar amounts so we can see how this works in an example.

Royalty Example

Izzy illustrator does the layout and pencils for *Maggot Man: Carrion Eater of Justice* issue 230. She has a royalty rate of 35% of 3% of the cover price from a shared "Royalty Pool," subject to a minimum threshold of 30,000 units.

The comic book begins selling, and Izzy does not yet receive a royalty. The only money she has received so far is her page rate. The issue she worked on now sells its 30,001st copy. Once the 30,001 copies of the comic book are sold, a Royalty Pool is created, and in this deal, 3% of the cover price of the comic book and all subsequent sales will be allocated to this Royalty Pool.

Now she's entitled to royalties. Royalties on 30,001 copies? No. Royalties from a shared pool of sales from one copy (the royalty is only derived from those issues sold that *exceed* the minimum threshold).

Okay, let's now make the math worth our while. Let's now assume that 50,000 copies of the comic book are sold. Now 20,000 copies would generate royalties (remember, issues sold have to exceed 30,000 copies in order to generate a royalty). Let's assume this comic book has a cover price of $3.00.

- 20,000 multiplied by $3 = $60,000
- 3% of $60,000 is $1800, which is the **Royalty Pool**
- The Royalty Pool is then split among the various creators (ink, coloring, writer), according to the formula above. Because Izzy has drawn the layout and pencils, her total percentage would be 35%. 35% of the $1800 Royalty Pool = $630

Bottom line: If the comic sells 50,000 copies and Izzy gets paid her page rate plus $630, it will be a while before she can make a down payment on that yacht.

Now 30,000 units might be an average print run for a large publishing company, but if the illustrator is working for a smaller publishing company, or an indie publisher, she may want to get figures for their typical print runs before she agrees to this number as the "minimum threshold." After all, if the small publisher only prints 5,000 books per print run, this illustrator will never begin to receive royalties if 30,000 units is the minimum threshold.

That's why for indie books, an illustrator royalty rate is often much higher and might not be subject to a minimum threshold. After all, on indie titles, the illustrator may be doing a lot of the heavy lifting—illustrating the entire book by himself or herself. Additionally, the illustrator may be taking a gamble that the book will sell at all. You know a Marvel or DC title will sell; you don't have that same assurance for a new series from a new publishing company.

From the perspective of the artist, it is crucial for any royalty participant to have the annual right to audit the books of the publishing company (the accounting pertaining to the royalties for the comics the artist worked on). After all, you want to make sure that you are being paid what they have promised they would pay you.

Delivery

Integrally related to the provision of services is the "delivery" clause. This specifies the schedule to which the artist must work as well as what materials and artwork he or she must send to the publishing company. This may sound straightforward—and it is—it is also one of the most important clauses in the agreement; I find that a majority of the problems that arise in the creative relationship stemmed from a misunderstanding of:

- What is to be delivered,
- When must delivery occur?

Ownership of the Work

The question of ownership is twofold:

1. Who owns the physical sketches, drawings, and other original art?
2. Who owns the intellectual property rights (like copyrights) in and to that art?

Make no mistake about it: these are two very distinct issues. Remember—just because somebody owns the physical artwork doesn't mean that they necessarily own intellectual property rights to that artwork.

From the hiring party's point of view, it is very often preferable to let a penciller keep her original sketches to sell at the latest Comic Con while the hiring party simultaneously keeps the copyright to the penciller's work. Additionally, the big publishers almost always require artists to work under work-for-hire agreements.[15]

EXAMPLE: WHO OWNS CAPTAIN COLUGO'S PENCILS?

Carmen Creator has hired The Penciller to sketch out the comic book for Carmen's newest issue of *Captain Colugo: The Flying Lemur of Liberty*. Because The Penciller's contract specifies that all work he or she does is work for hire, the copyright to his or her Captain Colugo pages is owned by Carmen. This means that The Penciller cannot make her own "Captain Colugo" comic book, T-shirts, or other derivative works, without Carmen's express permission. However, Carmen may decide to structure contract letting The Penciller keep ownership of the physical sketchbook and comic book pages, so that The Penciller can sell these to collectors on eBay or at comic book conventions. (See, Work for Hire, p. 39.)

BUYOUT BEWARE!

If you're an artist, be aware of the confusing term "**buyout**," an ambiguous word subject to several different meanings:

1. It can mean that all intellectual property rights are being transferred to the buyer (even though the illustrator may continue to receive royalties), or
2. It can mean that this is a one-time payment for all rights, and that there is no obligation to pay the artist royalties or other payments, regardless of how the work is used.

EXAMPLE: ILLUSTRATOR WORK-FOR-HIRE AGREEMENT

Okay, let's see how this all plays out with actual contract language.

In the following agreement, the illustrator is being engaged to provide all of the illustration and design work for the comic book. For larger publishing companies, this work is usually divided among several specialist artists, like pencillers, letterers, inkers, and colorists. Furthermore, comic book covers are often done by another artist entirely.

Even though this is a contract for an illustrator, with some modifications, it could be used to engage a writer to work on a project as well.

ILLUSTRATOR SERVICES AGREEMENT[16]

This Agreement, effective as of ________________, 20___ (the "Effective Date"), is made between Izzy Illustrator, residing at ________________ ______________________ (hereinafter, "**Illustrator**" or "**you**"),★1 and Comic Publishing Company, LLC, ★2 whose principal business address is ________________ ("**CPC**") in connection with services to be performed in conjunction with the comic book, tentatively titled "**The Adventures of Maggot Man, Issue #**"★3
(the "Comic Book"), a copy of the script thereto is attached as "Exhibit A."★4

1. Engagement

1.1. CPC hereby engages the services of Illustrator for the purpose of designing and illustrating the Comic Book and to create and deliver original Materials (as that term is defined below) for the same purpose.

1.1.1. "Materials"★5 shall mean all results and proceeds of Illustrator's services hereunder, including, but not limited to artwork, drawings, character designs, penciled artwork, writings, plots, stories, scripts, irrespective of the media in which they are contained.

1.2. Illustrator will render all such services in a conscientious and diligent manner and to the best of Illustrator's ability and comply with all of CPC's instructions and requests. Specifically, Illustrator agrees to provide the following services (the "Services"★6):

1.2.1. To develop and complete concept drawings of characters and locations that appear in the Comic Book;

1.2.2. To develop; complete; and revise page layouts, pencil sketches, lettering, ink, and color for the Comic Book;

1.2.3. To develop; complete; and revise pencil layouts, pencil sketches, lettering, ink, and color for the Comic Book cover★7

--------COMMENTS--------

1 Be sure to establish in the opening paragraph how each party will be named in the agreement (e.g.: "Illustrator," "Writer"), as well as how you can refer to the comic book (e.g.: the "Comic Property"). Note, all of these terms should be capitalized throughout the contract, as they are "defined terms." (See Defined Terms, p. 451.)

2 If you are hiring an artist, you are the publishing company in this agreement.

3 If this is a single issue in the series, it's important to specify the issue number.

4 It's often a good idea to attach a copy of the comic book script as an exhibit to the contract, that way there is no confusion over exactly what the Illustrator will be creating.

5 In this agreement, the defined term "Materials" does a lot of the work. As you'll see later, the Materials are created as a work for hire, so the publishing company owns all rights to the Illustrator's work in this deal.
Even though the Illustrator will only be working with the book's visuals, the way the defined term is drafted encompasses any narrative or literary contributions the Illustrator makes as well.

6 "Services" in this agreement means all of the work the Illustrator will perform. Both sides should make sure these services are clearly defined so that there are no unspoken expectations as to exactly what artwork the Illustrator will be delivering. In this agreement, the Illustrator is being asked to create most of the visual assets in the comic book: initial concept designs, layout, pencil sketches, ink, and color. Only lettering appears to be outside the definition of services. The fact that these tasks are often split among several artists, should give the Illustrator the impetus to negotiate a higher page rate than she might receive for merely providing pencil art.

7 Artists often get paid a higher rate for cover art.

1.2.4. To make any and all necessary changes based on the Comic Book's script (the "Script") as it may be amended from time to time;

1.2.5. To work closely with CPC regarding creative elements regarding the Comic Book, including "camera" angles and panel size;

1.2.6. To perform all services pursuant to CPC's specifications and in accordance with CPC's creative direction;

1.2.7. To provide at Illustrator's sole responsibility and expense, equipment, and/or supplies required to perform the services herein; <u>★8</u>

1.2.8. To perform all the services described above so as to comply with any and all schedule and budgetary constraints herein.

1.2.9. To deliver all Materials and other required artistic deliverables, as herein specified, necessary for CPC to create, print, publish, and exploit the Comic Book.

2. Compensation<u>★9</u>

2.1. Contingent upon the full and complete performance of all services hereunder, and as full and complete consideration for services rendered and rights granted hereunder, CPC shall pay Illustrator the following:

2.1.1. Page Rate: $450<u>★10</u> per completed, CPC approved, page, inclusive of penciling, inking, and coloring.

2.1.2. Royalty Rate:

2.1.2.1. **Single Issue Comics**: Contingent upon the sales of the Comic Book exceeding 30,000 units ("Minimum Threshold"<u>★11</u>), a royalty pool ("Royalty Pool") shall be created, consisting of 3%<u>★12</u> of the cover price of any Comic Book sold over the minimum threshold of 30,000 copies. Any comic book

8 Independent contractors are typically responsible for purchasing and maintaining their own materials.

9 Compensation on a work-for-hire agreement like this one is typically in two forms:

- A page rate, which is a fixed amount.
- A royalty rate, which is dependent on the success of the book.

10 Page rates for artwork vary quite considerably. (See Typical Page Rates, p. 157.)

11 In a publisher-owned comic book services agreement like this one, royalty payments often kick in only when the comic book has sold a certain number of copies, referred to here as the "minimum threshold."

reprinted within 12 months of its initial print run shall be included in the calculation of units applicable toward meeting the minimum threshold.

2.1.2.2. Such Royalty Pool**★13** shall be apportioned among and between all creative royalty participants in the following manner:

2.1.2.2.1. Plot & Script: 35%

2.1.2.2.2. Layout & Pencils: 35%

2.1.2.2.3. Ink: 15%

2.1.2.2.4. Colorist: 15%**★14**

2.1.2.3. Graphic novels: "Graphic Novel" shall mean any bound collection of reprinted Comic Book issues drawn by Illustrator, which exceeds 100 pages in length. Contingent upon the sales of the graphic novel exceeding 4,000 units**★15** ("Graphic Novel Minimum Threshold"), a royalty pool ("Graphic Novel Royalty Pool") shall be created, consisting of 5% of the cover price of any Graphic Novel sold over the Graphic Novel Minimum Threshold of 4,000 copies. Such Graphic Novel Royalty Pool shall be apportioned among and between all creative royalty participants in the manner and in the portions specified in paragraph 2.1.2.2, above.

2.1.2.4. **Special Characters:★16** "Special Character" shall mean a character originated and created by Illustrator, which may be worthy of further exploitation. The determination of "Special Character" status rests unilaterally with CPC, in its sole discretion. If CPC determines that Illustrator has created a Special Character, CPC shall pay to Illustrator

12 Once the 30,001 copy of the comic book is sold, a Royalty Pool is created, and in this deal, 3% of the cover price the comic book and all subsequent sales will be allocated to this Royalty Pool.

13 Once created, the Royalty Pool is then split among the various creators, according to the formula in this paragraph. Because the Illustrator in this agreement is providing layout, pencils, and ink, her total percentage would be 65%. So in this deal, if 50,000 copies of the comic book are sold, only 20,000 would generate royalties (remember, issues sold have to exceed 30,000 copies in order to generate a royalty). Let's assume this comic book has a cover price of $3.00. 20,000 · $3 = $60,000 times 3% = a royalty pool of $1800.
Of this royalty pool, the illustrator in this agreement would be entitled to $1170.

14 If the Illustrator is performing all of these roles, why not just say 65%? Well, you could. Nothing wrong with that... unless you may need to bring in additional artists. If you think you may need further artistic help down the line, it's safe to leave this breakdown in place to define how the illustrator's royalty split would be affected.

15 The minimum threshold tends to be much less for graphic novels than for issues of comic books because so few units are printed.

16 **Special Characters**. Not every publishing company recognizes "special characters." If the creator originates a new character all by him or herself, the publishing company could deem it valuable enough to pay an additional royalty to the creator any time that special character is incorporated into a royalty-producing property. The catch is that publishing companies often reserve for themselves the rights to declare who is a special character and what isn't.

a royalty rate in accordance with CPC's Special Character royalty rate policy, as such may be amended from time to time, on any derivative works sold, which contain such Special Character.

2.1.2.5. Audit Right:**★17** contingent upon Illustrator being entitled to share in any royalty stream contained in this paragraph, Illustrator shall have the right, upon 30 business days' notice to CPC, to audit those of CPC's financial records, which directly pertain to the exploitation of the Comic Book or other royalty-bearing product. Such audit shall be conducted no more than once per CPC's fiscal year and performed by a licensed CPA, at Illustrator's expense. Should such audit uncover an underpayment to Illustrator in excess of 10%, CPC shall bear the cost of such audit, in addition to immediately tendering any unpaid royalties to Illustrator.**★18**

2.1.3. Cancellation Fee:**★19** If the work and Illustrator's services hereunder are cancelled by CPC prior to the Comic Book's completion, but after its final form has been approved by CPC, a cancellation fee ("Cancellation Fee") shall be paid to Illustrator in the amount of 50% of the Page Rate defined herein. The Cancellation Fee is in the nature of a buyout, and no other royalties, residuals, or other forms of compensation shall be due or payable to Illustrator as a result of Illustrator's work hereunder. Notwithstanding anything in this agreement to the contrary, any Comic Book materials subject to a Cancellation Fee shall remain the property of Illustrator and not be subject to the Work For Hire or other intellectual property transfer provisions herein. Notwithstanding the foregoing, if CPC rejects the Illustrator's work, Illustrator shall still maintain ownership of her results and proceeds;

17 Whenever you have the right or the expectancy to receive a royalty, you should also have an audit provision. This allows you to check on the publishing company's accounting.

18 Typically, the cost of an audit is paid for by the person requesting it; however, if the audit uncovers any paid royalties in excess of 10% of what is owed, the publishing company must pick up the cost of the audit.

19 Distinguish the types of Kill Fees: Cancellation Fees and Rejection Fees. (See Appendix G: Compensation, p. 464.) Here, the company is only offering a Cancellation Fee, but not a Rejection Fee. Kills Fees have to be negotiated for and some publishing companies don't give them at all.

however, no Cancellation Fee, or other payment, residuals, or otherwise shall be made to Illustrator for her work hereunder.

2.2. Illustrator shall receive no payments for any work done unless and until it meets CPC's specifications and is delivered on time.

2.3. Illustrator shall receive no additional or increased compensation for hours worked***20** beyond the expiration of any period of service or for services performed at night, on weekends or during holidays.

2.4. Illustrator will not be reimbursed for any expenses incurred to perform the Services hereunder without the prior written approval of CPC.

2.5. Illustrator shall receive five copies of the Comic Book.***21**

3. Deliverables*22

3.1. Illustrator agrees to deliver to CPC all Materials in acceptable formats as follows:

3.1.1. Digital files (formats and resolutions to be determined, but no less than 300 DPI) such as PDFs, EPS files,***23** and native file formats for individual layouts and illustrations.

20 No overtime in this agreement!

21 Writers and Illustrators typically receive five to ten copies each of the published comic.

22 Work out beforehand in what file formats you are expected to deliver your artwork.

23 Note: It is important to specify file format and resolution (e.g. "EPS" and "PDF" files). Obviously, this depends on the needs of the publisher and/or the media in which Illustrator works. Adobe Illustrator files are vector graphic and not rasterized, which means they are not resolution dependent. If you're dealing with a resolution-dependent file, like Adobe Photoshop, you should make sure to specify the minimum DPI that the drawings must have.

4. Delivery Schedule and Specifications*24

4.1. Development

4.1.1. Illustrator shall prepare and execute Pencil sketch concept drawings for the Comic Book including locations, and characters (the "Pencil Sketch Materials") to be supplied to CPC by _______, 20__ but in no event later than _______, 20__.

4.1.2. Within three (3) days of receipt, CPC shall review and provide Illustrator with comments on the Pencil Sketch Materials. If so requested, Illustrator shall make revisions to the Pencil Sketch Materials based on CPC's comments (the "Revised Pencil Sketch Materials"), such revisions to be supplied to CPC by _______, 20__ but in no event later than _______, 20__.

4.1.3. Once CPC has approved the Revised Pencil Sketch Materials, Illustrator shall create colored and inked versions of the Revised Pencil Sketch Materials, integrating CPC's comments, if any (the "Colored and Inked Materials"). Illustrator will provide CPC with the Colored and Inked Materials by _______, 20__ but in no event later than _______, 20__.

4.1.4. Within three (3) days of receipt, CPC shall review and provide Illustrator with comments on the Colored and Inked Materials. If so requested, Illustrator shall make revisions to the Colored and Inked Materials based on CPC's comments (the "Revised Colored and Inked Materials"), such revisions to be supplied to CPC by _______, 20__ but in no event later than _______, 20__.

4.1.5. Within seven (7) days of receipt, CPC shall review and provide Illustrator with comments on the Revised Colored and Inked Materials. Approval of the Revised Colored and Inked Materials is contingent upon Illustrator making any suggested revisions to the Revised Colored and Inked Materials.

--------COMMENTS--------

<u>24</u> This agreement contains an expansive delivery schedule, which allows for quite a bit of back and forth between the editorial staff and the Illustrator. Some illustrator agreements merely provide for one delivery date.
This schedule is really quite simple: the illustrator creates some stage of the process (e.g. pencil sketches or layout), and then delivers that product form to the publishing company for its review, approval, and further notes. The illustrator then revises the work based on the notes and delivers a finished product form, at which point production moves on to the next stage. Calendar dates and review time periods are specified to keep everybody in the project on track. While the protracted deliver/review/revise process shown here may seem like micromanaging, it is actually advantageous to the Illustrator. Every step of the way the publishing company must give approval before the next step is taken on. The publishing company cannot later say that they did not like artwork that they approved at an earlier stage.

4.2. Page Art

4.2.1. Within seven (7) days of CPC's approval of the Revised Colored and Inked Materials and in consultation with CPC, Illustrator shall commence work laying out, drawing, inking, coloring, and lettering the pages of the Comic Book (the "Comic Book Pages"), based on (1) the Comic Book Script, which is subject to change, and its directions, panel sizes, and camera angles and (2) the Revised Colored and Inked Materials.**★25**

4.2.2. Illustrator shall initially draw and deliver the Comic Book Pages in pencil or an equivalent ("Pencil Drawn Pages"), five (5) pages at a time, for CPC to review and provide comments. After receipt of each five-page section, CPC shall have three (3) days to provide Illustrator with comments and request revisions. Once any requested revisions have been approved, Illustrator shall deliver inked, lettered, and colored versions of each five-page section of the Pencil Drawn Pages (the "Colored and Inked Pages").

4.2.3. CPC shall have three (3) days to provide Illustrator with comments and request revisions on each five-page section of the Colored and Inked Pages (the "Revised Colored and Inked Pages"). Illustrator shall commence work on any subsequent five-page section no more than 48 hours from receipt of CPC's approval on the preceding section.

4.2.4. The final pages of the Revised Colored and Inked Pages shall be delivered to CPC for approval by _______, 20__ but in no event later than _______, 20__.

4.3. Final Corrections

4.3.1. Once the final section of the Colored and Inked Pages has been approved by CPC, Illustrator shall make any corrections, additions, or revisions to the assembled

---------COMMENTS---------

25 With respect to Page Art, make sure that the Illustrator's tasks are carefully delineated because the publisher and the artist's expectations are not aligned. If you expect the Illustrator to provide pencils, inks, and lettering you should state that specifically to avoid any confusion.

sections of the Colored and Inked Pages (the "Final Corrections"), as requested by CPC, and to be delivered to CPC for approval by ________, 20__ but in no event later than ________, 20__.

5. Work-For-Hire, Grant of Rights★26

5.1. Illustrator acknowledges and agrees that the Comic Book, the Materials, and any and all of Illustrator's proceeds and results of Illustrator's Services, including without limitation ideas, storylines, dialogue, gags, character designs, specifications, drawings, designs, writings, and concepts, produced with respect to the Comic Book (the "Work Product") is "work made for hire"★27 within the meaning of the copyright laws of the United States and Illustrator has no claim to the intellectual property in the Comic Book or any derived benefits from the exploitation of the Comic Book, other than those stated herein. Illustrator acknowledges that such work made for hire relationship was established prior to Illustrator commencing Services hereunder.★28 For purposes of this paragraph, the term Comic Book shall include any and all methods and forms of distribution, media, and/or derivative works, now known or hereinafter invented, throughout the universe, in perpetuity.

5.2. For all purposes throughout the universe and in perpetuity, CPC shall be the sole and exclusive author of the Work Product. To the extent that the Work Product is not "work made for hire" for any reason or that authorship of the Work Product does not vest solely, automatically, and exclusively in CPC, then Illustrator assigns all right, title, and interest of any kind in the Work Product to CPC, including without limitation any and all worldwide copyrights for the full term of copyright and all renewals and extensions thereof, in the name of CPC, together with all present and future rights of every kind pertaining to the Work Product, whether or not such rights are now known, recognized or contemplated, in all media now known or hereafter developed.★29

<u>26</u> This is a publisher owned property, so the work is work for hire. In other words, everything is owned by the publishing company. (See Work for Hire, p. 39.). While this may seem unfair, a number of recent comic book cases have underscored the need for comic book creators and publishers to cleanly control all the rights to the Illustrator's work. (See Comic Book Cases, p. 486.) Of course, from the Illustrator's perspective, the initial visualization of the comic book character should be worth more than just a page rate. An artist who initially designs a character may want to negotiate a perpetual royalty from the use of the character in exchange for giving up all copyright rights to that character. At the risk of being redundant, remember that owning the copyright to a character and to the right to receive royalty can be separated.

<u>27</u> Make sure you understand the scope of what you're being asked to produce. Anything within the scope of a work-for-hire agreement is owned by the hiring party.

<u>28</u> Note: The law that governs work-for-hire relationship differs depending on the jurisdiction. In some jurisdictions, the parties must agree upon the fact that the relationship is a work-for-hire relationship prior to the work being created.

5.3. Illustrator hereby waives the exercise of any "moral rights," "droit moral," and any analogous rights, in and to the Work Product, however, denominated now or hereafter recognized.***30**

5.4. All licenses, rights, and privileges herein granted, transferred, or assigned by Illustrator to CPC are perpetual, irrevocable, and not subject to restraint, rescission, or injunction under any circumstances, including the termination of this Agreement, by breach or otherwise.

6. Physical Artwork*31

6.1. Notwithstanding anything herein contained to the contrary, once CPC has made use of Illustrator's Materials for the purposes of printing and publishing the comic book, CPC shall return to Illustrator all original physical artwork and other original physical Materials created by Illustrator pursuant to the Services performed by Illustrator hereunder ("Returned Physical Materials").***32**

6.2. Illustrator shall own these Returned Physical Materials (but not any of their attendant intellectual property rights), provided that:

6.2.1. Illustrator keeps affixed to the Returned Physical Materials an intellectual property notice,***33** which clearly identifies CPC as the owner of all copyright, trademark, and other rights in and to the Returned Physical Materials.

6.2.2. Illustrator does not make commercial use of the Returned Physical Materials, other than their sale as chattels.***34** For purpose of clarity, Illustrator shall have no other rights to convey in and to the Returned Physical Materials, other than their physical sale. Any other commercial exploitation of the Returned Physical Materials is expressly prohibited.

6.2.3. Illustrator shall only publicly display copies of the Returned Physical Materials within the context of

29 Note: Here we have what's called an "alternate assignment" clause. Its effect is to ensure that the comic creator gets the copyright to the Illustrator's work no matter what. So if for some reason the Illustrator's work is not deemed to be a work for hire, this clause transfers the copyright from the Illustrator to the creator anyway.

30 For an explanation of these rights, see Appendix A: A Comic Creator's Guide to Moral Rights & The Visual Artists Rights Act.

31 Comic book publishing is unique in that artists are typically allowed to keep the physical copies of their artwork, despite the fact that they may not have the intellectual property rights to their artwork.
Artists often make extra money at Comic Cons by selling their artwork to fans.

32 Remember, while it is common practice for comic artists to retain the physical copies to their work, this must be negotiated.

33 Publishing companies typically require an intellectual property notice, clearly identifying the publishing company as owner of the copyright and trademark rights in and to the artwork.

34 "Chattels" is personal property, like goods, that can be sold.

Illustrator's own portfolio or pursuant to the physical sale of the Returned Physical Materials.

6.3. CPC's failure to return the Returned Physical Materials shall not be considered a breach of this agreement. Additionally, CPC shall not be liable for reimbursing Illustrator for the loss of the Returned Physical Materials, unless such loss was caused solely by gross negligence or willful conduct on the part of CPC. If CPC has a duty to reimburse the loss of the Returned Physical Materials, as specified hereunder, Illustrator agrees to accept as full and complete compensation for such loss, a page rate commensurate with that paid to Illustrator for their initial creation, as specified in paragraph 2.2.1., herein.**★35**

7. Publicity

7.1. Illustrator shall not publish or disseminate any article, book, news story, or other publicity regarding the Comic Book, or Illustrator's services herein, without the prior written consent of CPC. Illustrator shall keep the terms of this agreement confidential to all third parties, with the exception of the Illustrator's legal advisers and financial professionals, or pursuant to a court order to disclose the terms herein.**★36**

7.2. CPC shall have the right to use, reproduce, display, disseminate, publish, print, and make any other uses of Illustrator's name, voice, signature, approved likeness, sobriquet, and/or approved biographical information in connection with the marketing, advertising, and exploitation of the Comic Book.**★37**

7.3. Notwithstanding anything herein to the contrary, Illustrator shall have the right to exhibit, display, and promote no more than five (5) pages of the Comic Book on Illustrator's website(s)**★38** for purposes of self-promotion and only so long as the pages are accompanied by the following copyright notice: "© 2026 Comic Publishing Company, LLC. All rights reserved." All other uses or displays of the Comic Book are hereby expressly reserved by CPC.

35 And if the publishing company loses the physical artwork, it is only liable to the Illustrator for the original page rate.

36 Publishing companies tend to be very secretive about the terms of their contracts. After all, if every artist knew what other artists were receiving, it would make the publishing companies ability to negotiate with each one of them individually a lot more difficult.

37 The publishing company wants to be able to use the illustrator's approved biography and likeness to promote the book while restricting the illustrator's ability to use the artwork for publicity without prior written permission from the publisher.

8. Representations and Warranties*39

8.1. To the best of Illustrator's knowledge and belief, Illustrator represents and warrants the following:

8.1.1. Illustrator has the legal authority and right to enter into and perform any of the duties and/or obligations under this Agreement, and that by entering into or performing any of the duties and/or obligations under this Agreement, no rights of any third parties are or will be violated;

8.1.2. Illustrator shall create the illustrations for the Comic Book by his or her own efforts, and they shall not be based on or copied from any other pictorial, dramatic, literary, or other material of any kind, unless such material is in the public domain;

8.1.3. Illustrator shall not, without the prior written approval of CPC, engage third parties to assist with the Services;

8.1.4. Illustrator's contributions to the Comic Book shall not defame or violate any rights of privacy, publicity, or any other right of any person;

8.1.5. Illustrator's contributions to the Comic Book shall not infringe upon the copyright, trademark, or other intellectual property right of any other person;

8.1.6. Illustrator shall make no attempt to diminish, impair, or otherwise encumber any of the proceeds and results of his or her services or any of the rights granted herein.

8.2. These representations and warranties shall survive the termination of this Agreement.

9. Termination

38 *Tip*: artists should try and get that prior written approval upfront, especially the right to include artwork on the artist's personal website.

39 These representations and warranties are fairly standard:

The illustrator must promise that he or she is free to enter into this agreement and nothing that he or she contributes is going to infringe any copyright or other third-party rights.

9.1. Illustrator's engagement under this Agreement may be terminated at any time by CPC, subject only to payment of any compensation accrued by Illustrator up until the date of termination, or Cancellation Fee, if such is applicable.**★40**

9.2. In the event of any breach by Illustrator, or as a result of Illustrator's illness, accident, mental, or physical disability or by reason of any governmental authority or law, labor dispute or force majeure, or other event beyond CPC's control, CPC shall have the right to terminate or suspend Illustrator's services without compensation or further obligation.

10. Approvals★41

10.1. CPC shall have sole approval rights over all creative decisions regarding the Comic Book, the Materials, and any other proceeds and results from Illustrator's Services under this Agreement.

11. Credit

11.1. If Illustrator performs all duties and obligations under this Agreement, Illustrator shall be accorded credit in the Comic Book as follows: "Illustrated by Izzy Illustrator."**★42**

11.2. Without limiting the foregoing, all other aspects of credit, including the look, order, placement, or media, and whether or not Illustrator shall receive credit, shall be in the sole discretion of CPC, its successors, assigns, or licensees.

11.3. Upon receipt of written notice from Illustrator, CPC shall, within a reasonable time, make good faith efforts to cure prospectively a failure to accord proper credit, if any, created after the receipt date of such notice.

11.4. Notwithstanding anything to the contrary in this Agreement, in no event shall Illustrator seek, or be entitled to, damages of any kind by reason of any breach or threatened breach of any of the credit requirements; nor shall Illustrator be entitled to seek to enjoin the distribution, advertising, marketing, or exploitation of the Comic Book, all such equitable remedies

40 Typically, the publishing company reserves the right to terminate the agreement at any time, subject to paying the Illustrator any monies due up to the point of termination.

41 It should come as no surprise that for a publisher-owned work, the publisher keeps all approval rights.

42 Being properly credited in the comic book is almost as important as being paid for your work. Make sure to negotiate this provision carefully.

being hereby expressly waived by Illustrator. No inadvertent or casual failure to comply with any credit requirements herein shall be deemed a breach of this Agreement.

12. Exclusivity

12.1. Commencing as of the Effective Date of this Agreement, Illustrator shall render all Services on a nonexclusive basis provided; however, that any services that Illustrator may render for third parties or on Illustrator's own account shall not materially interfere with the timely performance of Illustrator's Services and obligations with respect to the Comic Book hereunder.**★43**

13. No Partnership

13.1. Nothing in this Agreement shall be interpreted to create a joint venture, partnership, or agency relationship between the parties. Illustrator acknowledges and agrees that he or she is an independent contractor.**★44** Neither party shall do or suffer to be done anything whereby one party may be represented as an agent, partner, or joint-venturer of the other. Illustrator further acknowledges and agrees to indemnify and hold harmless CPC from any loss or damage that results from the violation of this provision.

14. Notice and Cure

14.1. CPC shall not be in breach of this Agreement unless and until CPC fails to cure the default, if any, within fourteen (14) days of receipt of written notice from Illustrator, in which case Illustrator may terminate this Agreement immediately. Notices shall be in writing and specify with particularity the nature of the other party's default. All notices shall be delivered by overnight courier, personal delivery, or in the form of a certified or registered letter.**★45**

15. Indemnification

---------COMMENTS---------

<u>43</u> If exclusivity is needed, the Illustrator may argue that he or she should be paid more.

<u>44</u> Although the Illustrator acknowledges his or her independent contractor status, only the facts of their working relationship actually determine whether he or she should be classified as an employee or independent contractor.

15.1. At all times, Illustrator shall indemnify, defend, and hold harmless CPC, its successors, licensees, agents, assigns, employees, and/or representatives from and against any and all liability, damages, loss, costs and expenses, of any kind (including reasonable attorneys' fees) from any action, claim, or demand (each, a "Claim") arising out of any breach by Illustrator of any warranty, representation or covenant contained in this Agreement.

15.2. At all times, CPC shall indemnify, defend, and hold harmless Illustrator, his or her successors, licensees, agents, assigns, employees, and/or representatives, from and against any and all liability, damages, loss, costs, and expenses, of any kind (including reasonable attorneys' fees), which may be suffered or assumed by Illustrator by reason of the development, production, and/or distribution of the Comic Book except to the extent indemnified by Illustrator in Section 15.1, above or from any claim that arises from a misrepresentation made by Illustrator herein.

15.3. Except for a failure to pay any compensation herein, CPC shall not be liable to Illustrator for damages resulting from the development, production or distribution of the Comic Book, or any derivative work therefrom, unless and until CPC has been provided reasonable notice and opportunity to correct or cure such matters.

16. Limitation of Liability

16.1. CPC, its respective parents, subsidiaries, and affiliates, and each of their respective officers, directors, shareholders, employees, agents, representatives, successors, licensees, and assigns (the "Contracting Parties") shall not be liable to Illustrator or any third party for any consequential, indirect, special, exemplary, incidental or punitive damages, regardless of the form of action, whether or not the excluded damages are characterized in tort, contract, negligence, or any other theory of liability, even if a party has been advised of the possibility of such damages and even if the damages were foreseeable. The maximum aggregate liability of the Contracting

45 If you're an Illustrator, be careful of one-sided notice and cure provisions like this one. If the publishing company defaults (doesn't live up to its contractual obligations), it has 14 days from when the artist notifies it in order to correct the problem before the default becomes a breach of contract. What if the Illustrator defaults on the contract, does he or she get 14 days to cure the problem as well? Not under this contract...!

Parties shall not exceed the total amount of compensation paid to Illustrator under this Agreement. If this limitation of liability is in any way disallowed by any applicable authority, the liability of the Contracting Parties is limited to the fullest extent permitted by law. Any personal injury to Illustrator or loss or damage to Illustrator's personal property shall be Illustrator's sole responsibility.

17. No Obligation to Utilize Results and Proceeds

17.1. Notwithstanding anything to the contrary contained herein, CPC shall not be obligated to use or continue to use Illustrator's services in connection with the Comic Book or any subsequent volumes of the Comic Book, and CPC may, in its sole discretion, use additional illustrators or other creative talent.**★46**

18. Assignment

18.1. CPC may assign all rights in and to any work performed hereunder in whole or in part to any firm, corporation or person, to be exploited in any and all media now known or hereafter created in any manner in perpetuity without any additional compensation due to Illustrator.

18.2. Illustrator may not assign any of his or her duties and obligations hereunder.

<u>**46**</u> While the publishing company has the right to utilize the Illustrator's services and artwork (and must pay under the contract), the publishing company is not obligated to use the artwork.

19. Option for Future Services*47

19.1 Illustrator hereby grants CPC an irrevocable option (the "Initial Option"), exercisable, if at all, within one year from the initial publication date of the first volume of the Comic Book, to engage Illustrator to perform the same services, with an equivalent delivery schedule, and for the same compensation, subject to Illustrator's professional availability.

19.2 Following the Initial Option, Illustrator hereby grants CPC a second irrevocable option (the "Second Option"), exercisable within one year from the initial publication date of the work created by Illustrator during the Initial Option, to engage Illustrator to perform the same services on a new issue of The Adventures of Maggot Man, with an equivalent delivery schedule, subject to Illustrator's professional availability, and contingent upon the parties agreeing to an increase in compensation, to be negotiated in good faith.

20. Remedies, Choice of Law

20.1. In the event of breach of this Agreement, the sole remedy of the nonbreaching party shall be limited to an action at law for monetary damages actually suffered.

20.2. Notwithstanding anything to the contrary in this Agreement, in no event shall Illustrator be entitled to seek to enjoin the distribution, advertising, marketing, or exploitation of the Comic Book or any sequel, remake, or other derivative work based thereon, all such equitable remedies being hereby expressly waived by Illustrator.

20.3. This Agreement shall be construed, interpreted, and governed by the laws of the State of New York. The federal or state courts of competent jurisdiction located in the State of New York, County of New York, shall have sole and exclusive jurisdiction to hear and determine any dispute or controversy arising under or concerning this Agreement, and both parties each hereby waive any objection and submit to the *in personam* jurisdiction and venue of such court.

--------COMMENTS--------

47 **Option for Future Services**. This clause does not always appear in illustrator agreements. It allows the publishing company to compel the illustrator to work for it on future books for essentially the same terms.
However, here the Publishing Company must agree to renegotiate compensation for every additional issue (after the first additional issue) it requests of the Illustrator.

21. Further Documents

21.1. The parties agree to execute and deliver all additional documents, papers, and other instruments that might be necessary to further the intent of this Agreement.

22. Entire Agreement

22.1. This Agreement constitutes the entire agreement between the parties hereto on the subject matter hereof and supersedes and replaces all prior and contemporaneous oral or written agreements, representations, and understandings. Illustrator warrants that he or she has not been induced into entering into this agreement by relying upon any statements, representations, or promises, whether oral or written, of CPC or its agents.***48**

23. Severability

23.1. If any provision of this Agreement is adjudged void, unenforceable, or unlawful, in whole or in part, by a court of competent jurisdiction, the remaining provisions shall continue in full force and effect.

24. Independent Legal Advice

24.1. Both parties have obtained independent legal advice in connection with this Agreement or have otherwise had an opportunity to consult with counsel and have voluntarily chosen not to do so.

25. Survival

25.1. The following clauses shall survive the termination of this Agreement, whether by breach or otherwise: "ENGAGEMENT," "COMPENSATION," "WORK-FOR-HIRE, GRANT OF RIGHTS," "PUBLICITY," "REPRESENTATIONS AND WARRANTIES," "INDEMNIFICATION," "ASSIGNMENT," "REMEDIES, CHOICE OF LAW," "SEVERABILITY," and "SURVIVAL."

48 The "Entire Agreement" paragraph is a seemingly innocuous creature. It's straightforward on its face, alerting the parties to the fact that the terms of the written contract that they are signing will govern over any other prior agreements that they may have had with respect to illustrating the comic book. In practice, however, things can get a little muddy. Let's say that you are an illustrator and that you have built up a wonderful relationship with the Publishing Company's editor. In fact, you decided to sign this agreement with them because the editor told you how excited the Publishing Company was, and how committed the publishers were to putting your book out by Christmas. Unfortunately, there's nothing in this Agreement that obligates the Publishing Company to publish by Christmas. As a result, despite your copious emails, video recordings, and sworn declarations with that editor to the contrary, the Publishing Company is simply not obligated to publish by Christmas. Remember, too, that editor may no longer be working for the Publishing Company in a year's time. So, any promises he or she may have made to you will undoubtedly be lost in the shuffle when a new editor takes his or her place. In my many years of practice, I've come to believe that there is no such thing as "institutional memory." If you want something to be a part of your deal, make sure it's in the written contract.

From the Publishing Company's perspective, the converse is also true: if you hired an illustrator with the understanding that they would provide pencils, inks, and coloring and yet your contract with them only specified that they would provide pencil art, this paragraph would limit the Illustrator's contractual obligation to just providing pencil art.

26. Counterparts

26.1. This Agreement may be executed in several counterparts, and all counterparts so executed shall be deemed an original, and all of such counterparts shall constitute one agreement. Scanned and facsimile copies shall be deemed originals for all purposes. If the Agreement is signed in counterparts, it shall only be effective upon delivery of one executed counterpart from each party to the other party.

In Witness Whereof, the parties have caused this Agreement to be executed by their duly authorized signatories to be effective as of the Effective Date. Any individual executing this Agreement on behalf of any party hereto does hereby represent and warrant that such execution is made with full authority, and that such party is bound by the terms hereof.

ILLUSTRATOR Izzy Illustrator	**Comic Publishing Company ("CPC")**
By: ____________________	By: ____________________
Date: ____________________	Date: ____________________
	Authorized Manager

With respect to Page Art, make sure that the Illustrator's tasks are carefully delineated. Many a project has been derailed because the publisher and the artist's expectations are not aligned. If you expect the illustrator to provide penciling, inks, coloring, and lettering, state that specifically to avoid confusion.

NEXT STEPS

Now that you've taken care of your collaborators, employees, and independent contractors, it's almost time to look for publishers. But first you need to give your comic book property once-over for hidden IP issues. On to the next chapter!

Notes

1 Fair Labor Standards Act of 1938, 29 U.S.C. § 201 et seq. (1938); 29 C.F.R. pts. 510–794, available at https://webapps.dol.gov/elaws/elg/minwage.htm (last visited Mar. 5, 2025).

2 Employment Law Guide – Wage Garnishment, U.S. Department of Labor, available at https://webapps.dol.gov/elaws/elg/garnish.htm (last visited Mar. 5, 2025).
3 Employment Law Guide – Child Labor Protections (Nonagricultural Work), U.S. Dep't of Labor (Updated Dec. 2016), available at https://webapps.dol.gov/elaws/elg/childlbr.htm (last visited Mar. 5, 2025).
4 Employment Law Guide – Child Labor Protections (Nonagricultural Work), U.S. Dep't of Labor (Updated Dec. 2016), available at https://webapps.dol.gov/elaws/elg/childlbr.htm (last visited Mar. 5, 2025).
5 Occupational Safety and Health Act of 1970 ("OSH Act"), 29 U.S.C. § 651 et seq. (1970); 29 C.F.R. pts. 1900 to 2400, available at https://webapps.dol.gov/elaws/elg/osha.htm (last visited May 9, 2025).
6 Family and Medical Leave Act of 1993 ("FMLA"), 29 U.S.C. §2601 et seq. (1993); 29 C.F.R. Part 825, available at https://webapps.dol.gov/elaws/elg/fmla.htm (last visited Mar. 5, 2025).
7 O-1 Visa: Individuals with Extraordinary Ability or Achievement, U.S. Citizenship and Immigration Services, available at https://www.uscis.gov/working-in-the-united-states/temporary-workers/o-1-visa-individuals-with-extraordinary-ability-or-achievement (last visited Mar. 5, 2025).
8 New York State Department of Labor, Independent Contractors, available at https://dol.ny.gov/independent-contractors (last visited May 09, 2025).
9 California Labor Code Section 3351.5(c). ("Any person while engaged by contract for the creation of a specially ordered or commissioned work of authorship in which the parties expressly agree in a written instrument signed by them that the work shall be considered a work made for hire, as defined in Section 101 of Title 17 of the United States Code, and the ordering or commissioning party obtains ownership of all the rights comprised in the copyright in the work.")
10 California Labor Code Section 3700.5.
11 Internal Revenue Service, Instructions for Forms 1099-MISC and 1099-NEC, available at https://www.irs.gov/pub/irs-pdf/i1099mec.pdf.
12 New York State Department of Labor, Independent Contractors, available at https://dol.ny.gov/independent-contractors (last visited May 9, 2025).
13 Graphic Artists Guild, Graphic Artists Guild Handbook: Pricing & Ethical Guidelines, 242 (16th ed. 2021).
14 Creator Resource, Page Rate Finder - Comic Book Publishers, Creator Resource, https://www.creatorresource.com/page-rate-finder-comic-book-publishers/ (last visited May 23, 2025).
15 "The economics of the comic book publishing industry means that the largest publishers require creators to operate almost exclusively under work-for-hire contracts because the publishers take most of the financial risk in producing a book." Sean McGilvray, Judicial Kryptonite?: Superman and the Consideration of Moral Rights in American Copyright, 32 Hastings Comm. & Ent L.J. 319, 335 (2010).
16 Although this is an agreement designed for an illustrator, it could also be used for a comic book writer, with a few modifications.

CHAPTER 9

Clearances and Licensing the Rights of Others

DOI: 10.1201/9781003496052-13

Copyrighted and trademarked materials appear everywhere: comic book illustrations and scripts, posters, sculptures, product labels, superhero logos, makeup and costume designs, and song lyrics; even the creative selection and arrangement of public domain elements can be protected by copyright. You need to make sure that you have the right to include any of these materials in your book (a process called *clearance*).

And while you're at it—did you base any of your comic book characters on a real-life person? Guess what: You may need that person's written permission as well.

Indeed, third-party-owned IP is the bane of the conscientious artist. Don't fall into the trap of thinking that just because you own a physical copy—or even the original—of a piece of art, you have the right to use it. Ownership of an issue of a comic created by somebody else gives you the right to read and sell that issue (or never read and keep mint in bag), but it doesn't give you the right to incorporate its plot or characters into your own work. And that original pencil drawing by Alex Ross that you purchased at the latest Comic Con? You can hang it in your house, but you can't put it in your book.

OVERVIEW OF THE CLEARANCE PROCESS

The first step is to switch off your artist brain and to look at your work like a lawyer. Really analyze your creative collaborations and how they were created. Before hitting publish, pinpoint what you—and any co-contributors—have added to your project. This means knowing exactly who inked which panel and ensuring that each contribution is locked down by contract or IP law. Next, scrutinize any third-party elements you've borrowed, whether that's illustrations sourced off the Internet, catchy song lyrics, or plot twists lifted from somewhere else. Distinguish between protected content that requires a license and bits that merely served as inspiration, come from the public domain, or fall under fair or nominative use. Then, if you're playing with generative artificial intelligence (GEN-AI), check for any legal gremlins hidden in its prompts, training data, or output, making sure your work retains that unmistakably human touch.

Next, if any external contributions are legally protected, secure the appropriate licenses—or better yet, consider a collaboration or exclusive license, and even round up some errors and omissions, insurance for extra peace of mind (it's like a safety net beneath your creative trapeze). After all that legwork, be sure to alert your stakeholders—like your ever-watchful publisher who expects every creative element to be spotless—and explain why extra permissions aren't needed because of fair use, or better yet, that you already have the replacement panels drawn and ready to swap out. Because, believe me, postponing a deadline is far better than wading into an expensive lawsuit—even if you eventually win. Finally, top it all off by registering your IP: Lock in the copyright and secure all the chain-of-title documents, so your work is legally sealed and ready for liftoff.

IP CLEARANCES

Think of IP clearance as your project's preflight checklist for intellectual property. It involves carefully scrutinizing every creative element to determine whether you need permission from a third party—and if so, securing that approval through a license. The process involves several essential steps:

- **Analyze Contributor Claims**: Examine any potential IP claims related to the contributions from your collaborators. Determine whether anyone involved in creating your work might assert rights over the material they helped develop.
- **Assess Third-Party Claims**: Identify any external intellectual property—such as trademarks, copyrights, or other protected content—that might require a license. This step is crucial to ensure that you are not inadvertently using someone else's work without permission.
- **Notify Necessary Stakeholders**: Inform all necessary parties, such as the publisher who expects you to have all rights secured. Explain why additional permissions may not be necessary or negotiate appropriate workarounds where needed.
- **Secure Licenses or Determine Alternatives**: Obtain the required licenses or permissions. If securing them is not feasible, explore alternative legal strategies to protect your project.

By performing this due diligence, you ensure that your creative project is free from legal turbulence before you launch it—and prevent a potential issue from escalating into a breach of contract.

CLEARANCES—STEP-BY-STEP

Analyze Contributor Relationships and Their Creative Contributions

In this first step, you need to take a close look at all of the relationships that help you create your book. Here, and in any IP analysis, it pays to put on your "tinfoil paranoia hat." In my experience as an attorney, when it comes to IP infringement—or perceived IP infringement—people are so emotionally involved in work that they feel they contributed to that they may sue—even when the potential recovery or likelihood of success is quite small. At this stage, don't look at your creative relationships from your point of view; look at them from the point of view of the people with whom you brainstormed and those who may have worked with you on creating your book. Ask: "Would *that* person believe that they contributed to my work? Would *they* think I used their work in mine?"

Ideas

Simply discussing or sharing an idea does not qualify someone as an author under copyright law; however, if a court believes you agreed to keep an idea confidential or that there was an implied contract between you and the concept's originator in which you agreed to develop the idea with them, you could be looking at a lawsuit. Review the following:

- **Source of Inspiration**: Consider whether any of your characters, plot elements, dialogue, or designs were inspired by ideas shared by people you met in writers' groups, classrooms, parties, or local "drink and draw" meetups.
- **Nature of the Ideas**: If the ideas you received were fairly generic or only minor modifications of concepts already well known in the comics industry, you might be protected against infringement claims.
- **Context of Disclosure**: Reflect on whether these ideas were disclosed in a situation where the provider might expect that any work you produce using their idea would be treated as a collaborative effort or that they would receive compensation if you use their idea.

If you answered "yes" or "maybe" to the above, you should have a discussion with that person to establish a clear and formal understanding of your arrangement.

Copyrights

Understanding how your copyrights were created and who may be a joint author or co-owner is critical.

- **Consider Your Creative Collaborations.** Before you pat yourself on the back as a comic book genius, ask yourself: Did you craft your character designs, panel layouts, dialogue, scripts, or any other copyrightable elements entirely on your own? Or did you join forces with another creative mind? Even if a friend only drew a few pages of your 100-page epic, they may very well be deemed a joint author. And if you hired someone to add that extra flair—whether through writing, inking, or penciling—make sure they sign a written agreement that clearly spells out who owns what. Trust me, those signatures are your first line of defense against future copyright conundrums. (See Appendix A, p. 335; "Joint Authors," p. 347; "Hiring Other Artists," p. 150.)
- **Watch Out for Work-for-Hire.** Now, add one more twist: Did you create any of your work while employed by someone else? If you're busy conjuring comic magic while on the clock for another company, they might claim ownership under the work-for-hire doctrine. In other words, if your creative genius is part of your job, someone else could end up being the actual copyright owner. So, double-check your contracts to ensure that you, not your employer, reap the rewards of your artistic triumph. This due diligence might not be as flashy as a superhero showdown, but it sure saves you from an unwanted legal battle down the road. (See Work for Hire, p. 350.)

Analyze Any Third-Party Intellectual Property

In step two, ensure you're not using unlicensed works in an infringing manner. Carefully assess all external content—examining not only copyrights and trademarks but also rights of publicity and idea rights—to confirm that any incorporated material serves as creative inspiration rather than a direct, unauthorized reproduction.

Ideas

In general, ideas are unprotectable unless there is a contract in place between the parties specifying that the idea will be treated as the property of one of the parties or that one party will pay the other for commercial use of the idea. Without a contract (but remember, the contract might be implied), we are all free to use each other's ideas. What this means is that if you read a comic book that inspires you to create a similarly themed comic book, you're probably within your rights to do so.

> **Example**: Assume you have never met the creators of the comic book series *The Walking Dead* (Robert Kirkman, Tony Moore, and Charlie Adlard). You read their comic book series and are inspired to create your own zombie-themed series. However, you set yours on a futuristic space colony on Pluto's moon, Charon. All of the characters are different than those in *The Walking Dead*, with the exception of your protagonist who is the Sheriff of the Charon colony (but that's where the similarity ends between your character and *The Walking Dead* protagonist Sheriff Rick Grimes). Like most zombie-themed creative properties, your book follows a similar pattern: Zombies surprise an ever-shrinking group of people, some of whom are eaten, that group of zombies is killed, the group runs off to their next destination, where new characters are added, and the pattern is repeated.
>
> If you publish your book, *Cannibal Corpses of Charon*, you might be accused of adding to the glut of zombie-themed books; you might even be castigated by the critics for being unoriginal because your hero character is also a sheriff, but you would almost certainly win were you to be sued for idea misappropriation by *The Walking Dead* creators.

Copyright

Keep in mind that you don't have to *intend* to infringe a copyright in order to do so. If you copy a legally significant amount of somebody's copyright-protected material, and what you include in your work is substantially similar to the work you copied, you could be an infringer. Take a close look at your sources of visual and narrative inspiration and make sure that, to the extent you have included someone else's material, your work is not **substantially similar** to their work. In other words, if you did include somebody's material in yours, are you using it for a fundamentally different purpose than the original, and not just to compete with the original? Did you change it significantly, or transform it, when you included it in your comic? (See Copyright Infringement, p. 44.)

Furthermore, if you've hired or engaged an artist or writer to work on your book, make sure you take the same careful approach with the materials that they created. If you have control or supervisory capacity over another artist, and you profit from their work, if they infringe somebody's copyright in making your book, you could be liable for vicarious copyright infringement. (See Appendix A: Vicarious Copyright Infringement, p. 373.)

> **Example**: With respect to your Zombies on Pluto book, whether or not you would lose a *copyright infringement* lawsuit brought by the creators of *The Walking Dead* depends upon how substantially similar the copyrightable elements in your book are to theirs (illustrations, dialogue, scene structure, character design, etc.).

Fortunately, there are exceptions to copyright's monopolistic protection. If you have included third-party copyrighted materials in your work, check to see whether or not any of the following apply:

- You only included a very little or insignificant amount. (See *De Minimis* Taking, p. 383.)
- The work you included was published in the United States prior to 1928. (See Copyright Duration, p. 361.)
- You significantly transformed the work you took and didn't compete in the same market as the original. (See Fair Use, p. 375.)
- You criticized, made social commentary about, or parodied the work you took. (See Fair Use, p. 375.)
- The creator or owner of the work gave you their oral permission to use the work. Obviously, written permission is best, but spoken permission may suffice to grant a nonexclusive license to use the work. (See Nonexclusive Copyright License, p. 30.)
- The creator of the work you took is the federal government; for instance, perhaps you copied some of NASA's photographs. (See What Is Not Protectable under the U.S. Copyright Law?, p. 341.)
- The work you took was created by an employee of yours and created within the scope of his or her employment. (See Work-for-Hire, p. 350.)
- You only use a short phrase, or a slogan, or a title. (See What Is Not Protectable under the U.S. Copyright Law? p. 341.) **Caution:** While short phrases and titles are not protected by copyright law, they may be protected by trademark law, see below.

Trademark

With respect to using third-party trademarks in their work, comic book creators need to be careful when they are showing those trademarks in a disparaging manner, are giving the impression that the trademark owners are endorsing or have sponsored the comic book, or are featuring the trademarks on their comics or merchandise in a manner that will confuse consumers as to who manufactured these items. (See Injuries to a Trademark, p. 413.) Fortunately, there are many defenses against trademark injury claims. If you have included third-party trademarked materials in your work, check to see whether or not any of the following apply:

- You depicted the trademark as actually occurring in a real-life location and in a manner that does not suggest sponsorship or affiliation with the trademark, for example, showing the Coca-Cola® logo on a billboard in Times Square in one of many billboards in the background of a New York City street scene.
- You only used a portion of the trademark and did so merely for the purposes of identifying the product, for example, one of your hero characters says, "Can we get a couple of Cokes with our burgers?" Here, you're using just the words and not the symbols or other indicia of the Coca-Cola Company.
- You use it as a comparison with other products in advertising, for example, in your comic you want to give a feel for the 1970s, so you show characters watching a television commercial which features "the Pepsi® challenge," a comparative advertising campaign which features both Pepsi® and Coca-Cola® being tasted by consumers.
- You parody or criticize the trademark. **Be careful of this one!** Although trademark theoretically should give way to broad First Amendment rights with respect to creative properties, some courts have not always seen it this way, for example, your comic book features "Battlin' Bullfrog," a talking frog character that drinks "Croak-a-Cola," and then burps the alphabet. To be safe here, only feature as much of the trademark as is necessary to convey your meaning. For instance, if you are drawing the "Croak-a-Cola" can, you might want to make the label green, as opposed to Coca-Cola®-red. For more on these defenses, see Defenses to Trademark Injury, p. 418.
- While parody can be a clever tool, be wary of overstepping boundaries. Even if you're putting a humorous spin on a famous mark, avoid using that parody as your own brand's trademark, as it could lead to infringement issues.[1]

Depictions

Did you model any of your characters after friends, family, colleagues, or even celebrities? If you're using someone's likeness for commercial purposes—like merchandising—you absolutely need written permission to avoid infringing on their right of publicity. Keep in mind that state laws vary, and if you make a celebrity appear to endorse your work without consent, you could be hit with a **false endorsement** claim. Depicting someone in a negative light may also open the door to **defamation** or **false light** claims, not to mention that using a copyrighted photograph as a basis for your drawing might trigger **copyright infringement** issues.

Even if your character's resemblance is subtle, if readers can draw a connection that might harm the real person's reputation, you should review your work for potential defamation risks. One generally safe approach is to significantly transform the likeness—imagine turning a real person into a quirky, half-monster caricature. However, unless you have a written agreement, avoid using an unaltered likeness on merchandise or in ads, or as the main reason someone would buy your comic. Remember, truth, social commentary, opinion, humor, and privilege are all strong defenses against defamation claims.

Generative AI (GEN-AI)is a powerful tool, but its use can raise significant legal and ethical questions. Investigate the following areas to make sure your **chain-of-title** is still intact.

- **Assess infringement in the prompts (visual or textual) used to generate content.** The prompts you input into GEN-AI tools are not immune to legal scrutiny. For example, if a textual prompt includes copyrighted song lyrics or a visual prompt incorporates an image of a recognizable character or logo, you may be inadvertently using protected material without permission. Careful review of your prompts is essential to avoid potential claims of infringement. Even descriptive prompts that seem generic could raise issues if they directly reference a specific creative work (e.g., "in the style of [famous artist]" or "resembling [specific movie poster]").
- **Investigate whether the GEN-AI's training dataset contains infringing material.** Many GEN-AI models are trained on vast datasets that may include copyrighted works. If the AI tool you're using was developed using copyrighted material without proper licensing, legal disputes could arise. For instance, if a GEN-AI image generator was trained on a database of famous photographs or artwork without the creators' consent, its output might inherit liability issues. Before using any GEN-AI tool, research whether its developers have disclosed information about the training dataset and any steps taken to ensure compliance with copyright law.
- **Evaluate whether the GEN-AI output demonstrates sufficient human-directed expression to qualify as authored by a human and, therefore, protectable under copyright law.** Copyright law generally requires an element of human creativity and expression. Purely machine-generated content may not meet this standard. For instance, if you use a text-based GEN-AI tool to generate a storyline with no substantial edits or input from you, the output might not be eligible for copyright protection. However, if you closely guide the tool by refining prompts, editing drafts, and adding personal creative decisions, the result is more likely to qualify as human-authored. Courts and legal scholars continue to explore this issue, but it's crucial to ensure your contributions are substantive enough to claim authorship.

Alerting Stakeholders and Negotiating Workarounds

After assessing potential IP claims and securing—or devising alternatives for—required licenses, the next crucial step is to update your key stakeholders. Inform your publisher or contracting parties, who expect every creative element to be fully cleared, about your findings, and explain why additional permissions aren't needed. This proactive communication helps ward off any unpleasant surprises down the road and sets the stage for negotiating creative workarounds if issues arise.

> **Example**: Imagine you're a comic book creator with a publishing agreement with Dee Press Inc. featuring a strict representations and warranties clause. Just as you're gearing up to send the files to the printer, you discover that your illustrator has modeled your formidable supervillain, Leper Maggot, on his former high school teacher, Mrs. Crabtree. To address this potential IP hiccup, you think that the artist can double down on the creative process and exaggerate the design so that the final product is unrecognizably distinct from any real-life individual. Present this as a practical solution to the publisher: Estimate how long it would take to redraw the panels featuring Leper Maggot—say, 2 weeks—and discuss whether this adjustment might set back the printing schedule. Don't be surprised if it does, but it's far better to delay a deadline than to face an expensive lawsuit, even if you eventually win in court. This level of due diligence ensures that both creative integrity and contractual obligations remain intact before your project takes flight.

Negotiate and Draft Agreements

For any of the intellectual property and other third-party rights issues you identify, you may need to negotiate and draft agreements that will ensure that you can use these materials in your comic book.

- If you worked with somebody to create copyrighted and trademarked materials, and that relationship was like a partnership, with each party contributing material collaboratively, you may need a collaboration agreement. (See Collaboration Agreement, p. 119.)
- If you hired or paid somebody to produce work for you, you should have them sign an Artist Services Agreement. (See Hiring Other Artists, p. 150.)
- If you want to use somebody else's preexisting artwork, writing, trademarks, or likeness in your comic, you should have them execute an artwork license with you. (See Licensing, p. 206.)

LICENSING

You've determined that you need to get permission for somebody else's artwork, script, trademark, or depiction. Now what?

Now you need to concern yourself with licensing. You may recall, a license is the permission to use somebody else's artwork, detection, trademark, and so on.

Many nonexclusive licenses can be granted orally; however, the commercial use of somebody's depiction is required to be in writing. As you might imagine, the best practice is to always get any license in writing. After all, the company spokesperson you're speaking with today may no longer be with the company several months from now when you land your publishing agreement. And trust me, publishers will want to know that you've secured *all* of the rights in writing.

At the heart of any license is the **grant of rights**. This clause needs to answer the following questions:

- What rights are being granted: Copyright? Trademark? Depiction? Any and all rights? What rights are being reserved by the owner?
- In what media are the rights granted: Comic books and graphic novels? Related advertising and promotion? Ancillary markets, like television, theater, and merchandising?
- For how long are the rights granted? Over what territories can the rights be exploited by you? How is the payment structured?

The following licensing agreement might be used for background design artwork for a splash page or a comic book cover. With some modifications, it could also be used to license a short story.

EXAMPLE: ARTWORK LICENSE AGREEMENT

This Agreement dated _______________, 20___ (the "Effective Date") is made by and between Beard-O-Brush, an artist, residing at _____________________ (hereinafter, "**Licensor**"**★1**), and Carlo Creator, a comic book creator, residing at _____________________ (hereinafter, "**Licensee**"**★2**). Licensor and Licensee may each be referred to herein individually as a "Party" and collectively as the "Parties." **Witnesseth:★3**

Whereas, Licensor is the owner of the Artwork (as defined below);

Whereas, Licensee is the creator of the Comic Book (as defined below);

Whereas, Licensee wishes to acquire the rights to use the Artwork on the cover of the Comic Book, and in any reprint of the Comic Book, as hereafter defined; and

Whereas, Licensor is willing to grant to Licensee, and Licensee wishes to accept, a limited license to the Artwork on the terms and conditions set forth in this Agreement.

Now, Therefore, in consideration of the premises, and of the mutual undertakings herein contained, the parties, intending to be legally bound, agree as follows:

1. **Defined Terms**

   (a) Artwork: the creative properties and other related intellectual property, their associated copyrights and trademarks, if any, created and/or controlled by Licensor and listed on Exhibit A.

   (b) Comic Book: the original comic book, tentatively titled, "**The Adventures of Maggot Man**," and any reprint or compilation thereof.

   (c) Limited Purpose:**★4** the acquisition by Licensee of the rights, throughout the Territory and Term, to use, or authorize

--------COMMENTS--------

1 LICENSOR—The person granting the license to you to include their work in your comic.

2 LICENSEE—The person receiving the license to use the artwork in their comic (you in this case).

3 The Recital section of a contract, often beginning with the word "WITNESSETH," gives the background of why the parties are entering into the contract. Courts usually give this section less legal weight in determining a contract's meaning, so try to avoid defining any terms here.

4 Here the rights being sought are just to incorporate the artwork in comic books. If additional rights, such as multimedia or merchandising rights were being requested, these defined terms would have to be adjusted accordingly.

others to use, Licensor's Artwork on the cover of the Comic Book, in any reprint or subsequent edition of the Comic Book, and in any format now known or hereafter developed, including without limitation comic books, graphic novels, and digital equivalents,**★5** and in any promotion, marketing, or advertising related directly thereto,**★6** and as otherwise outlined herein.**★7**

(d) Territory: worldwide.

(e) Term: commencing on the Effective Date and continuing for as long as some version of the Comic Book is being sold**★8** or until such time as this Agreement is terminated as provided herein.

2. Nonexclusive License★9

2.1. During the Term, and subject to the provisions of this Agreement, Licensor hereby grants to Licensee and Licensee hereby accepts a limited, nonexclusive license to use, and to authorize others to use, the Artwork for the Limited Purpose, and for other purposes as described herein.

2.2. The rights granted hereunder shall include the right to reprint, and authorize others to reprint, the Artwork, in whole or in part, as part of an anthology or other similar work published in book, comic book, graphic novel, or trade collection form (in both hard and soft cover), or their digital equivalents.

2.3. The rights granted hereunder shall also include the right to crop, edit, and alter the Artwork, at Licensee's sole discretion, so as to meet space restrictions or to enhance the effectiveness or function of the use of the Artwork.**★10** Licensor hereby waives approval over how the Artwork is incorporated in the Comic Book.**★11**

2.4. All right, interest, and title in the Artwork shall be retained by Licensor.**★12** Licensor may use the Artwork in any manner whatsoever or for any purpose, provided, however, that Licensor does not permit or authorize the publication

5 This grant language is more narrowly tailored to apply only to comic books and graphic novels, as opposed to movies, or merchandise, etc.

6 Because commercial use is usually treated separately from how rights are used within the Comic Book property, you may have to secure permission separately to use any right to promote or advertise your book.

7 In creating a definition for "Limited Purpose" make sure it encompasses all the rights granted in the Agreement.

8 Keep in mind that under the terms of this agreement, once the comic book is no longer sold, the license expires. Another variation—which may cost more money—is to request perpetual grant.

9 Non-exclusive license means the same rights can be granted to other third parties—including those who compete directly with your comic book, such as other comic book creators. If you want a more exclusive grant, or if you want the licensor to refrain from competing uses, you may have to pay more money for the licensed Artwork.

10 It is important to reserve for yourself the right to modify and edit the Artwork.

11 This is a pretty broad waiver of approval rights, and very favorable towards you, the Licensee. However, some Licensors may not want to waive approval or may only grant approval once they've seen how you plan to use their work.

12 Here, the contract clarifies that the Licensor retains ownership of the work that he is providing.

of the Artwork from the Execution Date until it has been published in connection with the Comic Book.**★13**

3. Payment

3.1. In consideration for the rights granted to Licensee herein, Licensee agrees to pay Licensor and Licensor agrees to accept the following payments, payable as follows:

3.1.1. $_______________ upon execution of this agreement, receipt of which is hereby acknowledged;

3.1.2. $_______________ upon receipt by Licensee of the Artwork, and in the manner specified in Section 4 below; and

3.1.3. $_______________ payable in the event that the Artwork is reprinted or included, in whole or in part, in any anthology and due upon publication of any such reprint or anthology.**★14**

4. Deliverables

4.1. Not later than _______________, 20___, Licensor agrees to deliver to Licensee the Artwork in the following formats:

4.1.1. A Photoshop file (PSD) suitable for reproduction of the Artwork, and no less than 300 dpi.**★15**

5. Copyright and Trademark Usage and Ownership★16

5.1. Licensee acknowledges and agrees that all right, interest, and title in the Artwork and any alterations, modifications, or improvements made to the Artwork by Licensee shall be retained by Licensor.**★17**

5.2. Licensee acknowledges and agrees that the Artwork is unique and original to Licensor and that Licensor is the owner of all underlying rights in the Artwork including trademarks, copyrights, and any rights in concepts, designs, and ideas. Licensee shall not, at any time during or after the Term, contest or dispute, directly or indirectly, Licensor's

13 This optional language is a "hold back" provision: it compels the Licensor to refrain from publishing the Artwork until you have published a comic book. Obviously, in many cases this will not be appropriate—such as when the artwork has been previously published.

14 A flat fee is often the easiest way to license Artwork. However, for certain deals, royalty provisions may be more appropriate (for instance, if the Artwork plays a primary role over several issues or is being used in the creation of merchandising). Additionally, for licensing of short stories, royalty payments are almost always a part of the deal—often both a page rate and a royalty are paid to the writer in such cases. For further ideas on how to structure these royalty provisions, as well as the audit clauses which should accompany them. (See Illustrator Services Agreement, p. 162.)

15 Obviously, adjust the file format and resolution to meet your needs... And the needs of your publisher.

16 This clause further underscores the Licensor's ownership of the underlying rights in the Artwork.

17 Be careful here! If you add to the artwork or improve upon it, such improvements will be owned by the Licensor under the terms of this clause.

exclusive right and title to the Artwork or the validity thereof, unless otherwise permitted by law. As between Licensee and Licensor, the Artwork and their associated rights and goodwill shall remain the complete and exclusive property of Licensor.

6. Credit, Copyright Notice*18

6.1. Licensee shall credit Licensor on all publications, if any, that utilize the Artwork under the terms of this Agreement, and Licensee shall include all notices, markings, and legends in connection with the Artwork as are, or may be required, by applicable laws and by Licensor in order to give appropriate copyright notice, such as: © (name of copyright owner, date of copyright).

6.2. Notwithstanding anything to the contrary contained in this Agreement, in no event shall Licensor seek, or be entitled to, damages of any kind by reason of any breach or threatened breach of any of the credit requirements herein, nor shall Licensor be entitled to seek to enjoin or restrain the exhibition, distribution, advertising, exploitation, or marketing of the Comic Book, all such equitable remedies being expressly waived by Licensor. No casual or inadvertent failure to comply with credit requirements shall be deemed a breach of this Agreement.

7. Representations and Warranties

7.1. Each Party represents and warrants that it has the right to enter into and perform under this Agreement.

7.2. Licensor represents and warrants the following:***19**

7.2.1. Licensor has the right to grant the rights herein;***20**

7.2.2. Licensor is the sole author of the Artwork, and the Artwork is original and created by Licensor;

7.2.3. The Artwork does not violate any rights of privacy, publicity, or any other right of any person;

<u>**18**</u> Not only is it important to give the Licensor credit and proper copyright attribution, but it is also critical for the licensee—you—to have the licensor waive the ability to sue you for a mistake in the credit requirements.

<u>**19**</u> Since you are the Licensee in this scenario, it's best to have the Licensor make absolute representations and warranties. In other words, the Licensor should state that the promises that they are making in this section are absolutely true (as opposed to merely being "true to the best of Licensor's knowledge and belief"). However, the Licensor may respond that these reps and warrants should be qualified with "To the best of Licensor's knowledge and belief..." because he might not know if his Artwork violates some obscenity law in another country. For more on this, see Representations and Warranties, p. 470.

<u>**20**</u> This is the warranty of authority—here, the Licensor is promising that he has the rights to grant and that he is the one empowered to grant the rights.

7.2.4. The Artwork does not infringe upon the copyright, trademark, or other intellectual property right of any other person;

7.2.5. The Artwork is not obscene or libelous; and**★21**

7.2.6. There are no third-party agreements by or on behalf of Licensor, her affiliates, or assigns that would violate or otherwise interfere with the exclusive rights granted to Licensee herein.

7.3. These representations and warranties shall survive the termination of this Agreement.

8. Publicity★22

8.1. Licensee shall have the right to use, reproduce, display, disseminate, publish, print, and make any other uses of Licensor's name and biographical information in connection with the marketing, advertising, and exploitation of the Comic Book.

9. Termination

9.1. Upon termination or expiration of this Agreement, all rights granted herein shall immediately revert back to Licensor, Licensee shall immediately cease all use of the Artwork, and all payments, if any, shall be accelerated and become due and payable.

9.2. Licensor may terminate this Agreement and all licenses granted therein, having provided Licensee with thirty (30) days' notice, and upon the occurrence of the following events:

9.2.1. If Licensee fails to publish the Comic Book in any form within ___ years of Licensor's execution of this Agreement;**★23**

9.2.2. Licensee fails to make any payments within thirty (30) days from the date they became due and fails to cure within 14 days of notice by Licensor.**★24**

21 You want to make sure that the work that you're licensing is free from potential infringement and other third-party claims.

22 Especially when it comes to using a famous cover artist's work, you may need the right to use the artist's name, photo, and other biographical info in publicizing your book.

23 Termination of a licensing agreement for failure to publish the comic book is fairly common.

24 Licensors will almost uniformly insist on terminating a license if they aren't being paid.

10. **Assignment.*25** Licensee may assign all rights in and to the Comic and its derivatives created pursuant to the Licensed Purpose, in whole or in part, to any firm, corporation, or person.

11. Indemnification*26

11.1. At all times, Licensor shall indemnify, defend, and hold harmless Licensee, his successors, licensees, agents, assigns, employees, and/or representatives from and against any and all liability, damages, loss, costs, and expenses, of any kind (including reasonable attorneys' fees) from any action, claim, or demand arising out of any breach by Licensor of any warranty, representation, or covenant contained in this Agreement.

11.2 At all times, Licensee shall indemnify, defend, and hold harmless Licensor, his successors, licensees, agents, assigns, employees, and/or representatives from and against any and all liability, damages, loss, costs, and expenses, of any kind (including reasonable attorneys' fees) from any action, claim, or demand arising out of any breach by Licensee of any warranty, representation, or covenant contained in this Agreement.

12. Notices*27

12.1. Except as otherwise provided herein, all notices shall be in writing and specify with particularity the nature of the other party's default. All notices shall be delivered by overnight courier, personal delivery, or in the form of a certified or registered letter.

13. No Partnership

13.1. Nothing in this Agreement shall be interpreted to create a joint venture, partnership, or agency relationship between the parties.***28** Licensor shall be acting solely as an independent contractor and not as a joint-venturer, agent, partner, or employee of Licensee.

25 The right to assign the licensed rights is critical. Without it, the publishing company would not have the right to publish your book (you will be assigning certain rights in your book to the publishing company; those rights include the right to publish the Artwork that is the subject of this agreement).

26 This indemnification provision ensures that both parties will be responsible for paying any damages the other party incurs which result from misrepresentations in his representations and warranties or his other breaches of this agreement.

27 How one sends a "notice" to the other party is important. The way this clause is drafted e-mail is not an acceptable form of notice, so any notice sent by e-mail might not be considered putting the other party on notice.

28 Remember: the law can see two people working together for a common business purpose as partners. You want to make sure that you are explicit in saying the Licensor is not your partner.

13.2. In the event that Licensor retains an associate or assistant in connection with the production or delivery of the Artwork, any costs or expenses incurred therefrom shall be Licensor's sole responsibility, and under no circumstances shall any such associate or assistant be, or be deemed to be, an employee or agent of Licensee.*29

14. Remedies, Choice of Law

14.1. In the event of breach of this Agreement, the sole remedy of the nonbreaching party shall be limited to an action at law for monetary damages actually suffered. In no event shall the parties be entitled to injunctive or equitable relief.

14.2. This Agreement shall be construed, interpreted, and governed by the laws of the State of New York. The federal or state courts of competent jurisdiction located in the State of New York, County of New York, shall have sole and exclusive jurisdiction to hear and determine any dispute or controversy arising under or concerning this Agreement, and both parties each hereby waive any objection and submit to the *in personam* jurisdiction and venue of such court.

15. Further Documents

15.1. Licensor agrees to execute and deliver all additional documents, papers, and other instruments that might be necessary to further the intent of this Agreement, including written releases from all persons whose likenesses may appear in the Artwork.

16. Entire Agreement*30

16.1. This Agreement constitutes the entire agreement between the parties hereto on the subject matter hereof and supersedes and replaces all prior and contemporaneous oral or written agreements, understandings, nor have the parties relied upon any writings or representations whatsoever not incorporated herein and made a part hereof. This Agreement may only be modified by a fully executed written amendment, signed by both parties, and containing the words "Agreement Amendment" in the title.

29 Does the Licensor need to hire other artists to help him prepare the work? This clause ensures that those costs are borne by the Licensor, not you.

30 This is one of the most important clauses in the contract. After the agreement is signed, parties often conduct their business relationship in a way which may be seen as a modification of the agreement—sometimes leading to unintentional results. The way this clause is drafted, the only way to modify this contract is to have a separate written, signed amendment, which clearly states that it is an amendment. This avoids the problem of "e-mail drift"—e-mail correspondence between the parties that inadvertently changes the contract's terms.

17. Severability

17.1. If any provision of this Agreement is adjudged void, unenforceable or unlawful, in whole or in part, by a court of competent jurisdiction, the remaining provisions shall continue in full force and effect.

18. Survival

18.1. The following clauses shall survive the termination of this Agreement, whether by breach or otherwise: "NONEXCLUSIVE LICENSE," "PAYMENT," "COPYRIGHT AND TRADEMARK USAGE AND OWNERSHIP," "REPRESENTATIONS AND WARRANTIES," "INDEMNIFICATION," "REMEDIES, CHOICE OF LAW," "SEVERABILITY," and "SURVIVAL."

19. Counterparts

19.1. This Agreement may be executed in several counterparts, and all counterparts so executed shall be deemed an original, and all of such counterparts shall constitute only one agreement. Scanned and facsimile copies shall be deemed originals for all purposes. If the Agreement is signed in counterparts, it shall only be effective upon delivery of one executed counterpart from each party to the other party.

In Witness Whereof, the Parties have caused this Agreement to be executed by their duly authorized signatories to be effective as of the Effective Date. Any individual executing this Agreement on behalf of any Party hereto does hereby represent and warrant that such execution is made with full authority and that such Party is bound by the terms hereof.

Licensor: Beard-O-Brush	Licensee: Carlo Creator
By: ______________________	By: ______________________
Date: ____________________	Date: ____________________

---------COMMENTS---------

EXHIBIT A—ARTWORK*31

The specific Artwork subject to this Agreement is as follows:

____:<u>**★32**</u>

The Artwork is subject to copyright registration [insert registration ###]<u>**★33**</u> and/or other such copyright and trademark registrations as are filed by or on behalf of Licensor, from time to time. Exploitation by Licensee of any additional artwork created by Licensor than that which is specifically enumerated in this exhibit shall require an additional license, mutually agreed upon and signed by all parties.

NEXT STEPS

You've put all the pieces together; you have an awesome comic AND you've protected it. Now, it's time to take your "Com-MECH" out for a test flight and find a publisher! Let's open the launch doors and blast-off!

Note

1 Jack Daniel's Properties, Inc. v. VIP Products LLC, 599 U.S. 140 (2023).

31 It is critical to clearly define which artwork is at issue. Is there may be several versions of the artwork produced by the artist. Therefore, a detailed Exhibit A in which samples of the artwork are attached, along with the appropriate copyright registration information, should help provide clarity.

32 Insert a picture of the artwork for clarity.

33 Insert copyright registration number.

CLEARANCES
COMPANY
COMIX
FILM
DVD

PART 5

Getting It Out There

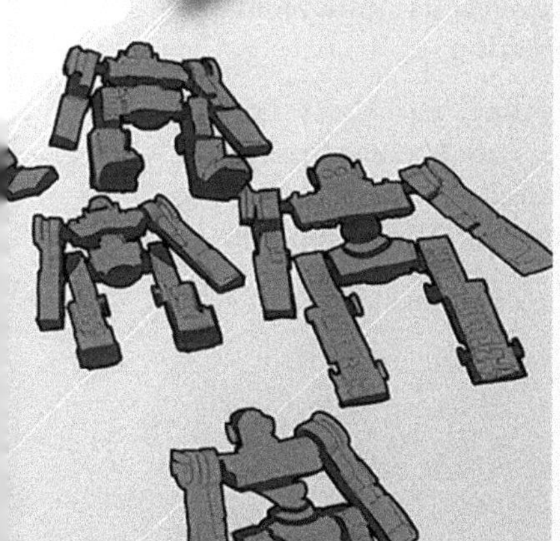

DOI: 10.1201/9781003496052-14

SECTION OVERVIEW

You did it! Whether you've crafted a 22-page burst of visual brilliance, a sprawling 300-page magnum opus, or a 12-issue mini-series destined for cult status, don't keep your masterpiece confined to your living room's "VIP only" list. The world is hungry for your creation—and here's how to serve it up.

If your comic isn't so esoteric that only a niche cadre of actuaries would care (yes, we're looking at you, *Two-Fisted Tales of William Morgan: The Father of Actuarial Science*), your first move should be to charm the big traditional publishers. Landing one of these deals not only gets your work into the hands of a wider audience but also makes your next project easier to market. If those gatekeepers don't bite, don't fret—self-publishing is no longer the fallback of last resort but a bold, modern alternative embraced by indie creators everywhere.

But don't be fooled—landing a publisher in today's crowded arena is like finding a rare holographic variant at Comic Con. Having a brilliant comic isn't enough; you've got to be a savvy self-promoter too. Dust off your social media magic and turn those posts into buzz. (See **Get Your Message Out**, p. 229.) You might even need to strut your stuff at the Comic Con circuit to catch the eye of publishers and industry insiders alike. (See **Landing a Publisher**, p. 240.)

Once your brilliance has intrigued a publisher, it's time to negotiate your deal. This isn't the moment to settle for the first offer that slaps your hand with a friendly handshake—arm yourself with a top-notch lawyer and hash out a deal that truly secures your rights and revenue. (See **Landing a Publisher**, p. 240.) And if the traditional path doesn't work out, fear not! Self-publishing is not a fallback; it's a formidable alternative embraced by indie creators aiming for both artistic freedom and a fatter paycheck. (See **Self-Publishing**, p. 301.)

Finally, despite your diligence and heroic efforts, sometimes legal issues slip through the cracks and the lawyers come-a'-knocking, with lawsuits firmly in hand. When that happens, you need to know how to deal with it before writing or saying a single thing to the other side of the dispute. (See **What Happens When Something Goes Wrong?** p. 320.)

CHAPTER 10

Get Your Message Out

DOI: 10.1201/9781003496052-16

Congratulations! You've completed your comic book—an impressive feat of creativity, resilience, and determination. But now the real journey begins. To bring your comic into the world and into the hands of fervent fans and discerning publishers, you must become its most passionate advocate; bring on your best barker's ballyhoo!

In this chapter, we'll walk you through every step of promoting your comic, from engaging with the community to pitching your work professionally. Additionally, we dive into essential crowdfunding topics that are key to ensuring your project's success. You'll learn how platforms like Kickstarter can serve not only as a source of funding but also as a vital market-testing tool. By tapping into these strategies, you can identify your ideal readership, refine your story's appeal, and turn early backers into long-term promoters of your work.

BALLYHOO LIKE A BARKER

No one can ballyhoo like you—and that's exactly why you need to step up as the most passionate promoter of your project. You're not just the creator; you're the beating heart of your comic book, and it's your enthusiasm that will inspire others to get on board. Promotion doesn't wait until you've landed a publisher or distributor; in fact, successful promotion is often the key to catching their attention in the first place.

You might land a publishing company or distributor—and yes, they'll have a vested interest in marketing your work—but keep in mind that, to them, your comic is a commodity. They'll weigh the costs and benefits of promoting your book based on projected returns. It's not personal; it's business. But here's where you come in: your role is to show them that their investment in your project is worth it, and no one can do that better than you.

To truly attract other artists, collaborators, and publishers—and to keep the momentum going once your comic is on shelves—you need to focus on being your own biggest fan. Create compelling pitch decks that visually showcase the essence of your story and characters to potential publishers. Build a vibrant online presence using social media platforms to connect with fans and industry professionals. Attend conventions like Comic-Con to network, pitch your project, and draw attention to your work.

A slick, visually appealing website can amplify your message, but it's your energy and dedication that will make the difference. Social media, conventions, and pitch decks are your tools, but your enthusiasm is the engine. Publishers and distributors notice creators who actively champion their own work, and they respect those who engage with the comic book community in authentic, entertaining, and generous ways.

Once your comic book hits stores—whether brick-and-mortar shops or online retailers—your continued efforts to promote it will drive sales and build your fanbase. This is where the comic book community can truly shine. When you show up with a presence that's magnetic, the community responds. Your persistence, creativity, and passion will keep the fire of your fandom burning bright, and the benefits will ripple throughout your career.

BUILD YOUR DIGITAL HQ—YOUR WEBSITE

Your website is your HQ—it's your portfolio, business card, and storefront rolled into one. Here's how to make it work for you:

- **Design That Reflects Your Style**: Build a visually stunning site that mirrors the aesthetic of your comic. Make sure it's mobile friendly, easy to navigate, and offers extras like downloadable wallpaper or sample pages. Fans visiting your site should feel like they've entered your comic universe.
- **Enable Direct Sales**: Fans love buying directly from creators, and many comic shops prefer it too. Use platforms like Shopify or Gumroad to seamlessly sell your work.
- **Connect Your Online Presence**: Cross-link your social media profiles, blog, and store on your website. In turn, make sure your social accounts link back to your site—it's a web of connections that lets fans easily explore everything about you and your comic.

Legal and Ownership Tips

- **Retain Ownership of Your Website**: If you hire a designer, make sure you own the final design via a work-for-hire agreement or copyright assignment. This ensures you control your site's look and feel.
- **Terms of Use**: If your website has interactive features like forums or downloads, protect yourself with a Terms of Use agreement. This document lays out the conditions upon which each user may utilize the material posted on your website and qualifies the types of materials that the user can upload. For instance, one condition of using your site would be that a registered user may not upload material owned by third parties or other potentially infringing material.
- **DMCA Compliance:**[1] If you do allow uploads to your website—for instance, letting people post pictures, snippets of comic book scripts, etc.—you need to be very careful. You could be held liable for copyright infringement for material that others post on your site!
  - The Digital Millennium Copyright Act (DMCA) allows certain website owners to escape liability for the infringing posts of their members. To be granted this "safe harbor," from a copyright infringement lawsuit, you must post on your website post proper "notice and takedown" procedures and designate an "agent to receive notice of claimed infringement." Notice-and-takedown procedures allow a copyright claimant, e.g. the owner of a copyrighted character, to contact you and instruct you to remove the claimed infringing material. If you do remove the material, you will not be held liable for copyright infringement (although the website member who posted the infringing material might still be sued).
  - For more information on registering an agent to receive notice of claimed infringement, see the United States Copyright Office at: www.copyright.gov/onlinesp/
  - Allowing user uploads (like fan art)? Protect yourself from liability under the Digital Millennium Copyright Act (DMCA). Post notice-and-takedown

procedures on your site and designate an agent to handle infringement claims. See the U.S. Copyright Office's guidance[2] for details.

- **Privacy and Data Compliance**: Make sure your website meets privacy standards by displaying clear cookie notices and a comprehensive privacy policy. These elements explain how you collect, use, and protect user data—information that is particularly important if you're gathering details such as email addresses for newsletters or other purposes. This transparency not only builds trust with your visitors but also ensures you comply with key legal frameworks like the GDPR (General Data Protection Regulation) and the CCPA (California Consumer Privacy Act).

INTERVIEW

WEB SLINGING TO SUCCESS

Interview with creator/musician Alan Robert

"Around 2009, I joined Twitter and started following some of my favorite comic artists and writers on there. At some point, I must've commented on a writer's post about some heavy metal music he was listening to, and he responded. We started going up and back about bands we liked and that sort of thing. At some point, after we became friendly on there, he mentioned that he liked the website I put together for "Wire Hangers" and asked to see some artwork. You see, it turned out that not only was this guy a comics writer, but he was also working for an indie comics publisher at a very high level. I really had no idea that the guy I was chatting with about Lemmy from Motorhead and Ozzy Osbourne was none other than the Editor-in-Chief of award-winning comics' publisher, IDW Publishing. IDW's Chris Ryall gave me my big break in comics and took a huge chance on me." [...]

"I have never sent out any physical materials." What I did was create a website that hosted my entire [comic book] pitch on one page. It was a scrollable page that had all of the details of the series right there. The user wouldn't have to click off of it to see more information. Everything was easy to access.

My goal was to make it as simple as possible for a publisher to scan the information in under three minutes. On this page, I had a brief introduction, the logline, some cover images, and character designs, plus an overview of the series—which was about six paragraphs long. Beneath that I broke down each issue of the 4-issue mini-series (one paragraph per issue). From there I described the format. For instance, "Wire Hangers is a full-color, open-ended horror series told in 4-issue story arcs." I described how the oil-painted covers would help distinguish the comic on the stands and draw new readers in."

***ALAN ROBERT** is the comic book creator of several IDW-published titles, including "Wire Hangers," "Crawl To Me," "Killogy," and the best-selling "Beauty of Horror®" series.*

ENGAGE, INTERACT, AND BUILD CONNECTIONS ON SOCIAL MEDIA

Alright, I hear you—social media isn't everyone's natural habitat. But trust me, when done right, it's like opening a portal to a multiverse of fans and industry professionals waiting to connect. Think of social media as a gigantic comic book convention—minus the overpriced snacks. Start by building bridges with other comic creators and professionals. Their fans could become yours, and you'll expand your circle of influence. Share posts that showcase your characters, plot twists, or creative process. Keep links to your website easy to find with tools like TinyURL or Linktree (because no one's clicking on a 200-character URL). Follow industry players like publishers and marketing directors—they may drop nuggets of wisdom (or opportunities) on their feeds. Instead of forums, consider starting a Discord server or private Facebook group where fans can discuss your work, share fan art, or connect with one another. Encourage user-generated content (like fan art or cosplay) and share it on your social media. This not only celebrates your fans but also expands your reach.

Oh, and witty posts grab attention, but genuine conversations grab hearts. Be memorable, not a monotone promo machine.

What to Share

Post content that showcases your characters, plot twists, and creative process. Platforms like TikTok, Instagram Reels, and YouTube Shorts are tailor-made for comic creators. Share videos of your process, humorous skits featuring your characters, or teasers for upcoming releases. Video content is highly shareable and engaging—it's an excellent way to grow your audience. Give fans a glimpse behind the scenes with Instagram Stories or TikTok videos. Encourage user interactivity—even cosplay—and amplify their contributions by sharing them on your channels. Genuine conversations grab hearts—don't be a monotone promo machine. Instead, be memorable, authentic, and engaging.

Your storytelling isn't just your talent—it's your superpower. Use it to turn your promotional and marketing strategies into an epic saga that no one can ignore!

Dedicate Time Wisely

Set aside 30 minutes daily—or spread it out—to interact with followers. Reply to comments, answer burning questions, and jump into discussions. Diversify your content with rich posts, including videos or LinkedIn articles, that reveal your creative journey or share exclusive updates. Witty posts grab attention, but sincerity builds community. Make sure to post on a regular schedule so fans know when to look for your content.

CONNECT AND SYNCHRONIZE YOUR PLATFORMS

Your social media accounts should function like the Avengers—a well-coordinated team, not random heroes doing their own thing. Link everything together: your website, blog, Facebook, X, Instagram, TikTok, etc. Your website should be the central hub, spotlighting your socials and making it easy for fans to navigate your digital universe. Think of it as your own comic book multiverse, where fans can hop between platforms without getting lost.

Host Events

Want to turn followers into superfans? Use platform-specific features to rally your troops. Facebook Events are perfect for announcing signings, workshops, or panels, while Instagram countdowns build hype for your next big release. TikTok challenges? Great for showcasing your art or connecting with other creators. Hosting something cool? Announce it like you're releasing the next blockbuster—your followers will feel part of the action. Attend conventions and host signings, workshops, or panels. Use social media to drum up excitement in advance, creating event pages and countdowns to rally fans.

Consider Crowdfunding

Kickstarter, Indiegogo, and Patreon are powerful platforms for creators. Use them to raise funds while connecting directly with fans. Sweeten the deal with rewards like signed copies, limited-edition prints, or sketches. Crowdfunding turns casual supporters into devoted superfans.

Track Engagement with Analytics Tools

Numbers don't lie—unless you're inventing fictional sales figures for a villain's evil empire. Use social media analytics tools like Instagram Insights and X Analytics to figure out what works and what doesn't. Which post got fans hitting "like" faster than The Flash? Which one fell flat? Study the data, refine your strategy, and focus on creating more of what resonates. It's like leveling up your storytelling skills—except the XP comes from likes and shares.

Find Common Ground Before the Big Ask

Picture this: you meet someone who could publish your manuscript. Instead of blurting out, "Will you read it and make me famous?", start with something more personal—find shared interests, like geeking out over a mutual favorite comic series or reminiscing about a convention you both attended. Look for shared interests, fandoms, or even mutual experiences—whether it's love for a certain comic series, a similar creative process, or attendance at the same convention. This creates a foundation of trust and rapport, making collaboration feel natural rather than transactional. People are more likely to engage if they feel a personal connection to your story or shared passion. Building genuine rapport makes your eventual ask feel less like a sales pitch and more like collaborating with an old friend. Bottom line? No one likes feeling hunted for opportunities. Make them feel valued first.

Run Targeted Ads

Start small with paid promotions on platforms like Instagram or Facebook. Target comic fans by narrowing your audience through interests (e.g., "graphic novels," "manga") and demographics (age, location). This strategy allows you to allocate your budget more effectively by focusing on users who are most likely to be engaged with your work. Additionally, consider testing different ad creatives and messaging through A/B testing, which can help identify the visuals and language that resonate best with your audience. Monitoring key performance metrics like click-through rates and conversions will provide valuable insights for optimizing your campaign over time, ensuring that your advertising efforts not only build awareness but also drive meaningful engagement.

CROWDFUNDING FOR COMIC BOOK CREATORS

Crowdfunding has flipped the script on financing comic projects. Instead of risking every dime on printing and distributing a comic that might leave readers wondering, "Who wants something this obscure?" creators can safely test their wild ideas to find out just how big the reader base is for, "The Unbearable Lintiness of Being," a graphic novel that explores the world of belly button lint through history. Using platforms like Kickstarter, Indiegogo, and Patreon, artists pitch their daring visions directly to fans, who back these projects with pledges in exchange for quirky, nonmonetary rewards (a belly button lint knitted scarf), exclusive art, behind-the-scenes secrets, and more.

This direct, two-way engagement not only opens up fresh funding streams but also transforms early backers into spirited advocates. Their support—and sometimes playful critiques—help validate and fine-tune the comic's concept before big bucks roll in. Essentially, it's a creative dress rehearsal where you discover if your potentially "disgusting" masterpiece is a hit or if it needs more tweaking before stepping into the spotlight.

Crowdfunding primarily falls into two categories:

- **Donation-Based Crowdfunding.** Also referred to as token crowdfunding, this method relies on backers donating funds and receiving rewards (such as digital issues, exclusive prints, or autographed hardcovers) that increase in value with higher donation levels. Unlike investors, these backers never receive a share of future profits. Popular platforms like Kickstarter and Indiegogo operate on this model, where rewards—not financial returns—are the primary inducement. It's important to note that, despite its allure, designing and executing an effective crowdfunding campaign requires significant preparation and effort.
- **Equity Crowdfunding:** An emerging avenue in creative financing, equity crowdfunding allows backers to invest capital in exchange for a share in future profits from the project. Although the process of setting up an equity-based campaign may resemble that of donation-based platforms, it is legally and functionally more akin to traditional securities offerings. Regulatory requirements under the JOBS Act and SEC Regulation Crowdfunding impose extensive documentation and legal compliance, making this option more complex and generally less common among comic book projects. **Note:** Most comic book creators typically pursue donation-based crowdfunding to avoid the legal intricacies associated with equity offerings.

COMMONLY CONSIDERED CROWDFUNDERS FOR COMIC CREATORS

Kickstarter: A leading platform for raising funds for creative projects, including comics, through all-or-nothing campaigns. **https://www.kickstarter.com/**

Indiegogo: Offers flexible funding options and a global audience, ideal for experimental projects. **https://www.indiegogo.com/**

Patreon: Perfect for creators seeking ongoing monthly support and building a dedicated subscriber base. **https://www.patreon.com/**

Ko-fi: Enables fans to make one-off contributions or support you through memberships, all without taking a cut from your earnings. **https://ko-fi.com/**

Buy Me a Coffee: A user-friendly platform that allows supporters to offer small donations, fueling your creative endeavors while building community. **www.buymeacoffee.com/**

Why Crowdfund? The Psychology and Strategy behind Building Your Audience

Crowdfunding isn't simply a way to raise funds—it's a powerful tool for discovering your audience, promoting your work, and fostering a passionate community around your creative vision. Whether you use Kickstarter, Indiegogo, Patreon, or similar platforms, the approach remains consistent: offering your fans a direct channel to support you and, in return, transforming them into advocates for your projects.

Understanding Your Audience: Who Are Your Fans?

Before launching your donative crowdfunding campaign, successful creators ask themselves: *Who is my ideal supporter?* This inquiry goes beyond mere demographics; it taps into the psychology behind why people support creative projects. Your fans aren't just paying for a comic—they're investing in a story, a creator, and an experience that resonates deeply with them.

- **Emotional Connection:** Supporters contribute because they feel a personal bond with the project. Whether driven by nostalgia, a taste for the unconventional, or admiration for a creator's vision, every contribution is a piece of an emotional investment.
- **Community Identity:** Crowdfunding platforms create a sense of belonging. Your supporters are more than just donors—they're early adopters, loyal enthusiasts, and the backbone of your creative journey.
- **Exclusivity & Ownership:** Offering limited-edition rewards, behind-the-scenes content, or personalized messages makes supporters feel like insiders, giving them a tangible stake in your project's success.

Turning Fans into Promoters

Once your ideal audience is identified, the next step is to activate and mobilize them. The most successful donative campaigns do more than collect pledges—they inspire supporters to spread the word. Here's how:

- **Social Proof:** People value recommendations from fellow enthusiasts far more than conventional ads. Encouraging your supporters to share their excitement on social media can generate authentic, organic buzz.
- **Gamification and Engagement:** Implementing stretch goals, exclusive rewards, and interactive updates keeps your community engaged and eager to recruit new fans.
- **Personalized Outreach:** A heartfelt "thank you" or a special mention can transform a casual supporter into a lifelong advocate.

Why Established Creators Use Crowdfunding

Even respected publishers and artists lean on crowdfunding—not solely for the funds but for the validation and community insights that come with it. Here's why:

- **Market Testing:** Crowdfunding allows you to gauge interest in your project, offering valuable feedback before committing to large-scale production.
- **Guaranteed Customer Base:** A successful campaign is a strong signal of demand, ensuring that your project enters the market with an already engaged audience.
- **Brand Awareness:** A crowdfunded project generates press coverage, social media chatter, and word-of-mouth marketing that often outperforms traditional advertising channels.

Crowdfunding isn't just about receiving donations—it's about building momentum, creating superfans, and setting the foundation for long-term success. Whether you're an indie creator or an established publisher, donative crowdfunding offers a unique opportunity to connect with your audience in ways that ordinary sales channels simply cannot match.

> **Example**: Imagine a comic series titled **"Maggot Man: Carrion Eater of Justice"**—a macabre anti-hero whose controversial style might prompt potential readers to wonder, "Is this too disgusting?" By launching a donative crowdfunding campaign, the creators can test this uncertain concept before full-scale production, inviting early adopters with exclusive rewards and community feedback to validate its appeal.

Creating a Successful Crowdfunding Campaign

A well-prepared crowdfunding campaign is as much a business plan as it is a marketing effort. Below is a step-by-step guide, adapted for the comic book creator:

1. **Establish Your Platform Account**
    - Create an account on your chosen crowdfunding site (e.g., Kickstarter, Indiegogo, or Patreon).
    - Ensure you meet all prerequisites, such as residing in an eligible country, having a valid bank account, and being legally over 18 years of age.
2. **Develop Your Campaign Strategy and Reward Tiers**
    - **Campaign Strategy:** Define your project's creative narrative, art style, and target audience.
    - **Reward Structure:**
        - Structure tiered rewards so that higher-level backers receive all the benefits of lower tiers.
        - Typical rewards for comic projects might include digital previews, sample pages or pilot issues, limited-edition prints, signed hardcovers, and behind-the-scenes content.
    - Ensure your fundraising goal accounts for platform fees (around 5% plus additional processing fees on sites like Kickstarter) and production/distribution costs.
3. **Design Your Campaign Materials**
    - Invest in a professionally produced campaign video that introduces you and the creative process behind your comic.
    - Develop an engaging landing page featuring high-quality artwork, sample pages, and a clear breakdown of how pledged funds will contribute to the project's production.
    - Think of your landing page as a hybrid of ad copy, a pitch deck, and an e-commerce storefront—this is often potential backers' first encounter with your project.
4. **Engage and Update Your Backers**
    - Communication is crucial: maintain regular updates via the platform, email newsletters, and social media channels.
    - Early momentum is vital; consider coordinating prelaunch donations from close networks (aiming for at least 30% funding at launch) to demonstrate commitment and encourage wider support.
    - Prompt, transparent communication not only aids in fulfilling rewards but also transforms backers into long-term advocates for your creative work.

Crowdfunding Tips and Tricks

- **Realistic Goal Setting:** Set achievable funding targets that are informed by the scope of your project. Remember, if you don't meet the goal in an all-or-nothing model, you receive no funds.

- **High-Quality Visuals:** Since comic books are a visual medium, your campaign should reflect the quality and style of your work. A compelling pitch video and professional sample artwork can make a significant difference.
- **Reward Fulfillment:** Carefully plan and execute the delivery of rewards. A record of timely and fulfilling campaigns enhances your credibility for any future projects.
- **Prelaunch Planning:** Leverage your personal network for early donations and use these initial funds to demonstrate campaign momentum—an essential factor in winning over more backers.

Crowdfunding platforms like Kickstarter, Indiegogo, and Patreon offer comic book creators a dynamic way to secure funding, validate creative ideas, and build a passionate audience—all while minimizing personal financial risk. Whether through donation-based models or, less commonly, equity crowdfunding, a well-structured campaign not only finances a project but also acts as real-time market research, guiding narrative development, production decisions, and long-term marketing strategies.

NEXT STEPS

Comic Cons are becoming a critical step in the quest to interest publishers in our work. So, let's leave our cosplay gear in our hotel rooms for now, grab our portfolio, and head to a Comic-Con and try to land a publisher!

Notes

1 17 USC §512(i)(1)(A).
2 U.S. Copyright Office. "Directory of Agents: Designation of Agent to Receive Notification of Claimed Infringement." U.S. Copyright Office, https://www.copyright.gov/dmca-directory/. Accessed 20 Mar. 2025.

CHAPTER 11

Landing a Publisher

DOI: 10.1201/9781003496052-16

LANDING A PUBLISHER

Publishing companies are the "Hollywood Studios" of the comic book industry: they produce a creative property and then promote it so that it gets the widest possible distribution; they have connections with merchandisers; and they look for ways to turn a successful comic book into revenue-generating sequels and spinoffs.

If you want your comic property to reach the largest audience, nothing beats working with a major publishing company. With powerhouses like Marvel, DC, Image, Boom!, Dark Horse, etc. behind you, your work gains immediate visibility, supported by the strength of their marketing and promotions departments. The prestige of having a well-known publisher on your side not only brings readers to your book but also opens doors to future opportunities with other publishers and projects.

In the past decade, however, crowdfunding and self-publishing have emerged as viable alternatives to landing a comic book publisher. Platforms like Kickstarter and Indiegogo allow creators to fund their projects directly through fan support, offering the freedom to retain creative control and ownership. At the same time, self-publishing provides a path to distribute comics digitally or in print, bypassing traditional gatekeepers and allowing creators to connect directly with their audience. These options have democratized the industry, giving aspiring creators more opportunities to share their stories with the world.

For creators seeking to work with a publishing company, it's essential to approach them in a way that demonstrates both professionalism and an understanding of their needs. This begins with crafting a compelling pitch deck. A **pitch deck** isn't just a showcase for your story—it's a tool to convince publishers that you're a professional who understands the business. Your pitch deck should include polished artwork, a clear outline of your story, and information about your target audience. Research the publishers you want to approach—understand their catalog, their style, and what they're looking for. Tailor your pitch to align with their preferences and be ready to articulate why your comic fits their vision.

Many comic creators want to interact with publishing companies in one of two ways:

1. They want the publishing companies to publish their creator-driven comic book or graphic novel.
2. They want publishing companies to hire them as artists and writers to work on the publishing company's comic book property. (See Working for a Publishing Company, p. 250.)

LANDING A PUBLISHER MAY BE A "CON" JOB

Perhaps you want a publishing company to hire you to draw its comics; perhaps you want to pitch them on publishing your book. Either way, getting your portfolio or comic book seen by publishers can be very difficult. Although some companies allow for online submissions, many comic book publishing companies have a "no solicitation" policy, which prohibits artists who are unknown to them from submitting their work.

Q: So how does one connect face to face with a publishing company?

A: Comic Con!

The Pros of Cons

Comic book conventions, or "Comic Cons," have been around since the 1960s, but it wasn't until the late 90s that they really started taking off; there are now hundreds, if not thousands, of Comic Cons worldwide. Now, they are some of the largest centers of comic book and pop culture fandom. In 2019 (just before the COVID pandemic), New York Comic Con alone took in over 260,000 attendees!

From the "City in Motion" to "The City That Never Sleeps," San Diego and New York are home to the two biggest Comic Cons in America. Organized and run by two different companies, the New York and San Diego Cons are attended by all of the major publishers, all the major merchandizers, many of the Hollywood studios, and any indie creator who can get themselves to one. Comic Cons feature informational panels for both professionals and fans, on topics that range from steampunk costumes to legal protection for comic books; I've been giving legal lectures at New York Comic Con for two decades, and I can honestly say that the level of professionalism and dedication shown by the attendees is nothing short of astounding.

And in addition to being great fun, Comic Cons are a great source of networking and connecting with other creators—potential publishing and distribution partners. If you are just starting out in comic book creation, you owe it to yourself and your project to go to a Comic Con to check out the competition, meet new colleagues, and learn innovative new techniques of publishing, printing, and the creation of art.

The best thing you can bring to Comic Con is a copy of your printed book. However, even if you haven't printed your book yet, going to Comic Con is still a valuable experience; after all, it can help you size up the other books on the market—before you spend $5000 on printing your "vampires versus zombies" graphic novel, it would be helpful to know how many other.

Working the Long Con

Preshow Strategy

A successful Comic Con experience requires careful preparation and a clear strategy. Here's how you can maximize your time and opportunities at the convention:

1. **Identify**: Begin by pinpointing the publishers you want to meet. Dive deep into their catalog and familiarize yourself with their direction in the

industry. Resources like comicbookresources.com and CBR.com can help you stay up-to-date on trends and insights. Understanding what makes a publisher's work unique and being able to articulate this during your conversations will make a lasting impression. Be sure to mention specific artists or writers whose work has inspired you.

2. **Reach Out in Advance**: Establish connections before the convention. Networking throughout the year can lead to relationships with professionals in the industry. If you've connected with someone from a publishing company, let them know you'll be attending Comic Con and would love the chance to meet them in person.
3. **Get "Pro" Show Badges**: Investing in a pro badge signals to publishers that you're serious about your craft. These badges also grant access to professional-only events, providing you with more opportunities to network with industry leaders.
4. **Pitch Deck**: If possible, prepare a pitch deck or other portfolio of examples to showcase your comic book property. See, Putting together a Pitch Deck, p. 245.

At the Convention

5. **Meet and Greet**: Treat Comic Con like a professional event—dress for success, not for cosplay. Present yourself and your materials in a polished, professional manner. Bring your pitch deck, digital samples of your work you can quickly email, and physical copies of self-published comics (if you have them). Additionally, print a well-designed business card that reflects your creative style—think of it as a mini portfolio. First impressions are vital, so ensure your materials are high quality and easy to share.
6. **Portfolio Reviews**: Many publishers offer portfolio reviews at Comic Cons. Take advantage of these opportunities, even if it means standing in long lines. Publishers often schedule reviews at specific times, so research the schedule in advance and plan accordingly. Listen attentively to feedback; it can guide your development and save you years of working in the wrong direction.
7. **Leverage Artist Alley**: Visit Artist Alley to connect with creators who share your journey. Speak with artists and writers—especially newer talents—to learn from their experiences and challenges. These interactions can be as valuable as connecting with publishers, offering insight into breaking into the industry and finding your footing.
8. **Long-Term Planning**: Comic Con should be viewed as one part of a larger strategy to market yourself as a professional. Success in the comic book industry takes time and persistence. Use the convention as a way to build connections, not as a quick solution. Proactively reach out to publishers and pitch ideas throughout the year.
9. **Connect Thoughtfully**: When interacting with publishing representatives, focus on brief, memorable exchanges rather than overwhelming them with

materials. Offer value during conversations and follow up after the convention to remind them of your meeting.

Follow Up

10. After the Con, maintain the connections you made by emailing them and connecting with them on social media. A few tips:
    a. **Offer Help First**: For example, you might write, "I remember you mentioned you're exploring new illustration techniques; I recently came across this free webinar that broke down some advanced concepts and thought it might be useful to you." Offering such a resource plays on the principle of reciprocity, nudging them to want to return the favor later.
    b. **Be Specific:** Instead of a generic "great meeting you," try something like, "It was great chatting with you about your passion for rare comic editions—your story about the 1960s collection was really memorable." A specific reference like this shows you were truly engaged and helps cement a more personal connection.
    c. **Suggest a Quick Chat:** You could include a line such as, "I'd love to continue our conversation—how about a quick 15-minute virtual coffee next week to exchange more ideas?" This gentle proposal builds commitment over time and makes future collaboration feel more natural.

COMIC BOOK INDUSTRY BUSINESS NEWS WEBSITES

- **Bleeding Cool**: https://bleedingcool.com/comics/ A prominent source for breaking news, rumors, and insights into the comic book world, covering everything from Marvel and DC to indie publishers.
- **Comic Book Resources (CBR)**: https://www.cbr.com/category/comics/news/ Offers detailed news, reviews, and analysis on comics, superheroes, and pop culture, making it a favorite among fans.
- **The Beat**: https://www.comicsbeat.com/ Focuses on comics, graphic novels, and industry news with strong coverage of creators, events, and cultural impacts.
- **Comics Experience** (https://comicsexperience.com/). Comics experience is a unique platform that serves as both a learning hub and a professional resource for comic book creators.
- **Variety**: https://variety.com Primarily focused on film and TV, variety also covers comic book adaptations, industry trends, and intersections with film, television, and broader entertainment.
- **The Hollywood Reporter**: https://www.hollywoodreporter.com Also focused on film and TV, The Hollywood Reporter features articles on comic book industry developments, adaptations, and insights on creators and major publishers.

INTERVIEW

Working the Long Con—A Writer's Perspective

"For comic book artists, you can set up a booth or table at a Comic Con to try to show your work to publishers." For writers it is a little bit different. There's a right way to do it, and a wrong way to do it. The right way to do it is to build relationships outside of Comic Con first—through networking, writing workshops, and online forums. For instance, Andrew Smith's comic experience (www.comicsexperience.com) is a great way to network with other comic book creators that you can rise up with.

- When you go to the Con, make sure you dress nicely; wear a suit and tie as if you're going to a job interview.
- Have a resume and know who you want to meet with.
- Have an agenda and move forward.
- Don't bring any ideas, and don't bring any spec scripts, *unless you have published comics*."

*Author **DAVID GALLAHER** has received multiple Harvey Award nominations and won The Best Online Comic Award for his work on High Moon for DC Comics*

PUTTING TOGETHER A PITCH DECK

A pitch deck's main goal is to sell your idea by showing that you're not only creative but also professionally savvy about the industry. It's not just about a compelling story—it's equally important to keep your presentation clear, concise, and in line with the publisher's submission guidelines, especially since they often receive hundreds of pitches. Additionally, don't overlook the business side. Make sure you own or control the intellectual property you're showcasing, and if your work has been digitally published, clearly state which rights are still available. This prevents any potential conflicts down the line.

Creative Components of a Pitch Deck

Crafting a comic book pitch deck requires a perfect blend of creative vision and professional preparation. To ensure that publishers see the full potential of your project, it's crucial to organize your pitch with both creative storytelling elements and necessary legal and business details.

1. **Title and Logline**: Begin with a strong title and a concise, one- or two-sentence summary that captures the essence of your story. Highlight the protagonist, their goal, the conflict, and the stakes—it's your elevator pitch.

2. **Description**: Provide a 2–3 paragraph synopsis, similar to the back cover of a book. Dive deeper into your story's core while keeping it brief and engaging.
3. **Character Profiles**: Introduce the key players in your story. Describe who they are, their roles, how they evolve, and their unique traits. Add concept art or visual references to bring them to life.
4. **Setting**: Offer a glimpse into the world of your story. If it's a fictional or unique setting, describe its rules and distinctive features. This helps the publisher visualize your narrative backdrop.
5. **Story Outline**: Map out the full narrative arc with a detailed beginning, middle, and end. For serialized works, include one page per issue, clearly marking where each starts and ends. Avoid leaving any resolutions up in the air.
6. **Art Samples**: Showcase six consecutive, polished, fully inked, and lettered pages from your comic. These samples should highlight your tone, style, and overall vision. Think of them as your proof of concept.

INTERVIEW

Working the Long Con—An Artist/Writer's Perspective

"The [publishing deal with IDW] happened pretty quickly after I put an animated teaser online and started using Twitter. One of the best tips I could probably give someone starting out is to have your pitch in the back seat ready to go, just in case an opportunity should arise. If someone bites, you definitely want to have your concept all fleshed out to make your best first impression quickly, instead of scrambling to put your pitch together at the last minute.

In comics, like most businesses, you often need to win over several different people inside the company in order for your project to get purchased. It goes through multiple review stages. It's very rare that you'll get the opportunity to pitch to the top dog who has the power to give you a deal on the spot. Usually there's someone looking for the talent or the concept, and then they'll bring in those properties into the company to be reviewed.

The first step to building my pitch was creating a logline for the book. I came up with something very simple and easy to understand. **A logline** is one to two sentences that summarize your core concept. It tells you who the story's about and their conflict or goal. For instance, my logline for "Wire Hangers" was—'A disfigured loner, haunted by his tragic past, emerges from obscurity with the power to heal. Only to discover that he just might be the key to unlocking the darkest government conspiracy of our time.'

I don't know if it was the best logline, but it seemed to be enough for me to get a publisher to bite and to ask for more. I think it was vague and mysterious enough to build some curiosity about the project. The best thing that can happen is the publisher asks to hear more. That's really the ultimate goal of the logline. It's a foot in the door. A good logline can also serve as a snappy one liner in which the publisher can pitch to his or her own internal team.

Remember, timing is everything. Being ready and prepared is probably more than half the battle, because you can develop all the buzz you want, but when that publisher asks you for your concise pitch and you don't have it ready, your opportunity is gone."

***ALAN ROBERT** wrote and illustrated several acclaimed graphic novels, such as Wire Hangers, Crawl to Me, and Killogy, all showcasing his knack for eerie storytelling and moody artwork. He is perhaps best known for his best-selling horror-themed adult coloring book series, The Beauty of Horror, which has earned him widespread recognition for its chillingly creative designs.*

Business and Legal Details

1. **Know Your Audience**: Identify your target demographic and genre. Is your comic for Early Readers (up to age 7), Kids (8–12), or Teens (13–17)? Show that you know your audience and how to captivate them. Consistency is key—don't pitch grinning ponies for kids if your story veers into angsty teen drama.
2. **Own or Control Your Intellectual Property (IP)**: Confirm that you own or control all aspects of your project. No borrowed ideas, licensed characters, or unclear rights. Publishers need assurance that they won't encounter legal roadblocks.
3. **Contractual Landscape**: If your comic has been published digitally, clarify what rights are available. Publishers often want exclusive rights for print editions, so they ensure there are no conflicts with previous agreements.
4. **Follow Submission Guidelines**: Publishers have specific rules—no AI-generated content, no mashups or existing properties, and strict adherence to formatting (e.g., PDF or JPEG, proper sizing). Tailor your pitch to fit their preferences and aesthetic requirements.
5. **Get Your Files Ready**: Your pitch deck should be polished and easy to review. Use PDFs or JPEGs, ensure file sizes meet guidelines, and include your contact information. Avoid external download links—attach files directly.
6. **Be Patient and Professional**: Once submitted, remember that publishers review hundreds of pitches. Don't rush them; make sure your work is polished, complete, and formatted perfectly before sending it in.

SUBMISSION POLICIES FOR THE BIG PUBLISHING COMPANIES

MARVEL

Although Marvel Comics periodically holds portfolio reviews at comic conventions, the company currently does not accept unsolicited submissions. If you send any of your work to them without their first having asked for it, they will destroy it. As one of the top two publishing giants of the comic book industry, it can afford to be choosy. As it says on the submission request page on its website: "if you have the right stuff... we'll find you."[1]

DC

DC Entertainment similarly refuses unsolicited artwork and scripts, "If you have questions about script or art submissions, we are not currently accepting any unsolicited submissions."[2]

DC Comics' Fan Works Submission Guidelines outline the terms for submitting original illustrations or artwork ("Fan Works") through the company's official channels. Notably, DC occasionally issues a call to action (CTA) inviting fans to create submissions centered on specific DC characters, comics, or series. These CTAs dictate the theme for submissions, requiring creators to stay within the bounds of DC's existing canon. For example, if a CTA requests art from the DC Originals Titans series, fans must stick to characters from that series and cannot create new characters, storylines, or mashups.

All Fan Works must comply with strict rules ensuring originality, adherence to DC's themes, and suitability for public presentation. Submissions, which must include the hashtag #DCFANART, may be featured on DC's platforms but offer no compensation.

IMAGE

Image Comics welcomes submissions[3] of creator-owned material, emphasizing that creators retain all rights to their work. They do not accept submissions featuring existing characters, AI-generated artwork, or physical art, and they do not pay page rates. Writers must submit a proposal that includes a cover letter, a one-page synopsis of the story arc, and at least five fully inked and lettered sequential story pages. Artists can submit samples of their work, which may be kept on file for future opportunities.

Submissions must be emailed to Image Comics and adhere to their detailed guidelines, which include providing a mock-up cover and ensuring the creative team is consistent throughout the project. Due to high submission volumes, image does not guarantee individual responses, and proposals without an email address will be declined. Accepted projects may change with creator approval, but the intellectual property always remains with the creator.

SUBMISSION POLICIES—*continued*

DARK HORSE

From an unsolicited submission perspective, Dark Horse is the mother lode; Dark Horse Comics accepts two types of unsolicited submissions:[4] art samples and story/series proposals from complete creative teams (writer-artist collaborations). Writers alone cannot submit proposals, and all submissions must include a signed submission agreement, a logline, a synopsis, a complete outline, and six consecutive pages of art. Art samples should be in JPEG or PDF format, with specific size requirements, and must not include AI-generated content. Submissions involving licensed or existing Dark Horse properties are not accepted.

NEXT STEPS

If the publishing company is interested in pursuing your talents further, here's what you do:

- If the publishing company wants to hire you to work on its properties. (See Working for a Publishing Company, p. 250.)
- If the publishing company is considering publishing your book. (See The Comic Book Publishing Agreement, p. 256.)

Notes

1 Marvel Entertainment, Submission Requests, https://help.marvel.com/hc/en-us/articles/34091098762260-Submission-requests (last visited Mar. 25, 2025).
2 DC Comics, Contact Us, https://www.dc.com/blog/2019/02/13/contact-us (last visited Mar. 25, 2025).
3 Image Comics, Submissions, https://imagecomics.com/submissions (last visited Mar. 25, 2025).
4 Dark Horse Comics, Submissions, https://www.darkhorse.com/Company/Submissions (last visited Mar. 25, 2025).

CHAPTER 12

Working for a Publishing Company

DOI: 10.1201/9781003496052-17

CREATING FOR THE BIG GUYS: MARVEL, DC, AND THE BRASS RING

Let's face it: every comic book artist has daydreamed about the big leagues—sketching Spider-Man's next epic pose for Marvel or creating Batman's brooding shadows for DC. Landing a job with one of these iconic publishers is like hitting the career jackpot and the prestige? Let's just say it opens doors. Once your name is attached to a well-known publisher-owned series, convincing someone to take a chance on your creator-owned comic becomes infinitely easier. It's the comic book equivalent of adding "NASA astronaut" to your résumé.

But let's not sugarcoat the hustle. Getting one of these coveted gigs takes more than just breathtaking pencils or inspired storytelling. It takes persistence, professionalism, and, frankly, a sprinkle of good old-fashioned luck. Sure, some companies roll out online submission forms for portfolio samples, or even host contests for aspiring creators, but don't count on these alone. Some publishers won't even look at unsolicited materials. Instead, the secret weapon? Networking. A well-timed handshake or a witty elevator pitch at a Comic Con can catapult you past the slush pile faster than any anonymous submission. (See Landing a Publisher, p. 240.)

If you do manage to catch the attention of an editor, expect to start with smaller contract jobs. Think of it as your audition—they're evaluating your skills and, perhaps more importantly, your reliability. Because here's the industry truth: a slightly less talented artist who delivers **on time, every time** will always beat out a brilliant artist who leaves editors hanging. Deadlines, it turns out, are the real superheroes of the comic book world.

WORK-FOR-HIRE AGREEMENTS: THE REALITY

If you're working on a publisher-owned comic book property, like Superman or Spider-Man, you will almost certainly be offered a work-for-hire deal. (See Work for Hire, p. 39.)

Despite most artists' understandable aversion to entering a work-for-hire deal where your employer is the author, if you want to write or draw stories based on somebody else's valuable intellectual property (e.g. publisher-owned characters and storylines), you should get used to them owning your work. It's simply the way the comic book industry is run, and for what it's worth, the film industry as well. The trick is not to run away from it, but, rather, not to give your copyright interest away without something valuable in return.

The bigger publishers sweeten the deal with page rates and even potential royalties. If you're lucky enough to invent a new character that makes the cut as a "**special character**," you might score bonus compensation. And here's a silver lining: comic book artists usually get to keep the physical artwork they create, even under work-for-hire contracts. That means you can sell those original pieces at Comic Cons nationwide. (Just don't try to license the copyright—if it's work for hire, it was never yours to license.)

WORKING FOR A PUBLISHER: KEY IP ISSUES

Know the Scope of Your Job

Before you start creating for the publishing company, understand clearly the **scope** of what it is they're hiring you to do. The reason for this is to avoid any confusion between your personal work and the work the publishing company has contracted for under its work-for-hire agreement.

For instance, if you are being hired to "design superhero characters," without reference to a particular series title, it may quickly become blurry as to who owns those character sketches you do at night at home. Are they your personal project? Are there more characters for the company that hired you? If you sense a potential for confusion on this issue, send a quick email to your employer before you start work, letting them know that you would like to work on your own property in your spare time. If you're dealing with an experienced publishing company, they have policies in place, which deal with this issue. Know these policies *before* you start drawing your own characters while in their employ.

Use Only Your Own Work Product

It's important not to include anyone else's work in the projects you create for the publishing company unless you have their express permission. Typically, if you're under contract, you have agreed to representations and warranties and indemnification clauses (often called "Reps and Warranties"). This means that if the publisher faces a copyright infringement lawsuit—perhaps because you traced an image from the web or used content from a generative AI—the company can transfer the legal costs to you (See Appendix G: Representations and Warranties, p. 470; Indemnification, p. 471). On the other hand, if the publishing company supplies third-party materials for your work, they are responsible for securing the necessary permissions, and you would have grounds to sue them if they fail to do so.

KEY CONTRACTUAL ISSUES

1. **Compensation.** Ensure you have a clear understanding of your compensation structure. Aim to negotiate both a per-page rate and a share of royalties. And if you're an independent contractor, don't forget a kill fee—because getting paid for a project that dies is better than getting ghosted. (See Hiring an Artist, p. 150.)
2. **Representations and warranties.** Remember those reps and warranties that we were concerned about above? Try to qualify them with the magic phrase "to the best of Artist's knowledge and belief." In other words, your work is free from IP infringement... as far as you know.

3. **Deliverables.** Know exactly what you need to deliver, in what format, and by when. Remember, publishing companies work on tight publishing schedules: missing a deadline is often worse than turning in mediocre work. Mediocre work might not get you hired again, but blowing a deadline can get you sued for breach of contract. And when you deliver excellent *and* punctual work, you get hired again and again and again.
4. **Loan-out company.** If you have a loan-out company and want to be an independent contractor, let the publishing company know this up front. It affects how they engage your services, whether or not they take taxes out from your paycheck, and how they treat you with regard to employee benefits. (See Loan-Out Companies, p. 109.)

Use IP Exhibits to Keep What's Yours... Yours

In the comic book publishing world, protecting your intellectual property (IP) is less about heroics and more about paperwork. Whether you're a writer crafting groundbreaking story arcs or an illustrator sketching your next iconic character, one thing's clear: safeguarding your creations is **mission critical**. The secret weapon? Attaching a robust exhibit to your employment contract—a legal fortress separating your work from theirs.

Here's how to armor it up:

1. **Provide an Exhibit of Your Existing Work:** Include a detailed list—in the form of an exhibit—that names all the work you've created and any projects currently in progress that might overlap with your publisher's properties.
   - **Names & Descriptions**: Catalogue all your projects, characters, storylines, designs, or concepts. Writers—yes, even those brilliant backstories. Illustrators—those heroic poses? They're yours. Be detailed—if it's not listed, it's harder to prove.
   - **Visual and Written Proof**: Writers, save those outlines, scripts, or drafts. Illustrators, gather your artwork, sketches, or portfolios. Because when it comes to IP disputes, evidence isn't just king—it's the entire royal court.
   - **Timelines**: Dates matter. Establish when and how you created each asset to show it's independent of any employment agreement.
   - **Ongoing Projects**: If your work is part of a larger venture—be it a self-published comic series or an unpublished masterpiece—it's worth letting the publisher know. These projects need their own spotlight in the exhibit.

2. **Clarify Duties and Ownership:** Clearly outline your responsibilities to the publisher and agree on who owns any new creations made outside of the assigned work. This ensures both you and your publisher understand which materials remain your property.

- **Outside Projects**: Specify that any characters, stories, or designs created outside your assigned work (like during personal time) remain your property.
- **Company vs. Personal IP**: Include language in the exhibit that makes it crystal clear which creations belong to the company and which stay under your ownership. Writers, for example, should ensure that any unrelated story concepts or scripts they come up with are excluded from company claims.

3. **Future-Proof Your Exhibit:** Add provisions for regular updates so you can refine the exhibit as your portfolio evolves. Writers may draft new ideas, and illustrators might develop new designs—keeping the exhibit current ensures that nothing slips through the cracks.

Skipping this step? Risky business. Even without a formal exhibit, you need some kind of documentation—say, an email thread with your employer—where both parties agree on who owns what and what's off-limits to whom. Otherwise, you could be fighting an uphill battle to prove ownership. I once spent *nine months* hashing out IP carve-outs for a writer working with one of the world's biggest media companies. Ownership of every asset they brought to the job—characters, concepts, you name it—was scrutinized in a long, back-and-forth negotiation. A well-drafted exhibit can save creators from future disputes and let them focus on what they do best—creating.

Special Characters

Comic book contracts can be as intricate as the storylines themselves, and the "Special Character Agreement" is one such plot device. In essence, if you single-handedly create a character and the company sees promise—perhaps as the next big thing in movies, games, or merchandise—you may be invited to sign this agreement. This designation comes with a bonus: extra royalties when your creation becomes part of a lucrative project.

WHAT DEFINES A SPECIAL CHARACTER?

Publishers who grant rights to creators of a "Special Character" usually define them as characters **originated and created by the Creator** that the publishing company deems worthy of further exploitation. But take note: the publisher **has the sole discretion** to determine whether your character earns this coveted status. Yep, the decision is all theirs—you don't get a say in the final judgment of whether you've just created the next Harely Quinn or just the next Arm-Fall-Off-Boy.

If the publisher does declare your character "special," it triggers additional compensation for you, the creator. You'll receive royalty payments based on the publisher's Special Character royalty rate policy. This policy can evolve over time, but the principle remains the same: the royalties apply to derivative works—think adaptations, spin-offs, or merchandise featuring your Special Character.

The catch? It's up to the company to decide whether your character qualifies as "Special." They've got the final say, which means some characters may ascend to stardom while others stay in the wings. It's less about corporate plotting and more about ensuring they can fairly manage creative rights across their expansive universes.

Special Character clauses hinge on three critical components:

- **Unilateral Determination:** The publishing company (CPC) calls the shots on whether a character qualifies as "special." This means you could create an incredibly unique and marketable character, but its status—and your extra royalties—are entirely at the company's discretion.
- **Royalty Payment Structure**: If CPC grants your character Special Character status, you're entitled to royalties on any derivative works featuring the character. These payments follow a set policy, which can be updated periodically by CPC. It's worth reviewing this policy closely to understand how your royalties are calculated.
- **Derivative Works Limitation**: Because the publisher defines what constitutes a Special Character, they also get a say in which uses generate money for the Special Character's creator. This clause clearly defines the media forms and specific uses of your Special Character that are eligible for royalty payments.

NEXT STEPS

What if you have your book already created and you need a publisher to print it and get it into the hands of your readers? In the next chapter, we will take a very in-depth look at the Comic Book Publishing Agreement.

- If a publishing company wants to hire you as an artist, review the Illustrator Services Agreement, p. 162, but this time, see it from the illustrator's perspective.
- If you're hiring other artists, see Hiring Other Artists, p. 150.
- Already written your comic and looking for a publisher? See Landing a Publisher, p. 240.
- Planning to self-publish your work? Dive into Self-Publishing, p. 301.

CHAPTER 13

The Comic Book Publishing Agreement

DOI: 10.1201/9781003496052-18

OVERVIEW OF A COMIC BOOK PUBLISHING AGREEMENT

Now that you've gotten a comic book publisher interested in publishing your creator-driven work (definitely a cause for celebration), let's take a look at the way your deal is likely to be structured.

The heart of the indie creator/publishing company relationship is the Comic Book Publishing Agreement. The first draft of this agreement will almost certainly come from the publishing company, but that does not mean it's fixed in stone. And don't let this first draft contract intimidate you; you may not understand all the legal terms, but at its heart, it's rather simple in purpose: for a defined period, the creator grants the publisher the right to publish the comic book in specified media.

The creator guarantees that they own the copyright and have the authority to license it, ensuring the publisher won't face legal issues related to infringement or defamation. In return, the publisher agrees to publish and distribute the comic and compensate the creator according to a predetermined formula, typically a percentage of the revenue the publisher earns.

The publishing agreement formalizes the business relationship between the publisher and the comic book creator and outlines the duties each party to the contract owes to the other. At a minimum, it must clearly establish:

- What rights you are licensing to the publisher; for how long, and in what media, and whether those rights are exclusive to the publisher
- What rights you retain, and in what media
- Your delivery date for your manuscript to be sent to the publisher and the specific expected deliverables to the publisher
- Who owns the copyright to your comic book property and its various parts
- Your expected compensation—including advances, royalty, page rate, residuals, option, and purchase fees—from each media and the formula by which each is calculated.

Example: In their comic book publishing agreement with Potto Publishing, Quill and The Penciller grant an exclusive license to publish, promote, and distribute their limited six-issue series, Maggot Man: Carrion-Eater of Justice, across print (in soft and hard cover, graphic novel and collected editions) in North America, and digital media, worldwide, for a defined term of five years. While Potto Publishing gains the rights to exploit the series in these channels, our creative duo smartly reserves all ancillary rights—such as film, video game, and merchandising adaptations—ensuring that only they control any side projects from their brainchild.

The deal mandates exacting delivery requirements: Quill is tasked with delivering the fully polished script, and The Penciller must supply the finalized artwork by a specific deadline, keeping those printing presses as relentless as a horde of comic book fans. Crucially, the agreement confirms that Quill and The Penciller jointly own the copyright to Maggot Man, ensuring that the publisher won't stumble into any legal hauntings over infringement or defamation issues.

On the money front, Potto Publishing commits to a nonrefundable advance plus a page rate for each creator and a royalty structure based on a transparent revenue-sharing formula—calculating from every copy or piece of merchandise sold, or, perhaps, a percentage of the profits with an escalating royalty. This compensation package not only rewards the creative efforts behind each issue but also motivates the publisher to maximize distribution, ensuring our dynamic duo gets their due for every flip through their horror-tinged masterpiece.

INTERVIEW

Mini-Series Success

"A short 4-or-5-issue mini-series is a lot easier to say yes to than a 16-issue run of a title that hasn't proven itself. Figure you can compile a 4–5 issue series into a trade paperback, too. That's much more reasonable from the printing costs perspective. Publishers want the least amount of upfront costs because they never know if something is going to connect with audiences or not."

ALAN ROBERT *is the comic book creator of several IDW-published titles, including "Wire Hangers," "Crawl to Me," and "Killogy."*

Strap in and steady your nerves—we're about to dissect every clause of this comic book publishing agreement. I think you're ready to stomach the legal fine print without flinching, so prepare for a deep dive into the nitty-gritty details that make or break your deal.

COMIC BOOK PUBLISHING AGREEMENT DEAL POINTS

Because of the importance of this agreement—it can act as a gateway agreement to other contracts, such as those with merchandizers, film studios, etc.—we'll analyze this deal in a bit more detail than some of the others we've seen.

Parties

The creator of the work is often referred to as the **Grantor**, **Licensor**, or **Assignor**, depending on how the rights are transferred to the publishing company.

For tax purposes, or to reduce your personal liability, you may want to form a "loan-out" company, which will take your place as a party to the contract after you transfer the rights to your comic book to your loan-out company. (See "Loan-Out Companies," p. 109.)

The publishing company is often referred to as the **Grantee**, **Licensee**, or **Assignee**, depending on how they receive the rights. Keep in mind that the publishing company will require the ability to assign its rights under the publishing agreement to its agents, affiliates, subsidiaries, etc. This means that even though you may be dealing with a familiar editor today, next year the publishing company may assign its rights under the agreement to another imprint, and you will have the same obligations to a new editorial team (and they to you).

Defined Terms

If the "devil is in the details," then defined terms are Satan himself. These linguistic imps lie in waiting to trip up the inexperienced reader with their duplicitous legalese. As we've seen, once a term is defined in a contract, it takes on that particular meaning, and not the ordinary meaning you might find in the dictionary! (See Defined Terms, p. 451.) So if the contract defines "Comic Book" to mean "any literary and/or graphic property, merchandise, audiovisual work, and derivative work thereof" and you give the publishing company the exclusive rights to exploit your "Comic Book," what you've actually done is given them the exclusive rights to exploit your comic book, and anything based on your comic book, including movies, novels, posters, merchandise, etc. Read and understand your defined terms; make sure the defined term for "Comic Book" only encompasses those media forms the rights to which you are willing to grant to the publishing company!

Some terms commonly defined in the comic book publishing agreement:

Licensed Property: this usually refers to the underlying comic book property that is the subject of the agreement. If this is a publishing agreement for the comic "Maggot Man: Carrion Eater of Justice," then that comic book is the Licensed Property.

Licensed Rights: these are the rights you're granting to the publishing company with respect to the Licensed Property. This definition may go into some detail as to the types of media in which the Licensed Property may be exploited (print publications, online access, video games, etc.). It is usually tied very closely to the Grant of Rights section; see below.

Territory: where the licensed rights can be exploited. This is often "worldwide, in all languages." However, if you've created a well-known licensed property, you may be able to impose some territorial restrictions, such as limiting publication to just North America.

Term: how long the publishing agreement is in effect. For newer creators, the publishing company usually requires rights for either the term of the copyright of the Licensed Property or for as long as the publishing company continues to keep the work in print. Try to include a proviso that allows the rights to revert back to you if the publishing company decides it no longer wants to print the Licensed Property.

Sell-off Period: once the term has expired, the publishing company typically gets a period of time (often 90 days to six months) within which to sell off any inventory it holds.

Grant of Rights

All the rights granted by the Licensor (you) to the Licensee (the licensee in this case is the Comic Book Publishing Company; however, as we've seen, the contract will undoubtedly give the publishing company the right to further assign those rights to other parties, like toy manufacturing companies). At a bare minimum, the publishing company will need the rights to publish, promote, distribute, advertise, and otherwise exploit the Licensed Property in comic books, graphic novels, and trade collections (hardcover or softcover). The right to exploit the comic online and through digital publication is now a fairly standard requirement as well.

Furthermore, most publishing companies, especially when dealing with newer artists, will want a host of other rights, such as the rights to exploit the Licensed Property in film/television and in merchandising. However, creators may want to reserve some of these other rights for themselves. (See Appendix G: Reserved Rights, p. 460.)

Copyright & Trademark

The heart of the grant of rights is your conveyance of certain exclusive copyright license in your work to the publishing company, for the duration of the term of the agreement. This, of course, means that you must have the ability to grant the exclusive copyright in the licensed property. If you created the work by yourself and haven't based it on anybody else's work, that shouldn't be a problem. However, if you worked with other authors and artists, or have based your work on another work, such as a novel, movie, or play, you will need to ensure that you have acquired the rights from these additional parties. (See Clearances and Licensing the Rights of Others, p. 198.)

If you have any trademark rights in your character or comic, you will also have to convey a license to the publishing company to use the trademark in conjunction with the publishing and promotion of the Licensed Property. However, unless you are assigning the entire property to the publishing company—in other words, selling it to them lock, stock, and barrel and keeping nothing for yourself, you need to maintain control over how your trademark is used. Additionally, you'll make sure that you get to keep any improvements to your licensed character or Licensed Property added by the publisher or its assigns. (See Trademarks, p. 2.)

Reserved Rights

Just as you are licensing some rights to the publishing company, there are probably some rights that you would like to keep for yourself. These reserved rights are often up for negotiation (and are often included as "granted rights" in the first draft of the contract you receive from your publisher; it's up to your mad negotiation skills to reserve them!). Creators often want to reserve the following rights for themselves:

- Video games
- Motion pictures and television
- Theatrical
- Merchandise and apparel
- Toys and action figures
- Apps
- Novels.
- Any rights NOT expressly granted to the publisher should be reserved by the creator!

Hold Back Period

Even if you reserve rights, the publishing company may want you to wait to exercise your reserved rights for a period of time, especially if your reserved rights could conflict with their publishing rights. The period of time that they may want you to hold these rights back is the "hold back period."

Right of First Negotiation

The publisher may further want the right to try to acquire your reserved rights from you if you decide to sell them. If the publishing company has included a right of first negotiation for itself, you will have to give them an opportunity to bid on the rights before you sell them to any third party.

> **Example**: In his comic book publishing agreement, Waldo Writer has reserved merchandising rights for himself. Now that the comic book is a huge success, Terrible Toys, Inc. wants to release Maggot Man action figures, with pus-shootin' action™! Because Waldo's reserved merchandising rights was subject to a two-year hold back, he must wait for that period to run before he can begin negotiations with Terrible Toys. Furthermore, if Waldo had granted the publishing company the right of first negotiation for the merchandising rights, he would have to deal with them first before starting discussions with Terrible Toys. In any merchandising deal, Waldo should include a provision stating that he will own the rights to any improvements or additions to the character created by the merchandisers. This way he can introduce Maggot Man's new pus-shootin' action, initially created for the action figure, into the comic story line, and maintain control over the goodwill of any trademark rights he may have in the character.

Credit

Credit in the comic world isn't just a nice courtesy—it's a mark of ownership, a stamp of recognition, and sometimes, the only proof that you actually created the masterpiece in question. A proper publishing agreement ensures that you're credited front and center, whether on the printed comic itself or on any spin-off products that emerge from your work. If the publisher slips up and forgets to give you the acknowledgment you deserve, they're contractually obligated to fix it—although they don't expect a lawsuit over a missing nameplate. The contract should also extend these credit responsibilities to third-party licensees, meaning that if your comic turns into a line of action figures or a best-selling graphic novel, your name should remain tied to its success. A properly drafted publishing agreement credit provision should include:

- **Clear attribution**—The publisher must credit the creator prominently on all published versions of the comic book and any related products.
- **Consistency across formats**—The credit should be formatted uniformly on comics, merchandise, promotional materials, and other licensed products.
- **Correction of errors**—If the publisher fails to provide proper credit, they must make corrections in future editions or materials after receiving written notice.
- **Third-party obligations**—The publisher must ensure licensees, distributors, and affiliates also uphold the credit requirements.
- **Limitations on enforcement**—While errors must be corrected, the creator waives rights to sue or block distribution over missing credits.
- **Approval rights for derived products**—The creator must have a review period before credits are placed on any merchandise or adaptations of their work.
- **Preserving IP rights**—The publisher must display all of the creator's copyright and trademark notices in a consistent manner. Consistent crediting and registration indicia strengthen the association between the creator and the comic property, helping protect copyright and trademark claims and ensuring the integrity of the brand.

Payment

Navigating payment models in the comic world can be as unpredictable as a plot twist in your favorite issue. You might see offers ranging from royalties—where you earn a percentage of the publisher's revenue after deducting expenses—to a steady page rate that pays you for every finished page regardless of sales. Or both. Some deals feature residuals that keep on giving when your work is reprinted or merchandised, while others build on net profit sharing, splitting whatever money remains after other costs. And here's an extra kicker: if the agreement bundles in audiovisual rights, a savvy studio might exercise its option to purchase those rights, potentially transforming your printed panels into a blockbuster franchise and adding a whole new revenue stream to your creative arsenal.

The payment provisions may be spread out over the course of the agreement in such clauses as "Royalty," "Net Profit," "Page Rate," "Compensation," "License and Payment," "Advance," "Recoupable Expenses," "Fee," etc. However, to get a complete picture of how much money you will receive when your book is published, you need to read all of these clauses in conjunction with each other.

PAYMENT MODELS

Figuring out which is the best payment model for you can be tricky, and you often don't have the luxury of choice. But at least you can understand how they work. Let's assume your comic book, "Combat Wombat: The Marsupial Marauder," is about to be acquired by a publisher and will be sold in the direct market for $5.00 an issue.

- **Royalty**: A royalty is the percentage of revenue paid to creators for each unit sold, and it may be based either on the cover price or on net sales after deductions. In trade publishing, it's common to see royalties calculated off the cover price—so a 10% royalty on a $5.00 comic would yield $0.50 per copy, whereas a net sales model that produces a lower per-unit figure would reflect deductions for expenses.
- **Page Rate**: A page rate is a fixed fee paid for every completed page of work, irrespective of the comic's eventual sales. For example, if Pedro is paid $50 per page on a 20-page comic, he earns $1,000 for that issue, independent of market performance.
- **Residual**: A residual is an ongoing, deferred payment made when the work is exploited in secondary markets such as merchandise or reprints, with industry standards generally ranging between 2% and 5%. For instance, if "Combat Wombat" is licensed for merchandise that generates $1,000, a 3% residual would provide an extra $30 to the creators.
- **Net Profit**: Net profit is the amount remaining from total revenue after all production, distribution, and overhead expenses have been deducted. For example, if each comic sells for $5.00 and $3.00 is deducted for costs, the remaining $2.00 per copy is the net profit to be shared according to the agreed contract terms.

Focusing on royalties, royalty rates, as well as the formulas with which they are computed, differ from publishing company to publishing company. One common form is the 50% royalty model that works like this:

1. The publishing company receives money from the sale of the creator's comic books and then deducts the following *recoupable expenses*:
    - Production, printing, shipping, promotion, and advertising costs
    - Agency fees (although sometimes you can convince the publishing company to treat this as part of its overhead and not deduct agency fees as recoupable expenses).
    - Taxes
    - Bad debts
    - Returns for credit and reasonable reserves (to be liquidated within six (6) months)
    - Costs of negotiating, monitoring, and enforcing third-party agreements related to the Licensed Rights and/or Ancillary Rights

2. Any *advances* to the comic book creator against the royalty, see below, are then deducted.
3. The remainder, if any, is split 50–50 with the comic creator as the *royalty*.

According to comic author Alan Moore, he and Dave Gibbons split an 8% royalty for their work on the iconic series "Watchmen."[1]

QUALIFY RECOUPABLE EXPENSES

Try to qualify the recoupable expenses the publishing company gets to deduct prior to splitting the royalty with you. Include language that ensures that those deductions are:

1. **"Directly attributable, verifiable, out-of-pocket third party"** deductions. In other words, it is fair for the publishing company to recoup any monies it paid to third parties to help it produce the comic book. However, it becomes a lot more difficult to control these costs if the publishing company is paying *itself* for the costs of getting the comic ready for production.
2. **"No deductions shall be taken by publishing company for general overhead."** The publishing company should not be allowed to deduct the costs of running its business (paying for new computers, salary, keeping the lights on, adding a pool table to the break room, etc.). Every party should bear their own costs for doing business.

Advance

This is short for "advance against royalties," which means the publishing company is loaning you money against your future royalties. So, if you have received an advance of $500, when your book starts making money, the publishing company will first deduct $500 from your royalty stream before you see your first dime.

You should try to negotiate an advance; for newer artists without a following, it may be the only money you see for a while from your work. When you're negotiating this clause in your publishing agreement, make sure the advance is "nonrefundable," which means that if your book does not sell, and your royalties do not even match the amount of the advance, the publishing company cannot require that you return your advance. One formula for an advance is 10% of the anticipated author's royalty stream from the first printing of the comic.

That being said, unfortunately, advances aren't as common in comic book publishing as they are in other published genres. However, some popular and proven creators can command advances.

Audit Rights

Whenever you have a net profit or royalty clause, always negotiate an audit right. This gives you the right to inspect the publishing company's books (usually once per year), to make sure that you're getting paid what you were promised.

A certified public accountant (CPA) will have to perform the audit, and you will have to pay for the CPA out of your pocket.

Try to negotiate a provision that allows you to have the costs of the audit paid by the publishing company if your CPA uncovers a discrepancy in the company's favor in excess of 5%. In other words, if you were supposed to receive $10,000 in royalties last year, according to the company's books, but the company only paid you $9,000, you would receive both the $1,000 difference as well as the cost of hiring the CPA.

Prohibition on GEN-AI

If you want to ensure that your work is not associated with Generative-AI (GEN-AI), you need to address it up front. Failing to include explicit prohibitions on the use of GEN-AI in your publishing agreement opens the door to a host of hazards, from unauthorized AI-driven modifications of your art to inadvertent use in training these systems or even being exploited in unsanctioned marketing campaigns. Make sure the agreement incorporates clear language that (1) prohibits any GEN-AI involvement in the creative process of your work, (2) bars the use of your intellectual propertyin training or enhancing AI systems, and (3) restricts GEN-AI usage in all marketing or promotional activities without your express written consent. These measures ensure that your distinctive vision remains under your human control, preserving the integrity and value of your comic book masterpieces.

Example: "Prohibition on the Use of GEN-AI in Connection with the Creator's Work.

The following provisions are incorporated into this Agreement to safeguard the integrity of the Creator's Work by strictly limiting the Publishing Company's use of Generative Artificial Intelligence ("GEN-AI").

a. **No GEN-AI in the Creative Process:** The Publishing Company shall not employ any GEN-AI systems, tools, or technologies in connection with, or in deriving enhancements, modifications, or adaptations of, the Creator's Work, which includes all original comic book content, characters, storylines, artwork, or derivative materials provided hereunder.

b. **No AI Training:** The Publishing Company shall not use the Creator's Work, whether in whole or in part, for the purpose of training, developing, or improving any GEN-AI systems—whether such systems are owned by the Publishing Company or any third party—and shall take all reasonable measures to prevent inadvertent use by subcontractors or service providers.

c. **No Marketing Use:** The Publishing Company further agrees to refrain from utilizing GEN-AI in any marketing, promotional, or advertising activities pertaining to the Creator's Work, with all such activities requiring the Creator's prior written approval.

d. **Binding on Licensees and Assigns:** The prohibitions outlined in this section shall extend to all licensees, assigns, affiliates, and third parties engaged by the Publishing Company. The Publishing Company shall ensure that any agreements, sublicenses, or assignments involving the Creator's Work explicitly prohibit the use of GEN-AI for creative processes, AI training, and marketing efforts. Any failure to impose these restrictions on third parties shall constitute a material breach of this Agreement, subjecting the Publishing Company to liability for unauthorized AI-related usage.

Merchandising

If you cannot reserve merchandising rights for yourself, make sure that the royalty rates that you would be receiving from the publishing company for exploitation in each media form are commensurate with industry standards.

Furthermore, you want to make sure that you maintain approval over all the creative aspects of merchandised products, to ensure that there's quality control and consistency across manufacturers. After all, you put a lot of time and effort into designing your hero's cape; you want to make sure that the manufacturers in Beijing get the costume color just right. If you have trademark rights in your character, this becomes extremely important. See "Approvals" below.

Accordingly, you may want to insert a provision that says that any merchandising agreement shall require your "prior written approval, not to be unreasonably withheld."

DON'T KNOW HOW MUCH TO CHARGE?

- **Creator Resource, Page Rate Finder for Comic Book Publishers** Available at: <https://www.creatorresource.com/page-rate-finder-comic-book-publisher>.
- **Graphic Artists Guild Handbook, 16th ed. Pricing & Ethical Guidelines** Available at: <https://www.amazon.com/Graphic-Artists-Guild-Handbook-16th-ebook/dp/B0CF13B7PX>.
- **Nick Macari, Comic Page Rates and Creator Budgets—UPDATED** Available at: <https://nickmacari.com/comic-page-rates-and-creator-budgets/> (last visited Apr. 2025).
- **Comichron, Comic Book Publishing Business Statistics** Available at: <https://www.comichron.com/>.

Licensor's Permitted Uses

If you want to make personal use of your Licensed Property, you should make sure to detail it in this clause. You may want the rights to:

- Sell original artwork and scripts for the property,
- Sell autographed copies of the comic book in limited numbers from your website,

- Create a fan site based on the Licensed Property, or
- Make a series of webisodes featuring your licensed character, taken from artwork that is a part of the Licensed Property.

Deliverables

These are materials you have to deliver to the publishing company in order for them to publish your work. Deliverables typically include both artistic and legal materials, such as:

- **Artistic deliverables**: you may be asked to supply original Photoshop files for all images, prepress files, script for the comic, character designs for advertising and promotional purposes, and any other artistic materials required in order for the publishing company to print, market, and distribute your book (and exploit any of the other rights you've granted to it in the Grant of Rights, above).
- **Legal deliverables**: all the material you need to prove to the publishing company that (1) you own the IP rights to the comic, and (2) they won't be sued if they publish your comic book. You will need to produce all of the contracts you have with the other artists and writers who have worked on your book, as well as chain-of-title materials.

Examples:

- Contracts with all writers and artists who helped you create the book. These contracts must give you the right to publish and exploit the final work and to transfer that right to the publishing company. (See Clearances and Licensing The Rights of Others, p. 198.)
- Proof of copyright registrations for the comic book. (See Copyright Registration, p. 363.)
- If the comic book features another company's trademarks or artworks, it requires licenses to use those materials.

FORMATS

You must make sure that the formats that you're being asked to deliver are ones you can deliver. Some older contracts may contain language that references file formats that not a lot of people use anymore. For instance, as of this writing, many younger designers are much more familiar with laying out a page using Adobe products (like InDesign), rather than the older Quark program. However, if your contract specifies that you must deliver your comic book layout as a Quark file, the failure to do so may result in your defaulting on the contract.

EXAMPLE: DELIVERING THE WORM

Quill is negotiating a comic book publishing agreement with Potto Publishing for his new limited-run superhero/horror series, "Maggot Man: Carrion-Eater of Justice." Quill wrote the script and worked closely with The Penciller, who provided the pencils. Lettering and inking were done by Beard-O-Brush. The comic book is based on *As the Worm Turns*, a sci-fi pulp novel from the 1970s and contains numerous lyrics from songs written by the band The Flaming Lips. For his legal deliverables, Quill will probably be asked to provide Potto Publishing with copies (or promise that he has copies) of the following:

- Agreements with The Penciller and Beard-O-Brush, in which it is clear that the work they performed was either as a work made for hire or, if either artist retained rights to their work, their contracts with Quill must allow him to grant the publishing company all the rights it needs to publish, promote, market, distribute, and otherwise exploit the comic book and any other rights granted to it by Quill. (See Artist Services Agreement, p. 156.)
- A license or option/purchase agreement from the copyright holder of the novel *As the Worm Turns*, (which would probably be either the author, the author's heirs, or the novel's publishing company) granting Quill the right to adapt the novel into a comic book, to exploit the same, and to transfer those rights to a comic book publishing company.
- A license from the music publishing company controlling The Flaming Lips' musical compositions granting Quill the rights to include the lyrics in the comic book, to exploit the same, and to transfer those rights to a comic book publishing company. (See Copyright Licensing, p. 29.)

INTERVIEW

Being on Time is Better than Being the Best

"I think a lot of the comic book industry is about reliability, because the deadlines are so crucial. Delivering the material on tight turnarounds is tough. It's almost like a bad joke that creators hand stuff in late and miss their deadlines. It's very frustrating for publishers. So if a publisher can find a creator that's going to deliver on time and also create projects with a built-in fan base, even if it's a small fan base, they know that they're going to make money and keep their schedule intact. They may love a concept from a creator and think the artwork is fantastic, but then it takes that creator six months to deliver one issue. It's just not gonna' cut it in the comic world."

***ALAN ROBERT** is the comic book creator of several titles, published by IDW Publishing, including "Wire Hangers," "Crawl To Me," and "Killogy."*

The Ability to Assign

If you used artists, writers, or third-party-owned IP rights to make your comic book, their contracts with you may be a part of your legal deliverables. All of their agreements with you **must** contain a clause that allows you to grant the bundle of rights they gave you to your "agents, licensees, and assigns." This allows the comic book publishing company (which is your licensee or assignee) to "step into your shoes" and exploit all the rights these artists granted to you.

If you can't assign to the comic book publishing company the rights that were assigned to you, the comic book publishing company can't publish the book, because if it does, it may be committing copyright infringement.

But that's not the worst part: ***the worst part is that you will have to pay for any legal damages the publishing company incurs in defending such a copyright suit.***

Why? You agreed to pay for their costs in the indemnification clause that will undoubtedly be contained in your publishing agreement! (See Indemnification, p. 471.)

Reversion and Termination

This clause specifies when and how you can get your rights back from the publishing company (the reversion) and whether or how either side can cancel the grant of rights or the contract (the termination).

From an author's standpoint, you want to get your book published. Not only do you want royalties from book sales, but a published and distributed book is also great publicity... it can lead to future deals with the same or other publishers. This is why it is important to set time limits within which the publishing company must publish your book. If they fail to publish in time, you get the rights back, which you can then offer to another publishing company. Of course, you will probably have to return any advances and other monies incurred by the original publishing company on your behalf.

Try to include in the contract the right to terminate the agreement for the following reasons:

- If the publishing company fails to publish and commercially distribute the issue(s) of the Licensed Property within one year of Licensor's delivery under the Agreement. In other words, once you deliver your comic book files in your legal deliverables, the clock starts ticking for the publisher. They have to publish within a year or grant the rights back to you.
- If the publishing company fails to meet its day-to-day financial obligations or is adjudicated bankrupt (subject to any provisions of any applicable federal laws) or shall make a disposition for the benefit of creditors.
- If the publishing company fails to account and pay royalties (in which case the Agreement should automatically terminate, the rights revert back to you, and all royalties and other payments are accelerated and payable to you immediately).

- If the publishing company defaults on any payment provision in the agreement and does not pay within five business days after notice of default.

GET BACK HERE!

Be careful of a reversion clause that says something like "if publishing company fails to utilize *any of its rights* under this contract within one year of the date hereof, the property shall automatically revert to the writer." This may look like a good reversion clause, but it actually gives wide latitude for the publishing company to hold on to the publishing rights even if it does **not** in fact publish the comic book. This is because you will be granting the publishing company the rights to "market, **promote**, distribute, and exploit" the comic book. Therefore, under this language, the publishing company could hold on to your publishing rights even though it only **promoted** your comic book at a Comic Con but held off on publishing it for a few years. The way around this is to make sure this clause is drafted so that only the publication and distribution of your comic book will stop the clock on your reversion right; with a clause like that, you can get your comic book rights back if the publishing company fails to publish and distribute your comic.

Approvals

This can be tricky. You, the creator, of course, want the right to approve anything that is based on your Licensed Property. However, the publishing company and any toy manufacturer may want the final say. One way to approach this is to carve out areas over which you have approval (character design, use of your trademarks and logos, etc.) while leaving the publishing company the right to approve other elements (perhaps script, dialogue, choice of cover artist). Even in those areas in which you do not maintain final approval, you should at least receive a right of "meaningful consultation." (See Approvals, p. 462.)

If you do have trademark rights in your character, you will need to maintain some kind of approval and quality control over the merchandising. Under trademark law, you need to retain some ability to control the way your trademark is used and maintain quality control... or else you risk losing your trademark! (See Trademarks, p. 2.)

Representations and Warranties

These are promises and statements of facts about the Licensed Property, its creator, and the publishing company. Each side is relying on the truth of these statements, and any misstatements here will be considered a breach of contract. (See Representations and Warranties, p. 470.). You will be promising the publisher:

- That the Licensed Property originated with you, you didn't copy it from anybody else, and the publishing company will not get sued by any other parties if they exploit the work under the terms of the publishing agreement.
- That the Licensed Property does not infringe any copyrights, defame anybody, or violate any third party's rights.
- That you will continue to protect the copyright, trademark, and other IP rights in your work against any infringers.
- That you are healthy enough to be able to carry out the terms of the publishing agreement.
- That you are not contractually prohibited by any third party from entering into the publishing agreement.

LIMIT YOUR KNOWLEDGE OF THE WORLD

You are promising that you have all of the copyrights, trademarks, rights of publicity, and any other IP rights needed for the publishing company to be able to exploit the comic book, and that the comic book does not defame anybody or violate these rights, *anywhere in the world*. That's a tall order, especially since laws vary widely around the world. For example, what is protected by the First Amendment here in the United States may be a violation of anti-blasphemy laws in other parts of the world. Therefore, whenever you have a reps and warranties provision that is asking you to promise that it doesn't violate rights worldwide, you should always qualify it by inserting the following: "To the best of the Licensor's knowledge and belief... "

Example: Waldo Writer has created a character, The Nietzsche Knight, an atheist crime fighter who spouts philosophical diatribes refuting the existence of God while bringing evildoers to justice. Waldo knows the publishing company has a strong distribution presence in the Middle East, a region in which many countries have anti-blasphemy laws.[2] Rather than doing a detailed analysis as to whether or not his character would violate the laws of any country, it may be easier for Waldo to qualify his representation and warranty by saying "To the best of Licensor's knowledge and belief, the Licensed Property, The Nietzsche Knight, does not violate any laws in the United States."

It is also important to note that no matter how well Waldo qualifies his representation and warranty, even a properly drafted one has no effect on whether or not his work *actually* violates the laws of any particular country. It only means that the publishing company isn't likely to win against Waldo for breach of a representation and warranty or breach of contract. Waldo could still be charged with a violation of the law within the country where his work is illegal.

The publishing company should promise you all of the following:

- That it is not on the verge of bankruptcy,
- That there are no contractual or business obligations that would prevent the publishing company from exploiting your work,
- That it has the distribution network it has discussed with you, and
- That it will not use your work to train AI systems (or other prohibitions you negotiate).

Publicity

Here, the publishing company wants to be able to use your name, likeness, and bio in promoting the book. The only real issue here is that these should be your "approved likeness and biography." In other words, you provide the bio, and possibly the picture, for them to use. Additionally, you may want the publishing copy to require your prior approval over any press release that contains your bio and likeness.

INTERVIEW

Show You Know the Market

"My pitch [web]page included a marketing plan. How I was going to be actively involved in pushing the book through organizing contests, creating a website for the book, scheduling interviews, and doing comic book signings around issue launch dates to help spread the word. That part—laying out the marketing plan—is actually pretty rare, I'd say."

From what I've seen in the industry, a lot of creators leave it up to the publisher to push the product. They may Tweet about it here and there or post some artwork from an issue. But if they're not the sole creator, I rarely see them involved. I never really see websites being built specifically for individual comic titles. Generally, they just use social media. But by creating my own sites, it's helped me a lot as a creator. It separates you from everything else out there, and you can connect with fans on another level. It also serves as a hub for everything going on with the book: interviews, sneak peeks at artwork, reviews, photos from signings, etc."

***ALAN ROBERT** is the comic book creator of several IDW-published titles, including "Wire Hangers," "Crawl to Me," and "Killogy."*

Author's Copies

Every author needs copies of his or her work. Typically, authors will receive several copies free of every issue of their publication. You may also want to include a clause allowing you to purchase copies of your published book from the publishing company at the publishing company's cost price.

Assignment

A contract assignment occurs when the rights and responsibilities outlined in a contract are transferred to a new party who was not originally involved in the agreement.

In the world of comic book publishing, a publisher might seek to assign a contract for several strategic reasons. If the company undergoes a merger or acquisition, it may transfer existing contracts to the new entity to ensure continuity in publishing. Similarly, if a publisher wants to streamline operations or focus on other genres, it might assign a comic book's publishing agreement to a third party better suited to promote and distribute the work. In some cases, financial difficulties or restructuring efforts may push a publisher to transfer obligations to another company that has the resources to fulfill contractual commitments, ensuring that creators continue receiving royalties and other benefits. But there could be trouble lurking in the waters of assignment...

Example: You've poured your heart and soul into your latest comic, *The Cosmic Koala Chronicles*, and you've just landed a publishing deal. Everything looks promising until—twist!—your publishing company merges, gets acquired, or decides to hand off your contract like a hot potato. What happens now? The fate of your intergalactic marsupial hero depends on the fine print of your contract.

1. **When Your Contract Says Nothing About Assignments**. If your publishing agreement doesn't mention assignments, the rules get murky. Generally, the company **can** transfer its rights (meaning your comic is still out in the world), but it **cannot** pass off its duties—like sending your royalty payments or managing distribution—without your consent. It's like trading a sidekick in a superhero team: the new partner may inherit the mission, but they don't automatically pick up the responsibilities unless the hero agrees.
2. **When Your Contract Explicitly Allows Assignment**. If your contract gives the publisher the green light to assign the agreement, they **can** move your contract to another company without needing your approval. However, rights and responsibilities don't always travel together. If your old publisher owed you unpaid royalties, the new company may not have to take on that debt unless the contract explicitly states otherwise. In essence, they inherit the spaceship but not the fuel costs.
3. **When Your Contract Allows Assignment but only with Obligations**. Some contracts permit assignments, but with strings attached for the publisher. In this case, the new publisher must take on all **rights** and **responsibilities** of the original agreement. This means that if your previous publisher had promised an exclusive launch campaign for *Cosmic Koala*, the new company can't skip out on that duty. Here, the new publisher gets everything—the perks, the obligations, and the commitment to keeping your comic thriving.

Okay, I think we're ready to dive into the contract itself!

EXAMPLE: COMIC BOOK PUBLISHING AGREEMENT

This Agreement ("Agreement") dated ______________, 20___ (the "Effective Date")★1 by and between Waldo Writer, residing at ________________ (hereinafter, "**Licensor**"),★2 and Comic Publishing Company, Inc., whose principal business address is __________________ (hereinafter, "**CPC**").

WITNESSETH

Whereas, the Licensor has created a six-issue comic book series, tentatively titled "**The Adventures of Maggot Man**," and consisting of text, lettering, cover art, and inked and colored illustrations,★3 and

Whereas, the parties wish respectively to publish and have published the six (6) issue series of "**The Adventures of Maggot Man**," and to exploit the other rights granted herein, upon the terms hereinafter set forth.

Now, Therefore, in consideration of the promises, and of the mutual undertakings herein contained, and for other good and valuable considerations, the parties agree as follows:

1. Defined Terms★4

1.1. "Licensed Property":★5 the script and illustrations for the comic book, or series of comic books, created and/or owned by Licensor, tentatively titled "The Adventures of Maggot Man," that is the subject of this Agreement, as well as the copyright, trademark, and other attendant intellectual property rights thereto necessary to effectuate the purpose of this Agreement. The script and fully illustrated, inked, and lettered pages of the first such issue of the series are attached hereto as "Exhibit A," and made a part hereof.★6

1.2. "Licensed Products":★7 the comic books, graphic novels, trade collections (in both soft and hard cover), and/or digital equivalents based upon and/or incorporating the Licensed Property.

1.3. "Licensed Rights":★8 throughout the Term and Territory, Licensee's exclusive rights to publish, print, manufacture,

--------COMMENTS--------

1 Effective Date. Even though the contract may be signed at a later date, the Effective Date will be the one that controls the Term and other timing issues.

2 The comic book creator is the LICENSOR; they are licensing certain rights to the publishing company.

3 Here the creator is supplying the publishing company with everything needed to create the six-issue series. If the creator needed the publishing company to supply elements, such as a cover artist or letterer, those labor costs would be deducted as expenses prior to the creator receiving a royalty.

4 Read these defined terms carefully. They hold the key to understanding what is being licensed and what isn't.

5 Licensed Property. Here this is the underlying intellectual property rights, scripts, and illustrations for the comic book property.

6 It's a good idea to attach any script or artwork to the contract to avoid confusion over which draft the parties have agreed to.

7 Licensed Products. These are all of the ways in which the comic book property may be exploited—in comic books, graphic novels in both the print and digital forms.

8 Licensed Rights. The publishing company is allowed to exploit the Licensed Products in any print or digital media. Note that this is not a right to exploit the Licensed Property in any print or digital media (that phrasing would allow the publishing company to turn the comic property into a movie), but rather this clause ties the publishers rights to the Licensed Products, the Licensed Products being only comic books and graphic novels. Be very careful here! Some publishing companies will try and grab all rights to your comic book as opposed to just the publishing and a few ancillary rights. That being said, granting all your rights to a publishing company is not a bad thing if that publishing company is compensating you well and has the power to fully exploit your comic property.

market, promote, advertise, distribute, sublicense (both in English and foreign language editions), and otherwise exploit the Licensed Products in any primarily print or digital media now known or hereafter developed. Without limiting the foregoing, these exclusive rights include: the right to have third parties publish and distribute the Licensed Products in digital media to end users by means of Internet downloads, iPod and mobile phone distribution, and other digital media now known or hereafter developed.

1.4. "Ancillary Rights":**★9** throughout the Term and Territory, Licensee's exclusive right to have third parties incorporate the Licensed Property into items of merchandise for sale to consumers, including but not limited to action figures, toys, apparel, posters, and sundries.

1.5. "Derived Product":**★10** Any product or media based on the exploitation of the Ancillary Rights.

1.6. "Reserved Rights":**★11** Notwithstanding anything contained herein to the contrary, the Ancillary Rights do not include the right to exploit the Licensed Products as a video game or other audiovisual works, such rights being expressly reserved to Licensor. Any rights not granted by the Licensor herein are expressly reserved by the licensor.

1.7. "Territory": worldwide, in all languages.

1.8. "Term":**★12** ongoing from the Effective Date so long as some version of the Licensed Products remain in print, or until such time as this Agreement is terminated as provided herein.

1.9. "Advance":**★13** a one-time, nonrefundable payment of $____________, applicable against Royalties, as such herein defined.

1.10. "Net Profits":**★14** any revenue actually received by CPC in the Territory and during the Term from the sale of the Licensed Products and any other exploitation of the Licensed Rights and Ancillary Rights, but not including all directly verifiable, attributable, out-of-pocket costs including any

9 Ancillary Rights. In addition to the rights to publish your comic book, publishing companies often want the right to engage in merchandising. In fact, if they're a reputable publishing company, they probably have relationships with merchandisers in place already. This can relieve you of a tremendous burden of having to shop your property around. However, if you're dealing with a smaller publishing company, you may not want to be so quick to grant these rights. Remember, whenever you grant merchandising rights, there are a different set of obligations that the publishing company must agree to (as well as a different set of royalty rates).

10 Derived Product. In this contract, any product that is made from the exploitation of the Ancillary Rights is a Derived Product. Action figures, toothbrushes, and Halloween costumes would all be Derived Products.

11 Reserved Rights. These are rights that you are NOT granting, but rather, reserving for yourself. In this agreement, you are specifically not granting the publishing company the right to make a movie or video game. Publishing companies may push back in the negotiations and ask for a holdback periods or rights of first negotiation with respect to your reserved rights. (See Holdback Provisions, p. 461.)

12 Term. How long the Agreement lasts. In this case, as long as they keep printing your comics.

13 Advance. Advances aren't common in comic book publishing. Still, it doesn't hurt to ask.

14 Net Profits. Caution! Because you will often be getting your print royalties based on the publishing company's definition of net profits, you need to make sure you understand how this definition works. Keep in mind, most net profit definitions are the subject of a great deal of tweaking by the publishing company legal staff and your editor may consider this provision non-negotiable.

Briefly, here's how the net profit calculation works: the publishing company gets in money from print sales, digital downloads, etc. It then deducts the cost of printing, promoting, marketing, and advertising your book. It gets to deduct other expenses, like bad debts. What's left over becomes the net profit, of which you will be paid a percentage (sometimes confusingly called a "royalty.")

associated production, printing, shipping, distribution fees, promotion, marketing, and advertising costs, taxes, bad debts, agency fees, returns for credit and reasonable reserves (liquidated within six (6) months), as well as any expenses arising out of the negotiation, monitoring, and enforcement of third-party agreements related to the Licensed Rights and/or Ancillary Rights, all of which CPC shall deduct prior to calculating issuing Royalties (as such are hereinafter defined). Notwithstanding the foregoing, CPC shall not deduct money from revenues or include as expenses, the following:***15**

1.10.1. CPC's general overhead expenses.

1.10.2. All costs related to Author's Copies (defined below).

1.11. Expenses and revenues derived from the exploitation of the Licensed Rights or Ancillary Rights shall not be cross-collateralized by CPC, its licensees, or assigns.

2. License

2.1. Licensor hereby grants to CPC and CPC hereby accepts an exclusive license to the Licensed Rights and Ancillary Rights in the Territory during the Term.

3. Royalty***16**

3.1. In exchange for the licenses and other rights granted herein, CPC shall pay the following royalty ("Royalty") to Licensor according to the following schedule:

3.1.1. Licensed Products—50% of Net Profits***17**

3.1.2. Derived Products—10% of the Derived Product's total retail sales amount, excluding any applicable sales tax.***18**

3.2. CPC will pay Licensor the Royalty as consideration for the licenses granted herein. During the Term, the Royalty shall be calculated on a quarterly basis and paid within 30 days of each quarter. Each payment will include a Royalty statement detailing CPC's Net Profits calculation.***19**

15 You may be able to negotiate a cap on the category of things that they can deduct from the revenue before becomes a net profit. For instance, here, they're not allowed to deduct their general overhead costs (i.e. the cost of keeping the lights on, general secretarial costs, their own marketing and promotion, etc.).

16 Royalty. In this deal, there are two kinds of royalties that the comic book creator may receive—royalties from Licensed Products and royalties from Derived Products—and each kind is treated differently.

17 Royalty for Licensed Products. This is the royalty for comic books and graphic novels. Basically, half of the Net Profits derived from the license sale of the comic book and all its forms. Obviously, this percentage can change depending upon the comic book creator's leverage.

18 Royalty for Derived Products. This is the royalty for merchandise and other items based on the ancillary rights. Here, the royalty is calculated little bit differently: it's 10% of the retail sales price. No net profit calculation is involved.

19 Knowing when to expect your money is critical; here, any Royalty payments should be made quarterly.

4. Interest in the Licensed Property*20

4.1. CPC acknowledges and agrees that the Licensed Property is unique and original to Licensor and that Licensor is the owner of all underlying rights in the Licensed Property including trademarks, copyrights, and any rights in concepts, designs, and ideas. CPC recognizes the great value of the goodwill and secondary meaning associated with the Licensed Property. As between CPC and Licensor, the Licensed Property and its associated rights and goodwill shall remain the complete and exclusive property of Licensor.

4.2. CPC acknowledges and agrees that all rights, interest, and title in the Licensed Property and any alterations or improvements made to the Licensed Property by CPC and/or its licensees and assigns shall be retained by Licensor.

4.2.1 **Credit:*21**

4.2.1.1. CPC will ensure that Licensor is credited as the creator of the Licensed Property on all Licensed Products in substantially the following form: "The Adventures of Maggot Man: created, written, illustrated, and lettered by Waldo Writer."

4.2.1.2. CPC will ensure that Licensor is credited as the creator of the Licensed Property on all Derived Products in substantially the following form: "The Adventures of Maggot Man: created by Waldo Writer."

4.2.1.3. Within a reasonable time after receipt of written notice from Licensor specifying a failure to accord proper credit in accordance with this section, CPC shall use good faith efforts to cure prospectively any such failure with regard to future publications, copies, Licensed Products, and/or advertising materials, if any, created after the date of CPC's receipt of such notice. CPC will make good faith efforts to contractually obligate

--------COMMENTS--------

<u>20</u> Interest in the Licensed Property. IP—like copyrights, and especially trademarks—must be carefully protected. This paragraph creates obligations on the part of the publishing company and its merchandisers to protect the creator's intellectual property by placing copyright and trademark notices on all merchandise. Furthermore, it clarifies that the licensor will own the IP rights to any improvements or modifications to the licensed property.

<u>21</u> Even though you may be delivering the comic with your name indelibly lettered on the first page, it is important to ensure that the Publishing Company has an obligation to keep crediting you both in the comic books and on any Licensed Products.

third-party licensees, publishing companies, and subdistributors with whom CPC is in privity of contract to make good faith efforts to comply with the credit obligations set forth herein, but shall not be responsible or liable to Licensor for the failure of any such third party to comply with the same. Notwithstanding anything to the contrary contained in this Agreement, in no event shall Licensor seek, or be entitled to, damages of any kind by reason of any breach or threatened breach of any of the credit requirements, nor shall Licensor be entitled to seek to enjoin or restrain the exhibition, distribution, advertising, exploitation, or marketing of the Comic Book, all such equitable remedies being hereby expressly waived by Licensor. No casual or inadvertent failure to comply with credit requirements shall be deemed a breach of this Agreement.**★22**

4.3. CPC shall contractually obligate its licensees and assigns:

4.3.1. To affix Licensor's copyright, trademark, and credit attribution notices to the principal face of all enclosure, packaging, and marketing materials relating to the Licensed Property or the Derived Products, such notice to be no smaller or less favorable than any marks identifying CPC or CPC's licensees or assigns, and

4.3.2. With respect to Derived Products, to allow Licensor a review and approval period with respect to the manufacture of all Derived Products.

5. Artistic Deliverables★23

5.1 For each issue of the Licensed Product,

5.1.1. Licensor agrees to deliver fully laid out, inked, lettered, and colored pages and cover art for the Licensed Property.**★24**

22 The Publishing Company will want to qualify what happens if it makes a mistake with these crediting requirements. In this agreement, the Licensor must send a notice to the Publishing Company pointing out the credit error. The Publishing Company must then fix the error on all future copies. One thing the Licensor gives up in this section is the right to sue the Publishing Company for damages or seek an injunction.

23 Artistic Deliverables. This is the page art, script, and other creative elements that you have to deliver to the publishing company in order for them to print and promote your book.

24 Here, the creator is supply everything. If any element will be supplied by others (e.g. cover art), this clause should specify that, and other sections of the contract would then detail approval rights over those additional elements and costs for those elements (which would be deducted as expenses before the Licensor received a Royalty).

5.1.2 Licensor agrees to deliver two (2) complete English-language copies of the Licensed Property's script.

5.1.3 Licensor agrees to deliver all artistic materials required by CPC to print, distribute, and market the Licensed Products including original ________ files for all pages, lettering, cover art, and prepress files, illustrations, drawings, and character designs.**★25**

5.2. All deliverables required for printing Licensed Products must be delivered to CPC prior to ________, time being of the essence.**★26**

5.3. From time to time, and at no additional cost to CPC, when reasonably requested by CPC, Licensor shall create and provide additional artwork necessary for the further marketing and exploitation of the Licensed Property.

6. Legal Deliverables★27

6.1. Licensor agrees to provide proof of copyright registration in the Licensed Property.

6.2. Licensor agrees to supply all contracts, if any, with other artists and writers who have contributed to the Licensed Property evidencing that Licensor has been granted all rights to those contributions and may assign those rights to CPC.

6.3. In the event that the Licensed Property is based on another work, Licensor agrees to provide CPC with any applicable license or option/purchase agreement with the underlying rights holder.

6.4. Licensor agrees to deliver all necessary permissions, licenses, and releases for any artwork, photographs, logos, and/or trademarks or other third-party materials incorporated into the Licensed Property.

6.5. Licensor agrees to provide depiction releases from any identifiable persons that appear in the Licensed Property.

25 It's important to know what file formats the publisher accepts so you can create accordingly.

26 Publishers work according to a publishing calendar and therefore are very deadline driven. Blow a deadline and they can terminate the agreement. It is more important to your editor that you deliver your manuscript on time, then you deliver something perfect, but two weeks too late. If you think you're going to come in late, let the editor know at the earliest possible moment.

27 Legal Deliverables. If you've been following along with the book, you should have most of the stuff already. Copyright registrations, contracts with other artists, etc. In other words, your chain of title.

7. Publicity*28

7.1. CPC shall have the right to use, reproduce, display, disseminate, publish, print, and make any other uses of Licensor's name, voice, signature, approved likeness, sobriquet, and/or authorized biographical information in connection with the marketing, advertising, and exploitation of the Licensed Products. Notwithstanding the foregoing, prior written approval is required before CPC may use Licensor's likeness and/or biographical material in a press release.

8. Representations and Warranties*29

8.1. To the best of Licensor's knowledge and belief, Licensor represents and warrants the following:

8.1.1. Licensor has the right to enter into this Agreement and to grant the rights herein;

8.1.2. Licensor is the sole author of the Licensed Property;

8.1.3. The Licensed Property does not violate any rights of privacy, publicity, or any other right of any person;

8.1.4. The Licensed Property does not infringe upon the copyright, trademark, or other intellectual property right of any other person;

8.1.5. The Licensed Property is not obscene or libelous; and

8.1.6. There are no third-party agreements by or on behalf of Licensor, its affiliates, or assigns that would violate or otherwise interfere with the exclusive rights granted to CPC herein.

8.2. CPC represents and warrants the following:

8.2.1. As of the Effective Date, CPC is capable of meeting its day-to-day financial obligations;

8.2.2. Neither CPC nor any of its affiliates has any business obligations or agreements with third parties that would

28 Publicity. The Publishing Company will want the right to use your authorized picture and likeness in its promotion marketing. The key here is to make sure that you provide the biography (that way it's authorized by you).

29 Representations and Warranties. These are promises that the parties are making that they can assume the other party will rely upon. In other words, if any of these things statement are inaccurate, they can because of the breach. As we've seen before, the creator is promising that he has all the rights to grant, and that he is under no conflicting contracts prohibiting him from entering into this agreement. Tip: try and qualify this section so that everything is "to the best of your knowledge and belief."

prevent or interfere with the publication of the Licensed Property; and

8.2.3. CPC has a distribution network sufficient to effectively distribute the Licensed Products.

8.3. These representations and warranties shall survive the termination of this Agreement.

9. Conflicting Publication

9.1. During the Term of this Agreement, Licensor shall not, without the written permission of CPC, publish or permit to be published any book, comic book, or graphic novel based on the Licensed Property and/or Licensed Products.

10. Termination and Reversion<u>★30</u>

10.1. Licensor may terminate this Agreement and all licenses granted herein, having provided CPC with thirty (30) days' notice and upon the occurrence of the following events:

10.1.1. If within one year of the Effective Date of this Agreement, CPC has failed to publish and/or commercially distribute the initial six (6) issues of the Licensed Property;

10.1.2. If within one year of the publication of the initial issue of the six (6) issues of the Licensed Property, CPC has failed to publish and/or commercially distribute the remaining five (5) issues of the Licensed Property;

10.1.3. If within one year of publication of the final issue of the initial six (6) of the Licensed Property, CPC has failed to publish a trade paperback compilation of the 6 issues of the Licensed Property;**<u>★31</u>**

10.1.4. CPC fails to account for and pay royalties and fails to cure within 14 days of notice by Licensor. In such an event, any late payments shall incur interest at the rate of one percent (1%) per month commencing from the date the payments originally came due;

<u>**30**</u> Termination and Reversion. Other than the Term expiring, how can the parties get out of the contract? Some typical "termination triggers" are the publishing company's failure to publish the book within a certain time or to pay royalties according to their scheduled obligation.

<u>**31**</u> Here, there are several termination triggers for nonpublication. In order to avoid the possibility of termination for nonpublication, the publishing company must: (A) Publish the first issue within a year of the Effective Date, (B) Publish the remaining issues within a year after that, and (C) Publish a trade paperback collection of all six years within one year after the final issue was released.

10.1.5. CPC fails to meet its day-to-day financial obligations, is adjudicated bankrupt, files a petition of bankruptcy or arrangement under any applicable federal laws or makes a general assignment for the benefit of creditors.

10.2. Upon termination or expiration of this Agreement, all rights granted herein shall immediately revert back to Licensor, and all royalty obligations, if any, shall be accelerated**★32** and become due and payable immediately. CPC's obligation to pay royalties shall survive termination or expiration of this Agreement and will continue for so long as the Licensed Products are being sold and/or remain in print.

10.3. Sell-off Period**★33**—CPC shall use reasonable business efforts to sell any unsold Licensed Products or Derived Products within its control within 180 days following the expiration of the Term of this Agreement ("Sell-off Period"). Any products, Licensed Products or Derived Products, remaining within the control of CPC beyond this Sell-off Period shall, at the election of Licensor, be destroyed, tendered to Licensor (at Licensor's shipping expense), or, upon the mutual agreement of both parties, subject to a subsequent extended Sell-off Period.

11. Approvals★34

11.1. CPC shall have the right to make editorial changes in the Licensed Product as it deems necessary or advisable, provided such changes do not substantially change the meaning of the text.

11.2. CPC shall allow Licensor meaningful consultation rights regarding the exploitation of the Ancillary Rights in the manufacture of any Derived Products, including any packaging, enclosure, and promotional materials. With regard to the Derived Products, licensor shall have sole approval rights over all creative decisions and decisions regarding the appearance of Licensor's intellectual property marking. Prior written approval, not to be unreasonably withheld, is required from Licensor before CPC may enter into any merchandising agreement regarding the Derived Products.**★35**

32 Make sure that upon termination, all royalty obligations become accelerated—in other words, all payments to you become due and payable right then and there, and all licenses that you granted revert immediately back to you.

33 Sell-off Period. What happens to unsold merchandise if the contract is terminated? Typically the publishing company and its licensees get a period of time after the contract termination, called the "sell-off" period, in which to try to sell the remaining items. During this sell-off period, of course they can't manufacture any additional items.

34 Approvals. The comic book creator should be aware that the publisher will want certain approval rights over the comic book. For instance, they need to ensure that nothing in the book violates their internal standards and practices guidelines, e.g. extreme graphic violence, obscenity, etc.

12. Licensor's Use of the Licensed Property*36

12.1. Notwithstanding anything herein to the contrary, Licensor shall have the right to exhibit, display, and promote the Licensed Property and/or Derived Products on Licensor's personal website(s).

12.2. Licensor shall have the right to keep and/or sell all original artwork derived from the Licensed Property that was created by Licensor for the purpose of creating Derived Products and Licensed Products.*37

13. Auditing*38

13.1. CPC shall maintain complete and accurate books of accounts and records regarding the licensing, production, and sale of the Licensed Products and Derived Products. Licensor, and his/her duly authorized representatives, shall have the right, upon reasonable advance notice, to examine CPC's books and records and all other documents and material, whether under the control or in the possession of CPC, with respect to the subject matter and the terms of this Agreement. For the purpose of extraction or to make copies, Licensor shall have full and free access thereto. All books and records shall remain available for inspection for at least five (5) years from the termination or expiration of the License granted herein.

13.2. If any mistake or underpayment by CPC of monies owed to Licensor is discovered, CPC shall correct the mistake and/or pay the difference, with such payments to include an interest charge calculated at the rate of one percent (1%) per month. If the examination reveals an under reporting or underpayment in excess of five percent (5%) of the amount owed to Licensor for any payment period, CPC shall pay the costs of such examination.

14. Author's Copies*39

35 Keep in mind that any merchandising agreement that features Licensor's trademarks must have a built-in provision, which allows Licensor a degree of oversight and quality control over both the marketing as well as the product design.

36 Licensors Use of the Licensed Property. Comic book creators often want to sell copies of the comic books on their own websites or at their booth at a Comic Con. This allows them to do so without violating the exclusive distribution rights to the publishing company.

37 Always try to negotiate the right to be able to sell your own physical artwork.

38 Audit. Any time there is a royalty or net profit position, you need a right to audit the financial records of the company promising to pay you in that fashion.

14.1. For every issue of the Licensed Property that is published, CPC shall provide Licensor with 20 free copies prior to its commercial distribution.

14.2. CPC shall provide 20 copies/units of every Derived Product, prior to distribution, and in the form licensed or sold to consumers.

14.3. If Licensor requests additional copies/units of either the Licensed Product or the Derived Products, CPC shall sell them to Licensor at a "most favored nations" price and in the form licensed or sold to consumers.

14.4. In addition, Licensor shall have the right to sell any copies/units purchased from CPC at a retail price of his/her choosing.

15. No Partnership

15.1. Nothing in this Agreement shall be interpreted to create a joint venture, partnership, or agency relationship between the parties other than that of independent contractors. Neither party shall do or suffer to be done anything, whereby one party may be represented as an agent, partner, or joint-venturer of the other.

16. Notices*40

16.1. Except as otherwise provided herein, all notices shall be in writing and specify with particularity the nature of the other party's default. All notices shall be delivered by overnight courier, personal delivery, or in the form of a certified or registered letter.

17. Indemnification

17.1. At all times, Licensor shall indemnify, defend, and hold harmless CPC, its successors, licensees, agents, assigns, employees, and/or representatives from and against any and all liability, damages, loss, costs and expenses, of any kind (including reasonable attorneys' fees) from any action, claim, or demand (each, a "Claim") arising out of any breach by CPC of any warranty, representation, or covenant contained in this Agreement.

---------COMMENTS---------

39 Author's Copies. Make sure to get free copies of each item the publishing company produces or commissions.

40 Notices. Take note: this notice provision does not allow e-mail as a proper form of notice. If the publishing company is in default of one of its obligations, letting them know via e-mail isn't sufficient.

17.2. At all times, CPC shall indemnify, defend, and hold harmless Licensor, his/her successors, licensees, agents, assigns, employees, and/or representatives, from and against any Claim arising out of any breach by CPC of any warranty, representation, or covenant contained in this Agreement, and for any Claim arising out of CPC's, its assigns' and/or licensees' acts of omission or negligence relating to the Licensed Rights or Ancillary Rights and/or based on the manufacture or sale of the Derived Products, including, but not limited to, any Claims for manufacturing defects, defective products, product liability, strict products liability, misrepresentation, false advertising, and unfair competition.

17.3. The party receiving notice of such action, Claim, or demand shall promptly notify the other party thereof.

18. Assignment

18.1. The Publisher may assign this Agreement and all rights and obligations hereunder to any third party, provided that such an assignment includes the obligation to pay royalties to the Author as specified in this Agreement. Any assignment that does not include the transfer of obligations to pay royalties shall be deemed void.

19. Remedies, Choice of Law

19.1. In the event of breach of this Agreement, the sole remedy of the nonbreaching party shall be limited to an action at law for monetary damages actually suffered. In no event shall the parties be entitled to injunctive or equitable relief.

19.2. This Agreement shall be construed, interpreted, and governed by the laws of the State of New York. The federal or state courts of competent jurisdiction located in the State of New York, County of New York, shall have sole and exclusive jurisdiction to hear and determine any dispute or controversy arising under or concerning this Agreement, and both parties each hereby waive any objection and submit to the *in personam* jurisdiction and venue of such court.

---------COMMENTS---------

20. Further Documents

20.1. The parties agree to execute and deliver all additional documents, papers, and other instruments that might be necessary to further the intent of this Agreement. Such documents may include, but are not limited to, certificates of authorship, short form assignments, etc.

21. Entire Agreement

21.1. This Agreement constitutes the entire agreement between the parties hereto on the subject matter hereof and supersedes and replaces all prior and contemporaneous oral or written agreements, representations, and understandings.

22. Severability

22.1. If any provision of this Agreement is adjudged void, unenforceable, or unlawful, in whole or in part, by a court of competent jurisdiction, the remaining provisions shall continue in full force and effect.

23. Survival

23.1. The following clauses shall survive the termination of this Agreement, whether by breach or otherwise: "LICENSE AND PAYMENT," "LICENSED PROPERTY," "REPRESENTATIONS AND WARRANTIES," "INDEMNIFICATION," "ASSIGNMENT," "REMEDIES, CHOICE OF LAW," "SEVERABILITY," and "SURVIVAL."

24. Counterparts

24.1. This Agreement may be executed in several counterparts, and all counterparts so executed shall be deemed an original, and all of such counterparts shall constitute one agreement. Scanned and facsimile copies shall be deemed originals for all purposes. If the Agreement is signed in counterparts, it shall only be effective upon delivery of one executed counterpart from each party to the other party.

---------COMMENTS---------

In Witness Whereof, the parties have caused this Agreement to be executed by their duly authorized signatories to be effective as of the Effective Date. Any individual executing this Agreement on behalf of any party hereto does hereby represent and warrant that such execution is made with full authority and that such party is bound by the terms hereof.

Licensor: Waldo Writer	CBC:
By: ______________________	By: ______________________
	Title: ______________________

EXHIBIT A

Insert the Artwork and Script for
Issue #1 "The Adventures of Maggot Man"

NEXT STEPS

What if you didn't land a publisher... or didn't want to? In the next chapter, we'll learn the ins and outs of D.I.Y. publishing.

Notes

1 "We got eight per cent between us for Watchmen. That eight per cent bought this house, the car, the worthless broken-down CD player in the corner and all the rest of it." Eno, Vincent (Richard Norris); Csawza, El (May/June 1988). John Coulthart, Alan Moore Interview '88, Feb. 20, 2006, https://www.johncoulthart.com/feuilleton/2006/02/20/alan-moore-interview-1988/ (last visited Apr. 21, 2025).

2 Blasphemy Law in Afghanistan, Wikipedia, https://en.wikipedia.org/wiki/Blasphemy_law_in_Afghanistan (last visited Apr. 21, 2025).

CHAPTER 14

Self-Publishing

DOI: 10.1201/9781003496052-19

OVERVIEW OF SELF-PUBLISHING

If traditional publishing remains elusive, don't fret—self-publishing has grown into a genuine contender! Gone are the days when you'd settle for the back door; today's digital age offers a slew of viable options that weren't this robust during my last book edition.

Let's not sugarcoat it: self-publishing is no walk in the park. You're not only channeling your creative genius but also donning the hat of a distributor. That means wrangling with printers, distributors, comic book shops, and digital comic book publishers—all while keeping your creative spirit intact.

Unlike traditional publishing, where someone else handles promotion, you're in charge of your own marketing empire. Embrace your inner social media maestro by tweeting, Facebooking, blogging, and diving into every comic-friendly online forum to shout out your masterpiece to the world.

There's even a benefit to self-publishing: if you do it well, you may even attract other publishers for your next book. And if you do it really well, you may not need them. I have several clients who couldn't get published until they did it themselves, and they did it so well that they stayed publisher/creators!

INTERVIEW

Being a Proactive Creator Attracts Publishers

"When you're just starting out, publishers like to see comic creators coming to them with a successful creator-owned property. They want to know that you have the wherewithal to create and publicize your own book from soup-to-nuts. They're looking for somebody who is in the driver's seat, with their own property and their ideas. Whether you are a writer or an artist, publishers are looking for somebody to come up with the ideas and then to drive it forward. Then, a publisher will take a look at you and say "You've worked hard, you've driven a project forward, let's give you a series. You brought enough attention to work and ideas that we should take a second look at you."

*Author **DAVID GALLAHER** has received multiple Harvey Award nominations and won The Best Online Comic Award for his work on High Moon for DC Comics*

This section will give you an overview of working with:

- Printers
- Distributors
- Comic Book Shops
- Digital Comic Publishers.

COMMON COMIC BOOK DISTRIBUTION TERMS

Ashcans: Early, prepress prototypes or rough editions of a comic—produced in very limited numbers on low-quality paper—intended solely for internal review, promotional preview, or copyright purposes rather than public sale.

Direct Market: A specialized distribution network in which comic books are sold directly to independent comic book shops (and select retailers) via preorders that are generally nonreturnable. This model contrasts with traditional newsstand distribution.

FOC (Final Order Cutoff): The hard deadline by which retailers must confirm or adjust their orders for an upcoming release cycle. After the FOC, print runs are finalized, and no order changes are permitted. *Reference:* Cosmic Comix FOC FAQ.

FOB (Free on Board): A shipping term indicating that once the product (comic) is loaded onto the delivery vehicle, the seller's responsibility ends, and the buyer assumes liability and associated transportation costs.

Floppies: An informal term for standard, single-issue, softcover comic books printed on lower-grade paper (typically around 22 pages), noted for their flexible binding and relatively lower production budget.

Initial Order: The first, often larger order placed by a retailer for newly released titles at the beginning of a sales cycle, setting the baseline inventory for that period.

In-Store Date: The official retail release date printed on a comic book, indicating when it is scheduled to be available for purchase on store shelves. Retailers use this date to coordinate promotions and displays.

Nonreturnable: A common stipulation in the direct market, whereby retailers cannot return unsold copies to the distributor for a refund, placing greater emphasis on accurate demand forecasting.

Pull List: A pre-established list of titles automatically ordered by a retailer each sales cycle (unless changed), ensuring consistent stocking of popular or standard issues. Retailers adjust the pull list via the Final Order Cutoff process if necessary.

COMMON COMIC —*continued*

Solicitations: Catalogs or order forms issued by publishers or distributors that detail upcoming comic book releases—including cover art, pricing, and other key information—used by retailers to decide on their orders.

Variant Covers: Alternate cover artwork for a comic issue produced in limited quantities for collectible appeal. Although the interior content remains identical to the standard version, variant covers offer fans a unique, often more exclusive design.

MAKING MONEY IN SELF-PUBLISHING

And when all is said and done, making money through self-publishing (especially with a printed title) can be difficult. To see why, let's follow the money as it goes from the comic book storeowner's wallet to yours.

1. The purchaser buys the book for $4.00
2. Retailer keeps approximately 40–50% of the cover price = ($2.00)
3. The distributor, who has sold the book to the retailer on a nonreturnable basis, might have bought it from you at 60–70% off the cover price. If the cover price is $4.00, and the distributor purchased it from you at 70% off the cover price, you will get $1.20 per book.
4. Keep in mind, however, that out of that $1.20 per book (if you're lucky), you have to pay printing costs, as well as any other production costs (which can be quite considerable). In fact, these costs can actually exceed the revenue from the sales of your book. In other words, you might be losing money!

As you can see, for a smaller "floppy comic" (single-issue, 22-page soft cover comic), the profit margins are often too small to make economic sense. Many artists self-publish only longer books and sell them for $15–$25 per book.

Have I scared you off yet? No? Great—let's learn about printers!

PRINTERS

The term **comic book printing** refers to the range of processes that transform your digital art or hand-drawn designs into a tangible comic book. It includes decisions about the printing method, paper stock, binding, finishes, and quality control. Just as you protect your intellectual property, you must make informed choices as to how your work is printed—because the printed version is what ultimately brings your story into readers' hands.

Between 2020 and 2025, the comic book printing industry navigated dramatic shifts that could rival any high-stakes crossover event—for example, the COVID-19 pandemic wreaked havoc on global supply chains, sparking recurring shortages of premium paper (whose prices soared as if Lex Luthor had cornered the market on pulp), specialized inks, and critical printing equipment, which led to intermittent production delays that even the most intrepid heroes couldn't avoid; meanwhile, fluctuating U.S. tariffs[1] on imported printing materials turned overseas printing into a financial wild card, where anticipated cost savings quickly fizzled into unexpected surcharges, and escalating international shipping fees compounded logistical headaches, nudging creators toward domestic printing for its predictable timelines despite the higher per-unit price.

Domestic Printing (U.S.). Domestic printing offers a suite of advantages that independent creators often find reassuring. With faster turnaround times and direct communication, you can often deal with problems more quickly, yielding less overall time spent waiting for your books to arrive—actually **with** covers this time. The trade-off, however, is often the higher price per unit because of materials and labor.

Overseas Printing (Asia/Europe). In contrast, overseas printing typically offers a lower cost per unit for large print runs. Yet, these benefits come with their own set of challenges: extended shipping times, an increased risk of sudden tariff adjustments, and more complicated quality-control procedures. These hurdles can lead to unexpected delays and complications, requiring creators to carefully balance cost savings against potential production setbacks.

Unless, of course, you're going straight to digital, in which case your route is much easier. See, Digital Distribution, p. 313.

WORKING WITH PRINTERS

Printing companies that cater to independent comic book creators, like anything else, vary in quality and price. Before you plunk down your hard-earned cash for a print run of 5,000 copies of your comic book, make sure to get a sample of the printer's work. Paper and print quality matter to comic book shops because they matter to shops' customers.

If you do a print run of 5,000 for a 24-page comic book, it can cost you around $1.50–$2.50 per comic. Keep in mind: for better quality paper and full-color interior pages, you pay more money. However, you can usually lower your per-unit printing costs if you have a larger print run than 5,000 copies.

One of the advantages of working with a publishing company is that it takes care of all of the printing requirements for your book. Furthermore, since publishing companies are repeat high-volume customers, the printers often charge a publishing company less than they would charge you for the same print run.

A SELECTION OF PRINTER SERVICES

1. **PrintNinja (USA):** Provides offset printing services for comic books and graphic novels with a range of binding and paper options. https://www.printninja.com
2. **Comix WellSpring (USA):** Offers short-run print services for comic projects with a focus on quality control and proofing. https://comixwell-spring.com
3. **QinPrinting (China):** Delivers customizable offset printing solutions for comics and related products at competitive rates. https://qinprinting.com
4. **48-Hour Print (USA):** Provides fast-turnaround online printing services for small comic runs and promotional materials. https://www.48hourprint.com
5. **Lulu (USA):** Offers print-on-demand services suitable for self-publishing comic books and graphic novels. https://www.lulu.com
6. **Blurb (USA):** Specializes in print-on-demand printing for comics and graphic novels with various binding and paper options. https://www.blurb.com
7. **PrintRunner (USA):** Supplies economical online printing solutions that cater to a wide range of printed materials, including comic books. https://www.printrunner.com
8. **Mixam (United Kingdom):** Provides professional offset and digital printing services from the UK, offering a variety of finishing options. https://www.mixam.com

PRINTER CONTRACTS

The contract with your printer will typically begin with a clear definition of the scope of work, specifying the technical requirements such as print run, paper type, color accuracy, binding, and finishing options. It should also include detailed delivery schedules and turnaround times, including procedures for ordering and approving the printer's proofs. Pricing details—including unit costs, payment schedules, any deposits required, and provisions for adjustments like change orders—must clearly be outlined, along with warranties and quality standards that govern the final product's acceptability.

Risk management provisions are another critical element; contracts usually include clauses on indemnification, limitations of liability, and remedies for defective work, as well as force majeure clauses covering events like supply chain disruptions or pandemics. Finally, they address the ownership and confidentiality of intellectual property, set forth dispute resolution procedures (including governing law and arbitration requirements), and codify termination or cancellation rights to ensure both parties have clear remedies in case of nonperformance.

Example: Imagine a comic book creator who, in their boundless optimism, skimmed over every clause in their printer's contract—especially that stealthy ***force majeure*** clause. They order a large print run of their latest masterpiece, *Excelsior! The Packing Material Avenger*—only to have their printer invoke the clause as an unforeseen pandemic swooped in, halting production and leaving comic stores as empty as a rogue's lair. But not to worry: when the pandemic lifts, the printer must get back to printing... better hope it's not too long.

DON'T GIVE A SHEET!

Before you place your order, don't just double-check, but triple-check that the technical specifications for your book are accurate. Make sure to order a printer's proof copy of your book before the final print run. Yes, it may cost a little bit more money, but it will save you a lot of money if you suddenly discover that one of your pages is upside down. Prepress formatting is obviously beyond the scope of this book, and there are many wonderful books on comic book creation that go into such subjects. That being said, keep in mind the key difference when placing your order: **pages** are not the same thing as **sheets**! In printing, a page is one side of the piece of paper, and a sheet is both sides of the piece of paper. This can be confusing as most standard comic books are around 22–24 pages. Placing print orders depends on the number of pages, not the number of sheets.

UPC and ISBN

If you plan to go beyond direct-to-fan sales—say, getting your latest issue or graphic novel onto retail shelves or into distributors' hands—you'll need to arm your release with the proper identification codes.

- A **UPC (Universal Product Code)** is that trusty 12-digit barcode you see on products in stores, used by cash registers to scan and track sales. Typically, you only need one UPC per series (not per individual issue), and you can snag one for under $10 from resellers such as BarCodesTalk—or opt for the official GS1 route if you're looking for a more formal setup.
- On the flip side, if you're releasing your work as a graphic novel or any other book-like format, you'll require an **ISBN (International Standard Book Number)**. Each edition or format—hardcover, softcover, or digital (like PDF, EPUB, or MOBI)—demands its own unique ISBN to help retailers manage inventories and catalog your work correctly. These can be purchased from official agencies like Bowker through MyIdentifiers, although they usually come in around $125 each (bulk discounts can ease the cost if you've got multiple editions in the pipeline).

In short, unless you're sticking exclusively to direct sales, where you might get away without these codes, investing in UPCs and ISBNs is essential for ensuring your comics seamlessly make their way into the broader retail ecosystem while every brilliant panel gets the proper star treatment.

Additional Printer Tips

- **Tailor to Your Project:** Every printer has its own strengths. For a large, meticulously designed run, the premium offset options like PrintNinja may be worth the expense. For a test run or a project where speed and cost are paramount, Mixam's model might work better.
- **Always Order Samples First:** Independent comic creators consistently recommend ordering sample packs when possible. This helps you verify paper quality, color accuracy, and binding options before committing to a full run.
- **Keep an Eye on Community Conversations:** The landscape is always shifting. Online communities, such as those found on Reddit's r/comicbooks or dedicated comic creator forums, are excellent resources for up-to-date, independent user reviews. They often share real-world experiences—including lessons learned on pricing, turnaround times, and customer service—that can be invaluable when updating your printer services section.

Okay, you've had your comic printed; now what? How do you get it into your readers' hands?

COMIC BOOK DISTRIBUTORS

Direct Market—Then and Now

In the good ol' days of bobby-soxers, malt shops, and career-shattering McCarthyism, comic books were sold in pharmacies and newsstands. As comic fandom exploded, specialized comic shops became the main outlets for titles, and by the early 1990s, publishers were distributing directly to these retailers using a handful of dedicated comic distribution companies. Unlike trade book channels (where unsold books might be returned to a Barnes & Noble or a local newsstand), unsold comics weren't returnable to the distributor—a key factor that forged a close bond between publishers and comic shops through deep discounts.

For decades, Diamond Comic Distributors, Inc. practically defined the direct market. Headquartered in Maryland and partnering with every major publisher—from Marvel and DC to Image and IDW—they created a model where, once a comic hit a retailer, it was essentially "sold." Publishers and creators loved this arrangement; it guaranteed that a comic absorbed the discount in exchange for nonreturnability, ensuring that each copy reached its dedicated reader.

While Diamond was synonymous with comic distribution for a long time, it started losing key publishers in the early 2020s[2] and, what was once considered an unassailable monopoly, now had serious competition. By 2025 severe delivery delays, financial missteps, and the unexpected turmoil during and after the COVID-19 pandemic have all taken a toll on Diamond's reputation. In early 2025, the situation reached a boiling point with a high-profile bankruptcy filing and contentious bankruptcy auctions that have unsettled not only comic shop owners but also major publishing houses that once relied completely on Diamond.[3] And in May of 2025, Diamond was sold to Ad Populum.[4]

New Avenues in Comic Book Distribution

As Diamond's long reign waned, the industry has seen the rapid emergence of alternative channels, both for physical and digital distribution. Here are some of the key new directions indie creators and publishers are exploring:

- **Alternative Distributors and Industry Partnerships:** Major publishers aren't sitting idly by. DC, for example, has pivoted toward Lunar Distribution, and Marvel has begun testing channels with Penguin Random House. These new partners promise agile supply chains, improved digital integration, and better customer service.
- **Direct-to-Consumer Sales:** The digital revolution gives every creator a chance to cut out the middleman. Platforms such as Kickstarter, Patreon, and custom e-commerce sites (powered by services like Shopify) enable creators to sell directly to fans. This model can yield higher profit margins and foster a tighter community around your work—reinforcing personalized marketing and immediate feedback loops.
- **Self-Publishing and Indie Consortiums:** With advancements in print-on-demand technology and digital distribution, more indie creators are embracing self-publishing. By banding together to form independent publishing cooperatives, creators can pool resources, share marketing efforts, and even negotiate better deals with alternative distributors. This collective approach not only mitigates the risks of a traditional print run but also allows for experimenting with hybrid business models that mix direct market exposure with digital accessibility.
- **Hybrid Distribution Models:** Some publishers are innovating by combining the best of both worlds: releasing an initial issue via direct market channels (to capitalize on the enduring value of comic book shop presence) while concurrently offering digital editions or limited print runs directly to consumers. This strategy can buffer against distribution disruptions and tap into today's fast-growing online markets.

OTHER DISTRIBUTORS BEYOND DIAMOND

When exploring distribution channels for comic books, it's essential to verify each resource by checking online reviews, Reddit discussions, and other industry feedback to ensure that the information is current and accurate.

- **ComicsProgress Directory:** A directory of wholesale suppliers for comics and graphic novels that focuses on non-Diamond channels. http://comicsprogress.com/knowledge-base/wholesale-suppliers-of-comics-and-graphic-novels/
- **Comic Distro:** A platform that connects independent publishers directly to local comic shops via a streamlined online interface. https://www.comicdistro.com/
- **Emerald Comics Distro:** Based in Seattle, this distributor offers both consignment and wholesale services for indie comic titles across the Pacific Northwest and beyond. https://emeraldcomicsdistro.com/
- **Lunar Distribution:** Providing swift fulfillment and robust logistical capabilities, Lunar Distribution serves both mainstream and independent publishers. https://www.lunardistribution.com/
- **UCS Comic Distributors:** A contemporary distributor offering a dynamic directory tailored to the needs of U.S. comic retailers and vendors. https://www.ucscomicdistributors.com/

Steps to Distribution

There are many new comic book distributors who have stepped in as Diamond Distribution stepped back from being the industry monopoly it was. Despite Diamond's reduced role, it is helpful to use it as an overview of how physical comic distribution worked for a long time (many new distributors are minor variations on this process). Most likely, you will have to pitch your book to the distributor with their required submission package. Broadly speaking, the steps are as follows (but you will have to check the requirements for each distributor you approach):

1. **Finalize Title:** Before any distributor commits to carrying your work, they must see something truly compelling. Even if you're self-publishing, expect to pitch your book formally; they will only pick up a title if it meets their standards for quality and market potential. Your comic or graphic novel should be nearly complete—a finely polished gem with minimal room for last-minute adjustments. This means your work should be virtually production ready when you approach the distributor, ensuring a smooth transition from pitch to production.
2. **Completed Distributor Product Information Submission Form:** In your submission, make sure to include the title, the issue number, and the total number of issues if your series is applicable; the names of all

creators; a concise synopsis; and the intended audience (whether All Ages, Mature Readers, or Adult Material). Also provide a clear description of its format—including whether it is in color or black & white, its size, and page count—as well as the retail price, keeping in mind that the distributor receives a discount off this figure. Additionally, indicate the printer or shipping origination and the country of origin (not where it's drawn, but where it will be printed), along with the ship date and the Order Increase Cutoff Date (which is the last day you can accept an increase in orders from the distributor, usually just before your print run is finalized). Finally, include any optional details such as the UPC code, any licensing restrictions, and any special discount information.

3. **Digital Assets and Informational Materials:** Provide high-quality digital copies of your title alongside comprehensive Product Information Sheets for each one. These materials allow Diamond's team to assess the artistic merit and market potential of your work—as if they're getting a sneak peek behind the curtain.
4. **Production Timeline:** Supply a detailed production schedule, typically covering six to twelve months, that demonstrates when you plan to release new material. This timeline is more than a calendar—it's a commitment to a consistent creative output that proves you're in it for the long haul.
5. **Marketing and Promotional Plan:** Lay out a thorough marketing strategy explaining how you'll drive retailer preorders and capture the interest of comic fans. Whether through social media outreach, targeted events, or other channels, your plan should show that you're ready to move beyond word of mouth and make a solid market impact.
6. **Company Background and Future Initiatives:** Offer additional context about your publishing business, including its history, prior successes, and future projects. Show your excellent social media reach! This backstory builds credibility and helps the distributor understand your long-term vision—after all, every great comic book hero has an origin story, why should the comic itself?
7. **Review Process and Approval Timeline:** Once your complete package is submitted, the distributor's purchasing team begins their review, which can take up to four weeks. If your title impresses them, they'll grant the green light to proceed, at which point you can start discussing sales terms.
8. **Catalog Inclusion and Order Volume Requirements:** With approval, your title is slated to appear in the distributor's catalog on a monthly basis—typically rolled out the first week of every month (Diamond's "Previews" was the standard for decades). Note that smaller or indie publishers might need to demonstrate a forecasted order volume high enough to spark retailer interest, adding a bit of pressure to prove your potential.
9. **Purchase Order Issuance:** After comic book retailers respond to the catalog and place their orders, the distributor aggregates these numbers and

sends you a purchase order. This is the moment when your careful planning transforms into tangible demand.

10. **Production, Shipment, and Payment:** Finally, produce the ordered quantity of comics and deliver them to the distributor. Once they've distributed your work to the comic shops and collected payment from the retailers, you receive your share of the proceeds—a rewarding finale to a well-executed process.

KNOW YOUR SHIPPING!

Indie creators are often unprepared for a distributor's shipping and reorder and invoicing requirements. For instance, when Diamond had multiple distribution centers, you'd have to know which ones to ship your comics to. Understanding when and how a distributor requires you to get them your comics is critical to dealing with them.

Self-Distribution to Comic Book Stores

Believe it or not, you can bypass distributors altogether and act as your own distributor. Of course, this takes a lot more time and effort, as you are now your own promoter and shipping company. Remember, the role of a distributor is threefold: it promotes the book, sells it to stores, and ships it on a certain schedule. So, in essence, if you're your own distributor, your work tripled. Not only do you have to make sure the comic book store gets your books, you have to make sure they know about your books in the first place!

In order to do that, you must make sure that you can be found. As one comic book storeowner told me: "I hate it when I see a comic book that I like and then have to spend a lot of time searching the creator's website just to find out how to purchase inventory for my store!" Remember, on a most fundamental level, your promotion and marketing are only as successful as the clarity of your message.

Comic book storeowners need to know:

- The genre and age demographic of your book
- How much will you charge the comic book store for your book (note this is different from the cover price that they will charge the consumer; remember the store owner is used to keeping 40–50% of the cover price)
- The quality of your book. If they've never seen your work before, you may want to send them a PDF copy, and then a printed sample upon request (remember, they are a brick-and-mortar store and will also want to make sure that the quality of your printing is up to snuff).

INTERVIEW

Prepare for Presales

"In the world of comics, it's all about the pre-orders. If you get a decent pre-order from retailers for your book, you'll have a better chance of succeeding. You may have a fantastic, original story on your hands, but if no one buys it, chances are the mini-series will either get canceled or only come out digitally. You really need to spread the word and do whatever you can to let retailers know that your book is coming out and their customers will want it. Do interviews. Host contests. Use social media. Do whatever you can to get people talking about your book. The publisher will only do so much. Remember, your first little book is a test. They have much bigger, more profitable books to promote.

It's important to remember that presales happen months and months before the release date. You can be working on issue 2 of the series, but issue 4 is being solicited at that time. So, you essentially have to send in your description for each book and cover artwork way ahead of time. So, you really can't make up a series on the fly. You have to have a lot of things planned out and a lot of pieces in place before you actually do the panel designs.

Also, every book has a pre-order number assigned to it by a publisher. Design a flyer that your fans can download from your website or through social media, so they can hand it to their local retailer to place their pre-order. You are essentially creating a little form that says, "Please order this book for me." It has the pre-order number already on it and some cover artwork, too. Doing that serves two purposes... posting another reminder that your book is coming out online, and also providing an easy way for retailers to notice your book through their very own customers."

ALAN ROBERT *is the comic book creator of several IDW-published titles, including "Wire Hangers," "Crawl To Me," and "The Beauty of Horror" series*

DIGITAL DISTRIBUTION

You want to bypass all of that "printing and looking for a distributor" stuff? Then digital distribution may be your ticket! Digital distribution is fast becoming the preferred means of self-distribution for the indie creator, with new distributors coming to market with increasing frequency. Even if you are self-distributing printed copies of your comic, digital distribution can add to your revenue stream. Right now, independent creators possess a veritable treasure trove of options to share their digital comics, whether you're looking to offer content for free or cash in through digital storefronts.

With digital distribution, you create an account with the digital distributor, upload your comic book files, and the distributor hosts them on its site. When potential readers "purchase" your comic book, you get a portion of the proceeds. How much the creator gets depends on the digital distributor.

Digital comics often need to be read by proprietary apps, provided by the digital distributor, although some distributors are recognizing the need to provide digital comics in already familiar formats, such as those used by Amazon Kindle and Apple.

Of course, just having a digital distributor doesn't ensure that readers will flock to your book. Digital distributors don't always promote titles as well as brick-and-mortar distributors do, leaving much of the comic's promotion and hype up to the individual creators. (See Get Your Message Out, p. 229.)

"I DON'T BUY IT"

Unlike physical comic book purchasing, the "purchaser" of a digital comic typically does not own the comic book file; rather, the reader licenses it from the distributor or the creator. In fact, readers who breach the license agreement with the digital distributor can find their digital comic subscriptions suddenly revoked, and the comics they paid for gone.

Know Your Rights!

All of the digital comics distributors require you to **represent and warrant** that you have all of the copyrights and other rights to your work. If you've been following along with this book, this should be a familiar mantra by now: make sure you have all of the rights before you publish and distribute your work!

Furthermore—again, it should be no surprise here—you will have to **indemnify** the digital distributors for any lawsuits or other damages that they incur because of your misrepresentations (like a misrepresentation that you have all of the copyrights that you promised you had in the representations and warranties). Not only will you have to pay the distributor's legal bills, but you will have to pay the legal bills of any of their licensees or assigns who get similarly injured.

If you are just jumping into the book for the first time at this section, you may want to review the following sections for this very important point:

- See Clearances and Licensing the Rights of Others, p. 198
- See Representations and Warranties, p. 470
- See Indemnification, p. 471

Hosting Services for Digital Comics

Independent creators have several choices when it comes to hosting their digital comics. The most popular platforms are designed specifically for webcomics.

For instance, **WEBTOON** and **Tapas** have become industry standards—with features like vertical scrolling, episodic uploads, and built-in community engagement—that help you build loyal readership. These platforms make it easy to get noticed, even if your comic is more niche than a secret society of caped crusaders. If you're aiming for a more boutique, curated vibe, consider platforms like **GlobalComix** or **ComicFury**. They allow you to upload your work for free while offering monetization options through premium content or advertising.

And for those creators who crave total creative control, setting up a customized website (using a CMS like WordPress with a comic-friendly theme) gives you the freedom to major digital storefronts including ComiXology Submit—now closely tied with Amazon's Kindle ecosystem—and Google Play Books. These platforms allow your comic to sit shoulder to shoulder with titles from major publishers, complete with interactive panel-by-panel reading modes that could rival a high-tech superhero gadget.

Beyond these heavyweights, **aggregators** allow you to push your comic onto multiple storefronts simultaneously. Services like Graphicly distribute your work to platforms such as iBooks, Kobo, and Barnes & Noble while letting you keep 100% of your royalties. Alternatively, if you prefer running the show via your website, tools like Shopify enable you to manage sales directly. Each choice comes with its own perks—so it's a bit like choosing your own adventure; know your audience, and pick the method that makes the most sense for your project and budget.

Encoding and Versioning Services

Before you share your comic with the world, it must be properly encoded. This step converts your beautifully rendered pages into popular digital formats such as PDF, EPUB, MOBI, CBR, or CBZ. Imagine it as translating your artistic genius into a language that the digital realm can comprehend. Tools like Adobe InDesign, Clip Studio Paint, or dedicated comic conversion services ensure that your files remain crisp, load quickly, and meet each platform's technical requirements (like optimal panel resolution and file size limits).

Versioning is equally important if you plan on releasing multiple editions—say, a free teaser versus a fully paid release or different versions optimized for mobile versus desktop reading. Modern encoding services often include versioning workflows that automatically handle file conversions and ensure consistency across various formats. This means if you ever need to tweak a page or add a bonus panel, your comic can be updated faster than a superhero can change costumes.

Digital Distribution Step-by-Step

Ready to blast off into the digital realm? Here's your step-by-step treasure map to digital distribution glory—your shortcut to turning pixels into paychecks.

- **Finalize Your Comic Content:** Ensure your artwork, panel layouts, and script are polished to perfection. Think of this as editing your comic until every panel sparkles like a freshly polished gem.

- **Digitize the Comic:** If you've created your comic traditionally, scan your pages in high resolution. For digital artwork, export your pages in a quality image format. Organize your pages in the correct order—which is crucial if you don't want your readers to experience your story out of sequence.
- **Encode and Version Your Comic:** Convert your master files into digital formats (CBZ, EPUB, etc.) and establish version control. This guarantees that whether readers are checking out a free preview or the complete version, they're getting the best quality your art can offer.
- **Select a Hosting Service:** Choose a hosting platform that aligns with your goals. Consider free community-centric platforms like WEBTOON or Tapas to grow your audience organically or build your own website for a more personalized approach.
- **Upload and Configure Your Comic:** Follow the uploader's guidelines—add metadata like title, issue number, creator info, genres, and tags. Schedule episodic releases if available to keep readers coming back for more.
- **Distribute Through Digital Storefronts:** If selling is part of your plan, register with digital distributors like ComiXology Submit or use an aggregator to list your comic across multiple storefronts. Include all necessary metadata (UPC codes, ISBNs, pricing details, etc.) for smooth cataloging.
- **Market Your Digital Comic:** With your comic online, it's time to announce it to the world! Use social media, email newsletters, and community forums to promote your work. Some platforms even offer built-in promotional tools to help track reader engagement and boost your reach.

POPULAR DIGITAL COMIC DISTRIBUTION SERVICES

- **ComiXology:** https://www.comixology.com/
- **GlobalComix:** https://globalcomix.com/
- **Tapas:** https://tapas.io/
- **WEBTOON:** https://www.webtoons.com/
- **ComicFury:** https://comicfury.com/
- **Shopify** (for self-hosted stores): https://www.shopify.com/

ADDITIONAL TIPS AND BEST PRACTICES

- **Stay Updated:** The digital comic market evolves rapidly. Subscribe to industry newsletters and join creative communities to stay informed about platform policy changes and new tech standards.
- **Leverage Analytics:** Most digital distribution platforms now offer robust analytics. Use these insights to track reader engagement, polish your SEO, refine your content strategy, and improve future releases.

- **Consider Multiple Platforms:** Diversification minimizes risk. Many creators start on free hosting platforms to build an audience and later expand into paid or aggregated channels to maximize revenue.
- **Seek Professional Assistance:** If technical aspects such as coding or file formatting become overwhelming, consider hiring professional encoding or versioning services. While it adds to your costs, professional-quality files can significantly improve the reader experience.

DIGITAL RIGHTS MANAGEMENT

Digital rights management (DRM) is like a bouncer at an exclusive club who only lets in those with the proper credentials—but for your digital comic masterpiece. Essentially, DRM is the software wizardry that controls who can access, share, print, or copy your work. And here's a plot twist for the reader: when you buy a DRM-protected comic, you're not really buying the comic outright. Instead, you're obtaining a license to read it—a license that can be revoked under certain contract stipulations (yes, all those lessons about licensing clauses and contractual "traps" are coming back to haunt you).

And unlike the physical comic, which can be purchased and then tucked safely into plastic bags for decades of safekeeping, the rights to a DRM-protected comic can be terminated. For instance, if you license a DRM-protected comic from a digital outlet, and that digital outlet goes out of business, poof! goes your comic book. Of course, if you read the click-through contract you "signed" before you downloaded the comic onto your e-reader, you might realize that you were made aware of just that eventuality.

However, if you're reading this book, you're not just a comic collector: you are a comic *creator*. So, let's switch hats for a second. Presumably, you want to ensure that your digital comics are *not* copied by pirates. After all, Bit Torrents are the bane of any royalty author's existence. In fact, using them to distribute comics without permission is copyright infringement. Imagine that the license to your comic book was granted to a reader who bypassed the software locks on your content and was now distributing your hard work royalty-free online. Wouldn't you want the online distributor to have the right to cancel that reader's account or downloads?

I would, but then, I'm personally kind of old-school about this. I put a lot of hard work into my writing, and I want to be paid for it. I've spoken to other authors who don't have a problem with their work being shared without further compensation to them. Either way, it's a personal choice, as well as a controversial one.

But bottom line, if you are going to be dealing with digital distributors, DRM is often built into the coding of the file format in which your comic book will be provided to the masses. Additionally, even artists who want to take a less restrictive approach to digital rights management may still want to include a digital watermark featuring their copyright notice.

So, what are your options when it comes to obtaining DRM for your digital comics? Here are a few approaches:

1. **Built-In DRM from Distributors:** Many digital distribution platforms—such as Amazon's Kindle Direct Publishing (KDP), Apple Books, and Google Play Books—include built-in DRM options. When you publish your comic through these channels, you usually just need to check a box to enable DRM protection. It's the easiest route if you're comfortable with the platform's terms and want a one-click solution.
2. **Third-Party DRM Services:** If you're selling your comic on your own site or need more control over your file's fortress, third-party DRM solutions might be for you. Services like Adobe Content Server, LockLizard Safeguard, and EditionGuard wrap your PDF, EPUB, CBR, or CBZ files in a robust DRM shield. This extra layer of security ensures that only authorized readers—those with the proper digital key—can access your work.
3. **Digital Watermarking as an Alternative:** For those who find DRM's strict regulations a bit too stifling (or worry about alienating your dedicated fans), digital watermarking may offer a more lenient path. By embedding a watermark (visible or invisible) with your copyright notice—or even buyer-specific information—on every page, you discourage casual sharing and can trace unauthorized copies if they surface. While it won't stop a determined pirate armed with the know-how to remove it, it might just make them think twice.
4. **Hybrid Approaches:** Some savvy creators opt for a hybrid strategy: applying DRM on premium releases while offering DRM-free versions for sample chapters or older issues. This way, your latest, most valuable work is protected, but readers still enjoy the freedom of DRM-free content when exploring your back catalog.

POPULAR DRM SERVICE PROVIDERS AND RESOURCES

- **Adobe Content Server:** https://www.adobe.com/solutions/ebook/digital-editions.html *A widely used solution for publishers needing robust DRM for ebooks and digital comics.*
- **LockLizard Safeguard:** https://www.locklizard.com/ *Specializes in PDF protection, preventing unauthorized copying and distribution.*
- **EditionGuard:** https://www.editionguard.com/ *Provides DRM solutions specifically geared towards self-published ebooks and digital comics.*
- **Digital Watermarking Solutions:** https://www.digimarc.com/ *Offers technologies to embed watermarks into digital media as a less intrusive form of protection.*
- **Platform-Based DRM Options**
  - **Amazon Kindle Direct Publishing (KDP):** https://kdp.amazon.com/
  - **Apple Books:** https://books.apple.com/
  - **Google Play Books:** https://play.google.com/books

NEXT STEPS

That's it—you're done! That is unless something goes wrong, and you need to sue someone for a breach of contract. Or even worse, you were sued by someone. If that's the case, take a deep breath and turn the page.

Notes

1 Rich Johnston, More Problems for the Comics Industry Over the 25% Taxes and Tariffs, Bleeding Cool (Nov. 29, 2024), available at https://bleedingcool.com/comics/more-problems-for-the-comics-industry-over-the-25-taxes-and-tariffs/; Rich Johnston, USA Imposes New Tariffs on Canada, Mexico & China, Including on Comics, Bleeding Cool (Mar. 4, 2025), available at https://bleedingcool.com/comics/usa-imposes-new-tariffs-on-canada-mexico-china-including-on-comics/; The Comics Journal, Comics and Trump's Tariffs 2.0: "They might fuck us up at any moment," The Comics Journal (May 1, 2025), available at https://www.tcj.com/comics-and-trumps-tariffs-2-0-they-might-fuck-us-up-at-any-moment/.

2 Marvel Comics, "Marvel and Penguin Random House Announce Exclusive Worldwide MultiYear Agreement to Distribute Marvel Comics and Graphic Novels," Marvel (Mar. 25, 2021), <https://www.marvel.com/articles/comics/marvel-penguin-random-house-announce-exclusive-agreement-to-distribute-marvel-comics-and-graphic-novels> (last visited Apr. 18, 2025).

3 Marcel Green, "Comics Industry Business Change: Diamond Distributors Bankruptcy Op-Ed," Screen Rant (02/19/2025), https://screenrant.com/comics-industry-business-change-diamond-distributors-bankruptcy-op-ed/ (last visited Apr. 18, 2025).

4 Universal Distribution LLC and Ad Populum Complete Acquisition of Diamond Comic Distributors and Related Assets," Business Wire (May 16, 2025), https://www.businesswire.com/news/home/20250516342658/en/Universal-Distribution-LLC-and-Ad-Populum-Complete-Acquisition-of-Diamond-Comic-Distributors-and-Related-Assets (as of this writing, "Diamond UK remains separate from this sale process").

CHAPTER 15

What Happens When Something Goes Wrong?

DOI: 10.1201/9781003496052-20

I sincerely hope that you'll never have to use this section of the book.

Much of this book is spent helping you to avoid lawsuits. That being said, you're not in control of who decides to file a lawsuit against you. Furthermore, there are many unscrupulous business-people who think nothing of taking advantage of an artist because they believe that they cannot afford an attorney to help them defend themselves.

In short, "suit happens."

For comic book creators, legal issues typically arise in three areas: intellectual property infringement suits, breaches of contract, and censorship.

Although you may, in many cases, represent yourself ***pro se***, it is almost always advisable to have an attorney representing you. In some cases, such as a lawsuit brought by or defended by a corporation or LLC, having an attorney representing you is a necessity.[1]

THE PROS

Pro se: When someone appears in court *pro se*, it means that they are representing themselves without the benefit of an attorney.

Pro Bono: An arrangement in which an attorney or law firm does not charge for the cost of legal services. However, a pro bono attorney may require the client to pay for the costs of filing a lawsuit and other related litigation costs. Attorneys are encouraged to perform a certain amount of pro bono work each year, and typically do so for indigent, charity, or low-income clients.

TYPICAL LEGAL ACTIONS INVOLVING COMIC CREATORS

Infringement of Intellectual Property

IP lawsuits usually stem from unpermitted use of copyright and trademark-protected materials. They are often litigated in federal court and are not something that you should handle without a lawyer. In fact, if you have a corporation or LLC, you are *required* to have a lawyer represent you in court. Details on intellectual property infringement and its defenses can be found in the appendices (next section):

- Copyright Infringement, p. 44
- Trademark Infringement, p. 414
- Fair Use, p. 375

Copyright Infringement

If someone appropriates your copyrighted work, you may have a copyright infringement battle on your hands. However, filing a copyright infringement suit in federal court can be a long-drawn, expensive odyssey—imagine trying to storyboard an epic comic book saga with endless revisions and a dwindling budget. The process demands deep-pocket legal support and can drag on for months or even years, making it a daunting adventure for independent creators battling unauthorized reproductions of their work.

Enter the Copyright Claims Board (CCB) as your trusty sidekick when facing unauthorized reproductions of your original panels and storylines. The CCB offers a streamlined, cost-effective, and speedy avenue for handling copyright infringement claims—an alternative to a federal court lawsuit—and may be ideal for artists and small businesses wary of the deep-pocket, drawn-out battles of traditional litigation. It's designed to be accessible and user-friendly, much like a well-organized utility belt, ensuring that you can protect your creative works without draining your resources.

However, every superhero has a weakness. The CCB caps damages, and its decisions don't set binding legal precedent, meaning if your infringement case involves blockbuster sums or complex issues, you might need the muscle of traditional litigation. Plus, because participation in the CCB is voluntary, a crafty defendant could simply opt out, potentially dragging you into further legal skirmishes. In short, if you're dealing with modest claims and need a no-frills, efficient remedy, the CCB is a cool option—but for those high-stakes scenarios, you might have to suit up for the full court fight.

Breach of Contract

Breach of contract lawsuits often result from one or both parties not performing their duties under an agreement, making misrepresentations within the contract, or delivering materials that don't meet the standards expected by one of the parties. Contract breaches, like most legal issues in this book, are incredibly nuanced and complex matters. If you are involved in a breach of contract or other litigation, seek the advice of an attorney. Small claims courts are set up to help litigants resolve issues under certain financial thresholds (often less than $5,000) and are set up to help litigants who don't have the benefit of a lawyer.

Performance is the successful fulfillment of a contractual duty. If a party to a contract fails to perform his duties under that contract, he may have *breached the contract*. There are two main kinds of breaches: *minor* and *material*.

A Minor Breach

A minor breach occurs when the damage to the aggrieved party is, well, minor. No surprise there. In the case of a minor breach, the contract still stands and the nonbreaching party must still perform.

Example: A printer that is contractually obligated to deliver 1,000 copies of your comic by noon delivers them at 1:00 p.m. instead. If the contract does not stipulate that "time is of the essence," the breach may be considered a minor one.

Remedy for Minor Breaches

The breaching party must remedy the particular breach and compensate the aggrieved party for any damages. For a minor breach, the aggrieved party, however, is not relieved of her duties under the contract.

Example: In the previous scenario, the printer that was late in delivering the comics must pay any expenses resulting from the one-hour delay. However, you must still pay the printer the agreed fee (minus costs that you incurred as a result of their delay).

A Material Breach

Unlike the minor breach, a *material breach* substantially affects the benefit the aggrieved party expected to receive from the contract. If there has been a material breach, the damaged party may consider the contract terminated, with no further obligation on their part to perform the duties they were obligated to perform.[2] Furthermore, the damaged party may pursue contract remedies in court.

Example: In the previous scenario, if the printer missed its deadline and failed to deliver the copies within a reasonable time, a court would likely find that a *major* breach of the contract had occurred. Other examples of major breaches might be:

- An artist failing to make changes requested by the writer who contracted her (even though she is obligated to do so under her illustrator's services agreement) or
- A publishing company's failure to pay a royalty as per its obligation under a publishing agreement.

Remedies for Breach of Contract

A party that has been hurt because the other party to the contract has breached that contract may sue for *breach of contract.* The chief remedy for a breach of contract is the award of money, usually referred to as "monetary *damages.*" The primary kinds of damages awarded for breach of contract are *compensatory* and *consequential.* The damaged party has a duty to *mitigate* damages, which means that they must try to minimize or reduce the amount of their losses.

Compensatory Damages

Compensatory damages compensate the hurt party by paying her an amount of money that will:

- Put her in the position that she would have been in had the contract been performed as expected, or
- Put her in the position she would have been in if she had never entered into the contract in the first place (in other words, a repayment for any of the expenses she has incurred as a result of relying upon the contract).

Consequential Damages

Consequential damages compensate the damaged party for the reasonably foreseeable losses that occurred as a result of—as a direct *consequence* of—the breach.

Example: In the previous scenario, the reasonably foreseeable damages for the printer failing to deliver the copies in a timely fashion might be the cost of express shipping to the comic bookstores that had expected your comic a week earlier. However, for consequential damages to be awarded, the printer would need to be aware of or have reasonably foreseen that the comic bookstores needed your timely comic delivery.

Implied Duty of Good Faith and Fair Dealing

Regardless of the specific duties and obligations of either party, keep in mind that there is an implied condition in *every contract* that the parties will behave in good faith toward each other.

In addition to damages, an aggrieved party may also be able to obtain injunctive relief. An *injunction* is a court order commanding something to be done.

Injunctions can also prevent something from being done. For example, a court can issue an injunction that compels a writer to transfer a copyright or that prevents a comic book from being distributed.

For employment and other service contracts, an injunction may not be used to force the employee who has breached the contract to continue to work for the employer. However, an injunction can be used to prevent the breaching employee from working for other employers during the term of the breached contract.

Example: If Beard-O-Brush is under contract with Pabulum Publishing to complete a comic book, and the artist decides to ignore his duties to the publisher and work on his friend's comic instead, the publisher may seek an injunction against Beard-O. The court could prevent him from working on another comic during the term of his contract with Pabulum.

But note carefully, while a court may prevent Beard-O from working for somebody else, he may **not** be compelled to continue to work for Pabulum (although Pabulum can sue for damages, if he doesn't work for them). This is because American law is a real stickler about forced servitude, ever since the 13th Amendment was ratified.

Censorship

Censorship is the suppression of speech by a state or federal government or a foreign country. We have a very strong First Amendment in this country, which protects artists and other speakers against government censorship of our political and religious speech. While a detailed analysis of the First Amendment is well beyond the scope of this book (indeed entire treatises are written on this one-sentence amendment from our Bill of Rights), the take-away here is that the censorship applies to *governmental action* against restriction of speech and not private contractual action. In other words, if you agree in a contract with your publisher not to publicize any news about the comic book you are working on, a court is likely to uphold that clause despite your well-meaning First Amendment defense to the contrary. Furthermore, First Amendment defenses often fail when they come up against charges of obscenity and child pornography.[3]

Even though we have had strong precedents in the United States protecting our political and religious speech, many other countries are not so forgiving. For instance, Tunisia has strong anti-blasphemy laws in its penal code, which prohibit "moral transgression," such as visually depicting the Prophet Mohammed in a negative fashion.[4] Whereas our First Amendment also protects speakers who want to espouse racist or discriminatory ideas, many other countries do not offer such protections.

> **Example:** Bolivia's Law 045 imposes administrative and criminal penalties on racist or discriminatory speech, particularly targeting public officials and media outlets, with the goal of protecting historically marginalized indigenous communities and promoting social cohesion. In contrast, the U.S. First Amendment provides broad protection for free speech—including offensive or hateful speech—limiting restrictions only to narrowly defined situations such as incitement to imminent lawless action. This difference reflects Bolivia's emphasis on collective rights and addressing past discrimination versus the U.S. focus on individual liberty and the preservation of open dialogue.

If you are charged with a crime like obscenity—in fact, if you are charged with any crime at all—get a lawyer to represent you. The stakes are simply too high to go *pro se*. Fortunately for comic book creators, there is an organization that specializes in representing victims of comic book censorship: The Comic Book Legal Defense Fund (CBLDF).[5]

Founded in 1986, the CBLDF provides legal referrals and, in some cases, pays for legal support for comic book creators and other individuals whose First Amendment rights are threatened when they make, sell, read, or distribute comic books. Their website has a host of information about banned comic books, a history of comic book censorship, and case summaries of key comic book censorship battles.

COMIC BOOK LEGAL DEFENSE FUND

www.cbldf.org

Comic Book Legal Defense Fund

15110 Boones Ferry Road, Suite 220

Lake Oswego, OR 97035

info@cbldf.org

The First Amendment

"Congress shall make no law respecting an establishment of religion, or prohibiting the free exercise thereof; or **abridging the freedom of speech, or of the press**; or the right of the people peaceably to assemble, and to petition the Government for a redress of grievances."[6]

Comic books and video games, like other literary, visual, and audio-visual works, are considered "speech" under the First Amendment.[7]

The First Amendment can be a powerful trump card to play in the defense of some types of IP infringement lawsuits—for instance, if you are sued for infringing a trademark by incorporating it into your comic. However, the First Amendment is not always an automatic defense card against the claim of copyright infringement. The US Supreme Court addressed this when they wrote: "Copyright law fosters free expression by protecting the right of authors to receive compensation for their work." In other words, your First Amendment rights don't give you the right to appropriate somebody's copyright with impunity.[8] In copyright, Fair Use provides a way to balance artist's rights versus the right of the public to create new works from old.

Obscenity Is Not Protected by the First Amendment

The obvious question is: what is considered obscene? U.S. Supreme Court Justice Potter Stewart famously declined to define the kinds of material that should be considered obscene, writing, "I know it when I see it."[9]

However, for our purposes, we need a little more than a judicial shrug of black-robed shoulders, so let's turn to a New York criminal law that defines obscenity as:

> **Obscene**. Any material or performance is "obscene" if (a) the average person, applying contemporary community standards, would find that considered as a whole, its predominant appeal is to the prurient interest in sex, and (b) it depicts or describes in a patently offensive manner, actual or simulated: vaginal sexual contact, a crime under the former sections 130.50, 130.45, and 130.40 of the penal law, oral sexual contact, anal sexual contact, sexual

bestiality, masturbation, sadism, masochism, excretion or lewd exhibition of the genitals, and (c) considered as a whole, it lacks serious literary, artistic, political, and scientific value. Predominant appeal shall be judged with reference to ordinary adults unless it appears from the character of the material or the circumstances of its dissemination to be designed for children or other especially susceptible audience.[10]

It is important to note that what is considered obscene differs from state to state and from community to community. New York's obscenity laws are more precise, explicitly listing specific sexual acts that qualify as obscene and requiring that the material lacks serious artistic, literary, or scientific value. In contrast, Alabama's approach centers on whether the material appeals to prurient interest, defined as exciting lustful thoughts, and considers community standards and commercial exploitation of erotica, allowing for a broader and more subjective interpretation of obscenity.

In other words, what may hardly raise an eyebrow in New York City may be deemed obscene by a court in rural Alabama. So maybe Justice Stewart did have something after all.

IF SOMEONE SUES YOU...

Whenever we create intellectual property, we run the risk of creating something another author believes too closely resembles her property.

In my experience, many of these claims involve authors who don't fully understand the difference between inspiration and infringement. I once had a potential client—an artist—call up my office and tell me that the producer of a very famous television show had come by the gallery where his work was being shown and started taking notes on the artist's work. Lo and behold, when the television series aired, one of its characters was a painter whose work was also shown in a gallery. The potential client told me, hurt and indignant: "Not only did the producer get the idea of making one of the characters a painter, but when the program copied my paintings—they changed them so much, even I couldn't recognize them!"

After viewing his paintings and the paintings that were featured on the television show, I talked to her about the idea/expression dichotomy (See Ideas v. Expression, p. 392) and ultimately declined to take her case. Another attorney took on her matter, sued the producer... and lost. However, the point is illustrative for several reasons:

- Many artists really don't want to believe that there's a difference between inspiration and infringement
- Despite the fact that the television producer had an excellent defense and ultimately won... *it still was sued*!

If you are sued, don't panic. Actually, before a lawsuit is filed against you, you will probably receive a "cease and desist" letter from your adversary's attorney.

Cease and Desist Letters

This is a letter that tells you (in your adversary's opinion) what you have done wrong and what rights you have violated. The letter also lets you know what you can do to rectify the problem.

> **Example:** Let's say that you are being accused of infringing the copyright in another comic book. The cease-and-desist letter will begin by telling you that the copyright to that comic is owned by your adversary. It will then inform you that you have infringed the adversary's copyright by using that copyright as the basis for your work. In the letter, your adversary will demand that you remove all of the infringing material, and then probably demand some form of payment for the unauthorized use of that literary material. The letter will usually conclude by saying that you have a certain time period within which to respond, and it will threaten further legal action (a lawsuit) if you do not comply with the terms of the letter.

Hopefully, if you follow this book's advice, you will already have a lawyer who can respond to the letter that you've received. But, if you have not hired a lawyer already, now is definitely the time to do so.

DO NOT TRY TO ANSWER THE LETTER YOURSELF!

If you have received a cease-and-desist letter, **do not try to answer it yourself**! Unless you are an attorney, you might not know how to write your response so as to avoid admitting facts that may be used against you in a lawsuit. On more than one occasion, I personally had to clean up a mess left by a client who had responded to a cease-and-desist letter before contacting me.

If you don't respond to the terms of a cease-and-desist letter or fail to reach an amicable agreement with your adversary, be prepared for the next step: they may decide to file—or aggressively defend—a lawsuit. This escalation is not something to take lightly, as it can dramatically affect your legal standing and financial stability.

Moreover, if you receive a cease-and-desist letter or find yourself facing litigation, your first priority should be to immediately cease any direct communications with your adversary. Let your lawyer handle all correspondence to ensure that every word is carefully managed and that you do not inadvertently compromise your case.

Once you have secured legal representation, all communications from the opposing party's attorney should be directed exclusively to your lawyer. That means they are not to contact you directly—unless your attorney explicitly authorizes it. This approach not only helps maintain a clear and professional channel for negotiations but also safeguards your legal rights by ensuring that all discussions are conducted through an expert who understands the nuances of your situation. In essence, stepping back and allowing your lawyer to do the talking is a critical step in protecting your interests and preparing a solid defense, should the situation escalate further in court.

If you can't afford a lawyer, try to get one through your local Volunteer Lawyers for the Arts or similar pro bono legal organization.

STATUTE OF LIMITATIONS—A TICKING CLOCK

Lawsuits have a time limit within which they must be brought, called a *statute of limitations*. For instance, copyright is a statute of limitations of three years from when the claim accrues.[11] Sending a cease-and-desist starts that timer running (if it hasn't started already). If you don't sue within the statute of limitations, you may have abandoned your claim forever!

LAWYERING UP

Finding the Right Lawyer

If you need to file or defend the lawsuit, you need to work with an IP litigator—one who also understands contractual disputes. In other words, the attorney who helped you sell your house may not be the right person for the job. And oddly, the attorney who helped you negotiate your publishing deal may not be the right attorney to help you litigate a breach of that same publishing agreement. One resource to help you find the right attorney is to call your state Bar Association and ask for referrals. Fortunately, IP litigators are easier to find than transactional lawyers with comic book experience.

Legal Fees

Under the American system, each party is responsible for paying for their own attorney. Which means that if someone infringes on your work, you still have to pay for your own attorney to file suit. Moreover, if someone sues you, you will have to pay your attorney, even if you win your case.

That being said, some causes of action allow you to ask for your attorney's fees if you win the case. Copyright infringement is one such law; however, in order to get attorney's fees awarded, you must have registered the copyright to your work before it was infringed (or within three months after your work was published). (See Copyright Registration, p. 363.) See why copyright registration is so important?

Most attorneys charge either by the hour or work on contingency (an attorney working on contingency typically gets a third of any money they recover from the suit). It is not unusual for an entertainment attorney to charge $450–$500 per hour. Remember, the more information you give them and the more homework you are willing to do, the cheaper it will be for you in the long run.

After the initial consultation, which is usually free, you will probably be billed by your attorney every time they talk to you over the phone—and many attorneys charge in either 6- or 15-minute blocks of time.

Pro Bono Legal Services Organizations

If you simply can't afford an attorney, contact your local Volunteer Lawyers for the Arts Organization. These nonprofit organizations provide volunteer attorneys to low-income artists and arts organizations. However, finding a pro bono attorney to help you with your entire matter is a difficult task.

For a state-by-state list of Volunteer Lawyers for the Arts and other pro bono legal organizations serving artists, see: https://vlany.org/national-directory-of-volunteer-lawyers-for-the-arts/

NEXT STEPS

We're done here! The next step is to create more comic book awesomeness. Of course, if you need more in-depth IP and contract info, help with comic book resources, why not turn the page and take a stroll through J.D. Esquire's very own **Law Library**.

Notes

1 *Michael Reilly Design, Inc. v. Houraney*, 40 AD3d 592, 593 [2d Dept 2007] ("Like a corporation or a voluntary association, the LLC may only be represented [in court] by an attorney.").

2 Siouxland Ethanol, LLC v. Sebade Bros., LLC, 290 Neb. 230, 237, 859 N.W.2d 586, 592 (2015) ("'material breach' is a failure to do something that is so fundamental to a contract that the failure to perform that obligation defeats the essential purpose of the contract or makes it impossible for the other party to perform under the contract." Whether or not a breach is material and important is a question of degree that must be answered by weighing the consequences of the breach in light of the actual custom of persons in the performance of contracts similar to the one involved in the specific case. On the other hand, substantial performance may be established as long as any deviations from the contract are relatively minor and unimportant.").

3 United States v Whorley, 550 F3d 326, 336 [4th Cir 2008] ("While § 1466A(a)(1) would clearly prohibit an obscene photographic depiction of an actual minor engaging in sexually explicit conduct, it also criminalizes receipt of "a visual depiction of any kind, including a drawing, cartoon, sculpture, or painting," that "depicts a minor engaging in sexually explicit conduct" and is obscene.").

4 Reuters, "Tunisian Loses Appeal Over Cartoons of Prophet," Reuters (Feb. 18, 2013), https://www.reuters.com/article/world/tunisian-loses-appeal-over-cartoons-of-prophet-idUSBRE85O0QO/ (last visited Apr. 17, 2025).

5 https://cbldf.org/.

6 USCA CONST Amend. I.

7 Brown v. Entertainment Merchants Ass'n, 131 S Ct 2729, 2733, 180 L Ed 2d 708 [2011] ("The most basic of those principles is this: "[A]s a general matter,... government has no power to restrict expression because of its message, its ideas, its subject matter, or its content.") (Discussing videogames).

8 Rogers v. Grimaldi, 875 F.2d 994, 998 [2d Cir 1989].

9 Jacobellis v. Ohio, 378 U.S. 184 (1964).

10 McKinney's Penal Law § 235.00.

11 17 USC §507b.

COMIC BOOK CASE LAW
INTELLECTUAL PROPERTY LAW
CONTRACT LAW

PART 6

The Law Library

DOI: 10.1201/9781003496052-21

THE LAW LIBRARY—APPENDICES A–G

The remainder of the book contains your very own portable law library. Here, you will find material that fleshes out and supplements the topics presented in the main part of this book.

A FEW WORDS OF CAUTION

This section is not intended to be an exhaustive treatment of intellectual property (IP) or contract law. It is intended to highlight those areas of the law most important to comic book creators. Copyright, trademark, rights of publicity, contract clauses, and other laws will be examined from the viewpoint of how they impact the comic book creator's ability to make and protect her comic.

- **Limited Scope**. Those areas of IP law that do not directly apply to the comic book creation process, such as patents and trade secrets, will not be examined.
- **Limited Jurisdiction**. Only United States laws are discussed in this book. It is critical to keep in mind, especially when dealing with IP and contracts that the laws of other countries may differ significantly from those of the United States. Accordingly, a comic that does not violate anybody's rights in the US may violate somebody's rights in another country, or that country's censorship laws! Before distributing a comic book outside the United States, it is good practice to have your book reviewed and your agreements analyzed by an attorney familiar with the IP and censorship laws of the country in which the comic book will be distributed.

APPENDIX A

A Comic Creator's Guide to Copyright Law

WHAT IS COPYRIGHT?

Copyright is actually a collection of legal rights, all of which protect "original works of authorship fixed in a tangible medium of expression."[1] Copyright protects:

- Literary works, such as scripts for comics, primarily text-driven comic books, movie screenplays, novels, magazine articles, and poems
- Pictorial and graphic works, like comic book art, covers, and comic books
- Sculptures
- Motion pictures, television shows, and other audiovisual works
- Musical works, including any accompanying words
- Dramatic works, such as plays, including any accompanying music
- Pantomimes and choreographic works
- Sound recordings
- Architectural works
- Other works of original authorship

Copyright is one of the easiest forms of intellectual property protection to obtain: just create an original work of authorship, write it down or record it in some way, and you automatically have a copyright in that work. Only a minimum amount of creativity is required. You don't even have to fill out a form or put a "C" in a circle to get copyright protection, *but you will get more legal protections if you do.* (See Copyright Registration, p. 363.)

> **Example**: You create a comic book. If you've written it yourself, and haven't based it upon anybody else's work, it's original to you. Because you've written it down, sketched it out, or saved it to your hard drive, you've recorded it. Smile—you've automatically been granted a copyright in your work without having to do anything else.

COPYRIGHTING CHARACTERS

Believe it or not, whether or not you can copyright a "character" is not always straightforward. For instance, a purely prose description of a character may be harder to copyright than an illustrated depiction.[2]

Purely Literary Characters

Purely literary, stock characters are generally not copyrightable. So, if your character has only been written down (and not illustrated), make sure that character is unique and detailed. Believe it or not, even a famous literary character like Dashiell Hammett's detective Sam Spade was initially found to be uncopyrightable.[3] As the court in *Gaiman v. McFarlane* pointed out:

> "[A] drunken old bum is a stock character. If a drunken old bum were a copyrightable character, so would be a drunken suburban housewife, a gesticulating Frenchman, a fire-breathing dragon, a talking cat, a Prussian officer who wears a monocle and clicks his heels, a masked magician [...] It would be difficult to write successful works of fiction without negotiating for dozens or hundreds of copyright licenses, even though such stereotyped characters are the products not of the creative imagination but of simple observation of the human comedy."[4] [...]
>
> "Even if the character is distinctive other authors can use the stock character out of which it may have been built without fear (well, without too much fear) of being accused as infringer."[5]

However, the court went on to point out:

> "Although Gaiman's verbal description of Cogliostro may well have been of a stock character, once he was **drawn** and **named** and **given speech** he became sufficiently distinctive to be copyrightable."[6]

So note, copyright protection will be "granted to a character if it is developed with enough specificity so as to constitute protectable expression,"[7] or if it is "highly developed and central" to the story,"[8] or if the character and the story are inseparable, so that the character constitutes the "story being told."[9] And as a story's plot becomes "more intricately detailed and characters become more idiosyncratic, they at some point cross the line into "expression" and are protected by copyright."[10]

Characters with both Literary and Visual Elements

Add some illustrations to your literary character, and now the equation changes.

Distinctive comic and cartoon characters—a blend of literary and graphic work—have long been protected by copyright law.[11] "As a practical matter, a graphically depicted character is much more likely than a literary character to be fleshed out in sufficient detail so as to warrant copyright protection."[12] Even parts of a character can be copyrighted if they significantly aid in identifying a character (e.g., like Freddy Krueger's "razor hands" in the Nightmare on Elm Street series).[13]

COPYRIGHT IN SELECTION AND ARRANGEMENT

When we think of what can be copyrighted, we often think of types of expression, like drawings, paintings, comic books, etc. In addition to these works, a *particularly creative arrangement or selection of materials may also be copyrighted*, despite the fact that what is arranged or selected may be in the public domain.
(See Public Domain, p. 340.)

Examples include:

- A collage made from scraps of 19th-century advertisements
- A selection of words, for example, in James Lipton's work "An Exaltation of Larks" Lipton was able to copyright the particular selection and arrangement of "terms of venery" (collective noun for a group of animals, like a "herd" of cows, or my favorite, a "murder" of crows).

Since it is the *creativity* of the selection and arrangement that is granted copyright (as opposed to the public domain elements themselves), the choices and organization of the elements must be sufficiently creative. For instance, the alphabetical listing of data is not creative enough to warrant copyright protection, nor is the chronological ordering of data.

COPYRIGHT RIGHTS

For comic book creators and other authors, copyright law gives the copyright owner the *exclusive* right to take his or her work and:

- Make **copies** of it
- **Distribute** it
- **Perform** that work publicly
- Publicly **display** the work
- Make **derivative works** based upon the original work

Anyone who, without the copyright owner's permission, performs any of the above actions may be infringing the copyright. (See Copyright Infringement, p. 44.)

COPYRIGHT TERMINOLOGY

Many of the following terms are taken directly from the federal copyright statute itself and may be helpful in interpreting copyright law. More definitions can be found in the United States Copyright statute, 17 USC §101.

See: https://www.copyright.gov/title17/.

Author

The **author** is the original copyright owner of a work. For instance, if you create a comic book by yourself, and it is completely original with you, and no one has hired you to write it, you are the author. However, under the work-made-for-hire rules, if someone else hires you to create the comic book, they would be considered the author, not you. (See Work Made for Hire, p. 350.) And to complicate things even more, work created by a GEN-AI program may fail the Copyright Office's human authorship requirement and be ineligible for copyright registration. See Using GEN-AI in Comics, p. 59; Copyright Registration, p. 363.

Audiovisual Works

Copyright law considers any film, video, or animated comic to be an *audiovisual* work.

> "'**Audiovisual works**' are works that consist of a series of related images which are intrinsically intended to be shown by the use of machines or devices such as projectors, viewers, tablet software, or electronic equipment, together with accompanying sounds, if any, regardless of the nature of the material objects, such as films or tapes, in which the works are embodied."[14]

Common Examples include:

- Animation, in whatever format
- Motion comics
- Movies
- Television programs
- Streaming video

Collective Work

A "collective work"[15] is a work, such as an omnibus edition, or comic anthology, or trade paperback, in which a number of contributions, constituting separate and independent works in themselves, are assembled into a collective whole. A collective work is a type of compilation work.

Compilation Work

"A 'compilation' is a work formed by the collection and assembling of preexisting materials or of data that are selected, coordinated, or arranged in such a way that the resulting work as a whole constitutes an original work of authorship. The term 'compilation' includes collective works."[16]

> **Example**: A comic book titled "RetroRanger: Groovy Flapper D-Day." This comic book is a compilation that features a series of short stories, each set in a different decade of the 20th century. To enhance the authenticity and immerse readers in the era, the comic book includes actual public domain advertisements from each respective decade. These advertisements are carefully selected and arranged within the comic book to provide historical context and verisimilitude. The comic is registerable, even if the ads are not.

Derivative Work

A "**derivative work**" is a work based upon one or more preexisting works, such as a translation, musical arrangement, dramatization, fictionalization, motion picture version, sound recording, art reproduction, abridgment, condensation, or any other form in which a work may be recast, transformed, or adapted. A work consisting of editorial revisions, annotations, elaborations, or other modifications, which as a whole represent an original work of authorship, is a "derivative work."[17]

Examples of derivative works in the comic book industry include:

- The illustrated comic book is based on a comic book script
- A movie that is based on a comic book
- A television series based on a comic book (or based upon the movie, which was based upon the comic book, and so forth)
- An action figure or other merchandise based on a comic book character
- A novel based on a comic book.

Graphic Works

"**Pictorial, graphic, and sculptural works**" include two-dimensional and three-dimensional works of fine, graphic, and applied art, photographs, prints and art reproductions, maps, globes, charts, diagrams, models, and technical drawings, including architectural plans.[18]

Literary Work

"'**Literary works**' are works, other than audiovisual works, expressed in words, numbers, or other verbal or numerical symbols or indicia, regardless of the nature of the material objects, such as books, periodicals, manuscripts, phonorecords, film, tapes, disks, or cards, in which they are embodied."[19]

Publication

In copyright law, **publication** is the act of distributing a copyrighted work to the public. Specifically, it is "the distribution of copies [...] of a work to the public by sale or other transfer of ownership, or by rental, lease, or lending. The offering to distribute copies[...]to a group of persons for purposes of further distribution, public performance, or public display, constitutes publication."[20]

The date of publication is a critical one in determining whether a work is still protected by copyright. Many comic books are created as works made for hire. For any work made for hire that you create today, copyright protection will last for 95 years from the first *publication* or 120 years from the year of creation, whichever expires first.

The publication of a comic book publishes all the components embodied in it including the artwork, the script, and any copyrightable characters.

Public Domain

If work is NOT protected by copyright, it is in the *public domain*. This means that it can be used by anybody without seeking permission from the original author. In fact, the Public Domain Review is a wonderful website and database of public domain images and literary works here: https://publicdomainreview.org/.

Some things are in the public domain by virtue of their nature, for example, facts, ideas, concepts, and works created by the federal government. Even formerly copyrighted works can fall into the public domain for a number of reasons, including:

- **Expiration of copyright**. Copyrights have a life span. When it runs out, the copyright dies and the artwork becomes part of the public domain, where it can enrich the work of other artists. It's the karma of copyright, man.
- **Copyright notice was not placed on the work**. Earlier versions of the copyright law required the © to be placed on the work when it was published. If a work was published prior to 1989 without proper copyright notice, the work may have fallen into the public domain. Be careful here: a number of exceptions to this rule apply. Don't automatically assume a pre-1989 work published without notice is in the public domain.
- **Failure to renew the copyright**. Earlier versions of the copyright law required authors to renew their copyright registrations with the federal government. If a copyright was not renewed, the work fell into the public domain.
- **Relinquished copyright**. Sometimes authors want their works to be in the public domain and have voluntarily given up their copyrights.

WHAT IS NOT PROTECTABLE UNDER U.S. COPYRIGHT LAW?

From scripts to artwork, from comic book covers to animation, copyright law protects the majority of the components used to make a comic book property, in most of its forms. However, there is a host of things copyright law simply will not protect. In general, copyright law will not protect the "building blocks" required to make a work of art. For instance, while you can register the copyright to a script or artwork, you will not be able to copyright a word. You can register the copyright to a novel, but not an idea, and so on. As SCOTUS[21] tells us:

> [C]opyright law is replete with escape valves: the idea-expression distinction; the general rule that facts may not receive protection; the requirement of originality; the legal standard for actionable copying; the limited duration of copyright; and, yes, the defense of fair use, including all its factors, such as whether the amount taken is reasonable in relation to the purpose of the use. These doctrines (and others) provide ample space for artists and other creators to use existing materials to make valuable new works.[22]

Bottom Line: Copyright protects the particular way an author has expressed himself; it does not extend to any ideas, systems, or factual information conveyed in the work.

Works That Have Not Been "Fixed in a Tangible Form" of Expression

If you want to protect something by copyright, you have to write it down, record it, paint it, save it to a hard drive, and so forth. To be copyrightable, it must be "fixed in a tangible form of expression" and must be "sufficiently permanent or stable to permit it to be perceived, reproduced, or otherwise communicated for a period of more than transitory duration."[23] So hand-drawn sketches would be copyrightable, but a sandcastle would not.

Example: If a writer improvises a character's speech, it will not be protected by copyright until she writes it down or otherwise records it.

It is important to note that you don't always have to fix your work "in tangible form" yourself. You could get someone else to do it at your direction or under your authority.[24]

Titles, Names, Short Phrases, and Slogans

These are the domain of trademarks, not copyright law. Copyright will not protect them. Nor will it protect:

- The name of an individual (including pseudonyms, pen names, or stage names).
- The title or subtitle of a work, such as a book, a song, or a pictorial, graphic, or sculptural work.
- The name of a business or organization.
- The name of a band or performing group.
- The name of a product or service.
- A domain name or URL.
- The name of a character.
- Catchwords or catchphrases.
- Mottos, slogans, or other short expressions.[25]

Example: You're trying to market your new zombie comic book, using the phrase "*The Crusin' Corpses*" on all of your promotional posters. Rather than turn to copyright law to protect that phrase, the best bet would be to try to register it as a trademark. Keep in mind that to be registered as a trademark, the phrase, word, or slogan would have to meet all of the requirements of a trademark, like identifying the source of a good or a service. (See Trademark Registration, p. 421.) However, the entire poster, phrase, and artwork *combined* could be copyrighted.

Familiar Symbols or Designs; Mere Variations of Typographic Ornamentation, Lettering, or Coloring

In other words, you will not be able to copyright a plain blue triangle. As in the previous example, you may be able to get trademark protection for a symbol that would otherwise not be copyrightable. However, if you made an animated film out of blue circles and the selection and arrangement of those simple shapes was significantly creative, you might be able to register the copyright to your animation (but not the blue triangles themselves). If you're confused, think of it this way: a blue dot might not be protectable under copyright law, but a pointillist painting is (unless it's from the 19th century, in which case any copyright it had has likely expired. Sorry, Seurat!).

Raw Data

Copyright protection is unavailable for raw data. For instance, you will not be able to protect:

- Mere listings of ingredients or contents.
- "Works consisting entirely of information that is common property and containing no original authorship."
- "Standard calendars, height and weight charts, tape measures and rulers, and lists or tables taken from public documents or other common sources."[26]

Historical Facts and Theories

Despite the fact that the author may have invested a good deal of time and money researching a subject, historical facts and theories are also unprotected by copyright law.

It may seem unfair, but just because you've spent time and effort laboriously researching a topic does not mean that you can copyright that research.[27] However, you certainly can copyright the text that contains that writing. As a result, you can't use copyright law to stop someone from reading your well-researched graphic novel and copying the facts and other data that you, alone, have uncovered. You may be able to sue for copyright infringement when that person copies the words, pictures, and structure that you've used to express your research.

> **Example**: You spend 10 years researching and drawing your book: *E.T. on the Grassy Knoll*, a groundbreaking graphic novel which demonstrates that John F. Kennedy was actually killed by extraterrestrials. Although your book will be protected by copyright, your actual theory will not be. Another artist could read your book and create his own book *Extraterrestrial Presidential Assassinations*. As long as he didn't copy your artwork, text, or other *expression*, he would not be infringing your copyright even though he developed his theory based upon reading your book.

Ideas, Themes, Concepts

Copyright Law Does Not Protect Ideas! This is, perhaps, one of the hardest concepts for many artists to grasp. Copyright only protects an idea's expression, not the idea or concept itself.

As a result, one of the problems copyright law must constantly struggle with is how to determine where an "idea" stops and "copyrightable expression" begins. As one court pointed out: "The line [lies] somewhere between the author's idea and the precise form in which he wrote it down... protection covers the 'pattern' of the work... the sequence of events, and the development of the interplay of characters."[28]

Example: The *idea* of a group of superheroes who have been forced into retirement by "anti-superhero" legislation is not copyrightable; it is capable of being expressed in any number of ways (e.g. *The Incredibles* or the numerous Marvel Comics featuring the "Superhuman Registration Act"). However, a fully-expressed comic book that is built around that idea—like *Watchmen* (Moore/Gibbons)—is protectable by copyright, and so is its constituent script and pictures.

For methods of idea protection, see *A Comic Creator's Guide to Protecting Ideas*, p. 390.

Procedures, Methods, Systems, Processes, Principles, Discoveries, or Devices

Systems, processes, methods, procedures, and devices may be protected, but not by copyright law. You need to turn to patent or trade secret law, not copyright law, for help.

Example: Beard O' Brush, invents a great new system for "flattening" comic book panels. He cannot use copyright law to stop other people from using his system (but he might use copyright to protect any code he writes to accomplish that task).

Work in Which the Copyright Has Expired

Copyright protection expires after a certain amount of time. (See Copyright Duration, p. 361.) Once a copyright expires, the copyright is in the *public domain,* and anybody can freely use the copyrighted work without the permission of the former copyright owner.

Works Created by the U.S. Government

Works created by the U.S. government are not protected by copyright.[29] A work of the U.S. government is "a work prepared by an officer or employee of the United States government as part of that person's official duties."[30]

Example: The Penciller wants to use photographs from NASA's Hubble telescope as her comic book cover for *Stellar D'Oro—The Cookie from the Milky Way*. She may do so without seeking NASA's permission because NASA is a federal agency and its images are generally not copyrighted. She must, however, be careful when using those images for commercial purposes, so as not to give the appearance that NASA is endorsing the particular product or service. Restrictions on endorsement fall outside of copyright law and must be analyzed under right of publicity, trademark law, or particular federal statutes that may prohibit the appearance of commercial endorsement by a federal agency.

In contrast to U.S. government works, *state* government works *may* (depending upon state law) be protected by copyright law. Nor does the law prevent independent contractors, working on behalf of the United States government, from owning the copyright to their works.

Be careful here. Even though the U.S. government cannot create a copyrighted work, it can *hold* the copyright assigned to it by others. This is why, when using material from the U.S. government, you should still verify that the material is not copyrighted.

GEN-AI Works without Sufficient Human Authorship (Caution)

The U.S. Copyright Office reinforces the **human authorship principle** in its Compendium of U.S. Copyright Office Practices, stating: "To qualify as a work of 'authorship' a work must be created by a human being. [...]Works that do not satisfy this requirement are not copyrightable"[31] A human may obtain a copyright for a work with GEN-AI elements, but the authorship of that work must be the product of a human. However, new software is allowing human creators to control the interim steps of an AI-generated work. When that happens, and the human has more control over how a graphic is created by GEN-AI, the Copyright Office has started to grant registration to such works. (See Chap. 3, Using Gen-AI in Comics, p. ##.)

Scènes à Faire

Scènes à faire (French for "scenes to be made") are common themes typical of an artistic genre that appear in numerous works. "*Scènes à faire* are unprotectable elements that follow naturally from a work's theme rather than from an author's creativity."[32] "Incidents, characters, or settings which are as a practical matter indispensable, or at least standard, in the treatment of a given topic are *scènes à faire*."[33] Furthermore, "thematic concepts... which necessarily must follow from certain plot situations" are not entitled to copyright protection.[34] In short, they're like ideas: "Under the [*scènes à*] *faire* doctrine, when certain commonplace expressions are indispensable and naturally associated with the treatment of a given idea, those expressions are treated like ideas and therefore not protected by copyright."[35]

Example: Quill is writing a superhero chase sequence: she has her characters battling over the skyline of Manhattan. Because this setting is so common to the super powered hero comic book genre, she need not be concerned that she will infringe the copyright of any particular book. Although the *scènes à faire* doctrine will allow her to use the concept of a skyline-showdown without fear of copyright infringement, she must be careful not to use the same dialogue, characters, or choice of panel layout that are used in another comic book, as these may be protected by copyright.

CREATIVE COMMONS COPYRIGHT LICENSES

Much of this book is designed to help you protect the monopoly rights in your copyright. And let me be clear: if you hope to sell your movie one day, you should maintain strong copyright protections over your work. However, sometimes an artist wants to contribute their work to the public at large in a manner that encourages remixing, repurchasing, and its inclusion as a building block for other works. This is where Creative Commons (CC) copyright comes in. CC is a system of copyright licenses that allows for various degrees of public use of the protected work, often with far fewer restrictions than traditional copyright licenses. Comic Creators may benefit from CC copyright licensing by being able to use a work protected by the CC license without paying licensing fees to the original creator. A database of CC images may be found in https://search.creativecommons.org/.

But don't just grab and go! A few key points first: CC is not the same thing as public domain! In fact, CC licenses require attribution for the original author and may limit the uses to which the CC-protected material may be used. It's important to identify the specific type of CC license that governs the protection of the work before a filmmaker includes it in their own. There are currently six kinds of Creative Commons licenses, each with varying degrees of permission:[36]

1. "**CC BY 4.0**": This kind of license allows both commercial and noncommercial use of the work. The scope of this license is quite broad: the work covered by the CC BY 4.0 may be used for purposes of distribution, remixing, adaptation, and building upon it in any medium. The original creator must be credited, if their name is given, as well as notice of their copyright in the material, a link to their material, and various disclosures, such as whether you modify the original work and which CC license governs their work.
2. "**CC BY-SA**": This license has a similar scope to the CC BY license, above, with the added requirement that any derivative works created from CC BY-SA works must be distributed under the same or compatible license.
3. "**CC BY-NC**": once more, the scope of use is similar; however, with the CC BY-NC license, the protected work may not be used for commercial purposes.
4. "**CC BY-NC-SA**": this license is a remix of numbers 2 and 3; not only you cannot use the final work for commercial purposes, but you must also allow your work to be governed by the same license as the work from which it is derived or uses.
5. "**CC BY-ND**": this license curtails the scope of what you may do with the covered work: you may copy and redistribute it, even commercially. However, if you decide to use the work and remix it, transform it, or build upon it, you may *not* distribute your final product.
6. "**CC BY-NC-ND**": the most restrictive CC license of all, this license allows only the *noncommercial* copying and distribution of the material.

Earlier versions of many of these licenses had slightly different requirements. Before using any CC-covered work, make sure you understand the requirements of the license under which it was granted. For more information on CC licenses, see https://creativecommons.org/.

COPYRIGHT OWNERSHIP

Who Is the Owner?

The person or entity that creates a copyrighted work is considered the "author."

- If two or more people jointly create a work, they may be joint authors.
- In addition to people, companies can be authors.
- When a work qualifies as a 'work made for hire'—whether created by an employee within the scope of employment or by an independent contractor under a written work-for-hire agreement—the company, and not the individual creator, is legally considered the author of the work. (See Work Made for Hire, p. 350.)

JOINT AUTHORS AND JOINT WORKS

Copyright law defines a joint work as "a work prepared by two or more authors with the intention that their contributions be merged into inseparable or interdependent parts of a unitary whole."[37] The authors of a joint work are, not surprisingly, called joint authors.

When two or more authors work together to create a comic book, copyright law may consider them to *be* **joint authors**. To be considered a joint author, each co-author must:

- Contribute copyrightable elements to the joint work, and
- At the time the work was created,[38] **intend to merge their own contributions** inseparably or interdependently with the contributions of the other co-authors to form a unified whole.
- Have some degree of control over the creative work (only some courts require this).
    - To figure out what the creators intended, courts may look to a variety of factors, including "whether the parties intended to be credited or billed as co-authors, the parties' view of decision-making and creative control, and the right to enter into third party contracts."[39]

Joint authors have certain rights under copyright law; if the authors want to change these rights, they need to do so by a contract between them, such as a Collaboration Agreement. (See Collaboration Agreement, p. 119) The contract must be in writing and signed by all authors.

Copyrightable Contributions Required for Joint Authorship

Copyright law generally requires that each joint author's contributions be copyrightable in its own right. If you have one writer and one "idea person" you have only one author—the writer—unless the agreement specifies otherwise. "To be an author, one must supply more than mere direction or ideas: one must 'translate [...] an idea into a fixed, tangible expression entitled to copyright protection.'"[40]

As one court pointed out:

> [...] the person with noncopyrightable material who proposes to join forces with a skilled writer to produce a copyrightable work is free to make a contract to disclose his or her material in return for assignment of part ownership of the resulting copyright.[41]

However, not all courts agree that each joint author must contribute copyrightable work. (See Spawning a Copyright, p. 350.)

> **Example**: Connor and Xander are working together on the comic Hypno-Robot-Zombie-Vampires from Venus. Connor just contributes the idea for the book, and Xander does all of the writing and illustration. Because ideas are not copyrightable, Connor cannot be considered a joint author. To share in the ownership of the copyright to the comic, Connor must do so by entering into a contract with Xander.

Is Everybody Who Contributes to a Work Considered a Joint Author?

Not everyone who contributes to a comic book is a joint author. Some courts require joint authors to have some sort of control over the project—to be the "mastermind" of the project, if you will. For instance, technical consultants and copy editors would not be considered joint authors.[42] In a case involving the authorship of the film Malcolm X, the 9th Circuit held that a technical consultant was not a joint author, even though he "helped to rewrite, to make more authentic" the script and the movie. "A creative contribution [without more] does not suffice to establish authorship of the movie."[43]

What Are the Rights of a Joint Author?

When someone is a joint author, he or she has the following rights (again, unless a contract says otherwise):

- Each joint author is entitled to an equal and undivided interest in the copyright with the other joint authors. **Note**: Their contributions do not have to be equal, and they will still share equally with other joint authors!

- Joint authors may grant nonexclusive licenses to the joint work. But ALL joint authors must agree to grant an exclusive copyright license to the joint work.
- Any joint author who sells or licenses the joint work must pay other joint authors an equal share of the money.
- Joint authors are not liable to each other for copyright infringement.
- Most courts require a signed contract to change a joint author's rights from those guaranteed by copyright law.

Example: Connor and Xander bring Natali in to create a comic book with them—again without a contract. This time Connor creates dozens of new pages, as does Natali. Everyone is a joint author. They are all excited and want to sell the comic. Connor and Xander go to New York and submit the script to Big Publishing, Inc., a major comic book publishing company. Back at home, Natali gets a call from her uncle, the president of Fly-By-Night Publishing, a would-be comic book company whose only claim to fame so far has been the production of several promotional comics for local car dealerships.

Fly-by-Night publishing offers to purchase nonexclusive publishing rights to the book for $100, and Natali accepts this offer over the phone without first talking to Connor or Xander. Can she do this?

Unfortunately, yes. Natali has granted a nonexclusive license to her uncle for $100. This means that he can publish the comic book. Of course, the other joint authors can also grant nonexclusive licenses to other publishing companies as well. However, the practical effect of Natali's grant is that Big Publishing, Inc. will never publish the comic book—no publishing company will invest money in printing, promotion, distribution, etc. as long as someone else has the right to make the exact same comic book as well. It is no consolation to her co-authors that Sally must split the $100 three ways with her other joint authors.

To avoid this disaster, the three of them should have had a contract that specified that any and all licenses must be granted only with the unanimous (or at least a majority) approval of the joint authors. (See Collaboration Agreement, p. 119.)

There is one consolation: online digital comic book publication is often nonexclusive, meaning that you can often publish your digital title on more than one online portal.

> **CASE SQUIB**
>
> **SPAWNING A COPYRIGHT**
>
> Does your contribution have to SPAWN a copyright in order to be joint author?
>
> There is some disagreement in the courts as to whether each putative author must contribute copyrightable content in order to be considered a joint author. The court handling the now-famous dispute between Neil Gaiman and Todd McFarlane over the question of joint authorship in the "Medieval Spawn" character reasoned that ideas alone might be enough:
>
> > The contents of a comic book are typically the joint work of four artists—the writer, the penciller who creates the artwork (McFarlane), the inker (also McFarlane, in the case of Spawn No. 9, but it would often be a different person from the penciller) who makes a black and white plate of the artwork, and the colorist who colors it. The finished product is copyrightable, yet one can imagine cases in which none of the separate contributions of the four collaborating artists would be. The writer might have contributed merely a stock character (not copyrightable, as we're about to see) that achieved the distinctiveness required for copyrightability only by the combined contributions of the penciller, the inker, and the colorist, with each contributing too little to have by his contribution alone carried the stock character over the line into copyright land.[44]
>
> However, other courts have held that contributing ideas alone are not enough to make someone a joint author:
>
> > a putative joint author's contribution must be independently copyrightable. As such, 'ideas, refinements, and suggestions, standing alone,' are not sufficient. Rather, a party asserting joint authorship must point to specific contributions that were fixed in a tangible medium.[45]

WORK MADE FOR HIRE

Normally, the person who creates a work is considered the author and will own the copyright as well. *Not so for a work made for hire.* The copyright to a work made for hire is initially owned by the employer or other hiring party, *not by the artist who created it.*

For comic book creators, there are only two ways a work gets to be a work made for hire:[29]

Employees: Any copyrighted work created by employees within the scope of their employment is considered work made for hire and is automatically owned by the employer.

> **Example**: Casey is employed full-time by SPAM Comics, Inc., drawing illustrations for marketing materials and writing ad copy for the comic books they publish. Anytime Casey creates marketing materials for their employer, the copyright to that work is automatically owned by SPAM Comics as it is in the scope of employment. Even if Casey creates that work at home, if it is for a SPAM Comics project, the copyright will vest initially with SPAM Comics. However, if Casey works on their own graphic novel—a project that is separate and distinct from any SPAM Comics projects—they will initially own the copyright to that graphic novel. To be on the safe side, Casey may want to document that their graphic novel project is not connected with any SPAM Comics project, nor does it use any elements that they created in the course of working on any SPAM Comics project.

Independent Contractors: For an independent contractor's work on a comic book to be considered a work made for hire, he or she must sign a written agreement explicitly stating that the work is a "work made for hire." Without both the signed, written contract and the clause that says the work produced is "work made for hire," the independent contractor's work is NOT a work made for hire. Additionally, the work created by the independent contractor must fall within a list of specifically enumerated types of work (comic books may be considered "collective works" and thus may fall within this category.)

> **Example**: Casey quits SPAM Comics and works as an independent contractor for several comic book publishers. Casey is commissioned on a project from Heroic Tales Publishing, creating cover art for a new comic book series. Casey does all the work at their home studio on their own equipment and, with the exception of the delivery date, on their own schedule. Casey is clearly an independent contractor. To own Casey's work product as a work made for hire, Heroic Tales Publishing better have a written contract with Casey, which Casey must sign. The contract must expressly state that any work they produce for them is considered "work made for hire," a "work for hire," or a "specially ordered and commissioned work." If Casey doesn't sign such a contract, at most, Heroic Tales will have an implied non-exclusive license to publish the work, but they will not own it as a work for hire.[46]

The Bad Old Days of Work for Hire

Back in the day, when Superman, Spiderman, and their superhero pals were just getting started, the 1909 Copyright Act was the law of the land. Under this old-school law, if an independent contractor created something at the "**instance and expense**" of the hiring party, it was considered "work for hire."[47]

> A work [was] made at the hiring party's "instance and expense" when the employer induces the creation of the work and has the right to direct and

supervise the manner in which the work is carried out. The right to direct and supervise the manner in which work is created need never be exercised.[48]

Fortunately for creators, that old law is not applicable to new works; today, work for hire is now a much harder relationship to form and requires more than just hiring someone for your benefit and at your expense. The new work-for-hire law—in effect since 1/1/78—is much more independent contractor-friendly.

Who Is an Employee for Purposes of Works Made for Hire?

Today an employee's work product (created within the scope of their employment) is automatically a work made for hire; it is critical to determine just who is an employee and the scope of their employment. This may not be as easy as you think. Merely writing the word "employee" on a contract does not automatically create an employee–employer relationship.

In determining who is an employee for work-made-for-hire purposes, courts will look at the following factors:[49]

- The hiring party's right to control the manner and means by which the product is accomplished.
- The skill required to make the product.
- The source of the instrumentalities and tools.
- The location of the work.
- The duration of the relationship between the parties.
- Whether the hiring party has the right to assign additional projects to the hired party.
- The extent of the hired party's discretion over when and how long to work.
- The method of payment.
- The hired party's role in hiring and paying assistants.
- Whether the work is part of the regular business of the hiring party.
- Whether the hiring party is in business.
- The provision of employee benefits.
- The tax treatment of the hired party.

Determining Scope of Employment

Let's face it, in today's world, most of us are gig workers with a side hustle. So, let's say you're employed by a comic book publisher to do whatever needs to be done on a particular day, which could mean anything from inking, coloring, and writing dialogue to managing social media when everybody else is at a convention. In other words, whatever they need you to do.

In a situation like that, how do you determine what your scope of employment is? If virtually everything is within the scope of employment, how do you know whether the graphic novel you're writing on the side would be owned as a work for hire by your employer? A court deciding on the issue might ask the following questions:

- Is the work you made the kind that you are hired to make? In other words, were you hired to create comic book content?
- When you created the graphic novel, was it within the time and location that was controlled by your employer?
- When you created the graphic novel, were you at least in part motivated by helping your employer or furthering your employer's interests?[50]

Work for Hire—Employee in California

If you sign a writer to an independent contractor work-for-hire agreement in California, you must treat them like an employee, which means you could be liable for unpaid taxes, disability payments, workers' compensation, and other costs attendant on an employer/employee relationship. Furthermore, in California, the presumption is that any person providing labor for money (like a paid crew member) is an employee and not an independent contractor, unless the hiring party can show:

A. The person is free from the control and direction of the hiring entity in connection with the performance of the work, both under the contract for the performance of the work and in fact.

B. The person performs work that is outside the usual course of the hiring entity's business.

C. The person is customarily engaged in an independently established trade, occupation, or business of the same nature as that involved in the work performed.[51]

This is the infamous "ABC" law that took effect in 2020. Under it, a plumber called to fix a leaky sink at the publishing company would be an independent contractor, but any professional artist working under the direction of the editor should be classified as an employee.

Type of Works That Qualify as Work for Hire

All work made by an *employee* within the scope of their employment qualifies as a work-for-hire. However, making matters more complex, only certain types of *independent contractor*-produced work qualify as work for hire:

- Contributions to a collective work
- Parts of a motion picture or other audiovisual work
- Translations
- Supplementary works
- Compilations
- Instructional texts

- Tests or as answer materials for a test
- Atlases[52]

This means that if you've hired an independent contractor to create a type of work that is not on the above list, it is **not** a work for hire, despite whether there is a written, signed, "work-for-hire" agreement.

You've probably noticed that comic books and graphic novels are not on that list. Don't breathe a sigh of relief just yet: courts have interpreted artwork for comics as "contributions to a collective work" and thus can be created as a work for hire by independent contractors.[53]

A CRITICAL ISSUE: WORK MADE FOR HIRE

This is one of the most important legal issues in this book!

From a publishing company standpoint, if it is hiring artists to work on a comic book series which it owns (e.g., Marvel Comics hires an artist to work on one of the many Spiderman books), all of the contributions of its artists and writers should be created as works made for hire.

Their contracts should:

- Explicitly state that the work these employees or contractors are performing for the publishing company is a "work made for hire," "a work for hire," or "a work specially ordered and commissioned," and
- The contracts should be signed by the independent contractor.
- It should be written before the work has been created. While it's true that some jurisdictions, like New York (2d Cir.), allow the contract to be written after the work has begun if and only if that written contract memorializes an agreement that the parties discussed and consented to before the work was started, some jurisdictions require the written contract first. Better to be safe and get it in writing right *before* the creative juices start flowing. No Exceptions.

Work Made for Hire/Copyright Assignment Clause

If you want to create a work for hire relationship, you should reinforce your work for hire language by including an "alternate assignment" clause to ensure that the copyright is effectively transferred from the comic book creator to the hiring part. This way, if the work isn't considered a work made for hire, the hiring party still gets the copyright through the alternate copyright assignment clause.

"But wait," you might be thinking, "if I can just get the copyright by having the creator assign it to me, why bother with all that work-for-hire stuff?"

That's because a work-for-hire arrangement is often the cleanest way to acquire a copyright due to a counterintuitive provision of U.S. copyright law: "Termination of Transfer." (See Termination of Transfer, p. 43.) In brief, any copyright assignment or license can be terminated after a certain period (often 35 years from the grant of the copyright), despite what the contract says! However, this isn't true for works for hire: the author and original copyright owner in a work made for hire is the contracting party, not the artist.

But since work-for-hire arrangements are situational (and require key facts to be established), it's a good idea to include a detailed copyright assignment clause, just in case.

> **Example**: "Artist acknowledges and agrees that all of their contributions to the Comic Book, including, but not limited to writing, illustrating, inking, and any other result of the artist's services provided under this contract (the 'Results and Proceeds'), are created as 'Works Made for Hire,' with all copyright and other rights thereto vesting initially in the publishing company. Accordingly, the publishing company shall be considered the sole and exclusive author and copyright owner of the Results and Proceeds and of the Comic Book. To the extent, if any, that ownership of the Comic Book produced hereunder or the Results and Proceeds of Artist's services do not immediately vest in the publishing company by virtue of this Agreement, Artist hereby immediately assigns to the publishing company all rights (including all rights of copyright) of every kind and character in and to the Comic Book and the results and proceeds of Artist's services. Artist hereby waives all 'moral rights,' 'droit moral,' and similar rights. All rights hereunder assigned shall be assigned in perpetuity, and such an assignment shall be irrevocable. This effect of this clause shall survive any termination of this Agreement."

TIP: If you are trying to create a work for hire, include a copyright assignment clause in every work-for-hire agreement. To ensure that the copyright is fully transferred to your publishing company, make sure that the language of this clause transfers all material that was made for your comic book even before the contract was signed. A phrase such as "Writer assigns the copyright to the work performed under this Agreement" might not transfer a script written by the writer prior to the agreement being negotiated and signed.

Duration of Work Made for Hire

Works made for hire have a shorter copyright life span than do works that are not made for hire. For any work made for hire created after January 1, 1978, copyright protection will last for 95 years from the year of first publication or 120 years from the year of creation, whichever expires first.

LICENSING AND ASSIGNING THE COPYRIGHT

A copyright license is the grant of a portion of copyright (usually limited by time, geography medium, etc.). The person giving the license is the **licensor;** the person receiving the license is the **licensee**.

> **Example**: Action Render Team, LLC., the **licensor**, grants a license to Mackerel Manufacturing, Inc., the **licensee**, to manufacture and distribute action figures based on A.R.T.'s "Maggot Man" comic book character.

An **exclusive license**, also known as an **assignment**, is a license that gives the licensee the exclusive power to a certain right. It is a transfer of ownership of a copyright or any of the exclusive copyright rights. Even if it is called a "transfer of ownership," that transfer may be limited in duration, scope, geography, or any other way you can think of. Once an exclusive license is granted, the licensor no longer has any power to grant another license to that right or to exercise that granted right herself. An exclusive copyright license must be in writing and signed by the licensor.[54]

> **Example**: Action Render Team, LLC is negotiating a publishing deal for its book *Wombats in Combat* with Pusillanimous Publishing, LLC. The publishing agreement grants Pusillanimous the exclusive rights to publish *Wombats* in comic books, soft and hard cover, and as a graphic novel. This is an assignment, because the rights to reproduce, distribute, and create derivative works are all granted to Pusillanimous. The assignment may be limited by territory (North America) or duration (as long as the books remain in print). Because it is a copyright assignment, it must be in writing and signed by A.R.T. to be effective.

A nonexclusive license is a license that may be granted to any number of licensees at the same time. A nonexclusive license may be granted orally or may even be implied from conduct. The holder of a nonexclusive license may not grant licenses to the work to others without the copyright owner's permission.

TO TRANSFER A COPYRIGHT, YOU MUST GET IT IN WRITING

The Law: "17 USC §204. Execution of transfers of copyright ownership (a) A transfer of copyright ownership, other than by operation of law, is not valid unless an instrument of conveyance, or a note or memorandum of the transfer, is in writing and signed by the owner of the rights conveyed or such owner's duly authorized agent...."

As one court put it: "The rule is really quite simple: If the copyright holder agrees to transfer ownership to another party, that party must get the copyright holder to sign a piece of paper saying so. It doesn't have to be the Magna Carta; a one-line pro forma statement will do."[55] However, that one-line statement must be clear and unambiguous, clearly transferring the copyright.[56]

Termination of Transfer

One seemingly odd wrinkle in copyright law is the termination of transfer provisions, which allows a valid and otherwise irrevocable copyright assignment or license to be revoked after a certain time by the copyrighted work's author or her heirs. Once a copyright transfer has been terminated under this provision, no new derivative works can be made from the terminated copyright. However, works prepared while the copyright license or assignment was in effect can still be exploited as per the original agreement. NOTE: Termination of Transfer doesn't apply to works for hire: the author and original copyright owner in a work made for hire is the contracting party, not the artist herself, so there is no interest in the artist for her to terminate.

> **Example**: Xander assigns the copyright to his patriotic comic book property *Captain Constitution and Bill O'Rights* to Mumble Publishing, which over a 35-year period makes a movie and a television series based on Xander's work. Even though the comic book acquisition agreement between Xander and Mumble explicitly states that the copyright transfer is irrevocable and lasts for the duration of the copyright, Xander can still revoke the copyright starting at the end of 35 years from when it was transferred! Mumble can still exploit any comic book, movie, or television series it had made *prior* to the termination, in accordance with the terms of the comic book acquisition agreement. However, once Xander revokes the copyright, Mumble can't make any more derivative works from the comic book (additional comics, spin-offs, video games, books, merchandise, etc.) without relicensing the copyright from Xander.

Unlike assigned copyrights, the copyright created as a work for hire is *not* subject to the termination-of-transfer provisions. That means that if a comic book artist signs work-for-hire agreement with the publishing company and then creates a roster of new characters as part of his assignment, all those characters will be owned by the publishing company. In 35 years' time, the artist will ***not*** be able to terminate this transfer... Because he never had the copyright the first place! Copyright law views the publishing company as the original author.

Of course, if you are hiring other artists to work for you, you *want* them to sign work-for-hire agreements so you will be deemed the author of their work. Whether work for hire is onerous or a business necessity depends upon whether you're commissioning the work or creating the work.

> **Example**: Connor is hired by Mumble Publishing on a work for hire basis to write the comic book *Marzi Pam: the Confectionery Crusader.* Thirty-five years later, he hears about Xander's success in terminating the transfer for *Captain Constitution*, as described in the earlier Example. Connor tries to terminate the transfer of rights to *Marzi Pam* but fails; unlike Xander, who assigned the rights in his comic book, Connor created his comic book as a work for hire for Mumble Publishing. When a work is created as a work for hire, the copyright originally vests in the contracting party (here, Mumble

Publishing). The law considers Mumble Publishing the author of *Marzi Pam* from the moment of the script's creation. Since Connor never had any rights in the comic book in the first place, he can't get the rights back.

CASE SQUIB: CAPT. AMERICA: COPYRIGHT CRUSADER

The termination of transfer provision has caused more fights in the comic book world than Red Skull's Nazi Army! For instance, Joe Simon, creator of Captain America, was able to use it to terminate his grant to Marvel Comics of rights in his star-spangled Avenger... even though he had signed an after-the-fact contract, stating that it was created as a work for hire!

Wait, what?! You may be asking yourself, didn't you just say that work for hire was not subject to termination of transfer?

Yes, I did. However, the facts are a bit strange here.

Captain America was created by Simon as an independently created project, which he then shopped around and sold to Timely Comics for fixed page rates of 25% of the profits.[57] In 1969, after several years of litigation against Timely's successors in interest, Marvel Comics, in which Simon contended that he was the sole author of Captain America, he finally dropped his case in exchange for a cash settlement. As part of the settlement Simon (and Marvel comic artist Jack Kirby, who worked on Cap'n as well) both signed agreements stating that Captain America had been created as work made for hire. He also assigned to Marvel "any and all right, title and interest he may have or control or which he has had or controlled in [Captain America]."[58]

Pretty iron-clad, right?

Nope. Enter the termination of transfer provisions, which state "Termination of the grant may be effected notwithstanding any agreement to the contrary, including an agreement to make a will or to make any future grant."[59]

Thirty years after he signed that settlement agreement, he again sought to terminate the transfer of his rights to Captain America. Understandably, litigation ensued.

Despite a contract signed by Simon in which he affirmed that he created Captain America as a work for hire, he was able to present evidence to the contrary that the character was not, in fact, created under a work-for-hire relationship. And since it was not a work-for-hire relationship, despite what his signed contract said, the copyright was transferred, and thus could be terminated. The court ruled:

CASE SQUIB—*continued*

> We hold that an agreement made subsequent to a work's creation which retroactively deems it a 'work for hire' constitutes an 'agreement to the contrary' under §304(c)(5) of the 1976 Act. Therefore, Simon is not bound by the statement in the Settlement Agreement that he created the Works as an employee for hire. Because Simon has proffered admissible evidence that he did not create the Works as an employee for hire [Simon could proceed with the termination of transfer].[60]

Marvel comics was forced, once more, to settle with Simon over the rights to Captain America.

This case is important for two reasons:

1. The termination of transfer provisions are extremely strong, even in the face of seemingly ironclad agreements to the contrary.
2. A court will look at the facts surrounding whether or not a work-for-hire relationship actually exists and will not merely rely on the parties stating that there was such a relationship.

So, in a sense, Captain America fought for both America's freedom and the freedom for creator's rights.

Termination of Transfer Statutory Provisions

The two sections of the copyright law that govern how and when a copyright transfer may be terminated are 17 USC §203 and 17 USC §304(c).

Generally speaking, §203 deals with licenses and transfers of copyright that happened after January 1, 1978. §304(c) deals with licenses and transfers of copyright that occurred prior to January 1, 1978.[61]

Any work that you transfer now[62] and assign to a publishing company or other licensee or assignee may be terminated:

> During a period of five years beginning at the end of thirty-five years from the date of execution of the grant; or, if the grant covers the right of publication of the work, the period begins at the end of thirty-five years from the date of publication of the work under the grant or at the end of forty years from the date of execution of the grant, whichever term ends earlier.[63]

To terminate the transfer to copyright, the owners of such "termination interest" must send a signed notice to the licensee or assignee terminating the right to the transferred copyright.

It's important to note that it's not just the original author who can terminate the transfer: if the author is dead, the author's spouse, children, and grandchildren may also serve notice to get the copyright back.

If you want to cancel a copyright grant under Section 203, your notice must include these details:

- **State the Reason:** Begin by clearly saying that you're canceling the copyright agreement under Section 203.
- **List the Affected Parties:** Provide the names of everyone whose copyright rights are being canceled. If their rights have been transferred to someone else, include the successor's name and the mailing addresses where the notice is being sent.
- **Give the Dates:** Include the date when the original agreement was signed. If the agreement also allowed for publishing a work, mention when that work was first published.
- **Identify the Work(s):** For every work affected by this cancellation, list its title and the name of the author (or all the authors if it's a joint work), and the original copyright registration number.
- **Describe the Agreement:** Add a short explanation that clearly identifies which copyright agreement or grant you're canceling.
- **Set the Effective Date:** Clearly state the date when the termination will take effect.
- **Include Information for Deceased Authors:** If you're canceling an agreement that was signed by a deceased author and the cancellation is being made by their heirs or successors, list those individuals' names and explain how they are related to the deceased author.[64]

Example: Beard-O-Brush creates a comic book: *Dino-Stores: Heart-Pounding Adventures in Jurassic Retail.* He assigns all the rights to *Dino-Stores* to Paleolithic Publishing in 2014, in exchange for a royalty from every book, film, video game, and other merchandise made from *Dino-Stores.* The publishing agreement he signs contains a clause that reads "Beard-O-Brush assigns all his rights in perpetuity, hereby waiving the right to terminate this copyright grant pursuant copyright law."

Seems pretty iron clad, right? After all, Beard-O is waiving his right to recapture his copyright!

Paleolithic Publishing finally publishes Beard-O's work in 2015. Thirty-five years after 2015, in the year 2050, Beard-O can terminate his copyright interest, *despite the apparently ironclad language in the agreement to the contrary.*

However, there's an important note here, if Beard-O signs a subsequent contract with Paleolithic Publishing, in which he revokes and re-grants the copyright (presumably for more money), this termination clock gets reset back to the beginning, and the 35-year period following publication, begins to run anew.[65]

TERMINATION TOOLS

Creative Commons.org has developed a "termination of transfer tool," which might help issue spot when you can terminate the transfer of your copyright.

See: https://rightsback.org/.[66]

Keep in mind however, that termination of transfer provisions are complex and a thorough discussion of them is beyond the scope of this work. If you need to terminate the transfer of your copyright interest, it is advised that you seek an attorney experienced in the matter to help you.

COPYRIGHT DURATION

Like a gallon of milk, every copyright has a "use by" date. After that date (called the "term of copyright"), the copyright expires, and the work goes into the **public domain**, where the work can be used by anybody, regardless of the wishes of the original creator (or their descendants).

No copyright permission is required to use a work whose term has expired and is in the public domain.

The copyright's life span is called a **term**[67]; and its duration has changed many times over the last hundred years. For the majority of the 20th century (pre-1978), a copyright was given an initial term, which could then be extended if the copyright was properly renewed with the government. Although the copyrights of modern works (created from 1978 on) no longer need to be registered or have that registration renewed,[68] for older works the renewal status of a copyright may need to be researched. How long the copyright lasts for a work is largely dependent upon:

- What kind of work is it (sound recordings have different terms; see chart below).
- When the work was made.
- If the work has been published.
- If the first publication was outside of the United States.
- If the work was first published in a country outside the United States that is not a party to certain international IP treaties.
- If the copyright to the work needed to be renewed and whether the copyright was, in fact, renewed.
- When the author of the work died.
- Whether it was a work made for hire.
- Whether the work was created anonymously or under a pseudonym.

To keep it simple, here are some of the more common copyright lifespans for works:

Copyright Duration of Works Originally Created on or after January 1, 1978

- These works are protected the moment they are created and embodied in a tangible form.
- The copyright lasts until 70 years after the author dies.
- For joint works, the term lasts for 70 years after the last surviving author dies.
- For works made for hire, the duration of copyright will be 95 years from publication or 120 years from creation, whichever comes first.

Copyright Duration of Works Originally Created Before January 1, 1978, but Not Published or Registered by That Date

- The duration is the same as the preceding section. The life-plus-70-year or 95/120-year terms will apply to these copyrights as well.
- In no case will the term of copyright for works in this category expire before December 31, 2002.
- For works published on or before December 31, 2002, the term of copyright will not expire before December 31, 2047.

Copyright Duration of Works Originally Created and Published between 1964 and 1977

- Protection started when the work was published with a copyright notice.
- The duration of protection is 95 years from date of publication with copyright notice.
- Copyright renewal was automatic.
- Registration was required.

Copyright Duration of Works Originally Created and Published between 1923 and 1963

- Protection started when work was published with a copyright notice.
- Protection is for 95 years from date of publication with copyright notice—but only if the copyright was properly renewed.
- Registration was required.

Copyright Duration of Works Originally Created and Published before 1928

- The work is likely in the public domain.

COPYRIGHT REGISTRATION

Registration is the most important step in protecting the copyright to your work; it is the process of filing your work along with information about it and its creator with the U.S. Copyright Office (**www.copyright.gov**) by submitting an online copyright registration form, paying a registration fee, and mailing in a sample of the work you're registering.

File Your Own © Registration (and Save $$)!

Some online services charge one hundred dollars or more to register a copyright; a lawyer might charge you several hundred. However, the government charges as little as $35 dollars. You want to save money? Try registering your copyrights by yourself. It really is quite simple. Give it a shot: go to www.copyright.gov. Once you set up an account, actual registration can take as little as ten minutes.

You know what? Why don't we let the Copyright Office explain it with their handy-dandy "**Copyright Registration Toolkit**": https://www.copyright.gov/intellectual-property-toolkits/copyright-registration-toolkit.pdf.[69]

Why Register the Copyright to Your Work?

Although registration is no longer a requirement of copyright protection, it does provide the following benefits:

- Copyright registration is usually required by publishing companies and other third parties who may have an interest in maintaining and protecting the comic book property.
- Registration establishes a public record of the copyright claim.
- Before an infringement suit may be filed in court, registration is necessary for works of U.S. origin.
- If registration is made before or within five years of publication, courts will start with the presumption that the copyright is valid and that all the facts stated in the certificate are correct.
- Registration allows the owner of the copyright to record the registration with the U.S. Customs Service for protection against the importation of infringing copies.
- If registration is made within three months after publication of your work or prior to an infringement of your work, you can seek *statutory damages and*

attorney's fees in an infringement lawsuit. Otherwise, you may be stuck with an award of actual damages and profits.

In other words, if you can prove that somebody willfully infringed your copyright after you had registered, you can ask the court to award you up $150,000.00 as well as legal fees you paid to your attorneys—even if you've never made a dime from selling your work before, and even if the infringer never made anywhere near that amount of money from selling the infringing work! Note, awarding you statutory damages is at the court's discretion, but you can't even ask for it if you haven't registered copyright. (See Copyright Infringement, p. 44.)

GRUW: GROUP REGISTRATION OF UNPUBLISHED WORKS

For visual, literary, or visual/literary works, the group registration option is a lifesaver for creators looking to register multiple works without the hassle. Imagine an author registering a bunch of essays, illustrations, or a mix of both—all in one go! The catch? Each work must be created by the same author(s), and the authorship statement for each work must match exactly. Oh, and don't forget to make sure the titles and file names match too, or you'll be in for some delays. This streamlined process is a godsend for comic book creators who churn out related works like there's no tomorrow.

Enter the U.S. Copyright Office's "GRUW" (Group Registration of Unpublished Works) option. You can register up to ten unpublished works if they meet the criteria: all works must be unpublished, created by the same author(s), and registered in the same administrative class. Each work needs its own title and must be submitted as an electronic file. Miss any of these steps, and your application might get the boot, requiring a new application with the appropriate fees and deposits. Just a heads-up, certain works like compilations, collective works, and architectural works aren't eligible for this group registration option.[70]

For more information on registering copyrights in comic books, comic strips, and cartoons, see: U.S. Copyright Office, (Information Circular 44) "Cartoons and Comic Strips": www.copyright.gov/circs/circ44.pdf.

LOOK OUT! GEN-AI and Copyright Registration

So, you used some GEN-AI to make your comic book. No big deal, right? RIGHT?!?

Actually, it is a big deal. Maybe a big enough deal that the Copyright Office will refuse to register your work. A long-standing Copyright Office policy restricts registration to works of "human authorship."

> **"300. The Human Authorship Requirement**." The U.S. Copyright Office will register an original work of authorship, provided that the work was created by a human being. The copyright law only protects "the fruits of intellectual labor" that "are founded in the creative powers of the mind." Trade-Mark Cases, 100 U.S. 82, 94 (1879). Because copyright law is limited to "original intellectual conceptions of the author," the Office will refuse to register a claim if it determines that a human being did not create the work. Burrow-Giles Lithographic Co. v. Sarony, 111 U.S. 53, 58 (1884).[71]

Comic creators who use GEN-AI must disclaim those AI components in their work in the copyright registration and the Copyright Office. The key to authorship is that it must be the product of a human mind; to paraphrase the U.S. Supreme Court in 1884, the work to be registered must be your own original mental conception, to which you give visible form.[72] "If a work's traditional elements of authorship were produced by a machine, the work lacks human authorship and the Office will not register it."[73]

However, you could get a registration on your comic book, even if its individual components are not registerable! Copyright law recognizes authorship in expressive, collection, selection, and arrangement of elements, even if those elements are not copyrighted. A collage of 19th century advertisements, for instance, would be registerable. Like the collage, your comic might be registerable, even if its individual panels were not. Which means that while your comic was protected by copyright, anyone could take the GEN-AI-created panels and put them on t-shirts, make their own comics with them, etc. Whatever was created by AI (without significant interim human authorship) drops out of the registration and is unprotected.

New Copyright Office rulings on AI are happening at a record pace and new software is allowing human creators to control the interim steps of an AI-generated work.[74] When that happens, and the human has more control over how a graphic is created by GEN-AI, the Copyright Office has started to grant registration to such works. At the time of this writing, it is still too early to draw the line where the line between human authorship (protectable) begins and unprotected GEN-AI ends. (See Chap. 3, Using Gen-AI in Comics, p. ##.)

Deposit Your Work—It's the Law!

Even if you don't want to register the copyright, it is a legal requirement that all copyrightable published works be deposited with the Copyright Office within three months of publication.[75] Failure to do so may expose you to a fines.

The Copyright Notice

Although it is no longer a requirement for copyright protection, it is advisable to include a copyright notice on all your copyrighted work to put would be infringers on alert that you are claiming copyright in your work. "Furthermore, in the event that a work is infringed, if the work carries a proper notice the court will not give any weight to a defendant's use of an innocent infringement defense—that is, to a claim that the defendant did not realize that the work was protected. An innocent infringement defense can result in a reduction in damages that the copyright owner would otherwise receive."[76]

How to Register Your Comic in Just 18 Easy Steps

You can register your comic book script and art separately, or together as a single work. If you want to do it yourself, here's what you do:

1. **Access & Account Setup:** Visit www.copyright.gov and click the Electronic Copyright Office (eCO) logo. Then log in or register as a new user.
2. **Initiate Your Claim:** From "Copyright Services," select "Register a New Claim" and click "Start Registration," using "Continue" after each selection.
3. **Work Type & Title:** Choose the appropriate category (e.g., Literary Work for text-based comics, Work of Visual Arts for pictorial works, or Single Serial Issue for a single comic periodical). Then click the "New *" tab to add the title (for Example, "The Naked Mole Rat's Revenge") and save it.
4. **Publication/Completion Details**: Indicate whether your work has been published. Provide the year of completion and, if applicable, the date and nation of first publication.
5. **Authors:** Enter the names and contributions of all authors by clicking "New" or "Add Me." For works made for hire, list the hiring party as the author.
6. **Claimant Information:** Specify who holds the copyright (for a self-created work, that's usually you; otherwise, provide the details of any transferee like a company or publisher).
7. **Disclosures & Limitations**: If your work includes previously registered or public domain material—or incorporates generative AI (GEN-AI) content—disclose this here. Clearly note which parts of your work were generated by AI and describe any creative human transformation applied.
8. **Rights, Permissions, & Contacts**: Provide contact information for managing copyright permissions, designate a correspondent for questions from the Copyright Office, and add the mailing address where the registration certificate should be sent.
9. **Special Handling (Optional) & Certification**: If you need expedited processing ("special handling"), select that option (additional fees apply). Finally, certify that you are the author, copyright claimant, or authorized agent by entering your name.
10. **Review & Submit**: Carefully review all entered information. Once satisfied, click "Add to Cart" to proceed to payment and complete your application.

You can submit an electronic copy of the work that you are registering, but even if you register online, if the Library of Congress requires a hard-copy deposit of your work, you must send what the Library defines as the "best edition" of your work.

Congratulations! In about six months, hopefully less, you should receive your copyright registration certificate. Don't worry however: "When the Copyright Office issues a registration certificate, it assigns as the effective date of registration the date it received all required elements—an application, a nonrefundable filing fee, and a nonreturnable deposit—in acceptable form, regardless of how long it took to process the application and mail the certificate."[77]

COPYRIGHT NOTICE

A copyright notice is a statement found on copies or phonorecords of a work, indicating that the copyright owner is asserting ownership. It usually consists of three primary elements that appear as a single, continuous statement:

1. The copyright symbol © (or ℗ for phonorecords); the word "copyright"; or the abbreviation "Copr."
2. The year of the work's first publication.
3. The name of the copyright owner.

Example: "Super Lative: The World's GREATEST Super Hero!" © 2025 Hy Perbolic.

In the case of a published work, a notice can prevent a defendant in a copyright infringement action from attempting to limit his or her liability for damages or injunctive relief based on an innocent infringement defense.

For a graphic novel, the copyright notice should be placed in one or more of the following places:

1. The title page
2. The page immediately following the title page
3. Either side of the front or the back cover
4. The first or the last page of the main body of the work

For a periodical comic book, the copyright notice should be placed in one or more of the following places:

1. Any location acceptable for books
2. As part of, or adjacent to, the masthead or on the page containing the masthead
3. Adjacent to a prominent heading, appearing at or near the front of the issue, containing the title of the periodical and any combination of the volume and issue number and the date of the issue.

For more information about copyright notice, see U.S. Copyright Office Circular 3, "Copyright Notice," at www.copyright.gov/circs/circ03.pdf.

COPYRIGHT RECORDATION, ASSIGNMENTS, AND TRANSFERS

Any contract or other document that transfers copyright ownership may be recorded at the Copyright Office. In other words, if you're putting together a comic and utilizing the work of other artists, you should record those illustrator services agreements, options, literary property purchase agreements, copyright assignments, and contracts containing copyright assignment or licenses clauses. In fact, the Copyright Office will record any document "pertaining to a copyright."

Why Record?

Recording a contract or other document pertaining to copyright ownership has several effects:

- It establishes a public record of ownership by giving the world constructive notice of the new owner. Constructive notice means that once the copyright in a work is registered, everyone is presumed to know the ownership and other registration information on file with the Copyright Office—even if they have not, in fact, actually looked up the registration records.
- It is necessary to prove a chain of title required by publishers, insurers, and other third parties.
- It determines priority of **conflicting transfers**;[78] If you fail to record the transferred copyright and the original copyright owner transfers that same copyright to a third party who then records that second transfer, you could lose the copyright. Although you could sue the original owner for a fraudulent transfer, you may be prohibited from getting the copyright from the second party to whom the copyright was transferred (called the "transferee").

SCRAMBLED TRANSFERS

Ella Scrambler, an eager comic book writer, has penned an exciting new story called "Al Bumen's Eggcellent Adventures." Keen to land a deal, she transfers the rights to her comic book to Sunny Side Up Comics on April 1, 2025.

A week after signing the agreement with Sunny Side Up Comics, Ella is approached by Massive Comics, Inc. with a far better offer. Realizing the opportunity, she quickly *scrambles* to transfer the rights to "Eggcellent Adventures" to Massive Comics, Inc. on April 8, 2025, despite having already assigned those rights to Sunny Side Up Comics. Massive Comics, Inc. is unaware of Ella's prior agreement with Sunny Side Up Comics.

SCRAMBLED TRANSFERS—*continued*

KEY POINTS

- Sunny Side Up Comics must record the copyright assignment with the Copyright Office within one month of the transfer (by May 1, 2025) to retain the rights to the comic book. Otherwise, they'll have a *tough break*.
- If Sunny Side Up Comics fails to record the assignment by May 1, 2025, and Massive Comics records its assignment first (for instance, on May 10), Massive Comics will own the copyright, even if Sunny Side Up Comics records their assignment on May 11. Looks like the *yolk's on them* if they miss that deadline!

Outcome: Regardless of which company secures the copyright, the losing company cannot recover the rights to the comic book unless the winning company agrees to sign them over. This situation may leave the losing company feeling a bit *thin-shelled*. However, the losing company has grounds for a breach-of-contract lawsuit against Ella Scrambler.

How to Record a Document

The Copyright Office does not determine the form of the documents to be recorded, so virtually any contract, from illustrator services to merchandising to publishing agreements, may be recorded.

A few basic requirements must be met. The document to be recorded must:

- Have original signatures of the parties who signed it (or proper certification of a photocopy)
- Be complete by its own terms
- Be legible
- Be accompanied by the correct fee, which is, as of this writing, $105 for one title; $30 for additional titles (per group of 10 or fewer titles)

Short Form Copyright Assignment

Keep in mind that recorded documents become publicly available, so any terms in a contract which is recorded will become known to anyone who views the recorded document. If you record the entire contract that contains the assignment clause, the entire world will also be able to read the contract clauses containing compensation, contact information, and other paragraphs that the parties might not want the public to access. For this reason, short form assignments and transfers are often used rather than the longer contracts that justify the transfer.

EXAMPLE: EXAMPLE SHORT FORM ASSIGNMENT

Date: ______

For one dollar in hand and other good and valuable consideration, the receipt and sufficiency of which is hereby acknowledged by all parties, the undersigned ______ (Assignor) does hereby assign and convey to ______ (Assignee), its successors, assigns, and licensees, the copyright to that [motion picture, video, screenplay, etc.] (the "Work"), currently titled: "______," and registered with the United States Copyright Office Registration #______. This assignment is perpetual in duration and applies to all derivative works of the Work and all copyrightable components which have comprised the Work. Agreed to and Accepted by:

Assignee: ______ Assignor: ______

Certificate of Authorship

A certificate of authorship is a key document in the chain of title of a comic book property that was created through the efforts of several people. This is a notarized statement by the writers and illustrators identifying them as authors of the comic book property. A certificate should be executed by all the property's authors. Don't forget that for a work for hire, the author is the hiring party!

EXAMPLE: THE CERTIFICATE OF AUTHORSHIP (WORK FOR HIRE)

"I, [writer or illustrator's name] certify that I have written the attached comic book [script/illustrations] as a work made for hire for [publishing company's name] ("Publishing Company"), pursuant to that [illustrator's/writer's] services agreement, dated ______, between me and the aforementioned Publishing Company. Accordingly, I understand and agree that the Publishing Company shall be considered the author of the attached [script/illustrations]. If a court of competent jurisdiction determines that the [script/illustrations] was/were not created as a work made for hire, I hereby assign all copyright, title, and interest to that/those [script/illustrations] to the Publishing Company with, full rights to assign said copyright in whatsoever manner the Publishing Company chooses. I waive any right to "droit moral" or other moral right, now known, or hereafter enacted.

I understand and agree that as full owner of the copyright to the [script/illustrations], the Publishing Company and its assigns, may make any modification or change whatsoever to the [script/illustrations] or its derivative works.

"I represent and warrant that nothing in the [script/illustrations] infringes upon any rights of third parties; the [script/illustrations] contain no defamatory material and does not infringe the privacy rights of any parties. All of the material not original with me which was used to create the [script/illustrations] was either provided to me by the Publishing Company or was in the public domain. I have the full right and power to execute this document, and nothing in the screenplay, or my services in connection with the creation of the [script/illustrations] does or shall infringe the rights of a third party."

Signed: Artist

Keep Your Records Clean

To maintain your credibility as a comic book creator, it's crucial to keep all documents related to your chain of title well organized and in a separate binder. Presenting a financier, publishing house, movie studio, insurer, or any co-production partner with an easy-to-follow, comprehensive file will help establish you as a trustworthy and reliable creator in the industry.

Copyright Infringement

Anybody who violates any of the exclusive rights of a copyright owner may be liable for copyright infringement. Keep in mind that *you don't have to intend* to infringe a copyright in order to be liable for copyright infringement!

In order to establish a case for infringement, the copyright owner must show:

1. That she is a valid owner of the copyright and registration
2. That the defendant, without the copyright owner's permission, copied a significant amount of protected expression, or otherwise violated the copyright owner's copyright.

And before we talk about how copyright infringement works, let me give you the best tool in your legal quiver if you ever need to sue an infringer: REGISTER YOUR COPYRIGHT BEFORE IT IS INFRINGED!

Proving Infringement

To prove copyright infringement, the copyright owner (the plaintiff) must prove both **ownership and copying**.

1. **Ownership**. That he or she owned a valid copyright.
2. **Copying**. That the defendant copied copyrightable elements of the plaintiff's copyrighted work. In order to show that the defendant actually copied the plaintiff's work, the plaintiff may present evidence that the defendant had access to the copyrighted work and the defendant's work is substantially similar to the portion copied from the plaintiff's work.

There must be copying of *copyrightable* material. Copying unprotectable elements is not enough. For instance, if all that was taken was an idea (which is not copyrightable), that would not be enough to prove copyright infringement, even if the plaintiff could show that the idea was directly taken from his or her copyrighted work.

Copying is composed of two parts, **access** and **substantial similarity**. "It is often impossible to demonstrate a copyright infringement by direct evidence as a defendant will rarely admit that he or she copied the plaintiff's work. Therefore, copyright infringement can be established by demonstrating inferentially that: (1) the defendant had access to the material; and (2) the defendant's work is substantially similar to the plaintiffs work."[79]

- **Access**. Although it's great if you can actually prove that the defendant copied your work, the evidence of copying is usually hard to come by. Recognizing that, courts will accept circumstantial evidence of the defendant's *access* to the copyrighted work. A plaintiff proves access by showing that the defendant had the opportunity to view or to copy the plaintiff's work. "Even where there is no evidence of direct access, 'an inference of access may still be established by proof of similarity so striking that the possibilities of independent creation, coincidence and prior common source are, as a practical matter, precluded.'"[80]
- **Substantial Similarity**. In addition to access, the two works (the plaintiff's copyrighted work and the defendant's work) must also be substantially similar. "[S]ubstantial similarity should be judged by the spontaneous response of the ordinary lay observer."[81] The test for "substantial similarity" is "whether an average lay observer would recognize the alleged copy as having been appropriated from the copyrighted work."[82]

INFRINGEMENT: NO "INTENTION" TO INFRINGE REQUIRED

Keep in mind that you don't have to *intend* to infringe a copyright to be liable for copyright infringement! It's what's called a "strict liability tort,"[83] meaning that all you need to do is actually violate one of the exclusive rights. Why you did it is largely irrelevant. Although if you knowingly and willfully reproduced work that you knew to be protected by copyright for your financial gain, you could actually be arrested and face much stricter civil and criminal penalties.

Because it is a strict liability tort, *you can be liable for copyright infringement even though you don't know you're copying somebody's protected work*! Which means that if you include somebody else's copyrighted material in your comic book without their permission—song lyrics, character design, lines of dialogue, etc.—and your publisher sends it to the printer to be printed, you can be sued for copyright infringement... and so can both your publisher and printer!

But it gets worse... there will be a clause in your contract with the publisher that obligates you to pay the publishers legal bills and damages if you've included material in your work that gets them sued! (See Indemnification, p. 471.)

So now you're looking at paying not just your legal bills, but your publisher's as well. But wait, there's more! The publisher has a similar clause in its contract with the printer. So if the printer gets sued, it passes that liability back to the publisher, who can pass that liability back to you. So now you're paying three sets of legal bills and damages! This is why it really does save money to look very carefully at where you have drawn your material from *before* you publish it.

Contributory Copyright Infringement

Even if you did not copy another person's copyrighted work, you can still be liable for copyright infringement. For instance, if you have knowledge of somebody's infringing activity and encourage, assist, materially contribute, or induce infringing conduct, you could be liable for **contributory copyright infringement**.[84]

Example: You're working with an illustrator to create your new superhero comic "Humongo-Phage—The World Devourer," about a gigantic intergalactic being who eats planets.

You encourage her to take a close look at Jack Kirby's seminal drawings of Galactus, give her copies of the character, and tell her to create a character that looks just like Galactus, but to "change the colors around a little bit." If her final product is substantially similar to the copyrighted Galactus character, she could be liable for copyright infringement, and you could be liable for contributory copyright infringement.

Vicarious Copyright Infringement

A somewhat related concept to contributory copyright infringement is the tort of **vicarious copyright infringement**. It's similar in that neither involves direct infringement by the wrongdoers, but here the relationship is one of a supervisor to a worker. Remember the concept of *respondeat superior* that we learned about when we were setting up our business entity? (See Respondeat Superior, p. ##.)

If you recall, an employer is responsible for the tortious acts of its employee which are committed during the scope of the employee's job.

In order to be liable for vicarious copyright infringement, you must have the right and ability to control a worker's infringing conduct, and you must directly benefit from your worker's infringing activity.

"One... infringes vicariously by profiting from direct infringement while declining to exercise a right to stop or limit it."[85]

> **Example**: Let's change the Example above a little bit. This time, you have hired the illustrator to create "Humongo-Phage—The World Devourer," but instead of giving her the Galactus materials to copy, she copied Galactus without your knowledge. Because she is your employee, you have the right to supervise and control her work. Furthermore, your company has made money from the sale of infringing Humongo-Phage merchandise. Therefore, if she is liable for creating an infringing character, you or company can be liable for vicarious copyright infringement.

What's especially concerning for employers about vicarious copyright infringement is that they can be liable without ever having knowledge that their worker was engaged in infringing activity[86] (although, with respect to Internet service providers and website owners, actual or constructive knowledge of infringing activity is required[87] to establish vicarious copyright infringement). Nor does an employment relationship need to be in place, merely the ability to supervise and control the infringing activity.[88]

Three-Year Statute of Limitations

Lawsuits have a "shelf life," called a statute of limitations. If you don't sue within that time period, your time is up: no matter how favorable the evidence in your favor, you can no longer sue over that claim. For copyright law, the lawsuit must be "commenced within three years after the claim accrued."[89]

Of course, the question then becomes "when does the claim accrue?" And on that subject, the courts are split over two ways of interpreting when the clock starts, so it really does matter where you bring your case:

> Under the **injury rule**, [...] a claim accrues at the time of each act of infringement, regardless of the copyright holder's knowledge of the infringement. In contrast, under the **discovery rule**, a claim for copyright infringement does not accrue until the aggrieved party knows or has reason to know of the injury that forms the basis of the claim.[90]

Penalties for Infringement

- Courts have a plethora of punishments in store for the copyright infringer, for instance—**Damages and Profits**.[91] A court may order an infringer to pay either:
    - The copyright owner's actual damages and any additional profits of the infringer, or
    - Statutory damages in a sum of not less than $750 or more than $30,000 as the court considers just.
    - For willful infringement, the court, in its discretion, may increase the award of statutory damages to a sum of not more than $150,000.
- **Costs and Attorneys' Fees**.[92] The court in its discretion may allow the recovery of full costs by or against any party... and the court may also award a reasonable attorney's fee to the prevailing party as part of the costs.
- **Injunctions**.[93] A court may issue injunctions halting the manufacture or distribution of infringing articles. (See Contract Anatomy: Remedies, p. 476.)
- **Impounding and Disposition of Infringing Articles**.[94] A court may order the destruction of all infringing copies of a copyrighted work. In addition to ordering the destruction of the copies, it can also order that the instruments that made the copies also be destroyed. This includes "all plates, molds, matrices, masters, tapes, film negatives, or other articles by means of which such copies or phonorecords may be reproduced."

- **Criminal Penalties**. Courts may also sentence willful copyright infringers to jail for periods ranging from one to ten years, depending upon the severity and amount of their willful infringement.[95]

COPYRIGHT SMALL CLAIMS AND THE COPYRIGHT CLAIMS BOARD

Protecting your copyright against infringers can be an expensive prospect involving the federal courts and tens of thousands of dollars in lawyers' fees. In fact, it's so expensive that many copyright holders choose not to sue if the amount that they could potentially recover is less than $30,000 or $40,000.

In 2020, Congress decided to address this issue by passing the Copyright Alternative in Small-Claims Enforcement Act of 2020 (CASE Act),[96] which established the Copyright Claims Board (CCB).[97] Functioning much like a small claims court for copyright disputes, the CCB offers a streamlined route to enforce your rights or defend your use of copyrighted material. It handles a wide array of issues—from claims of infringement of exclusive rights and declarations of noninfringement (helpful if you're wrongly accused) to misrepresentation disputes during the notice and counter-notice process under Section 512, and even related counterclaims.

Another perk of the CCB is efficiency: You don't need to wait for your copyright registration to be formally issued; simply having filed for the registration is enough to initiate a claim. Plus, you're not required to secure an attorney (though having one on board is usually a smart move).

That said, there are a few important caveats to keep in mind. Participation is entirely voluntary, meaning you can choose between the CCB and federal court, but you can't pursue your claim in both venues at once. Moreover, all parties involved must agree to the CCB process; if one party opts out, the case moves to federal court. Monetary damages here are capped at $30,000, ensuring that the stakes don't soar out of control.

DEFENSES TO INFRINGEMENT

Fair Use

Among creative professionals, fair use has achieved near-mythic status—widely recognized yet frequently misunderstood. Essentially, fair use is a legal defense that allows you to include portions of a copyrighted work without seeking permission from the owner (see Copyright Infringement, p. 44). The subtle nuance lies in determining exactly which elements—and precisely how much—can be used without venturing into infringement territory. It's a bit like walking a tightrope over a legal abyss: when deftly navigated, fair use offers a creative safety net, enabling you to engage with existing works while respecting the rights of their creators.

Categories of Fair Use

General categories of fair use include news reporting, criticism, comment, teaching (including multiple copies for classroom use), scholarship, or research. The 1961 Report of the Register of Copyrights on the General Revision of the U.S. Copyright Law cites Examples of activities courts have regarded as fair use:

"Quotation of excerpts in a review or criticism for purposes of illustration or comment;

- Quotation of short passages in a scholarly or technical work, for illustration or clarification of the author's observations;
- Use in a parody of some of the content of the work parodied;
- Summary of an address or article, with brief quotations, in a news report;
- Reproduction by a library of a portion of a work to replace part of a damaged copy;
- Reproduction by a teacher or student of a small part of a work to illustrate a lesson;
- Reproduction of a work in legislative or judicial proceedings or reports;
- Incidental and fortuitous reproduction, in a newsreel or broadcast, of a work located in the scene of an event being reported."[98]

FAIR USE FORMULA – 17 USC §107

In every fair use case, the courts must analyze the issue by applying the following four factors when looking to see if fair use is an appropriate defense:

In determining whether the use made of a work in any particular case is a fair use the factors to be considered shall include—

1. The purpose and character of the use, including whether such use is of the commercial nature or is for nonprofit educational purposes;
2. The nature of the copyrighted work;[99]
3. The amount and substantiality of the portion used in relation to the copyrighted work as a whole; and
4. The effect of the use upon the potential market for or value of the copyrighted work.[100]

Determining Fair Use

It's important to keep in mind just where the court is "looking" with respect to each one of the factors. To best understand what's going on here, let's define some terms:

The **Original Work** refers to a preexisting piece of copyrighted artwork from which a portion was taken without the permission of its owner. The **New Work** is art created by a different artist, who used a part of the Original Work to create their artwork for a particular purpose (known as "**secondary use**"), which may or may not be related to the Original Work's use.

Fair Use Factor #1

The purpose and character of the use, including whether such use is of the commercial nature or is for nonprofit educational purposes.[101]

This first factor is often considered: "the heart of the fair use inquiry."[102] Here the court analyzes the New Work and asks a few questions:

- "Okay, so you took a portion of the Original Work... What did you do with the portion you took?"
- "What kind of work is your New Work? Is it parody? Criticism? Commentary?"
- "Are you using this New Work for educational purposes or is your use purely commercial?"
- "Did the New Work *significantly* transform the portion of the Original Work that it took?"[103]

And, most importantly...

- "'Whether and to what extent' the use at issue has a purpose or character different from the original.[...] The larger the difference, the more likely the first factor weighs in favor of fair use. The smaller the difference, the less likely."[104]

TRANSFORMATIVE USE

"The fair use provision, and the first factor in particular, requires an analysis of the specific 'use' of a copyrighted work that is alleged to be 'an infringement'."[105] A court will give greater weight to a defendant who asserts a fair-use defense if they can show that their use is **transformative**. *The greater the transformative use, the greater the chance for fair use.* A transformative use

> adds something new, with a further purpose or different character, altering the first with new expression, meaning, or message [...] in other words, whether and to what extent the new work is transformative... [T]ransformative works... lie at the heart of the fair use doctrine's guarantee of breathing space...[106]

As the Supreme Court wrote, "The first fair use factor considers whether the use of a copyrighted work has a further purpose or different character, which is a matter of degree, and the degree of difference must be balanced against the commercial nature of the use. If an Original Work and a secondary use share the same or highly similar purposes, and the secondary use is of a commercial nature, the first factor is likely to weigh against fair use, absent some other justification for copying."[107]

To be transformative, you have to do more than just repackage the old, unlicensed work into a new form. You have to use the original for a different purpose, to create new meaning, often by providing insightful commentary or criticism; otherwise, the court may find that you're "free riding" on another's creations.[108]

Example 1: An artist decides to have a bit of fun and creates a caricature of Superman to represent American imperialism, which appears in several pages of a faux comic included in a book about 20th-century American foreign policy, cleverly titled "Just Us League." The use of Superman in this context isn't just to show off his bulging muscles and cape; it's a parody aimed at making a social and political statement by adding new meaning and expression to the original character while also making the additional point that Americans saw themselves as Superman, out to save the world (complete with the cape and a healthy dose of hubris). Now, imagine Superman with a smug grin, standing tall with one foot on a globe while a bald eagle perches on his shoulder, striking a pose that screams, "I'm here to save the day!" The transformative nature of this caricature shifts the original character's purpose and message from a superhero narrative to a critique of American foreign policy. While the book may be commercially available (because, let's face it, someone's gotta' pay for all this creativity), the parody's new purpose and message weigh heavily in favor of fair use, and given the highly transformative nature of the caricature and its added layers of meaning, the court is likely to find that this use of Superman falls under fair use.

Example 2: An artist decides to create a new superhero called "Capt. Hyperbolic," who is essentially Superman after a few too many cups of coffee. This character sports a similar getup and look, hails from the dead alien planet Cryptoon (you can never go home again), and works for the "Daily Pod-Net" as a podcaster and reporter, with his sound engineer, Jimmy Awesome. Capt. Hyperbolic has all the same abilities as Superman, except he becomes completely powerless whenever he puts on glasses (because, apparently, wearing glasses is his kryptonite).

In other words, Capt. Hyperbolic isn't parodying Superman so much a copying him and competing with the Superman brand; the overall look and feel of Capt. Hyperbolic is still substantially similar to Superman. The changes don't add a whole lot of new expression, meaning, or commentary. If the new comic book featuring Capt. Hyperbolic is commercially available; the commercial nature of the use may weigh against fair use, especially if the use is not significantly transformative. Given the similarities in purpose and character, and the lack of significant transformative use, the court is less likely to find that this use of Superman falls under fair use. The new character, Capt. Hyperbolic, may be seen as "free riding" on the original Superman character.

Findings that tip the balance toward fair use include:

- The New Work is educational, informational, a work of criticism, parody, or cultural commentary.

- The New Work is being used for nonprofit purposes rather than purely commercial purposes.
- The New Work significantly transforms the portion of the Original Work it took, by creating new meaning or new purpose, and is not merely a minor variation of the Original Work.

Fair Use Factor #2

The nature of the copyrighted work.

For the second fair use factor, the court turns its attention away from the New Work and fixes its gaze[109] on the Original Work.

The court asks the following questions:

- What kind of work is the Original Work?
- Does the Original Work have a lot of creative expression? Or,
- Is the Original Work more factual information, like a news story?
- Has the Original Work been published?

Tipping this factor toward the balance towards fair use would be:

- A finding which showed that the Original Works was primarily factual or informational, like a news story. News broadcasts, although protected by copyright, are themselves more prone to be used under fair use. As the U.S. Supreme Court has stated: "Copying a news broadcast may have a stronger claim to fair use than copying a [creative work]."[110]
- A finding that the Original Work had been published. Unpublished works are subject to greater protection under copyright law; the reason being that an author should have the right to control the first publication of his or her work. While the fact that the Original Work was unpublished may weigh against a finding of fair use, it, in itself, is not determinative.

Fair Use Factor #3

The amount and substantiality of the portion used in relation to the copyrighted work as a whole.

Now the court holds both the Original Work and the New Work side-by-side and asks the following questions:

- How much of the Original Work was taken and incorporated into the New Work?
- What percentage of the Original Work was taken?
- The portion of the Original Work that was taken—was it the heart of the Original Work? Or, rather, was it a portion that was ancillary, or incidental to the Original Work?

Findings that tend to favor fair use would include:

- Using a small or insignificant portion of the Original Work
- Using part of the Original Work that was incidental or ancillary
- Not using parts of the Original Work that are essential, critical, vital, or the "heart" of the Original Work

However, it does not help the fair-use defense trying to prove how much you did *not* take. "No plagiarist can excuse the wrong by showing how much of his work he did not pirate."[111]

Fair Use Factor #4

The effect of the use upon the potential market for or value of the copyrighted work.

Finally, the court examines the economic effect of the New Work on the Original Work. Unfortunately, this is one of the least uniformly interpreted factors. The court may ask:

- Does the New Work attempt to substitute for the Original Work in the relevant marketplace?
- Is the primary economic harm done to the Original Work caused by the New Work's criticism or parody of the Original Work?
- Is the economic harm that is done to the Original Work substantial?

Findings that tend to favor fair use would include:

- The New Work and the Original Work are sold to different types of consumers.
- The primary harm done to the Original Work is as a result of criticism or parody, rather than the New Work substituting for the Original Work.
- The economic harm done to the Original Work is relatively minor.
- The New Work does not compete directly for the same customer base.

Analyzing the Factors

Once the court has examined these four fair use factors, it steps back and looks at how they each interrelate, and which ones, given the facts before the court, should be given the most weight.

And, while these four factors *must* be considered by a court when analyzing a fair use question, they are not the only factors a court can consider; in other words, other relevant findings may be considered, such as intent by the creator of the New Work to deceive consumers, willingness to give appropriate attribution to the creators of the Original Work, bad faith on the part of either party, etc.

Examples of Fair Use

Two Examples may illustrate how a court may analyze whether an unauthorized use is fair or infringing.

Scenario #1: Beard-O-Brush is hired by a local car dealership to create a fun promotional comic that will be distributed along with the Sunday newspaper flyers. He creates a hero character called "Slasher," that is heavily modeled after Wolverine from the X-Men (metal claws, funky sideburns, X-Men style blue and yellow costume). Slasher even wears a big "X" on his belt because he is part of the "X-treme Team," a group of mutants dedicated to lowering auto sale prices (because all the superhero jobs were taken?). Marvel comics sues the car dealership and Beard-O for copyright infringement over their Wolverine character. Beard-O defends, asserting a fair use defense.

In determining whether his use was fair use, the court first looks to see **"purpose and character of the use."** Here, the court analyses what Beard-O did with the character he used. His use was clearly commercial, and not educational, and therefore Beard-O loses on this prong of the analysis.

Second, the court turns to the Wolverine character itself and looks to **"the nature of the copyrighted work."** Wolverine and the X-Men are creative works of fiction and thus are afforded the highest protection under copyright law (unlike works that are primarily informational, factual, or news related). This factor is also weighed against Beard-O.

Third, the court examines ***"The amount and substantiality of the portion used in relation to the copyrighted work as a whole"***—how much Beard-O took, and how important that character was to "Wolverine" as a whole. Here, Beard-O argues that he only took the claws, the hair, and the X on the belt—proportionately, this is at most only 20% of the character. The attorney for Marvel counters that these are all substantial parts of the Wolverine character—the heart of the character, if you will—and thus its importance should not be judged by its size alone. The court decides that this factor should also be counted against Beard-O.

Fourth, the court will look at ***"The effect of the use upon the potential market for or value of the copyrighted work"*** to see how Beard-O's unauthorized use affects the market for the Wolverine character. The court will take a look to see whether Beard-O's use of the character "usurps" the market for Wolverine.[112] The key here is whether the "defendant's use [acts] as a substitute for plaintiff's work in the marketplace."[113] Because Marvel has licensed its characters for use in other commercial properties, this factor, like the others, is counted against Beard-O. The court finds that Beard-O has not made a successful fair use defense and thus has infringed the copyright to Wolverine.

Scenario #2: Quill is writing a comic book about the media's treatment of the issue of global warming and wants to include narration and dialogue from an evening news story focusing on the world's biggest tire fire. Quill tries to get permission from Nosey News Networks, Inc. (NNN), the company that produced the footage, but they turn her down. She decides to use it anyway, copying the dialogue, voiceover, and shot sequence of a 1-minute clip from the 6-minute story and incorporating it into her panel art and script.

The clip she copies features a reporter who jokes about the impact on global warming, the tire fire will cause, saying: "Will the fire warm the globe or just cause a few paranoid scientists to get hot under the collar... over to you, Cathy." In her comic book, Quill adds captions with global warming statistics over the reporter's derisive commentary. The overall effect of Quill's editorializing and graphic additions makes the reporter seem extremely biased and ignorant of the issues. Even though Quill has been denied permission to use the clip, she nonetheless includes a copyright notice in her panel, properly attributing the clip to NNN.

Quill's comic book is printed and published, and she is sued by NNN. In court, she defends herself on the grounds that her use of NNN's clip was fair use. The court reasons as follows:

1. In determining whether her use was fair, the court first looks to see "purpose and character of the use." Quill used the NNN material to criticize the news program and as social commentary. Furthermore, her use was educational and in a very different medium. This factor is decided in her favor.
2. Second, the court turns to the NNN material itself and looks to "the nature of the copyrighted work." News broadcasts, although protected by copyright, are themselves more prone to being used under fair use. As the U.S. Supreme Court has stated: "Copying a news broadcast may have a stronger claim to fair use than copying a motion picture."[114] This factor is decided in Quill's favor as well.
3. Third, the court examines how much Quill took, and how important that clip was to the news broadcast as a whole. Quill copied 1 minute of dialogue and visuals of a six-minute broadcast. The court decides that this was a substantial amount, and, because the material contained the heart of the piece—the tire fire—the factor is decided in NNN's favor.
4. Fourth, the court looks to see how Quill's unauthorized use affects the market for the NNN news segment. The court holds that because NNN does not license its clips, the nightly news market is NNN's primary market. Quill's use does not have any appreciable effect on that market, and this factor is decided in her favor as well. Simply put, Quill's comic book is not a marketplace substitution for NNN News.
5. The court also points out that Quill's use was transformative—her captions recast the NNN material and provide social commentary. Furthermore, Quill acted in good faith by placing the NNN copyright notice below the materials used.

The court rules that Quill's unauthorized use is excused under fair use principles.

De *Minimis* Taking

De minimis is a fancy Latin phrase that means "of the least," or "of trifles." It refers to the taking of an insignificant amount of the copyrighted work, so trifling that a court will rule that no harm is done even though what was taken was taken without permission. This infringement defense underscores the fact that courts will rule that some infringement is just too harmless to worry about. Of course, it is up to the defendant to prove that the taking is *de minimis.* As the legal maxim goes: "*de minimis non curat lex*"—the law does not concern itself with trifles.

> **Example**: Penciller creates an odoriferous character named Scent-o-Pede: the vermiform villain of vengeance, with 100 meticulously-drawn legs. Each of the legs features a different shoe or boot, and one of them is a copy of Superman's boot. A court would most likely see this copying as *de minimis.*

The Doctrine of Independent Creation

This is not an exception to copyright law but a robust defense against infringement claims. It's a rule that allows two people to have copyright ownership in what is essentially the same work. If two authors come up with the same work independently of each other, and neither has copied the others' work, both works will be entitled to copyright protection—even though both works are substantially similar to each other. This is true because copyright is based on originality, rather than novelty. As long as the work originated with an author and is not copied from another author, that author may claim a copyright.

Example: Quill spent a year writing her graphic novel *The Platypus Papers.* Because she doesn't have any contacts in comic book publishing, her script sits on her hard drive without being seen by anyone but her mother. To her dismay, she visits her local comic book store and sees the new book *The Platypus Diaries,* produced by Monotreme Publishing, Inc. When she reads it, she is even more upset. The comic is substantially similar to her script. So much so, that if she could prove that Monotreme Publishing had seen her script, she would have a great claim for copyright infringement. However, because she can't prove that anyone has seen her script—let alone copied it—she should lose a copyright infringement lawsuit, should she bring one. She owns a copyright in her script, and Monotreme Publishing has a copyright in their script and comic.[115]

COPYRIGHT SEARCHES

Frequently, creators will need to find out copyright information concerning a particular work. For instance, you might want to make a comic book from somebody's copyrighted novel or use a copyrighted artwork as a background for a splash page. Or you might need to provide a publisher or distributor with a copyright search report. In short, at some point (hopefully, early on) you or your collaborators may need to conduct or commission a copyright search.

The process of researching a copyright and getting permission from the copyright's owners is called "clearing a copyright."

Copyright searches are an art form all to themselves. All too often, an author's contact information is difficult to find and may require a good deal of diligent investigative work. Remember, just because you can't find out who the author is doesn't mean that you're off the hook and that you are excused from getting permission to use the work. Unknown authors still have rights, and you don't want to get the author's contact information for the first time from her lawyer's cease-and-desist letter.

To clear a copyright, the comic creator needs to establish whether the particular work is still protected by copyright, and if it is, the comic creator needs to get contact information for that work's copyright owner so that they can attempt to negotiate a license to use that work.

There are four basic methods for researching the copyright to a work:

1. You can perform the research yourself
2. You can hire a lawyer to perform the search
3. You can commission the Copyright Office to perform a search
4. You can use a professional copyright research company

Often, your investigation will involve all these methods. Once you've identified the copyright owner, get permission to use the copyrighted work with a written copyright license signed by the rights holder.

COPYRIGHT SEARCH TIPS

- **Check out the Copyright Office website**: Visit the U.S. Copyright Office website at https://www.copyright.gov. For works registered or renewed since 1978, you can search the Copyright Office website for free at https://www.copyright.gov/public-records/.
- **Pay the Copyright Office to search for you**: If you can't find the information you need, or if the work was registered prior to 1978, you might want to commission a search by the Copyright Office itself. The Copyright Office charges an hourly rate and will provide you with an estimate of how long the search will take before it starts. Https://www.copyright.gov/forms/search_estimate.html
- **Hire a professional search company**: If all else fails, you can engage a professional copyright research company, such as Clarivate, to conduct a full copyright search report. This may be the most expensive option but given the fact that these companies search additional databases beyond those ones used by the Copyright Office, it is probably the most thorough option. Visit their website at https://clarivate.com/intellectual-property/brand-ip-solutions/trademark-searching/title-copyright-entertainment-searches/

Notes

1 17 USC §102(a) (2025).
2 "[M]any literary characters may embody little more than an unprotected idea [while] a comic book character, which has physical as well as conceptual qualities, is more likely to contain some unique elements of expression." *Olson v. Nat'l Broad. Co.*, Inc., 855 F.2d 1446, 1452 (9th Cir. 1988).
3 See *Warner Bros. Pictures, Inc. v. Columbia Broadcasting System, Inc.*, 216 F.2d 945, 950 (9th Cir.1954).
4 *Gaiman v. McFarlane*, 360 F.3d 644, 660 (7th Cir. 2004).
5 *Gaiman v. McFarlane*, 360 F.3d 644, 660 (7th Cir. 2004).
6 *Gaiman v. McFarlane*, 360 F.3d 644, 661 (7th Cir. 2004).
7 *Anderson v. Stallone*, 87–0592 WDKGX, 1989 WL 206431 [CD Cal Apr. 25, 1989] (citing to *Nichols v. Universal Pictures*, 45 F.2d 119, 121 (2d.Cir.1930), cert. denied, 282 U.S. 902 (1931).
8 *Anderson v. Stallone*, 87–0592 WDKGX, 1989 WL 206431 [CD Cal Apr. 25, 1989].
9 *Warner Bros. Pictures v. Columbia Broadcasting Sys.*, 216 F2d 945, 950 [9th Cir 1954].
10 *Suntrust Bank v. Houghton Mifflin Co.*, 268 F3d 1257, 1266 [11th Cir 2001].
11 "However, there has been no doubt that copyright protection is available for characters portrayed in cartoons, even before Nichols, e.g., *King Features Syndicate v. Fleischer*, 299 Fed. 533 (2d Cir.1924) (Barney Google's horse, Spark Plug); *Hill v. Whalen & Martell, Inc.*, 220 F. 359 (S.D.N.Y.1914) (Mutt and Jeff); see also *Empire City Amusement Co. v. Wilton*, 134 F. 132 (C.C.D.Mass.1903) (Alphonse and Gaston) (claim sustained against demurrer)" *Warner Bros. Inc. v. Am. Broad. Companies, Inc.*, 720 F.2d 231, 240 (2d Cir. 1983).
12 *Anderson v. Stallone*, 87–0592 WDKGX, 1989 WL 206431 (C.D. Cal. Apr. 25, 1989).
13 *New Line Cinema Corp. v. Russ Berrie & Co., Inc.*, 161 F Supp 2d 293, 302 [S.D.N.Y. 2001] ("[c]opyright protection is extended to the component part of the character which significantly aids in identifying the character.")
14 17 USC §101 (2025).
15 17 USC §101 (2025).
16 17 USC §101 (2025).
17 17 USC §101 (2025).
18 17 USC §101.
19 17 USC §101.
20 17 USC §101.
21 "SCOTUS," a.k.a., The Supreme Court of the United States. Not to be confused with POTUS, the President of the United States, or OTIS, Lex Luthor's henchman and founder of Otisburg.
22 *Andy Warhol Found. for the Visual Arts, Inc. v. Goldsmith*, 598 U.S. 508, 550, 143 S. Ct. 1258, 1287 (2023).
23 17 USC §101.
24 *Medforms, Inc. v. Healthcare Mgmt. Solutions, Inc.*, 290 F.3d 98, 107 (2d Cir. 2002) ("A work is considered "fixed" when "its embodiment in a copy... by or under the authority of the author, is sufficiently permanent or stable to permit it to be... reproduced[.]").

25 US Copyright Office Circular 33," Works Not Protected by Copyright," www.copyright.gov/circs/circ33.pdf, (Accessed October 6, 2020).
26 Circular 1, "Copyright Office Basics," U.S. Copyright Office, Circulars, https://www.copyright.gov/circs/ (last visited May 28, 2025).
27 See *Miller v. Universal Studios*, 650 F.2d 1365 (5th Cir. 1981).
28 *Hogan v. DC Comics*, 48 F.Supp.2d, 298 (S.D.N.Y. January 26, 1999).
29 See 17 USC §105, (2016). Subject matter of copyright: "United States Government works: Copyright protection under this title is not available for any work of the United States Government, but the United States Government is not precluded from receiving and holding copyrights transferred to it by assignment, bequest, or otherwise."
30 17 USC §101 (2016).
31 U.S. Copyright Office, Compendium of U.S. Copyright Office Practices § 313.2 (3d ed. 2021).
32 *MyWebGrocer, LLC v. Hometown Info, Inc.*, 375 F.3d 190, 194 (2d Cir.2004).
33 *Gaiman v. McFarlane*, 360 F.3d 644, 660 (7th Cir. 2004).
34 *Gaiman v. McFarlane*, 360 F.3d 644, 660 (7th Cir. 2004).
35 *Swirsky v. Carey*, 376 F.3d 841, 848 (9th Cir.2004).
36 Creative Commons, Creative Commons Licenses, CREATIVE COMMONS, https://creativecommons.org/share-your-work/cclicenses/ (last visited Jan. 17, 2025).
37 17 USC 101.
38 *Janky v. Lake County Convention and Visitors Bureau*, 576 F.3d 356, 362 (C.A.7 (Ind.), 2009).
39 *Brooks v Dash*, 454 F Supp 3d 331, 337 [SDNY 2020].
40 *Gaylord v. U.S.* 595 F.3d 1364, 1377 (C.A.Fed., 2010).
41 *Janky v. Lake County Convention and Visitors Bureau*, 576 F.3d 356, 362 (C.A.7 (Ind.), 2009).
42 *Aalmuhammed v. Lee*, 202 F.3d 1227 (9th Cir. 2000).
43 Aalmuhammed v. Lee, 202 F.3d 1227, 1233 (9th Cir. 2000).
44 *Gaiman v. McFarlane*, 360 F.3d 644, 659 (7th Cir. 2004).
45 *Corwin v. Quinonez*, 858 F. Supp. 2d 903, 910 (N.D. Ohio 2012) reconsideration denied, 3:10 CV 2163, 2013 WL 29806 (N.D. Ohio Jan. 2, 2013).
46 Effects Associates, Inc., v. Cohen, 908 F.2d 555 (1990).
47 *Archie Comic Publications, Inc. v. DeCarlo*, 258 F. Supp. 2d 315, 328 (S.D.N.Y. 2003).
48 *Martha Graham Sch. & Dance Found., Inc. v. Martha Graham Ctr. of Contemporary Dance, Inc.*, 380 F.3d 624, 635 (2d Cir. 2004).
49 17 USC §101 (2010).
50 "The Fourth Circuit, in a pair of decisions, developed a three-prong test to determine whether a work was created within the scope of an employment: (1) Is the work of a type the employee was hired to perform? (2) Was the work's creation substantially within the authorized time and space limits of the employee's job? (3) Was the creation of the work actuated at least in part by the purpose of serving the employer's interest?" § 5:69. William F. Patry, *Patry on Copyright* (Thomson/West, 2007–2024).
51 Cal. Lab. Code § 2775.
52 17 USC §101.

53 "Comic strips arguably qualify as works for hire under the 'contribution to a collective work' eligible category.' 17 USCA §101. A collective work is defined as 'a work, such as a periodical issue, anthology, or encyclopedia, in which a number of contributions, constituting separate and independent works in themselves, are assembled into a collective whole.' 17 USCA §101. Cf. Playboy, 53 F.3d at 558 ("Playboy magazine is a 'collective work')." Followed by: *Archie Comic Publications, Inc. v. DeCarlo*, 258 F. Supp. 2d 315, 334 (S.D.N.Y. 2003) judgment entered, 00 CIV. 5686(LAK), 2003 WL 21354692 (S.D.N.Y. June 11, 2003) aff 'd, 88 F. App'x 468 (2d Cir. 2004) and aff'd, 88 F. App'x 468 (2d Cir. 2004).

54 17 USC §204(a).

55 *Effects Associates, Inc., v. Cohen*, 908 F.2d 555 (1990).

56 *Weinstein Co. v. Smokewood Entertainment Group, LLC*, 664 F.Supp.2d 332, 341 (S.D.N.Y., 2009). ("the intention of a copyright owner seeking to transfer an ownership interest must be clear and unequivocal").

57 *Marvel Characters, Inc. v. Simon*, 310 F.3d 280, 282 (2d Cir. 2002).

58 *Marvel Characters, Inc. v. Simon*, 310 F.3d 280, 284 (2d Cir. 2002).

59 17 USCA §304 (2013).

60 *Marvel Characters, Inc. v. Simon*, 310 F.3d 280, 292 (2d Cir. 2002).

61 I realize that this runs the risk of being an overgeneralization, as these sections also deal differently with works depending upon their renewal terms, and whether or not they were unpublished. Such distinctions are, unfortunately beyond the scope of this work.

62 or transferred a time after January 1, 1978.

63 17 USC §203(a)(3)(2018).

64 See, 37 C.F.R. §201.10 (2013).

65 Section 203 would not prevent the parties to a transfer or license from voluntarily agreeing at any time to terminate an existing grant and negotiating a new one, thereby causing another 35-year period to start running 3 Patry on Copyright §7:46, citing to H.R. Rep. No. 1476, 94th Cong., 2d Sess. 127 (1976), copied from *General Revision of the Copyright Law Revision Part 6: Supplementary Report of the Register of Copyrights on the U.S. Copyright Law: 1965 Revision Bill*, 89th Cong., 1st Sess. 76 (House Comm. Print 1965).

66 Copyright 2017 Authors Alliance and Creative Commons.

67 For more on copyright duration, see the U.S. Copyright Circular 1, "Copyright Office Basics," www.copyright.gov/circs/circ01.pdf, and Circular 15a, "Duration of Copyright: Provisions of the Law Dealing with the Length of Copyright Protection," www.copyright.gov/circs/circ15a.pdf.

68 https://www.copyright.gov/circs/circ15a.pdf.

69 U.S. Copyright Office, Copyright Registration Toolkit, available at https://www.copyright.gov/intellectual-property-toolkits/copyright-registration-toolkit.pdf (last visited May 13, 2025).

70 U.S. Copyright Office, Circular 24: Group Registration of Unpublished Works (2021), https://www.copyright.gov/circs/circ24.pdf.

71 Compendium of U.S. Copyright Office Practices, Third Edition, Chapter 300, §306.

72 Burrow-Giles Lithographic Company v. Sarony, 111 U.S. 53, 60 (1884).

73 U.S. Copyright Office, *Copyright Registration Guidance: Works Containing Material Generated by Artificial Intelligence*, at 4 (2023), available at https://www.copyright.gov/ai/ai_policy_guidance.pdf.

74 Katelyn Chedraoui, This Company Got a Copyright for an Image Made Entirely with AI. Here's How. CNET, https://www.cnet.com/tech/services-and-software/this-company-got-a-copyright-for-an-image-made-entirely-with-ai-heres-how/(last visited Feb. 26, 2025).

75 U.S. Copyright Office, Circular 7D: Mandatory Deposit of Copies or Phonorecords for the Library of Congress (Revised July 2006), available at https://www.copyright.gov/circs/circ07d.pdf.

76 17 USC 407.

77 U.S. Copyright Office, Copyright Notice (Circ. 3), available at https://www.copyright.gov/circs/circ03.pdf.

78 17 USC §205 (2013) Recordation of transfers and other documents. [...] (d) Priority between Conflicting Transfers.—As between two conflicting transfers, the one executed first prevails if it is recorded, in the manner required to give constructive notice under subsection (c), within one month after its execution in the United States or within two months after its execution outside the United States, or at any time before recordation in such manner of the later transfer. Otherwise the later transfer prevails if recorded first in such manner, and if taken in good faith, for valuable consideration or on the basis of a binding promise to pay royalties, and without notice of the earlier transfer.

79 *Roginski v. Time Warner Interactive, Inc.*, 967 F Supp 821, 825 [MD Pa 1997].

80 *Roginski v. Time Warner Interactive, Inc.*, 967 F Supp 821, 826–27 [MD Pa 1997].

81 *Cabell v. Sony Pictures Entm't, Inc.*, 714 F. Supp. 2d 452, 458 (S.D.N.Y. 2010) aff 'd, 425 F. App'x 42 (2d Cir. 2011).

82 *Warner Bros. Inc. v. American Broadcasting Companies*, 654 F.2d 204, 208 (2d Cir. 1981).

83 *Twentieth Century Fox Film Corp. v. iCraveTV*, CIV.A. 00–121, 2000 WL 255989 (W.D. Pa. Feb. 8, 2000).

84 *Perfect 10, Inc. v. Visa Intern. Serv. Ass'n*, 494 F.3d 788, 795 [9th Cir 2007].

85 *Perfect 10, Inc. v. Visa Intern. Serv. Ass'n*, 494 F.3d 788, 802 [9th Cir 2007] (citing to *Metro-Goldwyn-Mayer Studios, Inc. v. Grokster, Ltd.*, 545 U.S. at 930, 125 S.Ct. 2764).

86 "One can be liable for vicarious copyright infringement even without knowledge of the infringement." In re Aimster Copyright Litigation, 252 F. Supp. 2d 634 (N.D. Ill. 2002). 14 A.L.R. Fed. 825 (Originally published in 1973)

87 17 USCA §512 [West].

88 "Even in the absence of an employment relationship, a defendant incurs liability for vicarious copyright infringement if he has the right and ability to supervise the infringing activity and also has a direct financial interest in such activities." *A & M Records, Inc. v. Napster, Inc.*, 114 F. Supp. 2d 896, 55 U.S.P.Q.2d (BNA) 1780 (N.D. Cal. 2000). 14 A.L.R. Fed. 825 (Originally published in 1973).

89 17 USC §507(b).

90 *Urbont v. Sony Music Entm't*, 863 F. Supp. 2d 279, 281 (S.D.N.Y. 2012).

91 See 17 USC §504 (2010).

92 See 17 USC §505 (2010).

93 See 17 USC §502 (2010).

94 See 17 USC §503 (2010).

95 See 17 USC §506 (2010); 18 USC §2319 (2010).

96 U.S. Copyright Office, Small Claims, U.S. Copyright Office, https://www.copyright.gov/about/small-claims/ (last visited Feb. 6, 2025).

97 U.S. Copyright Office, Copyright Claims Board, U.S. Copyright Office, https://www.ccb.gov/ (last visited Feb. 6, 2025).

98 U.S. Copyright Office, Report of the Register of Copyrights on the General Revision of the U.S. Copyright Law, at 24 (1961), available at https://www.copyright.gov/history/1961_registers_report.pdf.

99 *Cariou v. Prince*, 11–1197-CV, 2013 WL 1760521 [2d Cir Apr. 25, 2013] "We consider '(1) whether the work is expressive or creative,... with a greater leeway being allowed to a claim of fair use where the work is factual or informational, and (2) whether the work is published or unpublished, with the scope for fair use involving unpublished works being considerably narrower.'"

100 17 USC §107 (2025).

101 17 USC §107 (2025).

102 "The purpose and character of the use, including whether such use is of a commercial nature or is for nonprofit educational purposes." Judge Leval has variously described the first factor as "the soul of fair use,"1 and as the "heart of the fair use inquiry." Patry on Fair Use §3:1 (Quoting Judge Leval, Leval, 103 Harv. L. Rev. at 1116. See also *Blanch v. Koons*, 467 F.3d 244, 251 (2d Cir. 2006); *Davis v. The Gap, Inc.*, 246 F.3d 152, 174 (2d Cir. 2001) (Leval, J.)).

103 Cf. "But [the case law] cannot be read to mean that §107(1) weighs in favor of any use that adds some new expression, meaning, or message." *Andy Warhol Found. for the Visual Arts, Inc. v. Goldsmith*, 598 U.S. 508, 541, 143 S. Ct. 1258, 1282 (2023).

104 *Andy Warhol Found. for the Visual Arts, Inc. v. Goldsmith*, 598 U.S. 508, 529, 143 S. Ct. 1258, 1275 (2023).

105 *Andy Warhol Found. for the Visual Arts, Inc. v. Goldsmith*, 598 U.S. 508, 533, 143 S. Ct. 1258, 1277 (2023).

106 *A&M Records, Inc. v. Napster, Inc.*, 239 F.3d 1004, 1015 [9th Cir 2001].

107 *Andy Warhol Found. for the Visual Arts, Inc. v. Goldsmith*, 598 U.S. 508, 532-33, 143 S. Ct. 1258, 1277 (2023).

108 Patry on Fair Use §3:9 (citing *Campbell v. Acuff-Rose Music, Inc.*, 510 U.S. 569, 578–579, 114 S. Ct. 1164, 127 L. Ed. 2d 500 (1994)).

109 Although, exactly how Lady Justice can gaze with that blindfold over her eyes has defied legal commentators for centuries.

110 *Sony Corp. of America v. Universal City Studios, Inc.*, 464 U.S. 417, 455 n.40 (1984).

111 *Harper & Row Publishers, Inc. v. Nation Enterprises*, 471 US 539, 565 [1985].

112 *Lennon v. Premise Media Corp.* 556 F.Supp.2d 310, 327 (S.D.N.Y., 2008) ("In considering the fourth factor, [the] concern is not whether the secondary use suppresses or even destroys the market for the original work or its potential derivatives, but whether the secondary use usurps the market of the original work. The market for potential derivative uses includes only those that creators of original works would in general develop or license others to develop.").

113 Patry on Copyright, §10:150, Westlaw, (2010).

114 *Gottlieb Development LLC v. Paramount Pictures Corp.*, 590 F.Supp.2d 625, 632 (2008).

115 *Roginski v. Time Warner Interactive, Inc.*, 967 F.Supp 821, 832 [MD Pa 1997](Plaintiff failing to demonstrate that defendants' "Awesome Possum" character is so strikingly similar to Plaintiff's own "Awesome Possum" that there was no reasonable manner in which it could have been independently created.)

APPENDIX B

A Comic Creator's Guide to Protecting Ideas

THE LAW OF IDEAS

Without a doubt, copyright is the best way to protect a comic book property from being stolen. However, a creator may have only an *idea* for a comic book or graphic novel—a concept that has yet to be turned into a breathtaking work of sequential art—and copyright law does not protect ideas. In fact, even outside of copyright law, ideas can be very hard to protect legally: the law starts with the presumption that ideas are free for anyone to use.

Generally, for a creator to protect an idea when she is pitching it to a publishing company or another artist, the creator must get the other party to agree in a contract that the idea person will be compensated if their idea is used. And, unfortunately, even with a contract, some ideas may be so unoriginal that a court may not allow an artist to have a monopoly over that idea, even with a signed contract!

COPYRIGHT LAW DOESN'T PROTECT IDEAS!

"I have a copyright on my idea!" is a phrase that many artists utter, but it is a 100% legally impossible phrase. In fact, the copyright statute is quite explicit on the subject:

In no case does copyright protection for an original work of authorship extend to any idea, procedure, process, system, method of operation, concept, principle, or discovery, regardless of the form in which it is described, explained, illustrated, or embodied in such work.[1]

Example: Let's say that you are a writer with a great idea for a comic book character, and you're looking for an artist to help you illustrate it. You go to meetup groups looking for the right artist with whom to collaborate. You tell several artists about your character idea, take a look at their portfolios, and finally decide on somebody who seems like a good fit. But just as you finish up the comic book script and sit down to talk with your new partner, you see your character on the web... created by one of the artists you interviewed for the project!

You have timestamped emails showing that you sent your idea to the plagiarizing penciller before he created the project. Heck, you even have a Facebook post from him, in which he writes, "Thank you for telling me your comic book idea; it sounds great!"

It looks like you have a slam-dunk lawsuit for copyright infringement or idea misappropriation, right?

Not so fast. Unless your conversations rose to the level of creating a contract with this purloining painter, you may be out of luck. That's because the law really, really, really doesn't like giving anyone a monopoly over an idea. The plain and simple truth is that if you post your idea on the Internet or tell somebody your concept at a cocktail party, chances are you can wave (and waive) goodbye to owning that idea.

Why Is the Law so Hard on Ideas?

As the United States Supreme Court once said, "The general rule of law is, that the noblest of human productions—knowledge, truths ascertained, conceptions, and ideas—become, after voluntary communication to others, *free as the air to common use.*"[2]

This is because the law sees artistic ideas as building blocks for expressive works. Anyone who had exclusive rights to an idea would have a monopoly over that idea, which would frustrate the policy of copyright law, which is to encourage authors in the creation of new expressive works.

As the court pointed out while analyzing the difference between Superman and Capt. Marvel,[3] "A copyright never extends to the 'idea' of the 'work,' but only to its 'expression,' and that no one infringes, unless he descends so far into what is concrete as to invade that 'expression.'"[4]

Ideas vs. Expression

Okay, so we've seen that copyright law only protects expression, like writing and drawing, and it does not protect intangible ideas. What if you write down an idea—is that enough to protect it under copyright law?

Not quite. For instance, let's say you wrote down: "A super villain takes as a hostage someone that the superhero loves, and the superhero saves them." Would that have been protected by copyright law? After all, you typed it up and printed it out. That's a tangible means of expression, isn't it? Can't you just send your written idea to the copyright office for registration?

Well, if you were able to get it registered, the registration wouldn't be worth the paper it was printed on. All you've done is put an idea on paper. It's not *expressive* enough to be afforded protection. It's still just an idea, and ideas aren't protectable. I know what you're thinking: "Okay, smart guy, how much expression do I need in order for my concept to be protected?"

To answer that question, I have to toss up my hands, shrug my shoulders, and say, "I'm not sure."

Now, before you hurl this book across the room and complain to my publisher about my lack of copyright knowledge, let me point out that there is no cut-and-dry answer to the question of when the idea becomes expressed fully enough to be worthy of copyright protection. As a matter of fact, this "idea/expression dichotomy" is one of the great philosophical conundrums of U.S. copyright law. The more general and less specific a work is, the more likely a work will be seen as a mere concept and, therefore, not protected by copyright law. The oddly named but brilliantly minded Judge Learned Hand famously wrote:

> Upon any work... a great number of patterns of increasing generality will fit equally well, as more and more of the incident is left out. The last may perhaps be no more than the most general statement of what the [work] is about, and at times might consist only of its title; but there is a point in this series of abstractions where they are no longer protected, since otherwise the [author] could prevent the use of his 'ideas,' to which, apart from their expression, his property is never extended.[5]

The Copyright Golem

To understand this idea/expression dichotomy, it may be helpful to think of a sculptor's armature: a basic human form made from wire upon which any number of sculptures can be constructed. This is like the idea or concept—unprotectable by copyright.

Now, let's imagine the great superhero sculptor—"The Learned Hand"—is about to fashion a living golem upon this armature. He wraps a layer of clay upon the wire armature in preparation for building his homunculus hero. Meanwhile, as Learned Hand is sculpting, his archrival, Dr. Infringer, spies on Learned Hand and copies the superhero's work. At this point, there is still nothing unique or expressive that has been copied. This first layer of clay is required to bind additional, more expressive layers of clay to the armature. In comic book script terms, this first layer of clay is like using very plain and unexpressive language to describe a generic idea. It is given very little copyright protection, if any.

But the more the Learned Hand adds layers of musculature and unique flourishes to his clay creature's skin, scales, and costume design, the more it becomes an original and unique expression and subject to copyright protection. If Dr. Infringer copied the golem now, he would find himself on the losing end of a super battle—a super *copyright infringement* battle.

As you can see, the question of when form becomes ***expression*** is very case-specific and depends upon the work in question. In fact, it's an issue that courts struggle with virtually every single time they are presented with a copyright infringement claim.

In a copyright infringement lawsuit, if the plaintiff shows that the defendant copied his work without permission, the defendant will often try to rebut this allegation by pointing out that the only thing that was copied from the plaintiff was an unprotectable idea or concept. The court then has to figure out where along the copyright spectrum between idea (unprotectable) and expression (potentially protectable) the copying occurred. This philosophical tug-of-war, between concept and copyright, goes by the highfalutin name of "the idea/expression dichotomy."

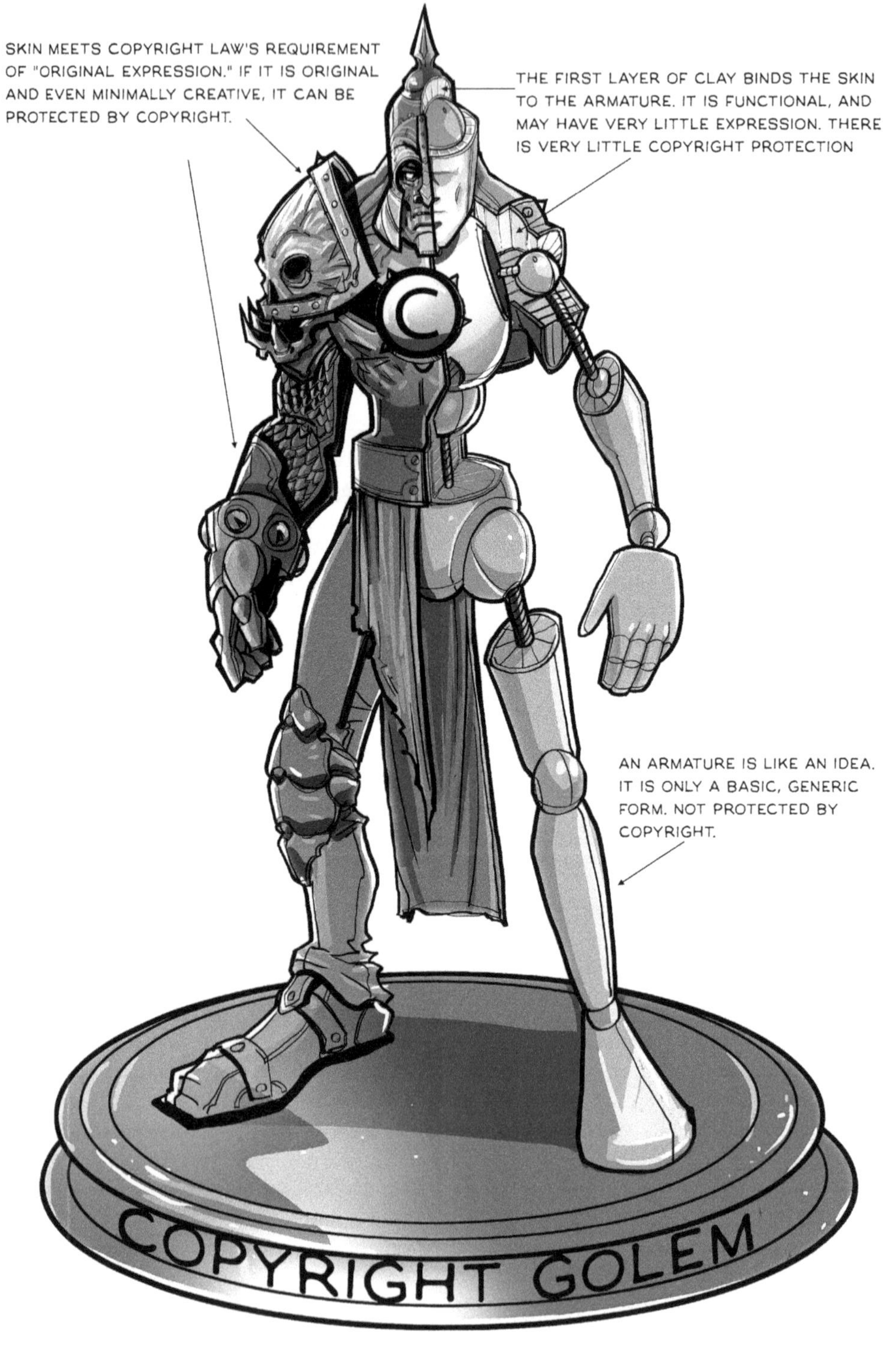
SKIN MEETS COPYRIGHT LAW'S REQUIREMENT OF "ORIGINAL EXPRESSION." IF IT IS ORIGINAL AND EVEN MINIMALLY CREATIVE, IT CAN BE PROTECTED BY COPYRIGHT.
THE FIRST LAYER OF CLAY BINDS THE SKIN TO THE ARMATURE. IT IS FUNCTIONAL, AND MAY HAVE VERY LITTLE EXPRESSION. THERE IS VERY LITTLE COPYRIGHT PROTECTION
AN ARMATURE IS LIKE AN IDEA. IT IS ONLY A BASIC, GENERIC FORM. NOT PROTECTED BY COPYRIGHT.
COPYRIGHT GOLEM

INTERVIEW

Pitch Execution, Not Ideas

"Keep in mind that ideas are a dime a dozen. Execution is everything. Don't worry about people stealing your ideas. However, if you are in a pitch meeting with a publisher and you don't have contracts, you want to make sure that you bring in **execution**, rather than just an **idea**."

AUTHOR DAVID GALLAHER *has received multiple Harvey Award nominations and won The Best Online Comic Award for his work on High Moon for DC Comics.*

Scènes à faire

Okay, so instead of just writing down the simple idea "A super villain takes as a hostage someone the superhero loves," let's say you began to put some meat on your golem's bones. Let's say you wrote down the following: "A supervillain takes as a hostage someone the superhero loves and threatens to injure the loved one unless the hero abandons his superpowers. The hero abandons his powers and confronts the supervillain. The hero manages to find a way to get his powers back just in time to fight the super villain, rescue his loved one, and destroy the villain's hideout."

Would this be enough expression to be protected by copyright law?

It depends upon what you're trying to protect: the phrases would probably be afforded very little copyright protection, as it is as utilitarian and un-expressive a phrasing of that idea as possible. But even if you could protect that small paragraph by copyright, the underlying concept of a "supervillain holding the hero's loved one hostage" is a plot sequence that is so clichéd that, as a *matter of law,* it would probably be found to be unprotectable. In the end, even if you had a copyright registration for the paragraph, it would not allow you to stop somebody else from making a comic book based upon the concept.

Copyright law has a term for that: *Scènes à faire*. This fancy French term means elements, themes, or scenes that naturally result from genre conventions so as to be unprotectable as a matter of law. In other words, these are standard conventions that naturally arise from the genre and cannot be claimed as original by any one creator.

SCENES À FAIRE

Copyright law does not protect "*scènes à faire*," which are:

- "Incidents, characters or settings which are as a practical matter indispensable, or at least standard, in the treatment of a given topic."[6]
- "Thematic concepts... which necessarily must follow from certain plot situations."[7]
- "[those scenes] which flow naturally from generic plotlines[...]."[8]

Examples:

- "[a] dinosaur zoo or adventure park, with electrified fences, automated tours, dinosaur nurseries, and uniformed workers, these settings are classic scenes a faire that flow from the uncopyrightable concept of a dinosaur zoo."[9]
- Police dramas that include foot chases, the morale problems of policemen, and characters such as drunks, prostitutes, vermin, and derelict cars.[10]
- And with superheroes, a non-exhaustive list might include "scenes that depict the superhero 'perform[ing] feats of miraculous strength,' wearing a 'tight-fitting acrobatic costume[ ],' battling 'wealthy megalomaniacal villains,' exercising the 'power of self-propelled flight,' or leading a double life are all unprotectable *scènes à faire*."[11]
- Similarly unprotectable:
- "Basic plot ideas are not protected by copyright law."[12]

Now, please don't misunderstand me. You could take that "hero-gives-up-his-powers-to-save-his-loved-one" concept and flesh it out with fresh dialogue, new scene sequences, expressive illustrations, etc., and have a comic book that is fully protected by copyright law. However, if another artist reads your comic book and is inspired to create her own comic book based upon that same concept, she could do so. That's the point of ideas: to inspire. What she couldn't do, however, is copy how you've expressed your ideas—the artwork, words, sequence of events, etc. (what copyright law calls your "original expression"). For more on this, see Copyright Infringement, p. 44.

The takeaway here is this: don't turn to copyright law to protect your ideas and concepts. And even if your work is very expressive, the ideas contained within that work are not to be protected by copyright law. ***Remember: inspiration is not infringement.***

That all being said, if you're really determined to protect a concept, as opposed to an expression, there may be a way to do it.

And that way is with a contract.

PROTECTING IDEAS THROUGH CONTRACT

Although we can't use copyright law to safeguard our ideas, we still have one superpower in our arsenal that will help us: the Almighty Contract. In general, here's how it works: if someone agrees not to exploit your idea and then they do, you may be able to sue them for breach of contract.

That's the basic idea, anyway. But from here on, it becomes more nuanced. For instance, the kind of contract you have matters (**express** or **implied**), as does when you enter the contract (**pre-disclosure** or **post-disclosure**), as does the **novelty** of your idea.

THE STATE YOU'RE IN

States, to differing degrees, offer contract protection for ideas, but because it's on a state-by-state basis, the laws differ drastically throughout the country. Make sure you know which state's law controls your contract for the protection of your idea.

Say you want to pitch your idea for a new comic book series to a publishing company. Let's take a look and see how and when your idea might be protected and when it might not.

No Contract

Let's start first with the worst-case scenario. You tell someone your story idea, but there is no contract between you two, or you post your idea online and a stranger sees it. That person who hears or reads your idea then decides to make their own comic book based upon your idea. Unfortunately, you have an almost impossible task ahead of you if you try to sue them for misappropriation of your idea (using your idea without permission): you would have to prove to a court that your idea is *so unique and original that it should be treated as your private property*. However, in practice, this often amounts to having to prove that your idea was so unique that no one else in the world had ever conceived it! As you can imagine, that's the very definition of a losing proposition.

No Contract = No Idea Protection: Without a contract, your idea is not protected.

- **A pre-disclosure agreement** is a contract you make with a party before you tell them your idea.
- **A post-disclosure agreement** is a contract entered into with the party after they have heard your idea.

Pre-disclosure Express Contract

Let's say you're about to pitch your comic book idea to a publishing company, but before you tell them your concept, you actually discuss the terms under which you agree to disclose your idea. Before they hear it, you both discuss and *agree* to specific contractual terms under which you will disclose your idea, including:

1. That they will treat the idea that you're about to disclose to them as your proprietary property,
2. They will not use it or disclose it to others without your permission, and
3. If they exploit your idea, they will pay you an agreed-upon amount of money.

Now you have an **express pre-disclosure contract** with the publishing company. Feel free to pitch away. If the publishing company uses your concept after they've agreed not to, you can sue them for breach of contract. However, they may still have some defenses, such as the following:

- **Independent creation.** They had developed an idea similar to yours through independent means (in other words, they didn't copy your idea but got it another way).
- **Generic**. Your idea was so **generic** that, as a matter of law, it should not be protectable.

But stop and think about this for a moment. How likely is it that a publishing company is going to expressly agree not to exploit your idea, no matter what it is, before they've heard it? Furthermore, most people just go to pitch meetings and pitch their ideas without ever talking about contracts beforehand. Therefore, to the extent that there is a contract in place, it is often an *implied-in-fact* contract.

IMPLIED VS. EXPRESS CONTRACTS

When you start to do business with others, you'll be faced with two types of contracts. The two flavors are the **express contract** and the **implied contract**. The second is the one that really causes unexpected problems.

- An **express contract** is one in which all the elements and terms of a contract (offer, acceptance, consideration, etc.) are specifically stated. (See What is a Contract?, p. 78) An express contract is usually, but not always, in writing.
- An **implied contract** is an agreement that arises based on circumstances or by the actions or behavior of the parties. In other words, the contract may be created because the parties are acting as though a contract is in place, even though the terms of the agreement are not fully discussed. When you pitch an idea to somebody in a business meeting, and the industry practice is that people who pitch ideas are expected to be paid for them, you may be entering into an implied contract with the person to whom you're pitching the idea.

For more on the elements of a contract, see Contracts: The Engine Which Drives the Deal, p. 77.

The Pre-disclosure Implied-in-Fact Contract

This is the scenario in which you pitch your idea to a publishing company, but no agreement regarding your idea is discussed first. Or maybe you talked about some aspects of the business relationship, but not all of the key terms. However, industry practice suggests that creative types, such as yourself, only pitch ideas to publishing companies if there's an expectation that if the publishing company uses your idea, you will be compensated. Now, even though you didn't discuss it, you may be able to argue that there was an implied-in-fact contract for the protection of your idea. However, for a court to find an implied-in-fact contract, you'll have to show:

1. That you submitted an idea to the publishing company, which the company received; and
2. Before you submitted your idea to the publishing company, you clearly conditioned your disclosure upon the company's agreement to pay for any of your ideas that the company used; and
3. That the company knew, or should have known, this condition upon which the disclosure was being made before the disclosure was made; and
4. That the company voluntarily accepted the submission on your terms and thereby impliedly agreed to pay you the reasonable value of any of your ideas it used; and

5. That in publishing your comic book, the publishing company actually used your ideas; that is, that the project was based substantially upon your ideas rather than on the company's own idea(s) or those from any other source(s); and
6. The ideas the company used had value.[13]

Many states require that your idea also be **novel,** that is *new* and *unique* as opposed to a mere rehashing of generic concepts.

The "Novelty" Requirement

Many states agree that to receive any protection at all, an idea must be novel, that is, new and unique, if it is to be protected by an implied contract. Let's take a look and see how this works in practice. Let's say a comic book creator wants to pitch an idea for a new comic book series to a small publishing company.

- *If there is a contract* between the creator and the publishing company for the protection of the idea, the creator's idea only needs to be novel *to the publishing company* or other party that is hearing the idea for the first time.[14]
  In other words, as long as the publishing company had never heard this particular idea before, the fact that other companies might have heard it would not destroy the contract between the creator and the publishing company. Again, the important thing is that the contract is entered into *prior to* the idea being disclosed.
- However, *without a contract* between the creator and the publishing company, the creator must prove that his idea was so novel that no one else in the world had ever conceived of it!

To make things even tougher, some ideas are deemed so lacking in novelty that even a contract won't protect them.

Determining an Idea's Novelty

So how do you figure out whether an idea is novel enough to be protected? One New York court[15] listed the following factors as among those courts will use to judge the novelty of an idea:

- The idea's specificity or generality, that is, is it a generic concept or one of specific application?
- How common an idea is it, that is, how many people know of this idea?
- How unique is the idea, that is, how different is this idea from generally known ideas?
- The commercial availability of the idea, that is, how widespread is the idea's use in the comic book industry?

However, as the court pointed out, an idea will not be considered novel if:

- It is merely a variation on a basic theme[16] or
- It is merely a clever or useful adaptation of existing knowledge.

Furthermore, just as in copyright law, the publishing company will not be liable to the creator if it can prove that it came up with its similar comic book concept through its own initiative or through wholly independent means.[17] (See The Doctrine of Independent Creation, p. 383.)

Post-Disclosure Agreements

And finally, there's the scenario in which you pitch an idea to somebody, and *after* they hear it, they agree to compensate you if they exploit it. In other words, they enter into a contract with you after they've heard the idea: a post-disclosure agreement. In this scenario, courts don't really look at novelty, which makes sense: since the receiving party has already heard your idea before entering into a contract, they can judge its novelty and value for themselves. For these reasons, courts often uphold post-disclosure agreements.

EXPRESS CONTRACTS CONTROLLING IDEA DISCLOSURE

Two common types of written express agreements that deal with idea disclosure are the **non-disclosure agreement (NDA)**—also known as an "NDA"—and a **submission release form**. These contracts are virtually the exact opposite of each other:

- Someone who signs an **NDA** is promising not to disclose or exploit an idea they receive unless they have a written agreement with the party telling them the idea.
- Someone who signs a **submission release form**, by contrast, is giving up the right to sue for idea misappropriation or breach of contract if their idea is used by the receiving party. <u>Publishing companies often require comic book artists to sign a submission release form before they're allowed to pitch an idea to them</u>.

Safeguard Your Ideas with an NDA

Like all agreements for the protection of ideas, an NDA is a contract in which the recipient of confidential information agrees that:

- Your idea is unique and valuable.
- Your idea is your proprietary information.
- They will keep this idea confidential.

EXAMPLE: NON-DISCLOSURE AGREEMENT

This Agreement dated ______________, 20___ (the "Effective Date") is made by and between Waldo Writer, residing at ____________________ ("**Writer**"), and Izzy Illustrator, residing at ____________________ ("**Recipient**"), for the purpose of protecting and preserving confidential information to be disclosed or made available by Writer to Recipient under this Agreement. The parties agree as follows:

1. Confidential Information

1.1. The information disclosed under this Agreement (the "Confidential Information"**★1**) includes, but is not limited to, the following:

1.1.1. All non-public information, whether written, oral, electronic, or otherwise, including ideas, concepts, characters, or designs, in connection with the comic book tentatively titled "The Adventures of Maggot Man"**★2** and created by Writer (the "Comic Book").

1.2. Recipient acknowledges Writer's proprietary rights in the Confidential Information, as well as the uniqueness of the Confidential Information.**★3**

2. Purpose

2.1. Recipient agrees to use the Confidential Information solely for the following purpose (the "Purpose"**★4**):

2.1.1. Evaluating a potential business relationship with Writer regarding services that Recipient may be asked to provide in connection with the illustration, creation, and/or development of the Comic Book.

3. Term

3.1. This Agreement shall be effective for five (5) years from the Effective Date of this Agreement.

--------COMMENTS--------

1 In a non-disclosure agreement, it is critical to identify information that is considered confidential and, therefore, subject to the agreement's protections.

2 Insert the title of the comic book here.

3 If possible, try to get the recipient to acknowledge your proprietary rights in the idea. This, understandably, may be difficult and is very situation-dependent. After all, unless the recipient knows a little bit about your idea, how can they base their decision as to whether or not they should consider it proprietary? Yet, if you disclose the idea to them without the protection of the NDA, it might be appropriated. To overcome this potential "Catch-22," you may have to dole out just enough information about your concept for them to realize that it is indeed unique (at least to them), have them sign the NDA, and then fully disclose all of your confidential materials.

4 NDAs are created for specific purposes. In this case, the purpose is for the writer to evaluate a potential business relationship with the illustrator.

4. Terms and Conditions

4.1. All Confidential Information is, and shall remain, the property of the Writer. The Recipient does not acquire any intellectual property, copyright or trademark rights, or any rights of ownership under this Agreement.**★5**

4.2. The Recipient shall not use the Confidential Information or disclose it to third parties during the Term of this Agreement, unless such use or disclosure of the Confidential Information is:

4.2.1. Required by judicial action after all available legal remedies to maintain the confidentiality of the information have been exhausted;

4.2.2. Provided to the Recipient by a third party who has a right to do so and without restriction on disclosure; or

4.2.3. Approved by the Writer in each specific instance.**★6**

4.3. Recipient shall protect the Confidential Information and prevent its unauthorized use, dissemination, or publication using the same degree of care (or greater) taken by Recipient to protect his/her own confidential information. The Recipient acknowledges that the unauthorized use of the Writer's information will cause great or irreparable injury to Writer and that it will be extremely difficult to determine the amount of compensation necessary to afford Writer adequate relief. For this reason, the Recipient agrees that the Writer will have the right to obtain injunctive relief in addition to any other rights and remedies he may have.**★7**

4.4. This Agreement shall be binding upon and shall inure to the benefit of both parties, their legal representatives, assigns, and successors.**★8**

5. Return of Information

5.1. If the parties hereto are unable to come to an agreement regarding a subsequent agreement to work together in

5 This clause underscores that the IP rights in the confidential information stay with the writer. If the writer and illustrator decide to work together and share the copyright in their joint work, the collaboration agreement, which outlines their new relationship, should very specifically supersede this paragraph.

6 There are several situations in which the recipient may be permitted to disclose confidential information. These include instances where the law compels disclosure, when a third party discloses the same information to the recipient without any confidentiality requirements, or if the writer provides approval for disclosure.

7 The recipient is obligated to treat the confidential information with a great deal of care. Furthermore, the recipient acknowledges that the writer may seek injunctive relief to prevent the confidential information disclosure, if necessary.

8 If the writer assigns the intellectual property of the confidential information to another party, for instance, a publisher, the illustrator will still be required to keep the information confidential, this time, protecting the publisher as well.

furtherance of the Purpose, the recipient shall return all Confidential Information immediately upon request and delete all electronic copies in the recipient's copies.*9

6. Choice of Law

6.1. This Agreement shall be construed, interpreted, and governed by the laws of the State of New York.

7. Entire Agreement

7.1. This Agreement is intended as the complete agreement on this subject matter and supersedes all other proposals, previous agreements, or commitments, whether oral or written, between Writer and Recipient. Neither party has relied on the statements of the other as inducement to enter into this agreement. This Agreement may only be modified by a written instrument executed by both the Writer and the Recipient.

In Witness Whereof, the parties have duly executed this Agreement:

Writer:	Recipient:
Waldo Writer	Izzy Illustrator
By: ______________________	By: ______________________

IDEA PRE-FLIGHT CHECKLIST

- The more novel your idea, the better. The more detailed your idea, the better.
- Try to avoid protecting an idea in the first place. The best protection comes from creating a copyrightable work and registering it with the United States Copyright Office. (See Copyright Registration, p. 363.)
- If you're going to be pitching your idea to a potential collaborator, try to get them to sign an NDA. (See Safeguard Your Ideas with an NDA, p. 401.)
- If you're going to be pitching ideas to a publishing company, be careful about signing a submission release.

9 If you can't arrive at an agreement to work together after the information has been disclosed and working relationships have been negotiated, you need to ensure that you can either get back your confidential information or that it will be deleted to avoid it falling into the wrong hands.

Bottom line: If you have a great idea for a comic book character, it's better to write a script or illustrate a character and protect them through copyright than to try and protect the idea itself. If you do want to try to protect the idea, use a contract.

Notes

1 17 U.S.C. § 102(b) (1976).
2 *International News Service v. Associated Press*, 248 U.S. 215, 250 (1918).
3 Although ultimately the court found that Capt. Marvel had infringed Superman, I think this case might have gone the other way if decided today.
4 *Nat'l Comics Publ'n v. Fawcett Publications*, 191 F.2d 594, 600 (2d Cir. 1951) supplemented sub nom. *Nat'l Comics Publications v. Fawcett Publications*, 198 F.2d 927 (2d Cir. 1952).
5 *Nichols v. Universal Pictures Corp.*, 45 F.2d 119, 121 (2d Cir. 1930).
6 *Hogan v. DC Comics*, 48 F.Supp. 2d 298, 309 (S.D.N.Y. 1999) (citing to *Hoehling v. Universal City Studios, Inc.*, 618 F.2d 972, 979 (2d Cir.1980)).
7 *Hogan v. DC Comics*, 48 F.Supp. 2d 298, 309 (S.D.N.Y. 1999) (citing to *Reyher v. Children's Television Workshop*, 533 F.2d 87, 91 (2d Cir.1976)).
8 *Thomas v. Walt Disney Co.*, C-07–4392 CW, 2008 WL 425647 (N.D. Cal. Feb. 14, 2008) aff 'd, 337 F. App'x 694 (9th Cir. 2009).
9 *Williams v. Crichton*, 84 F.3d 581, 589 (2d Cir. 1996) (analyzing whether or not Jurassic Park infringed upon the book Dinosaur World").
10 *Walker v. Time Life Films, Inc.*, 784 F.2d 44, 50 (2d Cir. 1986).
11 *Lewinson v. Henry Holt & Co.*, LLC, 659 F. Supp. 2d 547, 567 (S.D.N.Y. 2009) (citing to *Warner Bros. Inc. v. Am. Broad. Cos.*, 654 F.2d 204, 210 (2d Cir.1981)).
12 *Thomas v. Walt Disney Co.*, C-07–4392 CW, 2008 WL 425647 (N.D. Cal. Feb. 14, 2008) aff 'd, 337 F. App'x 694 (9th Cir. 2009).
13 William O. Knox, The Role of Novelty in A California Idea Submission Case, 11 UCLA Ent. L. Rev. 27, 28 (2004) (citing to *Mann v. Columbia Pictures, Inc.*, 180 Cal. Rptr. 522, 533 n.6 (Cal. Ct. App. 1982).
14 *Montz v. Pilgrim Films & Television, Inc.*, WL 2197421, C.A.9 (Cal.), June 3, 2010.
15 *Nadel v. Play-By-Play Toys & Novelties, Inc.*, 208F.3d 368 (2d Cir. 2000).
16 *Alliance Sec. Prods., Inc. v. Fleming & Co.*, 290 F. App'x 380, 383 (2d Cir. 2008) ("When 'an idea consists in essence of nothing more than a variation on a basic theme... novelty cannot be found to exist.'").
17 *Hollywood Screentest of Am., Inc. v. NBC Universal, Inc.*, 151 Cal. App. 4th 631, 646, 60 Cal. Rptr. 3d 279, 290 (Cal. Ct. App. 2007).

APPENDIX C

A Comic Creator's Guide to Trademark Law

OVERVIEW OF TRADEMARK LAW

"Look up in the air: It's a bird! It's a plane! It's... a trademark!"

When most people think of a trademark, they think of logos for products, like the distinctive "3D" look of Superman's name[1] (Superman® comic books,[2] Superman® brand candy[3]) or services (Superman Ride of Steel®[4]). This is fairly accurate, since trademarks and service marks are used (1) to identify and distinguish a trademark owner's goods and services from those sold by others and (2) to identify for consumers the source of those goods and services.

Furthermore, the image of cartoon comic book characters themselves can function as trademarks, as long as they identify the source of the work of entertainment or expression.[5]

A wide variety of things can be trademarked: colors, sounds, phrases, drawings, and smells. What they all have in common is that all trademarks must be distinctive enough to act as a source identifier for their owners.[6]

The policy of copyright law is to protect authors; the policy behind trademark law is to protect business interests, specifically "**goodwill**." Because of this, trademark rights start with a trademark's **use**, not from its creation. Although every state has its own trademark law to protect intrastate trademarks, the strongest trademark protection in the United States is granted by the federal government. And that protection is only granted after a *lengthy* application and approval process with the U.S. Patent and Trademark Office (**USPTO**), after you prove to its satisfaction that:

1. The mark is distinct,
2. Is or will be used in commerce, and
3. Doesn't conflict with other registered marks (as well as a number of other factors).

Once registered, you can bring the mighty power of federal law to bear against anybody who tries to use a trademark that is confusingly similar to yours, on goods or services similar to yours, in commerce.[7]

Unlike a copyright, a trademark is potentially perpetual in nature—it exists as long as you continue to use it, and it continues to identify its source. If it becomes a generic term—"aspirin," for instance, was once a trademark—then your trademark suffers the ignoble death of "**genericide**." To maintain a healthy trademark, you must police infringement by others and maintain tight control over how it is used by your licensors. If you trademark your superhero's name and then license your character to be used on lunchboxes, you should have a quality control provision in your merchandiser's manufacturing agreement giving you the right to review and approve the trademark's appearance on those lunchboxes and to destroy any non-compliant merchandise.

One of the strongest defenses against the charge of trademark infringement, tarnishment, or false endorsement (See Injuries to a Trademark, p. 413) is the assertion of your First Amendment rights as a creator.

It is beyond the scope of this book to go into ways to register your trademark, and for titles of a single artistic work, like a single issue of a comic book, it's almost impossible. So instead, I'm going to concentrate on the types of trademark *use* that get comic book creators into trouble: when they use or feature a trademark they don't own in their work and/or its marketing.

What Makes a Trademark?

Marks that distinguish goods are called "trademarks," and marks that distinguish services are called, not surprisingly, "service marks." Trademark rights begin with a trademark's use, and the first user of the trademark (often referred to as the **senior user**) has rights over subsequent users (often referred to as **junior users**).

The key to a trademark is that it has to be distinctive: it has to effectively distinguish your goods and services from those of other manufacturers and service providers. What this means for you is that you can protect your design through trademark law to the extent that your character is (1) distinct from other artists' comic book characters, (2) your comic book readers recognize that character as associated with you, and (3) you created and used this trademark first.

There are primarily two ways in which a mark can be distinctive:

Inherent Distinctiveness

The mark is **inherently distinctive**. Coined and fanciful terms and novel designs are usually considered inherently distinctive.

> Example: You create a superhero character named "Xortblort," whose insignia is a big Times Roman X on his chest. His fanciful name would probably be inherently distinctive if you tried to register it as a trademark, whereas a Times Roman "X" would not be.

Acquired Distinctiveness/Secondary Meaning

The mark has **acquired distinctiveness**, also known as "**secondary meaning**." What this means is that through successful marketing, promotion, advertising, publishing, and other exploitation by the mark's owner, the relevant customer base associates the mark with the mark's owner.

> Example: You create a superhero character with the power of super-strong bad breath and try to trademark just his name (not his image or logo design): "Halitosis Hero." The USPTO might find that the name is merely descriptive of your character, and thus not registrable unless you can show secondary meaning in the mark, in other words that a significant number of comic book readers identified the name "Halitosis Hero" with your character.

This is because marks that are "merely descriptive" are not registrable without secondary meaning. Of course, the design or look of the hero himself may be separately registrable as a trademark, despite the name being descriptive.

SECONDARY MEANING

If a mark is not inherently distinctive, in order to be accorded the legal right of a trademark, it must have acquired distinctiveness in the minds of the consumer. This acquired distinctiveness is also known as "secondary meaning."

> Secondary meaning exists when the trademark is interpreted by the consuming public to be not only an identification of the product, but also a representation of the product's origin. Secondary meaning is generally established through extensive advertising which creates in the mind of consumers an association between different products bearing the same mark.[8]

ACQUIRED DISTINCTIVENESS = SECONDARY MEANING

Example: You create a super-powered military character called "Mega-Soldier" and want to trademark just the name for military action figures. It is likely that this rather generic name would be seen as merely descriptive, rather than distinctive. However, with enough advertising and promotion, consumers might begin to associate the mark "Mega-Soldier" with your character. If you can show that enough consumers make the association between your Mega-Soldier Mark and you as the source of this mark, your trademark will have "acquired distinctiveness" and thus achieved "secondary meaning." You can now stop others from using a similar mark in a manner that would confuse consumers.

What Can Be Trademarked?

Anything that can act as a source identifier can be trademarked. A slogan, insignia, character design, catchphrase, distinctive packaging, melody, sound, color, and even smells have been trademarked.

Comic book creators often register the trademark in:

- Superhero designs
- Catchphrases
- Logos
- The title of the comic book series
- Publishing Company Names
- Superhero team names
- Trade dress (see below)

However, while trademarking a hero character's name or her logo is relatively straightforward, trademarking the title of a single book is not. This is one place where it's easier to be the creator of a serialized work like a comic book than it is to be the author of a solo graphic novel. To grant protection for a single-title work, "secondary meaning" must be demonstrated.[9]

Trade Dress

The overall distinctive look and feel of a superhero—which functions as a source identifier—is its "**Trade Dress**." In other words, when a consumer encounters the complete visual package that is Spider-Man or Superman, the superheroes' Trade Dress creates an association in the consumer's mind with Marvel and DC, respectively. Trade dress is not an article of clothing, so even though Spider-Man wears tights, he also has a trade dress.

If you think you own a protectable Trade Dress in your comic book character, file for registration at the USPTO. You must prove to the USPTO that your mark:

- is distinctive (or has acquired distinctiveness)
- is non-functional[10]

In order to enforce your trade dress rights, your mark must be clearly articulated, distinctive, and non-functional. Now, if another creator comes along and develops a character whose trade dress is similar to yours, and that similarity confuses or is likely to confuse consumers as to who owns which character, you can sue for infringement[11] and ask the court to enjoin the sale of this other character's merchandise.

STRENGTH OF A TRADEMARK

A trademark becomes *more* distinctive the *less* "on the nose" it is: the greater a creative leap that is required by the consumer to bridge the gap between the mark and its owner, the stronger the mark is.

Generic Marks

Generic marks are not registrable at all. So if you created a comic book hero character and tried to register the name "comic book hero," you would probably be rejected by the USPTO, because that is the categorical term for a hero in comic books, the class of goods for which you would be registering your mark.[12] It is important to note that trademark registration is very category-specific; there is a rock group called "Comic Book Heroes,"[13] but note that they have registered the mark for musical entertainment services, not for comic books.

No amount of secondary meaning will make a generic mark registrable.

Merely Descriptive Marks

Merely descriptive marks are not registrable without secondary meaning (see above). Here, the mark, while not the name of the category of good or service itself, only describes the good or service. For example, the name (but not the design) "Tights and Cape-Wearing, Super-Powered Man" would be hard to register unless you show that comic book readers identified and recognized this character as being connected with you or your publishing company.

Suggestive Marks

Suggestive marks hint at the nature or the quality of the good or service. These are registrable without showing secondary meaning (but there are other reasons why they might not be registrable). For example, if instead of "Halitosis Hero," we called our stinky breath hero above "Capt. Garlic," we would have a greater chance of registering his name.

Arbitrary Marks

Arbitrary marks are also registrable without showing secondary meaning. These are marks that use an ordinary word but with a meaningless context; for example, naming your super-strong time-traveling steampunk hero "Mr. Walnut." Walnuts typically have very little connection to time travel.[14]

Fanciful Marks

Fanciful marks are those that consist entirely of made-up words and are also registrable without secondary meaning. For example, my hero "Xortblort," above.

Goodwill

You may see the term "goodwill" associated with trademark terminology in a variety of licensing agreements. "Goodwill" is a term of art in trademark law; roughly speaking, it represents aspects that contribute to the customer patronage of a business.[15]

You can't assign a trademark without assigning the goodwill of the business along with it.

INJURIES TO A TRADEMARK

Copyrights can be infringed, but trademarks can be injured in a variety of different ways.

Trademark law protects commercial interests from a broad range of injuries: infringement, dilution, false endorsement, unfair competition, and more.[16] We'll focus on a few of these here.

This provision establishes that anyone who uses or reproduces a registered mark without permission—whether by directly copying it or creating a similar version—is liable if that use is connected to selling, promoting, or advertising goods or services in a way that could confuse consumers or mislead them about the source of the product.

It's important to note that the statute is chiefly aimed at protecting the commercial aspects of trademarks. That is, it mostly applies when marks are used in packaging, merchandise, advertising, or branding. In contrast, marks used within a First Amendment context—like in artistic work, commentary, or criticism—are generally not the target of this law, though if those marks are later used in connection with merchandising or core branding activities, they might still fall under its purview.

Trademark Infringement

When a junior user uses a mark that is the same or similar to yours, and that mark is **likely to cause confusion to your consumers**, you may be able to sue them for trademark infringement. What this means is that when your consumers (comic book readers and purchasers of action figures) encounter a mark that looks or sounds like yours but is being used without your permission by a junior user to advertise or brand their work, and your readers are or are likely to be confused as to whether that junior user's comics and toys are made by you, you may have a claim for trademark infringement.

> Example: You create a steampunk comic book character called "The Chartreuse Chanteuse"—French cancan girl by night, hero by day; her skin was stained in a distinctive yellow green paisley pattern after falling into a vat of magical absinthe. You register this distinctively featured character as a trademark for a line of handmade absinthe decanters, featuring the image of The Chartreuse Chanteuse.

You sell your marked products online and at steampunk, gaming, and comic book conventions around the country. Your first-year sales are impressive; people love your character so much so that when conventioneers see "The Chartreuse Chanteuse," they think of you and your company. In other words, it's acquired a secondary meaning.

But the next year you do the convention circuit, you see that another merchandiser has come out with its own line of handmade absinthe decanters. However, these competing decanters are marked with the logo "The **S**hartreuse **S**hanteuse." On these shoddy, knockoff decanters is a similar yellow-green steampunk heroine. Not exactly the same as yours, mind you; there are differences. However, if consumers are likely to be confused and think that this new interloper's products are yours, or vice versa, you can sue for trademark infringement.

Trademark infringement turns on the "likelihood of consumer confusion." The more the following elements are present, the more likely consumers will be confused by a junior user's use of your mark:

- You have an inherently strong mark.
- Both marks were used on similar goods and services.
- The junior user's mark is very similar to yours.
- There's evidence that your consumers were actually confused as to whose mark is whose.
- The junior user used similar marketing channels to those you use.

- Your consumers are not likely to exert a lot of care in selecting the goods and services both you and the junior user have marked (the thought being that the less a consumer typically cares about deciding whether to purchase your product or the junior user's, the easier it will be for the consumer to be confused).
- There's evidence that the junior user intended to use a mark that was similar to yours.
- If the junior user is using his mark on different types of goods or services than you use your mark on, the likelihood that your business will expand to encompass those additional goods and services in the future.[17]

As in all trademark disputes, the timeliness of who *used* the mark first, as well as who *registered* the mark first, are key factors.

Penalties for Trademark Infringement

When the defendant is found liable for trademark infringement, a court can order a host of remedies for the successful plaintiff, including:

- **Injunctions**—the court can order the losing defendant to destroy all of the infringing merchandise it created, stop distributing merchandise, and take other steps as required to correct the problem.[18]
- **Money damages**—whatever profits the defendant made and loss of sales you, the plaintiff, may have suffered as a result of the infringing activity—can be recovered by the successful plaintiff. The court even has the power to triple the amount of money the plaintiff should receive in egregious cases.[19]
- **Attorney's fees**—when federally registered trademarks are infringed, winning plaintiffs can also ask for their attorney's fees to be paid by the losing defendant.
- **Counterfeit[20] marks**—if the mark was not just infringed but was counterfeited (in other words, the defendant intended to create a confusing mark, like the makers of the Gucc**ci** bag), then the penalties are much higher. They include statutory damages,[21] *mandatory* treble damages,[22] and reasonable attorney's fees.[23]

INFECTED, POLLUTED... DILUTED!

"The term 'dilution' means the lessening of the capacity of a famous mark to identify and distinguish goods or services, regardless of the presence or absence of—(1) competition between the owner of the famous mark and other parties, or (2) likelihood of confusion, mistake, or deception."[24]

> Confusion leads to immediate injury, while *dilution is an infection, which if allowed to spread, will inevitably destroy the advertising value of the mark.*[25]

No! NO! Not the spreading infection of dilution... EEEEEEEK!

Dilution

If someone damages the distinctive quality of your trademark, you can sue them for diluting your mark... but only if you own a **famous** mark (e.g., Batman, the Hulk, etc.).

In dilution cases, the consumers often know that your mark and the junior user's mark represent different owners and maybe even different industries:

> **Example**: Batman is a comic book character protected by numerous trademarks; the character appears on merchandise, apparel, movies, and of course, comic books, just to name a few categories. However, what if a sports manufacturer invented a special rack which held baseball bats, and sold it under the title "Batman," but the manufacture **did not use** any of the DC comic book character's distinctive logos or designs? Let's further assume that consumers do not think that DC Comics was the source or affiliated with the baseball rack manufacturer.

No infringement, right? Under those facts, probably not. However, DC could still sue the sports manufacturer for **trademark dilution**. The theory being that the more unaffiliated "Batman" marks there are out there, the less effective DC's registered Batman will be in identifying DC as its source.

To sue somebody for dilution, you need to show:

1. "That you own a famous mark that is distinctive;
2. that the defendant has commenced using a mark in commerce that allegedly is diluting your famous mark;
3. that a similarity between the defendant's mark and your famous mark gives rise to an association between the marks; and
4. that the association is likely to impair the distinctiveness of your famous mark or likely to harm the reputation of the famous mark."[26]

There are two "flavors" of dilution: **blurring** and **tarnishment**.

Blurring

With trademark blurring, consumer confusion is not the problem. The problem is that the ability of your mark to identify with you or your company is reduced—diluted—because there is *another similar mark* on the market that is identified with a different company.

> **Example**: Loony Lawncare, LLC markets "Incredible Hulk" brand lawnmower bags, but does not use the Superhero design, just the name. Presumably, consumers know that Marvel is not in the lawn care business. But if Loony is allowed to keep this mark on its bags, when people see the phrase "Incredible Hulk," they might not think exclusively of Marvel, but of Loony as well. In a sense, Loony is piggy-backing on the time, effort, and money Marvel expended in making that phrase distinctive for its superhero products. Marvel can sue for dilution, through blurring. This is similar to the Batman/baseball bat rack example, on the previous page.

WHEN THE LINE IS BLURRED

"'Dilution by blurring' is association arising from the similarity between a mark or trade name and a famous mark that impairs the distinctiveness of the famous mark." 15 USCA §1125(c)2(b)[27]

HOW DO YOU KNOW IF A MARK IS FAMOUS?

Only famous marks can be tarnished or diluted under federal law.[28] But how famous does a mark need to be?

"A mark is famous if it is widely recognized by the general consuming public of the United States as a designation of source of the goods or services of the mark's owner."[29]

Trademark Tarnishment

When silver corrodes, it becomes tarnished. Your trademark can also become tarnished—its value is corroded—when someone uses your mark or a mark similar to yours in a scandalous or disparaging manner. It's almost like defamation of a trademark.

Example: A plumbing fixture company manufactures a new toilet and sells it under the mark "Aquaman." Even though most consumers would not assume that DC is now in the plumbing business, the mark might create a negative association between the Atlantean King and a less than royal throne. Even though there is no likelihood of consumer confusion, DC Comics could sue, asserting that Aquaman's trademark and trident are tarnished.

TARNISHED AND CORRODED

"'Dilution by tarnishment' is the association arising from the similarity between a mark or trade name and a famous mark that harms the reputation of the famous mark." 15 USCA §1125(c)2(c)[30]

False Designation of Origin and False Endorsement

In addition to protecting trademark owners from blurring and tarnishment, that same section of the Lanham Act also gives trademark owners two more weapons to combat threats to their mark: **false designation of origin** or source, known as "product infringement," and **false description** or representation, known as "false advertising."[31]

Example: A comic book plastic bag manufacturer sells its protective bags with the slogan "These bags are a MARVEL with COMICS." Marvel Comics might be able to argue that this conspicuous display of the words "Marvel" and "Comics" creates in the consumer's mind the impression that Marvel comics has endorsed this brand of comic book bag.

False Endorsement

If a trademark is used in such a manner as to create the erroneous impression that the product or service is being endorsed, sponsored, or is affiliated with another person or company, the trademark user can be sued for **false endorsement**.[32]

> Trademark law is not limited to confusion of consumers as to the source of the goods, but also includes confusion as to sponsorship or affiliation.[33]

Defenses to Trademark Injury

Maybe you want to comment on or criticize a company; maybe you want to reference another trademarked hero—can you do it? Can you incorporate someone else's trademark into your comic book without getting the owner's permission?

Good news! In most cases, it is *not* infringement to use somebody else's trademark in your comic books (as opposed to on your merchandise) for the following purposes:

- Parody
- Comedy
- Allusion
- Criticism
- News reporting
- Commentary[34]

In fact, to sue someone for trademark infringement, a plaintiff must show that the defendant used the plaintiff's mark "in commerce."

> Only a 'person who, on or in connection with any goods or services, or any container for goods, uses in commerce' a trademark or false designation of origin, can be found liable for trademark infringement.'[35]

DISCLAIM THAT USE

Prominent **trademark disclaimers** can also be helpful to help guard against infringement claims. Since trademark infringement turns on consumer confusion, disclaimers on a comic's cover or title page may alleviate confusion by alerting consumers to the fact that the trademark owner did not endorse or sponsor the use of their marks in your book.[36]

DISCLAIM THAT USE—*continued*

Example: "The reference herein to any trade name, trademark, service mark, or publisher, does not necessarily constitute or imply its endorsement, recommendation, or sponsorship by the owner(s) of such names and marks."

CONTEXT IS KEY

As in other areas of IP law, context is key: *how* a mark was used without the owner's permission determines liability—it is not the unpermitted use itself, but the manner of the unpermitted use that is determinative.

Trademarks and the First Amendment

The First Amendment can be a powerful defense against trademark infringement. For instance, a creator has a First Amendment right to reference the title of another creative work, as long as the reference is not misleading and is artistically relevant to the creator's work.[37]

Example: Moira creates a graphic novel called *Archetypes and The Avengers*, in which she tells the autobiographical story of a young woman falling in love with comic book heroes like Marvel Comics "Avengers." The novel's heroine becomes a hit in the cosplay scene and finally makes it as a successful comic book artist. Even though "The Avengers" is registered trademark,[38] it is directly and artistically relevant to Moira's narrative. As long as Moira steers clear of trademark tarnishment, false endorsement, or copyright infringement, she should be able to use The Avengers trademark in her title.

Trademark "Fair Use"

Just as fair use is a defense to copyright infringement, trademark fair use is a defense to trademark infringement. Simple, right?

Not so fast. To begin with, there are actually *two* separate defenses to trademark infringement that fall under the heading "fair use," and to make matters worse, neither of these trademark "fair use" defenses has anything to do with copyright's "fair use" defense.

CHECK YOUR DEFINITIONS

It's important to keep in mind that words can be defined very differently in different areas of law. "Fair use" of a trademark is a different doctrine altogether from "fair use" of copyright. The rules that apply to one don't apply to the other.

Classic Trademark Fair Use

Classic trademark fair use occurs when the senior owner of a trademark has chosen a mark that contains commonly descriptive language, and the junior user uses that descriptive language to describe their own product. For instance, a candy manufacturer selling "SweeTarts" brand candies cannot stop a juice maker from describing the flavor of its cranberry juice as "sweet-tart."

As the court in that case said, "That SweeTarts is an incontestable mark for sugar candy does not make [the candy manufacturer] the gatekeeper of these words for the whole food industry."[39]

When you use the descriptive terms of another mark to describe your goods, that is an example of classic trademark fair use.

> **Example**: You design a comic book character who is made of metal, and his superpowers include heating his body until its red-hot, and shooting steam from his pores. You name him Man-Iron. Nothing about his design is reminiscent of the Marvel comics Iron Man character. Since he has the properties of a steam iron, using terms "iron" and "man," would be permissible under classic trademark fair use (although, it probably wouldn't help your argument if you use those words in the same order that Marvel does).

Nominative Fair Use

"Nominative" fair use is different from "classic" fair use. In nominative fair use, you are using somebody else's trademark to identify the mark owner's products or services.

For example:

- You own the comic book shop, and you shoot a TV commercial in which you prominently display the trademarks of a variety of comic book publishers as they appear on the comic books, which sit on the racks in your store; or,
- In your graphic novel, you draw a scene that takes place in Times Square, NYC. You accurately depict portions of the many trademarks found on the billboards that stretch from horizon to horizon on 42nd St. Your drawings of portions of these trademarks would probably be considered nominative fair use.

In order to mount a successful nominative fair use defense, you must not be using the plaintiff's trademark in a way that appears as if the plaintiff is endorsing you, your products, or services.

Parody

Nobody likes to be the butt of a joke, not even a trademark. However, parody is one more defense to trademark infringement.

In one case, a pet toy maker sold a handbag-shaped doggie chew toy marked "Chewy Vuiton." Luxury handbag manufacturer Louis Vuitton responded by suing the pet toy maker for trademark infringement and trademark dilution. The court threw the toy manufacturer a bone when it decided in its favor, finding the company not liable for dilution:

> For trademark purposes, [a] 'parody' is defined as a simple form of entertainment conveyed by juxtaposing the irreverent representation of the trademark with the idealized image created by the mark's owner. [...] A parody must convey two simultaneous—and contradictory—messages: that it is the original, but also that it is *not* the original and is instead a parody.[40]

And the Hormel food company did not find it kosher when a puppet character in the movie *Muppet Treasure Island* was named "Spa'am, High Priest of the Boars," a name that sounded suspiciously like their product "Spam," America's favorite pork-based luncheon meat. When Hormel sued for trademark infringement, false advertising, and trademark dilution,[41] the court found for the parodical puppeteers, saying:

> No one likes to be the butt of a joke, not even a trademark. But the requirement of trademark law is that a likely confusion of source, sponsorship or affiliation must be proven, which is not the same thing as a 'right' not to be made fun of.[42]

Comic book parodies, as expressive works, are generally protected against trademark infringement claims.[43] However, be careful not to take the reasoning in the Chewy Vuitton case too far and use the parody you create *as your own trademark*. In the Jack Spaniels case,[44] the court found that the "Bad Spaniels" dog toy, which parodied Jack Daniel's whiskey bottle, tarnished Jack Daniel's trademarks but did not infringe them. As the Supreme Court pointed out, "Consumer confusion about source--trademark law's cardinal sin--is most likely to arise when someone uses another's trademark as a trademark."[45]

Trademark Registration

Registering trademarks might seem like a chore, but it's a superhero move for any artist wanting to protect their creative babies. Trademark rights actually start with a trademark's use, not just its creation. While states have their own laws to protect intrastate trademarks, the strongest armor in the United States comes from the federal government. This superhero-level protection is only granted after a long, epic quest through the application and approval process with the USPTO. You'll need to prove to their satisfaction all of the following:

1. Your mark is distinct, and
2. Is or will be used in commerce, and
3. Doesn't clash with other registered marks, and
4. Is not misleading or deceptive.

Once registered, you can unleash the mighty power of federal law to tackle anyone trying to use a trademark that's confusingly similar to yours on goods or services similar to yours in commerce.

Why Register?

Securing federal registration of your trademark provides you with some powerful tools:

- It gives you the right to use the "®" symbol, putting the world on notice that you have a federally registered trademark. It acts as a warning that you can hammer trademark infringers with the full power of federal law. If you didn't register your trademark with the federal government—let's say you only registered your mark with a state government—you can only put "TM" next to your mark. No federal registration, no "R in a circle!"
- Your mark will be listed on the USPTO databases and should show up in the trademark search for anybody trying to register a similar mark after yours.
- Once you register your mark, you are presumed to be the owner of that mark. Additionally, you are presumed to have the exclusive right to use that mark throughout the United States. Unlike copyright law, where independent creation is a defense, it doesn't matter if somebody else has never heard of your mark; you can stop them from using it if they started using the same mark after you registered your mark.
- You can record your U.S. trademark registration with the U.S. Customs and Border Protection (CBP) Service to prevent importation of infringing foreign goods. That's right, you can get the customs officials working for you to seize and destroy those knockoff action figures from Beijing that infringe your trademark.
- If you want to sue somebody for trademark infringement, you will need to have a federally registered mark in order to get into federal court. And trust me, federal court is where you want to be—and may need to be. If you prove that somebody has infringed your registered trademark, the court has a wide variety of remedies to help you out, including:

    – Injunctive relief. Someone has created T-shirts that infringe your trademark? The court may order all of the T-shirts destroyed.[46] But wait, there's more: not only will the T-shirts be destroyed, but also any "plates, molds, matrices, and other means of making the same," all related advertisements, signs, packaging, etc. In other words, not just the inventory was destroyed but also the infringer's entire means of making more. The court could order the losing defendant to issue "corrective advertising," alerting the world to its infringement.
    – Monetary recovery for you, including compelling the defendant to pay you its profits, the amount of money you lost, and maybe the reasonable cost of your attorney's fees.[47]

UNITED STATES PATENT AND TRADEMARK OFFICE WEBSITE: (WWW.USPTO.GOV)

But remember, this quest might not be available for single-issue work! However, for those who plan to launch a series, build a brand, or have recurring products or works, taking the time to register your trademark is like donning a cape and ensuring your creative works are shielded from any imposters. This quest requires skill, knowledge, and a lot of paperwork. That's why it's always a wise idea to work with an experienced trademark attorney to guide you through the labyrinth of regulations and help you protect what's rightfully yours.

Notes

1 USPTO serial number 71444138 (for magazine publishing).

2 USPTO serial number 75432535.

3 USPTO serial number 77578832.

4 USPTO serial number 75543613 for entertainment in the nature of an amusement park ride.

5 *Harvey Cartoons v. Columbia Pictures Indus.*, Inc., 645 F. Supp. 1564, 1573 (S.D.N.Y. 1986) ("the image of a cartoon character and some indicia of that character can function as a trademark to identify the source of a work of entertainment.").

6 15 USC §1127.

7 *DC Comics Inc. v. Unlimited Monkey Bus., Inc.*, 598 F.Supp. 110, 115 (N.D. Ga. 1984) ("Section 32 of the Lanham Act, 15 USC §1114(1), provides as follows: Any person who shall, without consent of the registrant—(a) use in commerce any reproduction, counterfeit, copy, or colorable imitation of a registered mark in connection with the sale, offering for sale, distribution, or advertising of any goods or services on or in connection with which such use is likely to cause confusion, or to cause mistake, or to deceive; or (b) reproduce, counterfeit, copy, or colorably imitate a registered mark and apply such reproduction, counterfeit, copy, or colorable imitation to labels, signs, prints, packages, wrappers, receptacles or advertisements intended to be used in commerce upon or in connection with the sale, offering for sale, distribution, or advertising of goods or services on or in connection with which such use is likely to cause confusion, or to cause mistake, or to deceive, shall be liable in a civil action [...]").

8 *E.T. Browne Drug Co. v. Cococare Products, Inc.*, 538 F.3d 185, 199 [3d Cir 2008] (citing 2 McCarthy on Trademarks §15:1).

9 2 McCarthy on Trademarks and Unfair Competition §10:2 (4th ed.) ("literary titles of single works which are inherently distinctive are not accorded immediate protection, absent proof of secondary meaning and consumer recognition.")

10 *Trademark Manual of Examining Procedure (T.M.E.P.)* §1202.02–1202.02(a)(i) Statutory Basis for Functionality Refusal.

11 1 McCarthy on Trademarks and Unfair Competition §8:1 (4th ed.).

12 Actually, you'd be registering your mark with respect to "comic books, in class 016," but the USPTO would still probably think this was too generic.

13 Reg. # 3187221.
14 Unless you are cracking them open with a tachyon-generating particle accelerator shaped like a British police call box. But WHO would do that?
15 Calboli, Irene, "Trademark Assignment "With Goodwill": A Concept Whose Time Has Gone" (2005).Faculty Publications. Paper 542. http://scholarship.law.marquette.edu/facpub/542.
16 15 U.S.C. § 1114 (2021).
17 In NY, the courts apply a similar test, called the "Polaroid Test," taken from *Polaroid Corp. v. Polaroid Electronics Corp.*, 287 F.2d 492, 495 (2d Cir. 1961) ((i) the strength of plaintiff's mark; (ii) the similarity of the parties' marks; (iii) the proximity of the parties' products in the marketplace; (iv) the likelihood that the prior user will bridge the gap between the products; (v) actual confusion; (vi) the defendant's good or bad faith in adopting the mark; (vii) the quality of defendant's product; and (viii) the sophistication of the relevant consumer group.) *Polaroid Corp.*, 287 F.2d at 495.
18 5 McCarthy on Trademarks and Unfair Competition §30:5 (4th ed.).
19 15 USCA §1117 [West].
20 15 USCA §1116 [West] "(B) As used in this subsection the term 'counterfeit mark' means—(i) a counterfeit of a mark that is registered on the principal register in the United States Patent and Trademark Office for such goods or services sold, offered for sale, or distributed and that is in use, whether or not the person against whom relief is sought knew such mark was so registered; or (ii) a spurious designation that is identical with, or substantially indistinguishable from, a designation as to which the remedies of this chapter are made available by reason of section 220506 of Title 36."
21 15 USCA §1117(c) [West].
22 15 USCA §1117(b) [West] (treble damages are three times the amount of actual financial loss suffered).
23 15 USCA §1117(b) [West].
24 *Moseley v. V Secret Catalogue, Inc.*, 537 US 418, 433, 123 S Ct 1115, 1124, 155 L Ed 2d 1 [2003] (citing to 15 USC §1127).
25 H.R.Rep. No. 104–374, p. 3 (1995).
26 *Louis Vuitton Malletier S.A. v. Haute Diggity Dog*, LLC, 507 F.3d 252, 264–65 [4th Cir 2007].
27 15 USCA §1125(c)2(b).
28 15 USCA §1125(c)1.
29 15 USCA §1125(c)2(a).
30 15 USCA §1125(c)2(c).
31 *Resource Developers, Inc. v. Statue of Liberty-Ellis Is. Found., Inc.*, 926 F.2d 134, 139 [2d Cir 1991](citing to 15 USCA §1125(a).)
32 15 USCA §1125a(1).
33 *Team Tires Plus, Ltd. v. Tires Plus, Inc.*, 394 F.3d 831, 835 [10th Cir 2005].
34 *Charles Atlas, Ltd. v. DC Comics, Inc.*, 112 F.Supp 2d 330, 335–36 [S.D.N.Y. 2000].
35 *Charles Atlas, Ltd. v. DC Comics, Inc.*, 112 F.Supp 2d 330, 336 [S.D.N.Y. 2000] (citing to Section 43(a) of the Lanham Act, 15 USC §1125(a).)
36 *Home Box Off., Inc. v. Showtime/The Movie Channel Inc.*, 832 F.2d 1311, 1315 [2d Cir 1987]("We have found the use of disclaimers to be an adequate remedy when they are sufficient to avoid substantially the risk of consumer confusion.")

37 *Rogers v. Grimaldi*, 875 F.2d 994, 998 [2d Cir 1989].

38 U.S. Serial # 72278015.

39 *Sunmark, Inc. v. Ocean Spray Cranberries, Inc.*, 64 F.3d 1055, 1058 [7th Cir 1995].

40 *Louis Vuitton Malletier S.A. v. Haute Diggity Dog*, LLC, 507 F.3d 252, 260 [4th Cir 2007].

41 [as well as a few other causes of action] *Hormel Foods Corp. v. Jim Henson Productions, Inc.*, 1995–2 Trade Cases P 71154 [S.D.N.Y. Sept. 25, 1995] affd, 73 F.3d 497 [2d Cir 1996].

42 *Hormel Foods Corp. v. Jim Henson Productions, Inc.*, 1995–2 Trade Cases P 71154 [S.D.N.Y. Sept. 25, 1995] affd, 73 F.3d 497 [2d Cir 1996] (quoting 2 J. McCarthy, Trademarks and Unfair Competition §31:38 at 670 (2d ed. 1984)).

43 *Charles Atlas, Ltd. v. DC Comics, Inc.*, 112 F.Supp 2d 330, 335–36 [S.D.N.Y. 2000].

44 Jack Daniel's Properties, Inc. v. VIP Products LLC, 599 U.S. 140 (2023).

45 Jack Daniel's Props. v. VIP Prods. LLC, 599 U.S. 140, 142, 143 S. Ct. 1578, 1581 (2023).

46 15 USC §1118.

47 5 McCarthy on Trademarks and Unfair Competition §30:57 (4th ed.).

APPENDIX D

A Comic Creator's Guide to the Right of Publicity and Other Privacy Rights

WHAT IS THE RIGHT OF PUBLICITY?

An offshoot of privacy law, the **right of publicity** is a person's right to benefit from the commercial exploitation of his or her own identity. Infringement of the right of publicity occurs from the unauthorized use of a person's identity (or likeness, voice, name, etc.) for commercial purposes (i.e., labeling goods and services with the unauthorized likeness or using the unauthorized identity in commercials and advertisements).

A celebrity's likeness is not the only part of his or her identity protected by their publicity rights. For instance, Johnny Carson won a suit against a company that was using the phrase "Here's Johnny" to advertise a toilet.[1]

Comic creators tend to run into problems with right of publicity laws in two main areas:

- When they attempt to create merchandise, such as action figures, T-shirts, and lunch boxes, that feature an actor whose publicity rights have not been obtained.
- When they use a celebrity's likeness as the basis for a character, and they predominantly use that celebrity-based character as a ploy to sell comic books and related products, rather than as an artistic or literary expression.

Duration of the Right of Publicity

Some states require a signed writing to convey the publicity right, and the duration and extent of the right of publicity protection differ from state to state.

- In California, your right of publicity lasts for 70 years after your death; lawsuits for misappropriation of your right of publicity therefore can be brought by your estate.
- In New York State, the right of publicity dies with you, unless you are a performer or personality with commercial value in your likeness (in which case that property right lasts 40 years).[2]
- Some states do not recognize the rights of publicity.

First Amendment and the Right of Publicity

The First Amendment greatly limits the extent to which the right of publicity can control areas outside of commercial exploitation of an image. Comics, movies, television, some art, news, literature, and educational uses are often not considered commercial use of a person's right of publicity.[3] Even TV commercials and other advertisements promoting comic books, movies, and television shows do not infringe the rights of publicity of the actors who perform in those movies and television shows being advertised. However, one must be careful: courts are not uniform in how they approach this issue, and using a celebrity's likeness in a video game without their permission has been ruled a violation of their rights of publicity—despite the fact that video games are protected by the First Amendment.[4]

A LEGAL TWIST—THE PREDOMINANT USE TEST

Spawn is a comic title that is no stranger to lawsuits. In 1993, creator Todd McFarlane added to the series a fictional Mafia Don character named "Tony Twist" Twistelli, based on famed hockey player "Tony Twist." The fictional character's appearance was quite different from that of the similarly named athlete. In fact, their names and the "tough guy" enforcer persona were the only similarities.

Unfortunately, McFarlane never obtained Twist's permission to use his name. Furthermore, the comic book creator admitted the character's name was based on hockey players. When the Twist character was used on merchandise sold at hockey games, the real Twist brought a suit against McFarlane for misappropriation of name and defamation.[5]

The Spawn case climbed the jurisprudential ladder all the way to the Missouri Supreme Court, which, after applying the predominant use test (see next page), held that "the evidence admitted at trial was sufficient to establish [McFarlane's] intent to gain a commercial advantage by using Twist's name to attract consumer attention to Spawn comic books and related products."[6]

Nor did a First Amendment defense help the undead hero battle the hockey enforcer: "On the record here, the use and identity of Twist's name has become predominantly a ploy to sell comic books and related products rather than an artistic or literary expression, and under these circumstances, free speech must give way to the right of publicity."[7]

That being said, outside of obvious commercial use, such as featuring an unauthorized likeness in a television commercial, courts and state laws are literally all over the map with regard to what triggers infringement.

For instance:

- A television news station broadcast an entire human cannonball act without the performer's permission. The court held that this may misappropriate the right of publicity.[8]
- A film portrayed Bobby Seale's participation in the Black Panthers without Mr. Seale's consent. In rejecting Mr. Seale's claim for infringement of the right of publicity, the court pointed out that a public figure had no exclusive right to his or her own life story. The court went on to state: "[I]n addressing right of publicity claims, courts have been mindful that the First Amendment provides greater protection to works of artistic expression such as movies, plays, books, and songs, than it provides to pure 'commercial' speech."[9]

- A television commercial that depicted a robot turning letters in a game show violated Vanna White's right of publicity.[10]

One rule of thumb may be:

- "The use of a person's identity in news, entertainment, and creative works for the purpose of communicating information or expressive ideas may be protected [by the First Amendment], but
- The use of a person's identity for purely commercial purposes, like advertising goods or services or the use of a person's name or likeness on merchandise, is rarely protected."[11]

Tests to Determine Infringement of the Right of Publicity

The difficult part is determining where to draw the line between commercial and noncommercial use. Courts across the country have developed a variety of tests to determine whether a use is primarily commercial or primarily expressive.

- **Transformative Test**. Does the work that allegedly infringes a person's right of publicity contain significant transformative elements so that the value of the work does not derive primarily from the celebrity's fame? In other words, "[a]n artist depicting a celebrity must contribute something more than a 'merely trivial' variation, [but must create] something recognizably 'his own,' in order to qualify for legal protection."[12]
- **Relatedness Test**. Is the work that allegedly infringes a person's right of publicity directly related to that person, like a life story? If so, then it may be protected under the First Amendment. However, if the name or likeness is used just to attract attention to that work and does not relate to the person himself, this may be a form of advertising and, therefore, require that person's permission.
- **Predominant Use Test**. If a product is being sold that predominantly exploits the commercial value of an individual's identity, under this test, that product should be held to violate the right of publicity and not be protected by the First Amendment, even if there is some "expressive" content in it that might qualify as "speech" in other circumstances. If, on the other hand, the predominant purpose of the product is to make an expressive comment on or about a celebrity, the expressive values could be given greater weight.[13]

When an artist is dealing with the gray area of rights of publicity, the best practice, as always, may be to seek permission.

OTHER PRIVACY RIGHTS

Creators need to be careful to avoid stepping on the privacy rights of people whom they depict. The extent to which privacy rights are recognized drastically differs from state to state. What a creator may do freely in one state may be actionable in another. As with most torts, consent is a valid defense to these causes of action.

There are four basic kinds of invasions of privacy:

- Infringement of the right of publicity (previously discussed)
- Intrusion upon seclusion
- Public disclosure of private facts
- False light

Intrusion upon Seclusion

Intrusion upon Seclusion[14] is, perhaps, what is typically thought of when we think of invasion of privacy.

For a comic creator to be liable for intrusion upon seclusion, all of the following elements must be present:

- The artist intrudes, physically or otherwise, upon the privacy, solitude, or personal affairs of his subject.
- The intrusion must be of the kind that is objectionable to a reasonable person.
- The intrusion must occur where the subject has a reasonable expectation of privacy.

Example: Inspired by the autobiographical graphic novel *Persepolis*,[15] Carla Creator is writing an indie comic about her own life experiences: she wants to tell the world about her former career working for a money launderer in the dry-cleaning industry. She tails her old boss, Gus Grimes, CEO of Clean As A Whistle, Inc., a dry-cleaning chain. Hoping to get some dirt on his money-laundering activities, she sets up her video camera in an apartment across the street from his house. She's going to film him and then write her graphic novel using the dialogue she captures and create her drawings based on the images she films. Using a video camera with a powerful telephoto lens and a powerful microphone, she peers into the window of his house, recording his secret business dealings.

Mr. Grimes may be able to sue Carla for the tort of intrusion upon seclusion. However, if Carla waited until Mr. Grimes was in a public park before photographing him, she might have a successful defense against this claim: she would argue that there is no reasonable expectation of privacy for conversations that occur in a public place.

Public Disclosure of Private Facts

A comic book creator can be sued if he or she publishes private facts about the subject. For a creator to be liable for **public disclosure of private facts**,[16] all of the following elements must be present:

- The creator writes a book that divulges private facts about the private life of the subject.

- The book is shown to others (this is referred to as publication, even though it is a book).
- The publication of these facts would be highly offensive to a reasonable person.
- There is no legitimate public interest in the disclosure of these facts.

Example: Carla Creator wants her readers to know everything about Gus Grimes—including the fact that he is Gay—a fact he has never been public about. Carla learned of this from a friend of hers who works as a nurse in Mr. Grimes's doctor's office, where Mr. Grimes was treated last year for HIV. She draws meticulous illustrations of the lab reports showing Mr. Grimes's medical condition and includes them in her graphic novel.

Once again, Mr. Grimes may be able to sue her for invasion of privacy, this time for "public disclosure of private facts." However, if Carla had obtained facts concerning Mr. Grimes' sexual preference from a *public* record, she would have a good defense. Furthermore, if Mr. Grimes were a politician running on a platform in which he publicly attacked homosexuality, Carla would be able to defend the lawsuit brought against her on the grounds that "outing" Grimes and showing the hypocrisy of his platform was in the public interest.

However, Carla may have also violated the Federal HIPAA law, which protects the privacy of medical records, and thus may be looking at jail time.[17]

False Light

False light[18] is similar to defamation in some respects. (See Appendix E A Comic Creator's Guide to Libel and Defamation, p. 433.) What is actionable here is publishing false information about somebody that attributes to that person viewpoints that he or she does not hold or actions that he or she did not take. For a comic book creator to be liable for the tort of publicly placing a person in a false light, all of the following elements must be present:

- The comic creator publishes **false** facts about the subject, and
- A reasonable person would find these false facts highly offensive if the false facts were told about him or her, and
- The creator had knowledge of or acted in reckless disregard of the falsity of the published facts, and
- If the published information is a matter of public interest or concerns a public figure, the creator must have acted maliciously.

In contrast to defamation, the false light tort requires a higher level of publicity not required by defamation. Unlike the requirements for defamation, a person placed in a false light does not have to show harm to his reputation but may only need to show he suffered mental distress or indignity from the false publication.

Example: Carla has tailed Grimes for days. Her video camera catches him heading into a McDonald's restaurant to use their bathroom. Knowing that Grimes is a strict vegetarian, she draws him going into McDonald's and gorging himself on hamburgers. She finishes the sequence with a panel of Grimes leaving the restaurant and patting his stomach. People reading her book assume that Grimes loves to stuff his face with cheeseburgers. When he discovers that people think he is a carnivore, Grimes suffers a nervous breakdown. The graphic novel portrays him in a false light, and Grimes would be able to sue Carla yet again.

Notes

1 *Carson v. Reynolds*, 48 CPR (2d) 57 (1980).
2 N.Y. Civ. Rights Law § 50-f (Consol., Lexis Advance through 2025 released Chapters 1–49, 61–125).
3 *Landwehrle v. Bianchi*, 75 Misc. 3d 1223(A), 2022 NY Slip Op 50649(U), ¶ 6 (Sup. Ct.). ("California's right of publicity law (Cal. Civ. Code § 3344) also provides for an exemption for matters related to news, public affairs, sports broadcast, or political campaigns (Cal. Civ. Code, § 3344(d)). Moreover, California courts have held that "expressive works, whether factual or fictional," are subject to First Amendment protections and, thus, a cause of action seeking to vindicate purported privacy rights may not be maintained. Finally, where advertisement of expressive works is merely an adjunct to the work and promotes the work, the action does not lie. Hence, even though Bianchi, as a California resident, would be subject to applicable California statutes, Bianchi's book of photographs is exempt from any liability imposed by California's right of publicity law."
4 *Hart v. Elec. Arts, Inc.*, 717 F.3d 141 (3d Cir. 2013).
5 *Doe v. TCI Cablevision*, 110 SW3d 363, 365 [Mo 2003].
6 *Doe v. TCI Cablevision*, 110 SW3d 363, 371 [Mo 2003].
7 *Doe v. TCI Cablevision*, 110 SW3d 363, 374 [Mo 2003].
8 *Zacchini v. Scripps-Howard Broadcasting Co.*, 433 U.S. 562 (1977).
9 *Seale v. Gramercy Pictures*, 949 F.Supp. 331, 337 (E.D. Penn. 1996).
10 *White v. Samsung Electronics America, Inc.*, 971 F.2d 1395 (9th Cir. 1992).
11 *Twist v. TCI Cablevision, Inc.* SC84856 (2003).
12 *Hart v. Elec. Arts, Inc.*, 717 F.3d 141, 160 (3d Cir. 2013).
13 *Doe v. TCI Cablevision*, 110 SW3d 363, 374 [Mo 2003].
14 Restatement (Second) of Torts §652B.
15 *Persepolis* by Marjane Satrapi.
16 Restatement (Second) of Torts §652D.
17 42 USC 1320d-6.
18 Restatement (Second) of Torts §652E.

APPENDIX E

A Comic Creator's Guide to Libel and Defamation

DEFAMATION DEFINED

There are two forms of **defamation:** slander and libel. **Slander** is the spoken form of defamation, and **libel** is a written, drawn, televised, or otherwise recorded form.

To be able to sue for defamation, the following elements must be present:

- A false and defamatory statement concerning another.
- An unprivileged publication of that statement to a third party.
- Fault amounting to at least negligence on the part of the publisher (fault amounting to "actual malice" in the case of a public figure). (See Defamation of Public Figures, p. 436.)
- Harm caused by the publication, or presumed harm because the statement falls within a special class of defamatory statements known as **defamation per se**.[1]

A comic book or novel that contains false statements damaging to someone's reputation may expose the producer to claims of libel and defamation.

Defamatory Statement

A defamatory statement is one that is both false[2] and that tends to "harm the reputation of another as to lower him in the estimation of the community or to deter third persons from associating or dealing with him."[3] Usually statements that are "merely unflattering, annoying, irksome, or embarrassing, or that hurt only the plaintiff's feelings"[4] do not support a defamation claim. Nor will humor or parody.

Some kinds of defamatory statements are considered especially harmful (called "defamation, *per se*"). Examples include:

- Accusations that the plaintiff has committed a crime.
- Statements that hurt the plaintiff's business reputation.
- Allegations that the plaintiff has a "loathsome disease."
- Accusations that the plaintiff has engaged in sexual misconduct.

Statements "Of or Concerning Another"

To sue somebody for libel, a plaintiff must prove that the libelous statement was aimed at him or her. The test, known as the "**of or concerning another**" test, looks to whether a reasonable person would assume the statement was made about or concerned the plaintiff.

Example: A nonfiction comic alleges that Chateau, Montana (population 1804), pharmacist Robert Martin poisoned all of his customers by filling prescriptions while he was drunk. If the allegations were false, a Chateau pharmacist named Robert Martin could sue the comic creator and the publishing company for defamation. After all, how many pharmacists named Robert Martin could be in Chateau? However, it would be unlikely that a Los Angeles (population 3.82 million) pharmacist with the same name would win such a suit, as there are undoubtedly more than a few pharmacists named Robert Martin in LA.

Defamation in Works of Fiction

Although most people associate defamation with fact-based titles, like an autobiographical graphic novel, narrative titles can create problems for comic creators as well. It may seem surprising that a work of fiction can give rise to a defamation claim—after all, unlike in a nonfiction graphic novel, the author is not trying to say that the story is real. Trouble usually occurs when a creator fictionalizes an actual person's life or creates a character that closely resembles an actual person. When faced with such a claim, a court may satisfy the "of or concerning another" test by asking whether a reasonable person reading the book would understand that the fictional character was, in actual fact, the plaintiff acting as described.[5]

To establish a connection between the fictional character and the real person of the plaintiff, a court may compare a host of characteristics, such as the names, backgrounds, physical characteristics, ethnic backgrounds, personalities, and ages of the plaintiff and the character. A court may place emphasis on whether the comic book creator knew and had a relationship with the plaintiff. A disclaimer stating that the comic book is a work of fiction and is not intended to represent actual persons may be given weight by the court but is not conclusive.[6]

Creators take heart: In cases involving fictional characters, similarity of names between fictional characters and real people, by itself, is usually not enough to transform coincidence into defamation.

Publication of Defamatory Statement

For a statement to defame someone, it must be **published** to a third party. "Published" does not mean printed in a book, nor does "published" have the same meaning as it does under copyright law ("the distribution of copies of a work to the public by sale"). For a defamatory statement to be published, it must be seen, heard, read, and so forth, by someone other than the person being defamed. Posting defamatory comments on social media counts as publication; no matter what bad thing you heard about someone doing at Comic Con, unless you have actual knowledge of their actions—like you witnessed the bad behavior yourself—you may want to think twice about posting. No matter how well-intended your post may be, if it's false, you may be hit with a libel suit.

Example: Quill posts the following tweet on her public Twitter account:

> Just witnessed utter chaos at #ComicCon today – saw Jason 'The Slipper' Jones blatantly snatch an exclusive, limited-edition comic right from a vendor's booth! Unbelievable theft, and totally dishonest behavior to lure fans into his shady collection.

Because this tweet is posted publicly, it is considered "published" under defamation law—it is read by multiple third parties beyond Jason "The Slipper" Jones. Even if Quill believes her observation is accurate, if the statement turns out to be false and harms Jason's reputation, he may have grounds to sue for libel. For instance, if Quill later learns that Jason did not commit any theft, and yet the tweet continues to circulate or is shared further, Jason could claim that the publication of this defamatory statement has damaged his reputation.

Republication

If a defamatory statement is published again after its initial publication, it is considered "republished." Generally, republishers may be sued for defamation as well. The Creator must be very cautious here! An interview subject who defames someone on the record may create republication liability when it is published in the comic, when that comic is turned into an animated film and shown in the theaters, or when digital versions of the comic are published for e-readers. Because the Creator has indemnified the publisher and everyone else down the line of distribution, those parties' legal claims and expenses will be passed on to the Creator.

There are exceptions to this rule of republication liability, but it is best to nip the problems in the bud by avoiding libel publication altogether.

Defamation of Public Figures

A public figure is a politician, celebrity, or other individual who has voluntarily placed him- or herself in the midst of the public controversy. Public figures have a much more difficult time proving defamation. To prove defamation, public figures must show the statement was made with **actual malice**.

Actual Malice Standard

In the context of defamation, *actual malice* is the knowledge that the statement was false or was made with a reckless disregard for its truth.

Example: The Action Render Team creates and publishes a "tell all" nonfiction graphic novel about popular rock singer Opie Um's decline into drug abuse. The novel depicts Opie's police record: he was arrested once carrying a small amount of marijuana, and his friends give interviews saying that he routinely went on benders. The novel's captions use phrases like "Opie slid into the dark depths of drug abuse and despair" and "there was a monkey on his back—a monkey named addiction!"

Opie sues for defamation. He produces evidence that the marijuana bust was the first and last time he ever took illegal drugs and that he was far from an addict. He proves that the "benders" his friends referred to were actually stories cooked up by his agent to cover up the fact that he was in South America doing missionary work—a fact that would hurt his public image with his hard-rockin fans. In short, Opie demonstrates that the statements made in the graphic novel were false.

Will Opie automatically win his suit? Not necessarily. Because he is a public figure, Opie will still have to show that the statements were made with knowledge that they were false or that they were made with a reckless disregard for the truth. This may be tough, considering the producer relied on police records of a drug arrest and interviews with Opie's friends.

DEFENSES TO DEFAMATION

There are a number of possible defenses to a charge of defamation:

- **Truth**. The most basic defense to defamation is truth. No matter how scandalous or injurious to a person's reputation a statement may be, it will not be considered defamatory if it is true.

  Example: The Action Render Team creates another nonfiction graphic novel titled *Prostitutes and the Policemen Who Love Them*, which features interviews with prostitutes naming the police officers with whom they have had sexual congress. Sergeant Lou Scivious, named in the book, sues A.R.T. for libel. At trial, A.R.T. shows footage of Officer Scivious handing money to, and entering a hotel room with, the call girl in question. A.R.T. produces evidence showing that Officer Scivious was not engaged in an undercover vice operation targeting prostitution. The court will most likely find that the film's statements about the officer were true, and therefore none of the members of A.R.T. will be liable for libel.

- **Consent**. If someone consents to the publication of a defamatory statement, they will not be able to bring a claim for defamation. *This is why any time you draw or write about a real living person for your graphic novel, you should get them to waive all claims of defamation.*

  Example: Quill interviews Dusty Rinkle, the owner of a retirement home under investigation. Prior to the interview, Rinkle signs an interview release form in which he waives the right to sue for defamation. The final graphic novel interweaves panels of Rinkle discussing the benefits of his retirement home with cartoons showing Rinkle burying little old ladies alive. If Rinkle sues, Freddy Filmmaker might win with a defense that Rinkle consented and waived his right to sue for defamation.

- **Note**, however, if Rinkle can prove that he signed the interview release because he relied on Quill's statement that he was going to be portrayed as the hero, he might be able to successfully argue that he was **fraudulently induced** to sign the agreement; therefore, he did not in fact consent.
- **Humor or parody**. This is generally protected by the First Amendment and is considered a form of protected opinion (see below). There is no libel when the material is clearly understood as parody, satire, humor, or fantasy and is not capable of a defamatory meaning.[7]

Example: Beard-O illustrates a *Mad Magazine* piece about Gus Grimes, insinuating that he is a crook. Because this is a well-known humor and satire magazine, the skit will probably not be considered defamatory.

- **Privilege**. Certain types of communications, such as judicial and legislative proceedings, are considered privileged and therefore immune from claims of defamation.

  Example: For her newest book on tobacco lobbyists, Quill transcribes congressional hearings in which Congressman Abe O'Lition accuses a tobacco industry lobbyist of having a second job of selling crack cocaine to children. The lobbyist sues Quill, who may successfully defend against the claim by virtue of the fact that the statement was made during the course of legislative proceedings.

- **Opinion**. Statements that reflect a point of view, or opinion, rather than specific allegations of fact are not considered defamatory. Also insulated from libel and slander are "vigorous epithets," "rhetorical hyperbole," "loose, figurative language," or "lusty and imaginative expressions."

  Example: The Action Render Team creates a nonfiction graphic novel about the history of New York pizza. In an interview with famous French chef S. Cargo, the gourmet badmouths the owner of Pete's Za, a popular New York pizzeria. Cargo says, "Pete's pizza is the worst I've ever tasted. If you looked up the word "disgusting" in the dictionary, you would find a picture of Pete. The man's an idiot!" Pete sues the Action Render Team and Cargo for libel. The court will most likely find that Cargo's statements are opinion and, therefore, not actionable as libel.

- **Fair Comment**. In matters of public interest, many states require that a reputation-damaging false statement be made with a certain amount of malice before it can be considered libel. However, this privilege does not extend to material that defames another and is not reasonably necessary to the development of the subject matter of the nonfiction graphic novel.

  Example: The Action Render Team creates a nonfiction graphic novel about a small dinner theater company's failure to pay the salaries it owes to the cast. They mistakenly say that the dinner theater manager is "holding out" on the cast. In fact, the manager is withholding the money because the cast had failed to show up for two shows, costing the theater money. The manager sues Jacob for defamation, claiming that the story A.R.T. created is one-sided. Since the story involves public interest, if they can prove that they didn't create the novel maliciously, A.R.T. may assert a fair comment defense.[8]

WATCH YOUR OPINION

Be Careful Here! Merely calling something an opinion does not insulate you from defamation. Whether a statement counts as an opinion depends upon whether it is falsifiable. In other words, can the statement be proven true or false? The statement, "In my opinion, Pete Za lied when he testified under oath," if false, may be defamatory, notwithstanding the use of the word "opinion," because it accuses Mr. Za of the crime of perjury, and whether he lied might be proven true or false.

In determining whether a statement is an opinion and therefore not defamatory, a court will take a look at the context in which the statement was made and the customary way in which the words used in the statement are typically uttered. The court may apply a "totality of circumstances" test to determine whether the statement is fact or opinion. This test will take into account (1) the specific language used, (2) whether the statement is verifiable, (3) the general context of the statement, and (4) the broader context in which the statement appeared.[9]

Examples of statements found to be opinion:

- Union officials who are "willing to sacrifice the interests of the members of their union to further their own political aspirations and personal ambitions."[10]
- An attorney was a "very poor lawyer."[11]
- A university vice president was the "Director of Butt Licking."[12]

Bottom Line: It may be counterintuitive, but the more inflammatory and hyperbolic a statement is, the more likely a court will find it to be opinion and not defamatory language.

So instead of saying, "Pete Za cheats on his taxes," you may be better off saying, "Pete Za would cheat an orphan out of her last dime."

MATTERS OF PUBLIC CONCERN: GROSS IRRESPONSIBILITY TEST

Good news for all of you political cartoonists out there: thanks to the First Amendment, matters of public concern are given greater leeway to reporters. In New York, if the allegedly defamatory material is of public concern, the allegedly defamed person will have to show that a news reporter acted with **gross irresponsibility** with regard to the accuracy of his or her reporting. Said one court:

Under this 'gross irresponsibility' standard, if an article is 'arguably within the sphere of legitimate public concern' or 'reasonably related to matters warranting public exposition,' the party allegedly defamed can recover only by establishing, by a preponderance of the evidence, that 'the publisher acted in a grossly irresponsible manner without due consideration for the standards of information gathering and dissemination ordinarily followed by responsible parties'.[13]

Gross Irresponsibility Test

In determining gross irresponsibility, courts look to whether the reporter:

- Followed "sound journalistic practices" in preparing the allegedly defamatory piece.
- Followed "normal procedures," including editorial review of the piece.
- Had any reason to doubt the accuracy of the source relied upon and thus had a duty to make further inquiry to verify the information.
- Could have easily verified the truth.[14]

SPECIAL RULES REGARDING DEFAMATION

- You can't defame a dead person.
- "Defamatory statements" are not limited to words alone. Pictures, videos, and audio may also contain defamatory material.
- An artist can be held liable for defamation even if she did not intend to defame somebody. The only intent that is required is the intent to publish a particular statement.
- Defamation requires publication: the unprivileged dissemination of the statement to a third party. In other words, an otherwise defamatory statement made only to the person it allegedly defames is not defamation. However, for artists, a comic book containing defamatory statements shown or distributed to the public would be considered "published."
- The liability for defamation extends beyond the initial publisher. Even those parties who disseminate the defamatory material can be held liable if they should have known of the defamatory content.
- Corporations may also sue for defamation when a graphic novel or comic book's false statements prejudice it in the eyes of the business community by accusing it of criminal business practices, dishonest conduct, or lack of integrity.
- Defamation law differs from state to state. Massachusetts, for instance, recognizes an exception to the rule that truth is an absolute defense to libel: statements that are reputation-damaging but true can still give rise to a libel claim if they are made with "actual malice" (ill will or malevolent intent).[15]
- In general, an artist has greater leeway regarding the kinds of statements she may publish when the statements concern a "public figure,"

such as a politician or actor, than when they concern somebody who is not in the public eye.

- Many states have **retraction laws** that allow the defaming party to retract her statements within a certain time period. If the statement is retracted, the defendant will be liable for fewer damages should she ultimately lose her case.
- Groups of under 25 people can be libeled, and if so, they can each sue! For example, if you say, "lawyers are all thieves," that's not libel. But if you say, "All the lawyers living in Kalawao County, Hawaii are crooks," you may be open to a libel claim. At 13 square miles, Kalawao County is the United States' smallest county and probably has fewer than 25 attorneys (one would hope).
- Generally, not defamatory are works "of fantasy, involving outlandish plot scenarios and characters with impossible powers. No reasonable reader of such a publication would take the events described as factual events."[16]

Notes

1 Restatement (Second) of Torts §558.
2 Although some states, such as Massachusetts, allow libel for harmful *true* statements published with "actual malice." See *Noonan v. Staples, Inc.*, 556 F.3d 20 (1st Cir. 2009).
3 Restatement (Second) of Torts §559.
4 Robert D. Sack, *Sack on Defamation*, §2.4.1, 2–12, (3d ed., PLI 2005).
5 *Bindrim v. Mitchell*, 92 Cal. App. 3d 61, 78 (1979). The test of whether a fictional character so closely resembles an actual person as to satisfy the "of and concerning" test is "whether a reasonable person, reading the book, would understand that the fictional character therein pictured was, in actual fact, the plaintiff acting as described."
6 For more on defamation in fictional characters, see Matthew Savare's excellent article, "Falsity, Fault, and Fiction: A New Standard for Defamation in Fiction" (Fall 2004). *UCLA Entertainment Law Review*, 12 (1).
7 *Salek v. Passaic Collegiate School*, 255 N.J. Super. 355 (App. Div. 1992).
8 *Bichler v. Union Bank & Trust Co. of Grand Rapids*, 745 F.2d 1006, 1012–15 (1984).
9 *Milkovich v. Lorain Journal*, 497 US 1 (1990).
10 *Gregory v. McDonnell Douglas Corp.*, 552 P.2d 425 (1976).
11 *Sullivan v. Conway*, 157 F.3d 1092 (7th Cir. 1998).
12 *Yeagle v. Collegiate Times*, 255 Va. 293, 26 Media L. Rep. (BNA) 2337 (1998).
13 *Chaiken v. VV Publishing Corp.*, 119 F.3d 1018 (2d Cir 1991).
14 *Chaiken v. VV Publishing Corp.*, 119 F.3d 1018 (2d Cir 1991).
15 "The defendant in an action for writing or for publishing a libel may introduce in evidence the truth of the matter contained in the publication charged as libellous; and the truth shall be a justification unless actual malice is proved." Mass. Ann. Laws ch. 231, § 92.
16 *Netzer v. Continuity Graphic Assoc., Inc.*, 963 F Supp 1308, 1325 (S.D.N.Y. 1997).

APPENDIX F

A Comic Creator's Guide to Moral Rights and The Visual Artists Rights Act

MORAL RIGHTS

Moral rights, sometimes referred to by the French name *droit moral*, are a collection of rights that allow the author of a work to have a say in how that work is used and whether it can be changed in any way. Moral rights may include:

- The author's right to be credited for the artwork or to refuse to be credited.
- The right of an author to prevent the artwork from being changed or altered in any way without the author's permission.
- The author's right to determine how the artwork is shown.
- The author's right to receive royalties from the artwork.
- The author's right to stop the artwork from being exploited in any way that damages the author's reputation.

In general, U.S. laws do not protect moral rights in and of themselves. They leave these sorts of protections to a combination of copyright, trademark, and unfair competition law. Other countries, notably France and other European countries, do protect moral rights; as a result, moral rights issues may come into play when the film is distributed in other countries.

Although moral rights generally cannot be transferred from one party to another, in some, but not all, countries, they may be waived (given up).

VISUAL ARTISTS RIGHTS ACT (VARA)

Although we don't recognize moral rights in this country, we do have a statutory variation called the Visual Artists Rights Act (VARA),[1] which is a part of the copyright statute (although, technically, it's not a copyright). VARA only applies to "works of visual art"... as that term is specifically defined in the copyright statute.

VARA and Comic Book Artwork

So, for a comic book artist, the takeaway is this: artwork that is prepared for a comic book, which is a periodical, is not considered a "**work of visual art**" (as copyright law uses that term) for purposes of VARA. Nor is artwork prepared for a graphic novel, which is a book. Nor is work that is created as work for hire.

However, if you've created a single or limited-edition drawing (under 200 copies) of a character—and this is the important part—and that drawing is not part of a comic book or graphic novel, your artwork might be protected by VARA.

Copyright law often defines things differently than a dictionary does.
For instance, a work of visual art under copyright doesn't mean a poster, but rather it is:

1. A painting, **drawing**, **print**, or sculpture **existing in a single copy;** in a limited edition of 200 copies or fewer that are signed and consecutively

numbered by the author; or, in the case of a sculpture, in multiple cast, carved, or fabricated sculptures of 200 or fewer that are consecutively numbered by the author and **bear the signature or other identifying mark of the author**; or

2. A still photographic image produced for exhibition purposes only (existing in a single copy that is signed by the author, or in a limited edition of 200 copies or fewer that are signed and consecutively numbered by the author).

Importantly, a "work of visual art" under copyright law **does not include:**

- Any poster, map, globe, chart, technical drawing, diagram, model, applied art, motion picture or other audiovisual work, book, magazine, newspaper, periodical, database, electronic information service, electronic publication, or similar publication.
- Any merchandising item or advertising, promotional, descriptive, covering, or packaging material or container.
- Any portion or part of the above.
- Any work made for hire.
- Any work not subject to copyright protection under this title.[2]

Example: Penciller draws a picture of "Man-a-Tee"—an herbivorous aquatic mammal superhero with the powers of a T-shirt. As long as this is a standalone image and not part of the comic book or graphic novel, she can claim rights under VARA. However, if she created the work as a work made for hire, as merchandise, for advertising or promotional use, as a poster, or for any audiovisual work, she cannot claim VARA rights.

Rights under VARA

Let's assume VARA applies to your drawing. What exactly are your new VARA-powered rights?[3]

1. **Right to Authorship and Attribution**
    - You have the right to assert your status as the artist of your work.
    - You may also stop others from using your name as the author of any visual work that you did not create.
2. **Right to Protection from Harmful Attribution**
    - If your work is distorted, mutilated, or otherwise modified in a way that could harm your reputation or honor, you can prevent the association of your name with that altered version.
3. **Right to Prevent Detrimental Modifications and Destruction (Subject to Limitations)**
    - You may prohibit any intentional alteration—such as distortion, mutilation, or other modification—that would be harmful to your reputation. Any such intentional change is considered a violation of your rights.

- You also have the right to prevent the destruction of a work recognized for its stature. Any intentional or grossly negligent destruction of such a work is similarly a violation of your rights.

In summary, if VARA applies to your work, you:

- Have the right to be credited as the creator of your artwork.
- Can stop others from falsely claiming you created work that isn't yours.
- Can disassociate your name from versions of your work that have been so altered they could damage your reputation.
- Enjoy, within certain limitations, the safeguard against the intentional or careless destruction or harmful modification of your artwork.

Waiver of VARA Rights

Like other copyright rights, your VARA rights may be given up (waived). As a matter fact, most intellectual property transfer clauses have language in them, which does just that. This is a stark contrast to moral rights laws in other countries, which can't be waived.

Waiving the rights under VARA requires an express agreement to such a waiver in writing, signed by the author. Such "written instrument" shall specifically identify:

- The work, and
- Uses of that work, and
- The waiver shall apply only to the work and uses so identified.[4]

Notes

1 17 USC §106A.
2 17 USCA §101.
3 17 U.S.C. 106(A); 17 U.S.C. §113(d).
4 17 USCA §106A.

CAUTION!

ONLY ONE JOINT AUTHOR IS NEEDED TO WAIVE ALL JOINT AUTHORS' RIGHTS UNDER VARA!

In the case of joint work prepared by two or more authors, a waiver of rights made by one such author waives such rights for all such authors! That's right, yet another reason for a collaboration agreement (see Collaboration Agreement, p. 119).

APPENDIX G

Contract Anatomy for Comic Book Creators

A NOTE ON "LEGALESE"

We attorneys take a lot of flak for confusing laypeople with our "legalese." It can be quite frustrating: a businessperson might make an offer to "sell" a widget, but a lawyer will "sell, convey, transfer, and assign all the rights in and to the widget, in perpetuity." You'd think we were being paid by the word. Quite honestly, some lawyers do use extraneous words. For instance, in the example above, the single word "sell" would probably work just fine.

However, there are times when a lot of seemingly duplicate words are necessary. This is especially true for contracts dealing with intellectual property, such as those in the comic book industry. There are many different ways a copyright can be transferred from one person to another. It can be mortgaged, it can be sold, it can be licensed, it can be assigned, security interests can be granted in the copyright, and so on. And all those transfers are not the same.

When a lawyer is drafting a contract, their greatest fear is that if they fail to be precise enough, that lack of precision will create a loophole that will be exploited when the parties decide they can no longer play nicely with each other.

A contract that says only that "Mr. Jones hereby licenses the copyright to his comic book to Mr. Smith" does not say anything about whether Mr. Jones may borrow money from a lender and use the copyright as collateral for the loan. If Mr. Smith wants to prevent that from happening, he needs to insert language into the contract that talks about mortgages, security interests, and so forth. However, for most purposes, using clear, simple language in the contract is the best way to draft. In fact, there are very few "magic" legal words that are required in contract law. Much of the time, if you can express the party's intentions in plain language, it will do the trick.

Contracts should be both **clear** and **precise**.

The best contract is one that is written in such a way that reasonably intelligent people, with no prior knowledge of the deal, can read and understand the obligations of the parties to the agreement.

CONTRACT ANATOMY

If you want to draw an awesome superhero, you must have a firm grasp of human anatomy. If you want to build a Formula One race car, you have to have a solid grasp of an engine's anatomy. Well, contracts have their own anatomy as well. And just as a mechanic will hoist an engine block out of a car in order to tinker with it, we're going to hoist up a sample contract to see how it works.

- In the head or **opening** of the contract, we meet the parties, special words are defined, and the duration of the contract is set out.

- The contract **body** introduces us to the services each party is going to provide for the other, the compensation (and how that compensation is computed), the all-important ownership of intellectual property rights, how artwork is approved and how it must be credited, and other deal-specific obligations.
- The **boilerplate** "belly" of the contract contains the drafting party's "standard terms," which tend to change very little from deal to deal but can have tremendous effect on the outcome of any disagreement that arises in the contract.
- The tail or contract **closing** provides signature blocks for the parties to execute the agreement and any attachments, schedules, or exhibits, which lay out the precise materials or obligations that are particular to this specific deal.

Once you learn to identify all of the common elements and clauses, you'll begin to see how they will work together like a finely tuned engine.

A DIVERSITY OF DRAFTING

Not every contract is going to have every clause that follows, and some contracts may refer to these clauses by different names from the ones you see below. Oh, and the language will differ from contract to contract, and drafter to drafter (See why I said some contracts may not be appropriate?). The more diverse the contracts you read, the better drafter you'll become.

Important note: The clauses provided in this section are mainly illustrative and are simplified versions to help you understand the effect of a particular clause; in other parts of the book, you will encounter more complete and complex agreements. But for now, I want you just to concentrate on how deal points are turned into contract language.

THE HEAD: THE OPENING OF THE CONTRACT

Like the beginning of the movie, the opening or "front" part of contract introduces our main characters and tells us a little bit about each one (the **parties**). The contract's opening situates us in time, letting us know when the obligations of each party begin (the **effective date**) and lets us know little about each of the party's motivations (the **recitals**).

Contract Title

The contract title should be a straightforward description of the transaction. You might want to leave the names of the parties out of it, as that can get cumbersome. The title is typically not part of the legal interpretation of the contract (because there's usually a clause that says that titles of paragraphs in the contract are not to be given legal effect).

Example: "Artist's Services Agreement"

Introductory Clause

The introductory clause lays out the type of agreement, the parties, whether or not they are companies or individuals, the effective date of the contract, and sometimes the addresses of the parties.

SAMPLE

1. This Artist Services Agreement ("Agreement"*1) is dated January 1, 2025 and is between Waldo Writer Publishing, LLC, a New York State limited liability company ("Pub Co."), and Amy Abigail Abhinandana Abrianna-Artist, an individual ("Artist"*2).

1 This is called a "defined term." Now, whenever you see the word "Agreement," with a capital "A" in this document, it refers to this agreement in particular, and not any other contract.

2 Defined terms can be tremendously efficient devices. You're going to refer to the parties a lot in this Agreement. Now instead of having to write Amy Abigail Abhinandana Abrianna-Artist each time, you can just refer to the illustrator as "Artist," because that's how you defined her.

Recitals

Often appearing in longer or more formal contracts, **recitals** are statements that provide background information and context about the contract. For instance, the recitals might state that the writer has created a comic book script and wants to hire an artist to illustrate it. Another recital might say that the artist has illustrated several comic books in the past and wishes to illustrate the writer's comic book for the fee and on other terms as are stated in the contract. It's important to distinguish the recitals from the terms of the contract itself because courts usually view the terms of the contract as controlling over the recitals. In other words, if there's a conflict between the explicit terms of the contract and the recitals, the court will typically say that the actual contract terms control.[1] You can often recognize a recital by the very old-fashioned-looking introductory words: "WHEREAS," or "WITNESSETH." "NOW THEREFORE" is the recital term that indicates the recitals are at a close.

EXAMPLE: "WHEREAS CLAUSE"

WHEREAS Pub Co. has created the comic book script tentatively titled "The Adventures of Maggot Man" (the "Script") and wishes to engage in services of Artist;

WHEREAS the artist is in the business of illustrating comic books and graphic novels and wishes to illustrate the Script, for the fees stated, and upon the terms and conditions herein;

NOW, THEREFORE, in consideration of the mutual promises herein, and for other good and valuable consideration, the parties hereto mutually agree as follows:

THE BODY OF THE CONTRACT

Now that we've established who our cast of characters are—the parties—and given a sense of what they want—the recitals—let's take a look and see how they are going to accomplish their goals.

Defined Terms

In contracts, we often speak in shorthand, and we often create our own lexicon by using shorter words to convey complex concepts. When we do that, we're creating a **defined term**. Remember before when we were identifying the parties? We decided to call the illustrator, Ms. Amy Abigail Abhinandana Abrianna, by the much shorter defined term "Artist." We need a translation guide to help us figure out what all of our shorthand means, so the first section of the contract body is usually a set of defined terms that we are going to use in the agreement.

DEFINED TERMS: PROCEED WITH CAUTION!

Defined terms are terms that are defined in the contract for the purpose of understanding the contract. They are Always Capitalized and defined in a "Definitions" or "Defined Terms" section of a contract or defined immediately after their first use in the contract, like this:

... Artist's work of sequential art (the "Comic Book").

Be careful here! Once a term is a "defined term," it takes on the defined meaning, which may not necessarily be the meaning you would find if you looked that word up in the dictionary. For example, let's say the contract says: "'Rutabaga' shall mean any derivative work based upon the Comic Book":

- Any use of the word "Rutabaga" in the contract will now mean a derivative work (note the uppercase "R"), and
- "Rutabaga" will *not* mean "a turnip with a large yellow root" (which is, of course, a rutabaga with a lowercase "r.")

Of course, this is a silly example, but defined terms can be tricky, especially when the defined term is close to, but not exactly, the same as its dictionary definition.

For example, everyone knows what a comic book is, right? But what if a publishing company uses the following definition in its publishing contract with Waldo Writer:

> 'Comic Book' shall mean the work of sequential art and accompanying script tentatively titled "The Adventures of Maggot Man," in whole or in part, produced by Waldo Writer, or any part thereof, and all derivatives of such work(s) and their or its parts, now or hereafter in existence, in any medium whatsoever, whether now known or hereafter in existence.

Here the term Comic Book means *not* only the comic book Waldo is currently making *but also* **any** work derived from that comic book, any animated television series, graphic novel, app, movie, or action figure, and so forth! That's because a phrase like "all derivatives of such work(s) and their or its parts, now or hereafter in existence, in any medium whatsoever" encompasses virtually anything that can be made from your comic book!

Remember you must be extremely careful when granting rights that include the term "derivative works!" For instance, if you're only granting print rights, make sure the grant qualifies the term derivative works with a phrase like:

> 'Comic Book' shall mean the work of sequential art and accompanying script tentatively titled "The Adventures of Maggot Man," in whole or in part, produced by Waldo Writer, or any part thereof, and all **print or digital** derivatives of such work(s), *such as reprints, graphic novel versions, and trade collections (hard or softcover). No other derivative work rights, whether audiovisual, or otherwise, are granted herein.*

<u>SAMPLE</u>

1. **Defined Terms:**
   a. "**Comic Book**" shall mean the work of sequential art tentatively titled "The Adventures of Maggot Man, Issue #1," in whole or in part, produced by Pub Co. Writer, or any part thereof, and all print or digital derivatives of such work(s), such as reprints, graphic novel versions, and trade collections (hard or softcover), based upon the Pub Co.'s script, attached hereto as Addendum A.

b. "**Comic Book Property**" shall mean the collection of intellectual property rights in the Comic Book, and in any derivative work thereof.

c. "**Net Profits**" shall mean the revenues actually received by Pub Co. from Pub Co.'s exploitation of the Comic Book,*3 less all directly attributable, verifiable, out of pocket third party costs associated therewith, including but not limited to production, promotion, and advertising costs, bad debts, taxes, returns for credit, and reasonable reserves (to be liquidated equally over the next four accounting periods), and costs of negotiating, monitoring, and enforcing third party agreements related to exploitation of the Comic Book and the Comic Book Property, but excluding any allocation of Pub Co.'s general overhead.

d. "**Original Artwork**" shall mean the physical artwork (e.g. pencil on paper, paint on canvas, etc.) produced and created by Artist pursuant to this Agreement. Expressly excluded from this definition are the copyright and other intellectual property rights to such physical artwork, as well as any digital files or reproductions containing such artwork.

e. "**Royalties**" shall mean 10% of Net Profits,*4 as that term is herein defined.

3 We explore this in more depth when we deal with artist services agreement, but note that the artist receives her royalty from the net profits of the issue of the comic book on which she works, but not on every issue of the comic book.

4 As you can see, sometimes defined terms are defined with reference to other defined terms. In this case, the defined term "Royalties" depends upon the defined term "Net Profits."

Engagement

In a services contract, like an illustrator or writer agreement, the **engagement** paragraph does the "heavy lifting" by listing the specific duties that the worker is providing for the hiring party. It typically provides some detail on how and by when those duties must be accomplished. Sometimes it's easier to understand the engagement paragraph if each task is broken down into a series of steps (e.g., preliminary sketches must be delivered, reviewed, and accepted by the hiring party before the artist can go on to the next stage of production).

The engagement paragraph in a services contract may also contain the **term**, which is the time during which the worker is engaged to provide services. The term may also be defined as **exclusive** or **nonexclusive**; if the term is exclusive, the worker cannot perform services for anybody else during the term.

Be sure to state any additional or unusual duties on a separate attachment at the end of the document (often called an exhibit or schedule, see p. 484). For instance, if you need your writer to provide thumbnail sketches for the illustrator, you should state this explicitly in either the engagement section or a rider attached to the contract.

SHALL/MAY

Be careful how you phrase terms of obligation in the contract. The words "may" and "shall" do not mean the same thing.

- "**Shall**" means something is obligatory must be done in the manner specified.

Example: "Artist shall deliver preliminary sketches on March 1, 2015." If the artist doesn't deliver the sketches by March 1, she is in default or breach of contract.

- "**May**" means something is permissible or is subject to a number of variations.

Example: "Artist may deliver preliminary sketches on or about March 1, 2015." Artist is permitted to deliver the sketches by March 1, but is not obligated to.

If there is no other language as to when she must deliver the sketches, the contract would be unclear on this point and a court might be forced to fill in the blank with any terms parties used when dealing with each other in the past or with the oh-so-vague "a reasonable time."

EXAMPLE: ENGAGEMENT CLAUSE

1. **Engagement**
   a. Artist is hereby engaged to create a work of sequential art for the first issue of the Comic Book.
   b. The services to be rendered by Artist shall include all services usually and customarily rendered by comic book illustrators, including but not limited to: creating character designs, pencil roughs, and providing penciling, layout, inking, and coloring of all pages★**5** in the Comic Book. Artist's results and proceeds★**6** hereunder shall be known as the "Work."

c. The Artist shall work closely with Pub Co. in preparing the Work, according to the delivery schedule herein, and in matters of artistic judgment, Pub Co. has final say.***7** Artist's services are unique and the loss of such services cannot be fully compensated by monetary damages.***8**

5 A list of all of the duties should appear in the engagement. You may want to be more specific, providing delivery dates for each set of pages.

6 "Results and proceeds" means all of the Artist's work under the contract.

7 Since Pub Co. is hiring Artist, it has final approval over the artwork.

8 The "unique" services recitation, coupled with the statement that money isn't sufficient to replace the loss of Artist's services may help the Pub Co. get an injunction against the Artist if she breaches the contract to go work for someone else. (See Contract Anatomy: Remedies, p. 476.)

Delivery

What materials the artist must deliver, when she must deliver them, and how the publishing company must approve them is sometimes part of the engagement paragraph; however, it may be clearer to include these stages in a separate paragraph, especially if payment is being made at various steps. The materials being delivered are called the **deliverables**.

EXAMPLE: DELIVERY CLAUSE

2. Delivery

a. Artist shall draw pages 1–24 of the Comic Book in pencil, or its equivalent ("Penciled Pages"***9**), and shall deliver the Penciled Pages to Pub Co. for review within one month of execution of this agreement.

9 Defined terms can also appear in the sentence next to their definition, as opposed to in the defined term section. For sections where there are a lot of defined terms, this may make the contract clearer.

b. Upon receipt of Penciled Pages from Artist, Pub Co. shall have five business days to review and comment upon the Penciled Pages. The format for delivery for all Penciled Pages and their revisions shall be Adobe PDF, PSD, or EPS files. All raster-based files must be at least 300 dpi.***10**

c. Within two weeks after receiving Pub Co.'s comments and corrections regarding the Penciled Pages, Artist shall, if so directed, prepare up to one (1) revision of the Penciled Pages, ("Revised Penciled Pages"), incorporating Pub Co.'s comments, and deliver them to Pub Co. for review.

d. Upon receipt of Revised Penciled Pages from Artist, Pub Co. shall have five business days to review, comment upon, and approve the Revised Penciled Pages. If Pub Co. fails to give approval within five days, either party may terminate this contract, and the termination provisions in paragraph ## shall apply.

e. Upon approval of the Revised Penciled Pages, Pub Co. shall pay Artist the sum of forty-five hundred dollars ($4500.00), and Artist shall immediately commence work on the inking of the Revised Penciled Pages.

f. [...]***11**

<u>10</u> Important to specify the format for the deliverables

<u>11</u> *Note:* This step-structure can be repeated indefinitely to account for all the stages of a comics creation (inking, coloring, lettering, etc.)

Rights Granted or Granted Rights

IP rights are the heart of the comic book property. The "Rights Granted" paragraph must be very carefully tailored to the specifics of the deal.

The rights granted must address:

- Who owns the copyright and other IP rights in the work created under the contract
- Who owns the copyright and other IP rights in any underlying work (like a short story upon which the comic is based)
- The scope within which these rights may be exploited (what media, territories, duration, etc.).

Keep in mind that copyright and trademark licenses and assignments should always be in writing and signed by the rights owner. **Remember** to be extremely careful when granting rights that include the term "derivative works!" (See Derivative Works, p. 28.)

For a more complete discussion of IP rights, see Intellectual Property, p. 15.

EXAMPLE: GRANT OF RIGHTS CLAUSE [PARTIAL]

A. Grant of Rights*12

a. Licensor hereby grants to CPC and CPC hereby accepts an exclusive license to the Licensed Rights and Ancillary Rights throughout the Term and Territory.

b. Such Licensed Rights include the Licensee's exclusive rights to publish, print, manufacture, market, promote, advertise, distribute, sublicense (both in English and foreign language editions), and otherwise exploit the Licensed Products in any primarily print or digital media now known or hereafter developed. Without limiting the foregoing, these exclusive rights include the right to have third parties publish and distribute the Licensed Products in digital media to end users by means of internet downloads, iPod and mobile phone distribution, and other digital media now known or hereafter developed.[...]

EXAMPLE: WORK FOR HIRE CLAUSE WITH ALTERNATE ASSIGNMENT OF RIGHTS

Work for Hire/Assignment of Rights*13

a. **Work for Hire:*14** Artist acknowledges that all work created by her under this agreement, and all of her results and proceeds are to, were created as a Work for Hire, and any Work to be created shall be considered a Work for Hire. Artist agrees that Pub Co. owns and shall own without limitation throughout the universe, exclusively and in perpetuity, free and clear of any and all claims, liens and encumbrances, all rights, title and interest of every kind whatsoever, whether now known

12 This is part of a grant of rights clause which conveys exclusive rights to certain Licensed Products defined elsewhere in the publishing agreement. Because the rights are being assigned, and the work was not created as a work for hire, the grant of rights can be terminated in accordance with copyright's termination of transfer provisions.

13 This is an example of a work for hire rights provision in which the artist is left with no copyright interest in the property.

14 If it's work for hire, you need to say this specifically and not just in the title, as titles are typically given very little legal effect.

or unknown, the copyrights therein, and all renewals, extensions, or reversions of copyright now or hereafter provided, of the Comic Book Art, with Pub Co. to be deemed the author thereof. Additionally, Artist acknowledges that such Work for Hire arrangement was agreed to prior to the performance of services hereunder and the creation of any Comic Book Art. Such results and proceeds including but not limited to designs, plans, and sketches of the look and feel of the comic book and its characters; the page layout or other visual illustrations of the script; inking and coloring of the Comic Book Pages (including cover), and sketches of several different versions of objects or characters that may or may not appear in the Comic Book, concepts, words, writings, concepts, ideas, "gags," and dialogue, which are composed, submitted, or interpolated by Artist in connection with the preparation or production of the Comic Book, and any and all elements thereof, in whatever form.

b. **Alternative Assignment:*15** To the extent, if any, that the Comic Book art, or any and all results and proceeds of the Artist's services hereunder, is not recognized as a Work for Hire, Artist hereby irrevocably grants and assigns to Pub Co. and its successors and assigns, without limitation throughout the universe, exclusively and in perpetuity, free and clear of any and all claims, liens, and encumbrances, all of Artist's rights, title and interest of every kind whatsoever, whether now known or unknown, the copyrights therein, and all renewals, extensions, or reversions of copyright now or hereafter provided, in the Comic Book Art in addition to any and all results and proceeds of Artist's services hereunder.

c. **Waiver of Droit Moral and Visual Artist Rights Act:** Artist hereby waives any moral rights, droit morale, or analogous rights***16** she may have under the laws of any nation or state, including those rights currently embodied in the Visual Artists Rights Act of Title 17 of the US copyright law.

d. This Paragraph #5 shall survive the termination or expiration of this Agreement, by breach or otherwise.***17**

15 In most work for hire clauses, you will also see an alternate copyright assignment. This means that, if for some reason the work for hire status is faulty, the Artist still transfers the copyright to her work to the contracting party.

16 Different countries recognize, to different degrees, an artist's right to attribution and integrity of her work. Here the artist is being asked to waive (give up) those rights. (See Moral Rights, p. 399.)

17 This is called a survival clause, and it means that even if the contract is terminated for some reason, the work is still considered a work for hire and owned by Pub Co.

You will need to keep your IP grants clean and straightforward in order to preserve your chain of title. Good news: the great thing about rights grants is that they can be tailored to fit any licensing scenario, usually by adding a few paragraphs.

Intellectual Property Qualifiers in Comic Book Transactions

In the dynamic realm of comic book publishing—where bold visuals meld with imaginative storytelling—intellectual property qualifiers play an indispensable role. These clauses clearly delineate the scope and limitations of rights granted for publication, merchandising, adaptations, and licensing, ensuring that both the creative team (writers and illustrators) and the publisher can maximize the commercial potential of the work while safeguarding the creator's long-term interests.

Reversion of Rights

The **reversion of rights** clause functions much like a well-timed boomerang for creative property. If the publisher fails to publish the book within a certain agreed-upon term, or the option for an animated adaptation expires, the rights should revert back to the original creators. This clause ensures that the creative team can reclaim their work and pursue alternative avenues for monetization.

Reservation of Rights

Reservation of Rights in the comic book publishing industry, Reservation of Rights is essentially a "save the best for later" strategy that emphasizes the importance of timing. Typically, while the publisher secures the exclusive rights to print and distribute the comic, the creators—be they the writer, illustrator, or both—retain ("**holdback**") key ancillary rights, such as those for merchandise, digital spin-offs, or video game adaptations.

However, in many contracts, the publisher also insists on implementing holdback periods on these reserved rights. Even though the creators legally keep these rights, they can only exploit them after a specified delay. For instance, while the writer and illustrator might reserve the rights to license character merchandise, the publisher might require that these rights become exercisable only six months after the comic's initial release. This arrangement helps ensure that the market isn't flooded with competing products from the outset, thereby preserving the commercial impact of the initial publication.

Through this strategic timing, both parties work together to maximize the long-term value of the property. The publisher's holdback periods provide a buffer that protects the primary release while allowing the creators to eventually tap into additional revenue streams in a controlled and mutually beneficial manner.

Right of First Negotiation

This qualifier obligates the rights owner to negotiate exclusively with a designated party before offering the comic's rights for sale or license to others. For example, if a publisher decides to explore a digital adaptation, the agreement might require the creators to first enter into negotiations with a preferred streaming platform or digital distributor, giving that platform an exclusive shot at acquiring the rights to the online version of the comic before any other party is approached.

Right of First Refusal

Under a Right of First Refusal clause, if a third party—say, a film studio interested in adapting the comic into a motion picture—makes an offer, the original creator or their designated partner (like a merchandising agent) gets the first opportunity to match or decline the offer. This ensures that the creative team maintains a measure of control over the direction of further adaptations whether that means taking the offer or leaving it open for another party under certain negotiated terms.

Right of Last Refusal

Finally, the Right of Last Refusal provides the holder with a final opportunity to match a competing offer within a specified timeframe before the deal is concluded. In a comic book scenario, if multiple parties are vying for the rights to develop a TV series based on the comic, the studio with which the publishing company has a relationship might contractually be given the final chance to match the best offer.

Reserved Rights

The reserved rights are those rights that are not being granted under the agreement. For example, when granting the rights to publish a comic book, a creator often reserves the right to adapt the comic to make a movie or other audiovisual work, theatrical rights, and the right to create a text-only novel (as opposed to graphic novel). Because these rights are reserved by the creator, the publishing company, which may have the exclusive right to publish the comic book, and perhaps also to create merchandise, does not have the right to make a text-only novel, film, or stage play.

Creators are cautioned that with the increasing popularity of comic book movies, more and more publishing companies are seeking audiovisual rights as part of their publishing deals and not letting the creator reserve these rights.

EXAMPLE: RESERVATION OF RIGHTS CLAUSE

##. Reserved Rights. Notwithstanding any other provision herein, with respect to derivative works of the Comic Book Property, Artist reserves exclusively for herself all rights to create and exploit motion pictures and other audiovisual works, novelizations, and theatrical works, based upon the Comic Book and the Comic Book Property, in any media now known, or hereafter invented, throughout the universe.

Important note: If you remember, we showed a work for hire clause in a previous example, which would not typically be in the same agreement as a reservation of rights clause. This is because when an artist creates a work for hire, all of the rights are vested in the hiring party, and there's nothing left for the artist to reserve.

Holdback Provisions

Reserved rights are often subject to holdback provisions. A holdback provision requires a copyright or other rights owner to refrain from licensing certain rights for a limited period of time.

Example: As we've seen with the Reserved Rights paragraph, publishing companies often try to acquire the greatest number and scope of rights from a comic book creator; the creator very often reserves certain rights for herself, such as the right to turn the comic book into a novel. To ensure that the creator does not execute her reserved rights in a manner that competes with the comic book being released by the publisher, the creator's reserved novelization rights are typically subject to a holdback period, which prevents the creator from exploiting those rights for certain number of years.

Important note: This is another clause that would not be in a work-for-hire agreement; there are no rights for the creator to hold back because they vested in the hiring party at the moment they were created.

EXAMPLE: HOLD BACK PROVISION

Holdback. Artist agrees to refrain from exploiting, and to "holdback," the rights listed in clause #6 ("Reserved Rights") for a period of two years from the date of execution of this agreement.

Reversion of Rights

Creators will want to get back those rights that they've granted if the publishing company has not exploited those rights within a certain period of time; in other words, if the publishing company fails to publish a creator's comic book, the creator should get those rights back. This clause specifies how, if at all, those rights will automatically revert to the creator.

Important note: yet another clause that would not be in a work-for-hire agreement; again, there are no rights to revert back to the creator, because they vested in the hiring party at the moment they were created.

EXAMPLE: REVERSION OF RIGHTS [PARTIAL]

> **Reversion of Rights.** If this agreement is terminated through the Pub Co.'s breach, or because Pub. Co. fails to publish or cause the Comic Book to be published within one year of execution of this agreement, all rights herein granted shall immediately revert back to Artist. Notwithstanding any termination of this agreement, the Pub. Co.'s obligation to continue to pay royalties to Artist shall survive expiration or termination of this Agreement and will continue for so long as Pub. Co continues to exploit the Comic Book.

Ownership of Materials

Especially if the agreement is work for hire, the parties need to be very clear on who owns the physical materials produced by the artist. Industry custom is that artists get to keep the physical work produced (pencil sketches, India-inked pages, canvas paintings, etc.), regardless of who owns the copyright to the work. In fact, make sure that this clause only transfers rights to the physical materials—like the hand-drawn pages—and not the copyright or other IP rights to the comic. However, if the contract is a work-for-hire agreement, this **must** be expressly agreed upon by the contracting party in this paragraph.

EXAMPLE: OWNERSHIP OF MATERIALS CLAUSE

> **Ownership of Materials.** Notwithstanding the foregoing, as between Artist and Pub Co., Artist shall retain ownership of all Original Artwork,*18 in its physical form, including but not limited to sketches, pencil roughs, finished pencil drawings, inked drawings, and colored pages. Artist may sell, transfer, or dispose of the Original Artwork in her sole discretion. Nothing in this section shall be deemed to transfer ownership of copyright, or any other IP right in the Original Artwork to Artist, all of such rights being expressly retained by Pub Co.

18 Remember, this should be defined in the definitions section.

Approvals

Here we specify who has creative control and final approval over work. It should come as no surprise that the contracting party typically reserves creative control. That means the publishing company may have creative control over the artist's work if the Pub Co. is commissioning a new book from the artist. For comic properties and characters already in existence, copyright owners will have to negotiate this provision carefully to make sure that merchandisers, publishing companies, video game developers, and other licensees agree to follow the owner's creative bible with respect to how the character may be depicted.

If two authors are collaborating (i.e., an artist and writer), this provision should deal with how disagreements are solved between the two. In some instances, it's as simple as specifying that the party who initiated the project—the party with the initial idea for the comic book—gets final approval. However, that can sour the relationship and leave one party feeling powerless. It's often helpful to carve up approval into spheres of influence. For instance, the artist might have final approval over the look of a comic book character, whereas the writer may have final approval over the character's literary origins, biography, dialogue, and plot.

Types of Approval

There are several different ways to create an approval mechanism for resolving creative differences. Here are a few common strategies:

- **Unilateral approval**. One party must approve the decision.
- **Meaningful Consultation**. This is generally toothless, as the party consulted does not have final say but only a right to "consult" with the decision-makers.
- **Mutual approval**. Both parties must approve the decision; if there is no tiebreaker provision, it is difficult to resolve differences with this method.
- **Mutual approval with third-party tiebreaker**. Both parties must agree; if they can't agree, a predesignated third person decides which party prevails.
- **Mutual approval with one-party tiebreaker over certain types of decisions**. The illustrator gets to approve decisions involving design, and the writer gets to prove decisions involving story content and dialogue. Everything else must be subject to mutual approval.

EXAMPLE: FINAL APPROVALS CLAUSE [WRITER WITH FINAL APPROVAL]

Final Approval Authority

a. Final approval over all key creative and business decisions related to the Comic Book—including, but not limited to, plot development, character design, script revisions, page layout, artistic style, and budgetary considerations—shall be exclusively reserved for **[Writer's Name]** ("Writer").

b. The Illustrator shall have a meaningful consultation right on all creative input and collaborate in good faith with the Writer throughout the development process. However, the ultimate authority to make binding decisions in these areas, ensuring consistency with the agreed-upon vision and narrative, shall remain solely with the Writer.

c. All approvals must be documented in writing, whether through physical or electronic communication, to ensure clarity in decision-making.

d. Any disputes regarding approval decisions shall be resolved through good faith discussions between the Writer and Illustrator. If resolution is not reached within three business days of discussions, beginning on the day one of the parties hereto sends notice of a disagreement to the other, the Writer's determination shall be final and binding, subject to any applicable Guild and Union requirements.

Compensation

Next to the rights paragraph, the compensation paragraph is the most critical—certainly for the party granting the rights. There are a number of different ways in which artists are paid (don't laugh, artists are paid sometimes—and it is the goal of this book to make sure that they're paid more often!). The compensation paragraph may deal with several different forms of payment, depending on the deal.

Typical forms of payment to the artist in the indie comic book world are:

- Flat fees
- Page rate
- Royalties
- Advances against royalties
- Salary
- Bonuses
- Reprint fees

- Residuals
- Kill fees

Broadly speaking, **compensation** falls into three types.

Fixed Compensation

Flat fees, **salaries**, **page rates**, and other forms of payment that are not dependent upon how many units of the comic book or other licensed property are sold. These fees are computed based on the number of pages created, number of illustrations delivered, etc.

Contingent Compensation

Royalties, **residuals**, **bonuses**, and other compensation that comes from a percentage of the sales or licenses of the comic book property (usually sales minus agreed-upon expenses). If an artist is receiving any form of royalties or residuals, it is important that their contract also contains an **audit clause**, giving them the right to review the pertinent financial records of the person promising to pay them to make sure they are getting the money they were promised.

Royalty computations must be clearly defined in the contract. If one party is receiving a royalty, they need to be able to look at the contract and know exactly what percentage they will be receiving, and what costs and expenses, if any, will be deducted prior to royalties being calculated. In the comic book industry, the creative team that produces the comic often has to share from a **royalty pool**, which means that once the comic generates royalties, these royalties must be further divided among the creative team, according to contractually specified proportions. Bottom line here, a royalty provision should be drafted clearly so that everybody can understand the formula by which royalty payments will be made to each party receiving them. We will deal with specific royalty formulas when we unpack the Artist Services Agreement. (See Artist Services Agreement, p. 156.)

Deferred Compensation

Deferred compensation is one form of contingent compensation of which you should be very wary. Deferred compensation is a flat fee that you receive at a later date, typically when the comic book starts generating revenue, and all of the comic book production expenses have been repaid. To quote Popeye's friend Wimpy, deferred compensation is like saying, "I'll gladly pay you Tuesday for a hamburger today." And just like Wimpy's hamburger-IOU, deferred compensation may never be paid. It is similar to a royalty in that you have to wait until the comic book makes money. However, with a royalty, the more money your comic book makes, the more money you receive, because royalties are based on a percentage. However, deferred compensation is typically fixed fee (e.g. $500 as opposed to 5%), so someone who is paid deferred compensation is taking all the risks of a royalty, without any benefits (like the increase in royalty payments from an increase in sales). As a result, if you need to settle for a deferred compensation rate, it is in your best interest to negotiate a higher rate to offset the risk of not being paid.

Kill Fees

YOU MAY HAVE TO ASK TO BE KILLED!

Be careful: kill fees are not always provided for in contracts, and some companies have policies prohibiting them. Additionally, many kill fees come with the price of the client keeping your work even though they killed it (which is another way of their having their cake and eating it to).

Kill fees are the booby prizes of compensation; kill fees are paid when a client rejects your work but wants to compensate you something for your time. Obviously, the kill fee will be much less than the actual compensation you would've received had they accepted your work. In general, there are two kinds of kill fees:

- **Cancellation fee**—a cancellation fee may be paid to the artist if the project is canceled for reasons unrelated to the artist's poor performance: for example, if the publishing company simply decides not to put out the comic book that the artist is working on because there are too many comics of that type on the market currently.
- **Rejection fee**—a rejection fee may be paid to the artist if the artist's work is not acceptable to the client: for example, if the publishing company asked the artist to draw in a realistic style, and the artist delivers a cartoon-style drawing instead. Rejection fees are usually less than cancellation fees.

EXAMPLE: COMPENSATION CLAUSE

Compensation:

a. **Page Rate:** Pub Co. agrees to pay Artist according to the following page rate schedule, in accordance with the delivery schedule herein:
   1. Completed penciled page (roughs plus revisions): $200 per page
   2. Completed inked page (roughs plus revisions): $100 per page
   3. Completed colored page (roughs plus revisions): $100 per page
   4. Completed lettered page (roughs plus revisions): $40 per page

b. Royalty:**★19** With respect only to issue #1 of the Comic Book, and conditioned on the delivery and approval of all of Artist's deliverables pursuant to paragraph #, Artist shall receive a Royalty of 10% of the Net Profits (as such are defined in ¶#, "Net Profits") from the Comic Book.

c. Kill Fee: If the work and artist's services hereunder are canceled by Pub Co. prior to the Comic Book's completion, but after its final form has been approved by Pub Co., a kill fee ("Kill Fee") shall be paid to Artist in the amount of 50% of the Page Rate defined herein.

The Kill Fee is in the nature of a buyout, and no other royalties, residuals, or other forms of compensation shall be due or payable to Artist as a result of Artist's work hereunder. Notwithstanding anything in this agreement to the contrary, any Comic Book materials subject to a Kill Fee shall remain the intellectual property of Artist***20** and not be subject to the Work for Hire or other intellectual property transfer provisions herein.

<u>19</u> Remember, the terms Royalty, Comic Book, and Net Profits were all defined in the beginning part of the contract.

<u>20</u> If the artist's work is "killed," the artist needs to be sure that the publishing company can't use it. If the publishing company does want to use the artwork in the future, it must license the artwork from the artist, and compensate this artist for the artwork's use.

Condition Precedent

A condition precedent is an express contractual requirement that must be satisfied, such as the occurrence of an act or event, before a duty to perform arises. If the condition is not met, the promise by the other party does not have to be fulfilled.

Example: A publishing contract between the comic book creator and the publisher includes a condition precedent requiring the creator to secure Andre the Artist to illustrate the cover of the comic book. If the creator is unable to secure Andre the Artist, despite the contract's existence, the publisher is not obligated to proceed with the agreement and can treat it as though the contract had never been formed (subject, perhaps, to any agreed-upon reimbursements or preliminary work completed before the condition failed).

<u>EXAMPLE: CONDITION PRECEDENT</u>

Condition Precedent. The parties acknowledge and agree that this Agreement shall not become effective unless and until the Creator secures Andre the Artist to illustrate the cover of the comic book. In the event that the Creator is unable to secure Andre the Artist for this purpose, this Agreement shall be deemed null and void, with neither party bearing any further obligations or liabilities arising hereunder.

Credit

This clause deals with how an artist is credited, and on what product forms the artist must be credited. For instance, in addition to having her name appear on the opening splash page of the comic book, does the artist also get credit in the videogame that's made from the comic book? Is she credited as an illustrator AND a co-creator?

The credit clause must also provide for what happens if credit is mistakenly dropped. A typical provision *eliminates* the ability for the artist to sue for breach of contract in case of a mistake in the credits, leaving a right to have future copies of the comic book printed with the correct credits as the sole remedy for the artist. This is known as a *waiver of injunctive relief.*

EXAMPLE: COMIC BOOK CREDIT

Credit

a. Artist shall be accorded a credit in the Comic Book credits on all versions and future copies prepared of the Comic Book, in every media in which the Comic Book may be read, in substantially the form of "Created, written, illustrated, and lettered by: Amy Abigail Abhinandana Abrianna."

b. The appearance and placement of such credit shall be in Pub Co.'s sole discretion. All other aspects of such credit shall be in the sole discretion of Pub Co.

c. Artist acknowledges that other artists may be brought in at a later date to create artwork for additional issues of the Comic Book, and if Artist does not create additional artwork work for the subsequent issues those additional artists may receive sole artist credit on those issues, with Artist receiving only a character "designed by" credit, in the substantially following form: "Maggot Man character designed by Amy Abigail Abhinandana Abrianna."

d. Within a reasonable time after receipt of written notice from Artist specifying a failure to accord Artist proper credit in accordance with this section, Pub Co. shall use good faith efforts to cure prospectively any such failure with regard to future Comic Books, reprints, copies, and/or advertising materials, if any, created after the date of Pub Co.'s receipt of such notice. Pub Co. will make good faith efforts to contractually obligate third-party licensees, publishing companies, and sub-distributors with whom Pub Co. is in privity of contract to make good faith efforts to comply with the credit obligations set forth herein but shall not be responsible or liable to Artist for the failure of any such third party to comply with the same.

e. Notwithstanding anything to the contrary contained in this Agreement, in no event shall Artist seek, or be entitled to, damages of any kind by reason of any breach or threatened breach of any of the credit requirements, nor shall Artist be entitled to seek to enjoin or restrain the exhibition, distribution, advertising, exploitation, or marketing of the Comic Book, all such equitable remedies being hereby expressly waived by***21** Artist. No casual or inadvertent failure to comply with credit requirements shall be deemed a breach of this Agreement.

21 Waiver of injunctive relief.

This paragraph deals with how the parties can promote and publicize each other's involvement in the project. Typically, a publisher will require the right to use an artist's authorized biography and picture in connection with the promotion or marketing of the comic book. Unfortunately, what is also typical is that the same publishing company may restrict the artist's right to promote their work on the book. How and whether an artist gets to Tweet, Facebook, blog, or promote their own work at Comic Cons is dependent upon how this clause is drafted.

And, believe it or not, as between two private, nongovernmental parties, a contract that prohibits one party from talking about their creative work *does not* violate the artist's First Amendment rights.

EXAMPLE: PUBLICITY CLAUSE

Publicity

a. **Grant of Publicity Rights.** The Artist grants the Publishing Company the irrevocable right to use the Artist's name, image, likeness, voice, personality, personal identification, and authorized biography in connection with the Comic Book Property. The Publishing Company may employ this information for the promotion, publicity, advertising, marketing, and exploitation of the Comic Book Property in any medium now known or later devised. This includes, but is not limited to, printed materials, websites, digital content, blogs, podcasts, and social media posts—whether written, video, or audio.
b. **Approval Process.** The Artist agrees that any public communications regarding the Comic Book Property—including press releases,

interviews, social media posts, blog entries, videos, podcasts, or similar content—must be coordinated with and approved in advance by the Publishing Company. The Artist shall refrain from publicly criticizing their involvement or disclosing confidential details about the Comic Book Property, the Publishing Company, or its affiliates without such prior written consent.

THE BOILERPLATE BELLY

Standard Terms and Conditions

Ahhh... the "Standard Terms and Conditions," that term alone makes you want to plunge your face into a fish tank full of pepper-spray and piranhas rather than read through this murky legalese.

I can always tell when somebody starts to read the "boilerplate" section of the contract: their eyes glaze over, their reading pace accelerates, they race through pages just to get to the end of the document.

Yup, it's a great place for us lawyer-types to bury sneaky-but-powerful legal material.

... Just sayin'...

These clauses, too often merely glanced at and forgotten, are quite controlling. For instance, they affect where you can sue the other party and what you have to do before you can sue them. They even determine whether you still have the right to sue in the first place—the clause may restrict the parties to using arbitration to settle disputes. The point is that these provisions really do matter.

NOTWITHSTANDING...

"Notwithstanding anything herein to the contrary... " or "Notwithstanding the foregoing... " are legal phrases to put you on your guard. They mean "what your about to read will be the rule, even if everything I've said before or after contradicts it." For example, let's say the contract has the following clause: "You will transfer your copyright to me in exchange for one million dollars. Notwithstanding the foregoing, you will also transfer the copyright to me if I give you a plate of pancakes, which shall be considered full and complete payment for all rights." Now, despite the "one million dollars" language, all I have to do is bring you a short stack of silver dollars—the kind you eat with butter and maple syrup—and I own your rights.

Termination

How does the contract deal with what happens when things go wrong? Sometimes it's nobody's fault—a flood destroys the artist's house and materials or sometimes the project is stymied because of creative differences. Sometimes fault plays a part, and one party simply fails to perform their duties under the contract. This paragraph often defines *force majeure* events: those situations that are outside of the parties' control that could hamper, delay, or cancel the project (think fires, earthquakes, floods, death or incapacity of one of the parties, etc.).

When such an event occurs, this paragraph determines for how long the contract may be suspended—"put on hold" until the situation resolves—or is terminated. If the contract is terminated, this provision should also deal with how compensation is calculated when it is terminated. Double-check your termination provisions! *They often conflict with kill fee provisions and IP ownership by Artist if the project is terminated. Can you spot the conflict in the section below*?

EXAMPLE: SUSPENSION AND TERMINATION CLAUSE

Suspension and Termination.

a. The Agreement may be suspended immediately for the duration of the event in question in case of *Force Majeure* like earthquakes, floods, labor controversies, acts of God, and similar unforeseeable events.

b. Pub Co. reserves the right to discharge Artist at any time. If this Agreement shall be terminated under any of the provisions herein contained, Artist and Pub Co. shall each be relieved of any further obligations hereunder, except that such termination shall not relieve Pub Co. of any obligation to compensate Artist which accrues prior to such termination, unless such termination was occasioned by Artist's failure, refusal, or neglect to perform services or obligations hereunder ("For Cause"), nor shall such termination relieve Artist of Artist's obligations pursuant to Artist's representations and warranties hereunder.

c. Should Artist be terminated For Cause, Pub Co. shall have no further obligation to pay Artist Royalties, hereunder.

d. Notwithstanding termination, Pub Co. shall own without limitation throughout the universe, exclusively and in perpetuity; free and clear of any and all claims, liens, and encumbrances; all rights, title, and interest of every kind whatsoever; whether now known or unknown; the copyrights and all renewals, extensions, or reversions of copyright now or hereafter provided, in the Comic Book and the Work in addition to any and all results and proceeds of Artist's services hereunder.

Did you see it? Paragraph D in the previous Suspension and Termination Clause would conflict with any other provision in the same agreement that would allow the Artist to retain their intellectual property if the project is cancelled!

Representations and Warranties

The representations and warranties section of a paragraph is one of the most critical provisions of an artist's contract, and yet it is one of the most frequently skimmed over and unread. Representations and warranties are promises made by each party that the other party may rely on.

For instance, an artist, writer, or other IP creator will always be asked to represent and warrant that the creative material they have included in their comic book originated with them—they must promise that they haven't plagiarized, used GEN-AI, or infringed anybody else's copyright or trademark. Furthermore, the language with which this paragraph is drafted is typically very strict: the artist promises that her work will not violate any laws *anywhere* in the world.

EXAMPLE: CREATOR REPRESENTATION AND WARRANTY

Representations and Warranties. The Creator hereby represents and warrants to the Publisher that:

a. **Originality and Ownership.** The Work, entitled [Insert Comic Book Title], is an original creation of the Creator (or Creators, if a collaborative effort between writer and illustrator) and has not been previously published or distributed in any form. The Work is solely conceived and executed by the Creator(s) without any other party holding ownership rights or interests.
b. **Authority and Unencumbered Rights.** The Creator has the full, clear, and unencumbered right and authority to enter into this Agreement and to grant the rights specified herein. The rights conveyed are free of any prior contracts, liens, or encumbrances. Furthermore, during the term of this Agreement, the Creator agrees not to enter into any other agreements or understandings that would conflict with the rights granted to the Publisher under this Agreement.
c. **Compliance and Content Standards.** Throughout the world, the Work is free from libelous, obscene, or otherwise unlawful content. It does not infringe upon any statutory or common law copyright or any other third-party right and contains no material that would violate any individual's or entity's rights to privacy, publicity, or any other proprietary interest.

d. **No AI-Generated Content.** The Creator further represents and warrants that the Work, including [Insert Comic Book Title] and all its derivative or ancillary elements, is completely free of any content created, generated, or derived from artificial intelligence platforms (including, without limitation, ChatGPT or any other generative AI technologies). No AI technology has been—and will be—used in the development of any part of the Work, including narrative, dialogue, artwork, character development, or plot elements. The Parties acknowledge that inclusion of any AI-generated content is expressly prohibited under this Agreement. Should any breach of this warranty occur, such breach shall be deemed material, thereby entitling the Publisher to pursue all legal remedies available under law, including termination of the Agreement, damages, and injunctive relief.

Indemnification

Coupled with the representations and warranties provision is the indemnification clause. This provision says that if one of the parties injures the other by breaching the contract or making false representations and warranties, the injured party will be compensated by the injuring party. When you indemnify someone, basically you're saying "Don't worry, I got your back!" Although rather straightforward in meaning, the effects of the indemnification clause can be surprising. Keep in mind that typical indemnifications cover legal bills and reasonable attorney's fees.

For instance, a licensee will typically ask to be indemnified for:

- IP infringement lawsuits arising out of their use of the licensor's material
- Breaches of contract by the licensor
- Falsehoods in the representations and warranties made by the licensor

Example: The Worm Turns

Artist designs the look of the "Maggot Man" character and incorporates a fast-food company's logo into the costume. The comic book is published by Arms Akimbo Publishing, who also licenses the rights to make Maggot Man action figures to Maquette Manufacturing. The fast food company sues Artist, Arms Akimbo, and Maquette for trademark tarnishment from the unauthorized use of its logo. Artist would have to pay not only for her own legal bills but also for the legal bills of the publishing company and the manufacturing company, who have both been injured as a result of her misrepresenting that she had all of the rights.

This is because most indemnification clauses also pass the injuries of any licensees (like Arms Akimbo and Maquette) on to the party making the indemnification, here, the Artist.

Best of Knowledge and Belief

If you are worried about your ability to indemnify a publishing company, you may want to try the following:

- Try limiting any knowledge-based representations and warranties to "best of knowledge and belief." For example, "To the best of Artist's knowledge and belief, Artist has not included any infringing material in the Comic Book."
- Try to limit indemnification to payment of legal costs after the case has been lost and appeals exhausted. In other words, try to make sure you don't have to pay to defend frivolous lawsuits.
- Build in a cure period for those breaches that can be cured.
- Try to avoid absolute obligations ("Artist shall...") and replace them with good faith obligations ("Artist shall use **reasonable business efforts** to...")

Make sure there is reciprocal indemnification; the publishing company should indemnify you for liabilities it creates which injure you as well!

EXAMPLE: INDEMNIFICATION CLAUSE

Indemnification*22.

a. The Artist agrees to indemnify and hold Pub Co. and Pub Co.'s licensees and assigns***23** harmless from and against any loss, liability, judgment, cost, or expense of any kind and character suffered or incurred by Pub Co., including reasonable attorney's fees, by reason of any breach or alleged breach of any of the foregoing warranties by the Artist or of the Agreement in general.

b. Pub Co. agrees to indemnify and hold the Artist and Artist's licensees and assigns harmless from and against any loss, liability, judgment, cost, or expense of any kind and character suffered or incurred by the Artist, including reasonable attorney's fees, by reason of any breach or alleged breach of any of the foregoing warranties by Pub Co. or of the Agreement in general.

22 Many indemnification provisions are one-sided, with the duty to indemnify resting solely on the artist's shoulders. Double check your contract and make sure that the duty to indemnify each other for damages is reciprocal.

23 Keep in mind that for most indemnification provisions, you're not only indemnifying the other party to the contract, but also anybody that they license your work to, like other publishing companies, merchandisers, movie studios, etc.

Assignment and Delegation

Contract rights and duties can both be transferred to new parties, who were not parties to the contract when it was made. This is called a contract *assignment.*

> **Example**: You originally agreed with Arms Akimbo Publishing that it would publish a comic book. Arms Akimbo then assigns and delegates your contract to a scented manga comic company: Manga-Nifty-Scent Publications. Now it is Manga-Nifty-Scent Publications that has the right to publish your comic, and the obligation to pay you as per your deal with Arms Akimbo.

Unlike publishing companies, artists are typically not allowed to delegate their creative duties to other artists (but you can always assign your rights to receive money to somebody else). This makes sense, doesn't it? If the artist is doing her job right, her services are unique.

An assignment clause specifies who can assign their rights and delegate their duties under the agreement. Keep in mind that not every assignment clause actually uses the word "delegation," often conflating the two separate legal concepts of assignment—a transfer of rights—and delegation—the transfer of duties.

Assignments can be a double-edged sword. When your contract is silent on assignments, the rules get murky. Generally, the publisher might transfer its rights—meaning your comic continues to appear on the market—yet they cannot unilaterally delegate crucial duties like processing your royalty payments or managing distribution without your consent. This situation is much like trading out a beloved sidekick: the mission persists, but the unique qualities that made the original team effective may not transfer automatically.

Conversely, if your contract explicitly permits assignment, the publisher can shift the agreement to another party without your approval, though it's important to note that rights and responsibilities don't always travel together. For instance, any unpaid royalty obligations might not be inherited by the new publisher unless the contract explicitly states otherwise—essentially, they might take control of the spaceship without picking up the fuel costs.

An effective assignment clause will clearly delineate who can transfer their rights and delegate their responsibilities, safeguarding your interests while providing the publisher with the flexibility to adapt to mergers, acquisitions, or strategic restructuring.

EXAMPLE: ASSIGNMENT CLAUSE

Assignments

a. Artist may not assign any of her rights under this Agreement, except the right to receive money. Any purported assignment of rights shall be void.

b. The Publisher shall have the right to assign***24** its rights and obligations under this Agreement to any third party, provided that such third party agrees in writing to assume all of the Publisher's payment obligations and duties***24** stipulated herein. Upon such assignment, such assignee shall effectively step into the shoes of the Publisher, assuming all duties and liabilities as if originally party to this Agreement. The Publisher shall promptly notify the Author/Artist of any such assignment.

24 Assignment provisions are often one-sided, with the contracting party retaining the right to assign and delegate, while prohibiting the artist from doing the same. This actually makes sense—in order to do its job and effectively exploit the Comic Property, the Publisher needs to be able to license or assign the rights to other companies (printers, distributors, possibly merchandisers, etc.)

25 When a duty is delegated, the party assuming the obligations—the delegatee—now must perform the duties delegated to it. However, if it fails to perform, the original delegating party is still obligated to perform its duties.

No Encumbrances

On those projects in which the artist keeps or maintains an IP ownership interest—in other words, *not* a work for hire—this paragraph obligates the artist to maintain healthy copyright, trademark, and other intellectual property rights. This is because the other party is relying on the strength of those unencumbered rights as part of the value of the license in those rights granted to them by the artist. Trademark rights, for example, can be lost if they're not diligently maintained. Trademarks and copyrights both can be used as collateral for a loan (and thus, "encumbered" by security interests).

In a **no encumbrances** paragraph (sometimes called a "**no impairment of rights**" clause), the artist promises that they will not hamper or impede their own IP rights in the subject of the contract.

EXAMPLE: NO ENCUMBRANCES CLAUSE

No Encumbrances: Artist has not granted, assigned, licensed, or in any manner encumbered, diminished or impaired any such rights, other than to Pub Co.; that Artist has not committed or omitted to perform any act by which such rights could or will be encumbered, diminished or impaired; and that there is no outstanding claim or litigation pending against or involving the title, ownership and/or copyright in the Property, or in any part thereof, or in any rights granted herein to Pub Co. Artist further represents and warrants that no attempt shall be made hereafter to encumber, diminish, or impair any of the rights granted herein and that all appropriate protection of such rights will continue to be maintained by Artist.

Notice and Cure

I'm a big fan of **notice and cure** provisions: they give the parties a chance to fix problems before they turn into lawsuits. Here's how it works: the **injured party** is required to send a notice to the party doing the damage (called the **defaulting party**), alerting them to the problem.

A clock then starts, and the defaulting party now has a period of time in which to cure the default—or risk breaching the contract. In other words, the defaulting party is given time to fix the problem. If the problem is not fixed within a certain specified time period, only then can a lawsuit be filed or arbitration started.

EXAMPLE: NOTICE AND CURE PROVISION

Notice and Cure

a. Neither party shall be liable to each other for damages of any kind in connection with damages for any breach of this agreement (except for failure to pay the money consideration herein specified) occurring or accruing before the defaulting party has received notice from the complaining party and has failed to cure such a default within the time period specified in this paragraph.
b. All notices shall be written and specify with particularly the defaulting party's default. Notices shall be delivered in the form of a certified letter, overnight courier, or personal delivery. Once such notice has been received by the defaulting party, the defaulting party shall have ten business days within which to cure such a default specified in the notice.

Remedies

When things go wrong, it's essential to consider the mechanism for dispute resolution. Will the parties take their disagreements to court or opt for arbitration? Keep in mind that while arbitration can be a faster process, an arbitrator's decision is generally very difficult to appeal compared to a court ruling.

A critical issue is whether either party is giving up the right to specific legal relief. For example, if you suffer an injury that cannot be fully remedied by money—such as having your unique comic book character infringed upon—you might normally seek an equitable remedy, like an **injunction**, from a court. An injunction could, for instance, prevent a publishing company from printing infringing material. However, many contracts in the creative industry require the artist to **waive this right to seek injunctive relief**, leaving them only the option to pursue monetary damages through litigation.

Additionally, the agreement should clearly specify which state's law will govern any potential breaches, as legal interpretations can vary widely from one jurisdiction to another; some contracts may even require a party to travel to another state to initiate legal proceedings.

My Place or Yours?

If a lawsuit is a battle, the jurisdiction is its battleground. Jurisdiction controls the location and kind of court that will hear a lawsuit. The laws can, and do, differ from state to state. Whether you sue in New York, as opposed to Los Angeles, may make the difference between winning and losing your case.

The choice of law or forum clause in the contract is the parties' attempt to control the jurisdiction of the lawsuit. There are tremendous advantages in having a lawsuit brought in the jurisdiction of your choice. Often, it's the home-court advantage. The cost of litigating in the state far away from your home state may influence you on settling or trying your case.

- But sometimes it's the other way around. For instance, a publishing company that's based outside California and New York might still want California or New York law to apply to the contract. Because many of the top comic book titles are published in New York and California, courts in those states have generated a lot of case law that applies to comic books in particular and publishing in general. By choosing one of these jurisdictions, both parties may benefit from an established body of entertainment law. This allows all parties to anticipate, to some degree, how a lawsuit might play out in the courts, its possible outcomes, and the measure of damages the loser will have to pay.
- In addition to determining which state's laws apply, the choice of forum clause often lists the **venue** in which any dispute must be brought. Venue is the geographic region—such as a county—over which a trial court has

jurisdiction. The venue answers the question: Within this state, which trial court will hear the dispute?

- Forum clauses are not always enforceable; however, they are a strong factor in the court's decision to allow a lawsuit to proceed in a particular court.

EXAMPLE: REMEDIES; CHOICE OF LAW

Remedies; Choice of Law

a. In the event of breach of this Agreement, Artist waives any rights to injunctive or equitable relief and agrees not to seek the same. Pub Co.'s sole remedy in the event of such a breach is limited to an action at law to recover monetary damages.
b. This Agreement shall be governed by the laws of the State of New York applicable to contracts that are entered into and fully performed therein, without reference to conflict of laws provisions. The Parties agreed to the exclusive jurisdiction of the state and federal courts sitting in the State of New York, County of New York, as the jurisdiction for the resolution of any disputes that might arise hereunder and agree to accept service and be subject to the jurisdiction of the courts therein.
c. Both parties have been given ample opportunity to consult an attorney of their choosing and have either done so or have chosen voluntarily not to do so.

Audit and Accounting

If you are receiving royalties, residuals, net profits, or any other contingent compensation, you're going to want to be able to keep track of the other side's financial records to make sure you're getting paid what you are owed. This provision specifies how frequently the parties must provide each other with a detailed accounting of profits, costs, and revenue streams. It also regulates how often a party can send a certified public accountant to perform an audit of the other party's financial records.

In a typical audit provision, the party with audit rights has the right to hire a CPA to perform an annual audit. If the audit uncovers an underpayment of more than, say, 5%, the party being audited has to pick up the cost of this audit (as well as make good on the underpayment that was discovered).

EXAMPLE: AUDIT CLAUSE

Accounting and Audit

a. Pub Co. shall keep complete and accurate financial records relating to the exploitation of the Comic Book and shall send Artist a semiannual Royalty statement and, if applicable, Royalty payment. Artist shall have the annual right, upon 30 days advance written notice, to cause a certified public accountant, at Artist's expense, to inspect the books and records Pub Co. keeps with respect to the accounting of the exploitation of the Comic Book.

b. In the event that such inspection reveals an underpayment by Pub Co. of the monies owed to the Artist, Pub Co. shall pay the difference. If such underpayment shall be in excess of 5% of the amount owed Artist for any payment period, Pub Co. shall also reimburse Artist for the directly attributable and verifiable out-of-pocket third-party cost of such inspection.

Right to Withhold

The "Right to Withhold" clause authorizes the publishing company to deduct taxes and other legally required contributions directly from the employee's paycheck. If you have an independent contractor relationship, this may not be included.

This provision ensures that all statutory deductions are made in compliance with applicable laws, thereby streamlining the payroll process and relieving the worker from having to manage these obligations independently. Additionally, by delineating this authority, the clause safeguards the company's adherence to government regulations while providing clarity regarding the worker's net compensation.

EXAMPLE: RIGHT TO WITHHOLD

Right to Withhold. The Artist agrees that the Pub Co. is allowed to withhold taxes★**26** or other deductions of the fees to the extent necessary to comply with all applicable federal and state laws.

26 The right to withhold taxes may not be applicable if the party being engaged has their own loan-out company and is acting as an independent contractor. For more on this issue, see Loan Out Companies, p. 109.

Relationship of the Parties

This clause clarifies that the parties, while working together, are not partners. You want to be very careful becoming a general partner with somebody, as you may be liable for their debts and legal liabilities that they incur in furtherance of the partnership. (See General Partnership, p. 106.)

<u>EXAMPLE: RELATIONSHIP OF THE PARTIES</u>

Relationship of the Parties. Nothing contained herein shall constitute a partnership between, or joint venture by the Parties or constitute either of the Parties as an agent of the other.

Further Documents

Whether it's a copyright assignment, a recordation of the transfer of ownership, or other legal document, no matter how well you plan the logistics of your legal deliverables there's always a document or two that you have to prepare for the future. The Further Documents paragraph obligates the party or parties to execute additional documents that further the intent of the Agreement at some unspecified future date.

<u>EXAMPLE: FURTHER DOCUMENTS</u>

Further Documents. The Artist agrees to execute all additional documents that might be necessary to further the intent of this Agreement. Such documents may include, but are not limited to: certificates of authorship, short form assignments, etc. In case of the Artist's failure to comply with this provision within ten (10) calendar days after receiving the documents, Pub Co. shall be deemed to be, and the Artist hereby irrevocably appoints Pub Co., the true and lawful attorney-in-fact*27 of the Artist, to have the right to execute and deliver these documents either itself or via an attorney of its choice in the name of the Artist, which right is coupled with an interest.

<u>27</u> The further documents paragraph usually contains a power of attorney giving the rights to the contracting party to execute documents on behalf of the artist, should the artist not comply within a specific period of time.

Third-Party Beneficiaries

A **third-party beneficiary** to a contract is someone who is not a party to a contract but who could nonetheless sue to enforce the contract. To become a third-party beneficiary, a person has to prove that the contract was made for his immediate benefit. A **Third-Party Beneficiaries** clause lists those additional parties who benefit by the proper enforcement of the contract. Conversely, a "**No Third-Party Beneficiaries**" clause specifically states that no other parties are beneficiaries to the contract (other than the contracting parties themselves).

Example: Waldo Writer (owner of Pub Co.) signs a publishing agreement with Arms Akimbo Publishing to publish his new book "The Adventures of Maggot Man." Waldo hires Amy Artist to illustrate the book. In her artist's services contract with Waldo, Waldo specifies that Amy's services are for the benefit of Arms Akimbo. If Amy breaches her contract to Waldo, Arms Akimbo, as a third-party beneficiary, may be able to sue Amy, even though Arms Akimbo is not a party to the contract.

EXAMPLE: NO THIRD-PARTY BENEFICIARIES CLAUSE

Third-Party Beneficiaries. Studios, Merchandisers, and other Licensees of Pub Co.'s rights in the Work are hereby designated as third-party beneficiaries of this Agreement. These third-party beneficiaries shall have the right to enforce the terms of this Agreement to the extent that their rights and interests are affected, in accordance with the terms and conditions set forth herein. The Author and Publisher acknowledge and agree that the rights granted to these third-party beneficiaries are intended to benefit and protect their interests in the Work.

---ALTERNATELY---

No Third-Party Beneficiaries. This Agreement is intended solely for the benefit of the parties hereto. No other person or entity, including but not limited to Studios, Merchandisers, and other Licensees, shall have any rights, interests, or claims under this Agreement as a third-party beneficiary or otherwise.

"Merger," "Integration," or "Entire Agreement" Clause

The Merger (or "Integration" or "Entire Agreement") clause declares that this written contract is the full and final word between the parties—it trumps every handshake, late-night brainstorm, or whispered side promise that might have taken place before. In plain language, it wipes the slate clean of any prior negotiations or informal understandings, ensuring that only what's inked on the contract is enforceable. Essentially, it's a no-nonsense way to say, "What you see here is what you get," so don't expect any surprise bonus clauses to magically appear later.

And it's in virtually every professionally drafted agreement.

Make sure everything you've been promised is in the contract—if it's not, do not sign the contract. Once you've put down your "John Hancock," the written agreement (and not your prior discussions) is what controls the relationship of the parties, not any of the communications leading up to it.

> **Example**: Alex negotiates a deal with Dermatobia Comics to publish his new series, *Boris the Battlin' Bot-Fly*. Early in the discussions, Dermatobia Comics casually promises that if the series becomes a hit, Alex's work will even be adapted into an animated show with a bonus licensing deal to boot. However, when the final contract is drafted, it includes a "Merger" or "Entire Agreement" clause, making it clear that only the terms written into the document are enforceable—superseding any handshake, late-night brainstorm, or whispered side promise. This means that if the bonus licensing deal or animated adaptation scenario isn't explicitly detailed in the contract, any statements Dermatobia Comics made about that possibility simply aren't binding.

EXAMPLE: MERGER CLAUSE

Entire Agreement. This Agreement constitutes the entire agreement between the Parties and supersedes all previous and contemporaneous agreements and understandings related to the subject matter hereof. Artist hereby warrants that the execution of this Agreement has not been induced by, nor do any Parties rely upon or regard as material, any representations or writings whatsoever not incorporated herein and made a part hereof. Artist further warrants there has been no reliance in the execution of this Agreement on Pub Co.'s statements, if any, relating to the treatment and appearance of Artist's work in the Comic Book. Only a written amendment, signed by both parties, shall modify the duties and obligations herein.

Severability

If any clause in the contract violates the law, the Severability clause allows the offending paragraphs to be deleted from the contract without destroying the validity of the contract. The offending clause simply falls out of the contract and the contract is interpreted as though the clause had never been included in the first place.

EXAMPLE: SEVERABILITY CLAUSE

Severability. If any provision of this Agreement is adjudged void, unlawful, or unenforceable, in whole or in part, by court of competent jurisdiction, the remaining provisions shall continue in full force and effect.

Counterparts

In the old days of contract law, each original copy of a contract had to be signed by all parties to the agreement in order for it to have strong evidentiary value. In today's email-friendly society, contracting parties may not live near each other, and in fact may never have met. Accordingly, a "counterparts" provision allows both parties to sign different physical copies of the contract, with both signed versions together being viewed as originals. Obviously, the copies must be the same version of the contract, but you can sit in New York City and sign your copy of the executable version of the contract, while the other party is sitting on a beach in Maui and signing her copy of the same version. Each signed version is considered an original.

EXAMPLE: COUNTERPARTS PROVISION

Counterparts. This Agreement may be executed in counterparts, each of which shall be deemed an original, and all of such counterparts shall constitute only one agreement. The agreement is signed in counterparts; it shall only be effective upon delivery of one executed counterpart from each party to the other parties.

Survival

A clear and unambiguous survival clause allows certain provisions to survive the termination of a contract. For example, when a party commissions an artist to create illustrations on a work-for-hire basis, the agreement will typically point to the "WORK FOR HIRE/RIGHTS GRANTED" provision within the survival clause. This survival clause will state that if the contract is terminated for any reason, the rights transferred to the contracting party under the agreement will remain with the contractor.

Other clauses that are earmarked to "survive" contract termination: GRANT OF RIGHTS; APPROVALS AND CONTROL; PROMOTION/NAME AND LIKENESS; REPRESENTATIONS, WARRANTIES, AND INDEMNIFICATIONS; REMEDIES; ASSIGNMENT; CHOICE OF LAW; SEVERABILITY; and SURVIVAL (because you have to have the survival clause survive, of course). Ensure that your survival clauses are fully consistent with every other term in the contract. They must not conflict with any other provisions; otherwise, the contradictory terms could render your agreement ineffective or unenforceable.

EXAMPLE: SURVIVAL CLAUSE

Survival. If this Agreement is terminated for any reason, including breach or otherwise, the following sections shall survive such termination: WORK MADE FOR HIRE/ASSIGNMENT OF RIGHTS; PUBLICITY; REPRESENTATIONS AND WARRANTIES; REMEDIES; INDEMNIFICATION; ASSIGNMENT; REMEDIES; and SURVIVAL.

CONTRACT CLOSING

You flip to the last page of the agreement and you say to yourself: "I can see the signature block up ahead... the end of all this legalese is in sight! What could be simpler than just signing my name?"

... Somewhere in the darkness a lawyer rubs his hands and cackles with fiendish glee. "Now we've got him!"

Signature Block

The signature block contains the signature lines for the parties executing the contract, the date on which they're executing the agreement, as well as additional identifying information, such as Social Security numbers of employees, EIN numbers of businesses, addresses, and other contact info.

Believe it or not: the signature block of the contract can be fraught with peril! For instance, if you have a limited liability business, e.g. an LLC or Corporation, and you are contracting with an artist to draw your book, you want to make sure that you sign the artist services agreement in your capacity as officer of that company, and not in your personal capacity.

Example

____

Jeremy Jodhpur, President, Tally Ho Publishing, LLC

—**NOT**—

____

Jeremy Jodhpur

Failure to sign in your capacity as an officer of the business may mean that you are personally obligated under the contract (as opposed to your company being obligated under the contract). In other words, for this deal, you may have just destroyed the limited liability protection, which was one of the purposes of forming a company the first place. (See The Company as Owner of the Project, p. 109.)

EXAMPLE: SIGNATURE BLOCK

PUB CO.:	Lender*28 (f/s/o Artist):
______________________	______________________
Churlish Comics Publishing, Inc. Carl Churlish, President of Churlish Comics Publishing, Inc.	Abhinandana Studios, LLC Amy Abigail Abhinandana, Managing Member of Abhinandana Studios, LLC
Date:______________________	Date: ______________________

28 In a loan-out agreement, the term "Lender" refers to the loan-out company. This is because the loan-out company is "lending" the services of the artist.

Inducement

If you're contracting with an artist's loan-out company (see Loan-Out Companies, p. 109), you need to include an inducement clause to make sure that the artist can't escape her obligations merely by folding their company. After all, it is the loan-out company (called the "Lender") and not the artist which is signing the agreement with you. You need assurances that the artist will abide by the terms of the contract between her loan-out company and you. The **inducement clause** states that the artist will perform as though she (rather than her loan-out company) were the contracting party. It will also state that in the event of a default by the loan-out company, the artist will render services directly to you and indemnify you for any damages caused by the loan-out company.

EXAMPLE: INDUCEMENT CLAUSE

Inducement

a. If Lender should be dissolved, wrapped up, or for any reason whatsoever should fail or refuse to perform as specified under this Agreement, I shall personally perform in the Lender's stead and be personally bound by all of the terms and conditions and covenants herein.

b. I will look solely to Lender and not to you for all compensation and payment for all services performed under this Agreement, and all rights granted herein.

c. You may join me personally in any action against Lender, without being first required to resort to or exhaust any rights or remedies against Lender, in the event of a breach or threatened breach of the Agreement by Lender.

By: ______________________

Amy Abigail Abhinandana, Artist*29

29 Inducement clause should also be signed, but this time the loan-out company owner should sign it in their personal capacity (as opposed to in their capacity as an officer of the loan-out company.) After all, they are being personally bound to perform the contract should their loan-out company fail to.

ATTACHMENTS—EXHIBITS AND SCHEDULES

Exhibits and schedules to a contract are those additional documents that follow the signature block and become part of the agreement. An *exhibit* is a separate document, such as a copyright registration or another agreement. A *schedule*, by contrast, is a writing that could've been incorporated into the main agreement, but for purposes of clarity has been moved to a separate document. Examples of the schedule include a list of deliverables, or even a set of illustrations, such as character design templates.

You may want to refer to any exhibit or schedule in the body of the contract to ensure that it will be considered a part of the contract by a court interpreting the agreement. Additionally, you may see introductory clauses incorporating the attachment such as:

EXAMPLE: SCHEDULE A—CHARACTER DESIGNS

This Schedule A is a part of that agreement between Pub Co. and Artist dated January 31, 2026. The Artwork that is the subject of this agreement is that illustration of the character "Maggot Man," as depicted below, and subject to copyright serial number VA######.

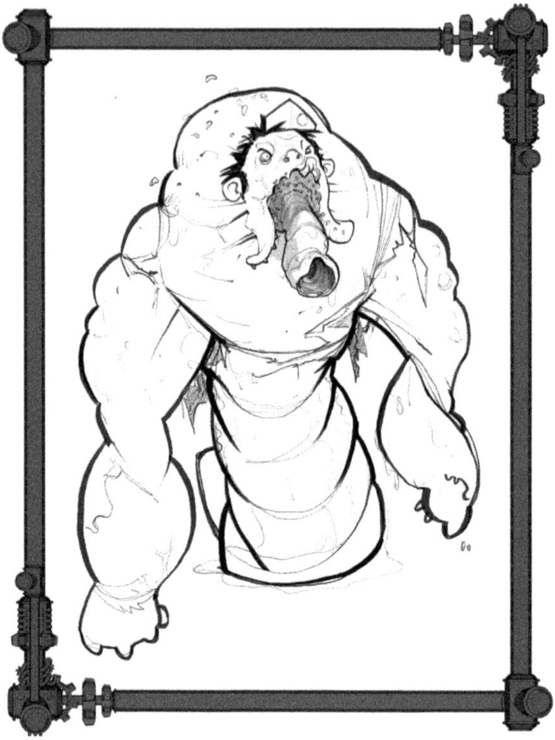

Obviously, not every agreement will have every clause, and you will see a lot of variations on a theme. But that's what the rest of the book is about!

Note

1 Williams v. Barkley, 165 N.Y. 48, 57, 58 N.E. 765, 767 (1900) ("Where the recital in an agreement is so inconsistent with the covenant or promise that they cannot be harmonized, the latter, if unambiguous, must prevail, because it is the most important. The promise is what the parties agreed to do, and hence is the operative part of the instrument, while the recital states what led up to the promise and gives the inducement for making it. When the explanation of the reason for the promise is at variance with the promise itself, the latter, if clear and unambiguous, must prevail, as it is the transaction between the parties. The rule governing the subject is well stated in a late English case as follows: "If the recitals are clear and the operative part is ambiguous, the recitals govern the construction. If the recitals are ambiguous and the operative part is clear, the operative part must prevail. If both the recitals and the operative part are clear, but they are inconsistent with each other, the operative part is to be preferred.")

APPENDIX H

Famous Comic Book Cases

Sometimes the greatest fight a superhero must face is in the courtroom; since its formative years, the American comic book industry has been rife with such two-fisted legal dust-ups. Here are just a few of the more famous cases.[1]

---------CASE STUDY---------

SUPERMAN BATTLES WONDERMAN

Detective Comics v. Bruns Publications, 111 F.2d 432 (2nd Cir. 1940)

Facts: It's a bird! It's a plane! It's... Wonderman?? Having just introduced Superman in *Action Comics*, *Detective Comics* (aka *DC*) was less than pleased when rival *Bruns Publications* introduced their own superhero with super strength, a secret identity, a "skintight acrobatic costume" (red, not blue), who liked to crush guns and leap over buildings while battling against "evil and injustice."[2] *DC* sued for copyright infringement and won. On appeal, *Bruns* argued that Superman was already an imitation of common archetypes, with countless analogues in the literary and mythological heroes of olden times.

In fact, *Bruns* argued, Supes was nothing more than "the presentation of a general type," lacking the originality necessary for copyright protection.

What did the court say? Superman may have been little more than "a comic Hercules," but he was just that, a bit more than a mere "presentation of a general type," which was enough to deserve copyright protection.[3] While the court may not have held the work in high regard,[4] they recognized there was "an original arrangement of incidents and a pictorial and literary form," and *Bruns* had clearly, in the court's opinion, done more than just copy some "general types and ideas."[5] That said, you can't copyright a "benevolent Hercules," only "the incidents and literary expressions original with the author," so that while *DC* still prevailed, they only had a copyright in Superman, not "the mere character of *a* 'Superman'."

Why is this case important? This case shows that just because there may be few original ideas left in the world, that doesn't mean your ultra-referential, archetype-fueled, comic masterpiece can't still be protected by copyright law. All that is required is that your expression and/or arrangement of your material have some spark of originality. On the other hand, general types and ideas, by themselves, are not the "proper subject" of copyright.[6]

---------CASE STUDY---------

"THE MAN OF STEEL" BATTLES THE "BIG RED CHEESE"

National Comics Publications v. Fawcett Publications, 191 F.2d 594 (2d Cir. 1951)

Facts: In a fight between Superman and Captain Marvel, who wins? That question is at the heart of this landmark comic book case. *National Comics Publications* (or *DC*, as it was known at the time) was the publisher of *Action Comics,* in which Superman, the original "Man of Steel," first took flight (well, this early incarnation couldn't actually fly—that came later—but he was a most prodigious leaper). Not long after Superman's initial debut, a rival comic publisher, *Fawcett Publications*, unveiled its own superhero, Captain Marvel, in the pages of *Whiz Comics*. *DC* sued *Fawcett* for copyright infringement, alleging that *Fawcett* had deliberately plagiarized their creation (well, *DC* didn't actually "create" Superman—Jerry Siegel and Joe Schuster did that—but they did own all the rights). The trial court agreed that the Superman character was not "a mere delineation of a benevolent Hercules," but instead embodied "an arrangement of incidents and literary expressions" (the "proper subjects" of "copyright"!).[7] The Captain Marvel creative team admitted that they had been instructed to imitate Superman "as closely as possible," and, as far as the court was concerned, the "only real difference" between the superheroes was the color of the costumes.[8] Even so, *DC* lost the case—the court decided that the publication of the strips in a newspaper without the proper copyright notices (a requirement of the 1909 Copyright Act) meant that the Superman stories had been abandoned and were now in the public domain.[9] Round One to *Fawcett*.

What did the appeals court say? On appeal, the renowned judge Learned Hand (a jurisprudential superman in his own right) had no trouble finding that *Fawcett* was guilty of copyright infringement: "it takes scarcely more than a glance at corresponding 'strips' of 'Superman' and 'Captain Marvel' to assure the observer that the plagiarism was deliberate and unabashed."[10] What's more, Hand concluded that *DC* had at least tried to comply with the legal notice requirements, and he wasn't going to penalize them for someone else's mistake—which was lucky for *DC,* who may have ended up forfeiting their copyright in Superman.[11] Round Two to *DC*.

Why is this case important? In the comic universe, the ultimate showdown of Superman vs. Captain Marvel rarely has a clear victor, but in the courtroom, Captain Marvel was soundly defeated (*Fawcett* ended up settling the case out of court and shutting down its entire comic book division). This case is a cautionary tale: if you copy someone's original work, it may not matter that essential details are different (i.e., throw in a new name, costume, alter ego, and a wizard called Shazam); you may still be found guilty of copyright infringement. As Judge Hand put it, "a plagiarist can never excuse his wrong by showing how much he did not plagiarize."[12]

TOO LATE TO WIN

Netzer v. Continuity Graphic Associates, 963 F. Supp. 1308 (S.D.N.Y. 1997)

Facts: At its heart, this case is a "cautionary and perhaps generational tale of the falling out between two formerly close associates," Neal Adams, a comic book artist, and comic writer Michael Netzer, an Israeli transplant, whose birth name was "Michael Nasser"[13] (keep this name in mind). Together, they formed the classic joint author equation in comics—"I can write it, you can draw it."[14]—devising a female superhero called Ms. Mystic. In 1982, after Netzer left for the Middle East, *Pacific Comics* published the first of two *Ms. Mystic* comics, which credited Adams as the sole copyright owner. Netzer learned of the publication in 1983, saw a copy in 1984, and in 1985 spoke to Adams, who assured him the copyright attribution was "a mistake" and that no money had been made from the comic. In 1993, Netzer sued, asserting his copyright claim over *Ms. Mystic* despite Adams' warning that "negative things" might happen if he did. In that same year, Adams' company, *Continuity Graphic Associates*, published *Crazyman*, a comic book series about a "crazy" man with derangement-fueled super strength who just so happened to face off against a terrorist villain with the aliases "Mike Nasser" and "Abu Netzer"—sound familiar? In this case, Netzer asserted 18 (!) claims, 15 of which related to the co-authorship of *Ms. Mystic* and other related fraud, contract, and tort claims, and the final three alleged libel, violations of his right of privacy, and intentional infliction of emotional distress, all connected to the terrorist character in *Crazyman*.

What did the court say? The first matter before the court, which proved decisive, was whether Netzer had failed to bring his lawsuit within the three-year statute of limitations window set by the Copyright Act of 1976.[15] The clock started to tick at the moment that Netzer learned that Adams claimed sole copyright ownership—when he saw that first issue of *Ms. Mystic*—in which case, his claim was way overdue. Netzer argued, in vain, that Adams' misconduct had led to the delay in bringing the suit, but the court felt that Netzer had not satisfied his own obligation of due diligence to dig a little deeper. Ultimately, the court did not want to "trivialize the statute of limitations by promiscuous application of tolling doctrines,"[16] especially since "certainty and repose are essential to the functioning of the copyright market."[17] The other fraud, contract, and tort claims were either swallowed up as part of the underlying (and now defunct) copyright claim or were knocked out by their own statutes of limitation.

All that was left were the "Crazyman Claims."[18] Because the comic was "patently a work of fantasy, involving outlandish plot scenarios and characters with impossible powers,"[19] the court didn't believe a reasonable reader would think the comic book was saying Netzer was actually a terrorist, so it couldn't be defamatory—and, at the very least, a defamatory statement should expose you to public "obloquy, contumely, [and] odium" (all of which sound quite nasty, but I'm going to have to take the court's word for it).[20] As for violating his right of privacy, the court concluded that the use was merely incidental and thus "insufficient to establish liability."[21] Furthermore, connecting his name to a fictional terrorist was not sufficiently "extreme and outrageous" to support his tort claim for intentional infliction of emotional distress.[22]

Why is this case important? The moral of this case probably has something to do with tardy birds and very fortunate worms. Netzer may well have had a valid co-authorship claim, but we'll never know—the court couldn't get to the merits of the case because Netzer had waited too long to file his lawsuit. Also, if you are angry at someone, putting their name or likeness into your comic book is just asking for trouble. Adams got away with it, but you may not be so lucky.

---------CASE STUDY---------

COPYRIGHT LAW WAS A STAKE THROUGH HIS HEART

Hogan v. DC Comics, 48 F.Supp.2d 298 (S.D.N.Y. 1999)

Facts: *Matchsticks* tells the macabre story of a half-vampire, half-human named Nicholas Gaunt, a young man with pale skin and dark hair who must make the ultimate choice between good and evil. *Dhampire* tells the macabre story of a half-vampire, half-human named Nicholas Gaunt, a young man with... ok, you get the picture. Francis Hogan had tried on several occasions to entice *DC* to publish his creepy vampiric comic, *Matchsticks*, but couldn't get them to bite. Around the same time, *DC* commissioned Nancy Collins' graphic novel, *Dhampire*. Hogan sued *DC* for both copyright infringement and for the misappropriation of his idea—and failed to draw blood on either front.

What did the court say? The court began with a close examination of the two works, their origins, and *DC's* interactions with the two authors. To prove his work was infringed, Hogan had to show "(1) ownership of a valid copyright, and (2) copying of constituent elements of the work, that are original."[23] To show "copying," Hogan had to show either direct or indirect access to *Matchsticks* along with substantial similarity between the two works. Even though Collins denied seeing Hogan's comic book, her editors at *DC* definitely had, which was enough to show "a reasonable possibility" of access.[24] As for the similarity determination, the court noted that copyright protects "the expression of ideas" and not "the ideas themselves." The court employed the "ordinary observer test" to see if an "average lay observer" would see that *Dhampire* had been appropriated from *Matchsticks*, comparing both the specific protectable elements and the "total concept and feel" of the works.[25] The half-vampire idea and everything that flowed "predictably" from that idea, even if similar, were not sufficiently original, not even in the way the elements were combined.[26]

A character can be protected too, so long as it is not a "stock character," too indistinct and undeveloped to be copyrighted[27] and while the name of the main character, "Nicholas Gaunt," was a pretty significant similarity, the other shared characteristics (pale skin, taste for blood, etc...) didn't add up to "substantial similarity."[28] A "shared [name], by itself, is insufficient to establish substantial similarity between the characters."[29]

Hogan's other claim was that *DC* had misappropriated his idea, which required a showing that the parties had "a legal relationship" and that his idea was novel.[30] Novelty isn't all that easy to establish—even "clever or useful" adaptations of existing ideas won't cut it. Not that it mattered anyway, because there was convincing evidence that Collins had come up with her idea independently.

Why is this case important? The substantial similarity analysis can be very fact-intensive—it can also be very hard to prove there was infringement even if the similarities seem a little suspicious—and that's largely by design—the last thing anyone wants is for courts to start handing out monopolies over ideas and stock characters. Would a well-drafted NDA have prevented this? Perhaps, but getting *DC* or any large publishing company to sign would be a losing battle in and of itself.

---------CASE STUDY---------

DYNAMIC TENSIONS

Charles Atlas v. DC Comics, 112 F.Supp. 2d 330 (S.D.N.Y. 2000)

Facts: Most comic book fans are familiar with "*The Insult that Made a Man out of Mac*," the *Charles Atlas* ("*Atlas*") advertisement in which a bully kicks sand in scrawny Mac's face, Mac buffs up with some help from Mr. Atlas, the bully gets his comeuppance, and all the beach beauties swoon over the new "Hero of the beach."[31] In this case, though, it was the corporate beefcake, *Charles Atlas, Inc.*, complaining that *DC Comics* had effectively kicked sand in its face by publishing Grant Morrison's *Flex Mentallo* story in their *Doom Patrol* comic in 1991. Morrison's *Flex Mentallo* closely mirrors the ad's storyline, even to the extent of using similar artwork, dialogue, and the same leopard skin trunks favored by Mr. Atlas himself. The stories diverge dramatically at the end, when the now-muscle-bound Flex beats up the woman he is with, declaring, "I don't need a tramp like you anymore!"[32] *Atlas* sued for trademark infringement, alleging that *DC* had violated the Lanham Act's unfair competition and trademark dilution provisions. In essence, *Atlas* claimed that the "sexist and vulgar portrayal" of Flex Mentallo "tarnishe[d]" their trademark and that the misappropriation of their ad would be likely to confuse the gravamen of a trademark infringement claim.[33] *DC* had three arguments why the plaintiff's case should be thrown out: (1) the claim was time-barred by the statute of limitations; (2) the comic books did not meet the requirement of having been used "in commerce"; and (3) as parody, the comic books were protected by the First Amendment.

What did the court say? The court analyzed and agreed with each of *DC*'s arguments: (1) The statute of limitations for bringing a trademark infringement case is generally six years from the publication of the infringing work, and this lawsuit was already two years overdue. The court was not impressed by Atlas's attempt to "profess ignorance of the publication of the very comic books in which it ha[d] placed millions of dollars of advertising over several decades." (2) To establish trademark infringement or dilution under Section 43(a) of the federal Lanham Act, *Atlas* had to show that *DC* used their trademark "in commerce."[34] The court recognized that a parody of a trademark is often seen as a "non-commercial use" and thus not actionable (unless the parody is being used to promote a rival product).[35] (3) Finally, the court dived into *DC*'s constitutional defense. In cases like this involving expressive works, courts must balance free expression interests against the public's interest "in avoiding consumer confusion."[36] As a parody, the *Flex Mentallo* comic book took the *Atlas* ad "to an absurd conclusion"[37] and while the court may not have found it particularly "funny," it was "precisely the type of expression of ideas that the First Amendment [was] designed to protect."[38] As for a likelihood of causing confusion, the court applied a multi-factor test[39] and found that the risk of confusion was minimal—noting that because comic fans are "extremely conscientious and knowledgeable" about comic history, they would have no trouble distinguishing between the original ads and Morrison's parody.[40]

Why is this case important? This case is a good reminder that corporations can be very protective of their trademarks (and litigious!), particularly if they think the use makes them look bad. The good news for comic book creators is that the First Amendment is a powerful defense against trademark infringement claims—particularly when the comic book is commenting upon, or making fun of, the trademark. But beware, your freedom of speech is always balanced against the public interest in avoiding consumer confusion, and that clever parody of yours won't seem that funny anymore if a court finds you liable for trademark infringement.

--------CASE STUDY--------

CAPTAIN AMERICA: COPYRIGHT AVENGER

Marvel Characters v. Simon, 310 F.3d 280 (2nd Cir. 2002)

Facts: In 1940, Joseph Simon sold his patriotic superhero, *Captain America*, to *Timely Comics* (now part of *Marvel*). After the initial 28-year copyright term expired, Simon sought a declaration that he was the author of the *Captain America* comic books and character. He eventually entered into a settlement agreement with the owners of *Timely* in which he acknowledged that his work was done as "an employee for hire"[41] (which, if true, would mean that Simon never owned the rights). The 1976 Copyright Act, though, gave authors like Simon an opportunity to reclaim their copyright by filing notices of termination[42]—a second bite, as it were, of that juicy *Captain American* apple. *Marvel* sued, arguing that this new termination right couldn't help Simon because the settlement clearly stated that Simon was not the "author" as far as copyright was concerned[43]—and while the 1976 Act allowed terminations "notwithstanding any agreement to the contrary," it excluded works "made for hire."[44] *Marvel's* basic premise was that the settlement agreement precluded Simon from asserting his termination rights. The trial court agreed, and Simon appealed.

What did the court say? Looking at the legislative history of the 1976 Act, the Second Circuit Court of Appeals concluded that Congress's intent was "to protect authors from unequal bargaining positions."[45] With that in mind, the court decided that an agreement after the fact that a work was created as a "work for hire" was just the kind of "agreement to the contrary" that could be disavowed under the statute.[46] Thus, trying to avoid termination by using the magic words "work for hire" in a subsequent agreement wasn't worth much unless there was an actual work-for-hire relationship when the work was created—and there was plenty of evidence that Simon was not an employee for hire. And it's not like there was much reason to feel sorry for *Marvel*: they had all the benefit of a 28-year renewal term and still had the right to exploit all the *Captain America* properties created before the effective date of the termination.

Why is this case important? This case shows that sometimes David beats Goliath, with a little help from the Copyright Act of 1976. Simon won this particular legal bout, but it was not a clear knockout—in fact, those three infamous words ("work for hire") in the settlement agreement very nearly stopped the fight in the first round.

---------CASE STUDY---------

THE WINTERS OF OUR DISCONTENT

Winter v. DC Comics, 30 Cal.4th 881 (2003)

Facts: In the 1990s, *DC Comics* published a mini-series featuring Jonah Hex, a disfigured Civil War veteran turned bounty hunter. In Volume 2 of the series, *Autumns of Our Discontent*, we are introduced to the villainous Autumn brothers, Johnny and Edgar: the half-worm, half-human spawn of a supernatural worm creature. At the end of Volume 5, our surly anti-hero, six-shooters ablaze, teams up with some singing cowboys to kill the evil Autumn brothers and their invertebrate brethren. But as worms will turn, the two aggrieved brothers would rise up to seek retribution—the Winter brothers, that is.

Johnny and Edgar Winter are successful recording artists and musicians who just so happen to be tall and thin with albino features and a predilection for black top hats—much like the Autumn siblings (except for the musical talent part). The Winters sued *DC* for the misappropriation of their names and likenesses under California's right of publicity statute.[47] The California right of publicity is essentially "the right of a person whose identity has commercial value—most often a celebrity—to control the commercial use of that identity."[48] In addition, the brothers claimed that they had been falsely portrayed as "vile, depraved, stupid, cowardly, subhuman individuals who engage in wanton acts of violence, murder and bestiality for pleasure and who should be killed"[49] (for some reason, "spawn of a supernatural worm creature" didn't make the list).

What did the court say? The Supreme Court of California recognized that "[a]n obvious tension exists" between the statutory right to prohibit others from using a celebrity's likeness and the First Amendment to the U.S. Constitution.[50] To decide if the free speech rights of the *Jonah Hex* creators trumped the statutory rights of the Winter brothers, the court employed a "transformative" balancing test, which asks, "whether the work in question adds significant creative elements so as to be transformed into something more than a mere celebrity likeness or imitation."[51] Conversely, a "literal depiction or imitation of a celebrity for commercial gain... without adding significant expression" would be a direct trespass of the right of publicity and would not be "protected expression" under the First Amendment.[52]

In other words, even though the evocation of the Winter brothers was "less-than-subtle," it was hardly literal—unless, of course, the Winters are actually depraved "half-human and half-worm" murderers[53] in which case DC has more to worry about than an annoying lawsuit. As the court cautioned, "the right of publicity cannot, consistent with the First Amendment, be a right to control the celebrity's image by censoring disagreeable portrayals."[54] *DC* prevailed because they sold depictions of "fanciful, creative characters, not pictures of the Winter brothers," and that made "all the difference."[55]

Why is this case important? As a general matter, celebrities may be less than pleased if you portray them as cowardly, subhuman, murderous nematodes (image is everything, after all), and, in a majority of states, they can sue for violations of their statutory or common law right of publicity—and sometimes they win.[56] This case provides an excellent example of how the First Amendment can be your very own constitutional shield—but only so long as the celebrity depiction is transformed into something more than mere imitation.

- - - - - - - - -CASE STUDY- - - - - - - - -

ARCHIE AND WORK FOR HIRE

Archie Comic Publications v. DeCarlo, 258 F. Supp. 2d 315 (S.D.N.Y. 2003)

Facts: Beginning in the early 1950s, comic book artist Daniel DeCarlo did freelance work on three titles, *Josie*, *Sabrina the Teenage Witch*, and *Cheryl Blossom,* published by *Archie Comic Publications* ("*ACP*"). Years later, DeCarlo initiated a series of lawsuits against *ACP* in which he claimed he owned the copyright to his contributions.[57] He lost every time. In 2003, *ACP* sued DeCarlo's estate to essentially "quiet its title to these properties" by getting the court to declare once and for all who owned what and to bar the DeCarlo heirs from bringing any more lawsuits or serving any more copyright termination notices. Specifically, regarding *Josie*, the court had to decide if DeCarlo's ownership claim was barred because a different court had already ruled against him—it was—and as for *Cheryl Blossom*, DeCarlo's claim failed because he had assigned all his rights and interests in the property in a 1988 Agreement. The more challenging issue for the court was whether DeCarlo's contributions to *Sabrina* were "works for hire," which would mean *ACP* owned everything from the very beginning.

What did the court say? Just when you figure out the *who* and *how* of a copyright question, along comes the *when* to make things even more confusing: in this case, most of DeCarlo's work had been created before January 1, 1978 (the effective date of the 1976 Copyright Act) and was thus covered by the earlier 1909 Copyright Act, but a few stories came later and were governed by the 1976 Act. Under the 1909 Act, the work of an independent contractor like DeCarlo is a "work for hire" if it was created at the "instance and expense" of the hiring party.[58] Here, the "instance" part of the test was met because *ACP* not only "induced the creation" of the *Sabrina* works, but it also had total editorial control.[59] As for "expense," it was enough that DeCarlo was paid. The heirs might have won if there was evidence of an agreement to the contrary stating that DeCarlo owned the copyright, but all they had was a voucher agreement and some copies of check endorsements, none of which specifically related to DeCarlo's work on *Sabrina* (the originals had been lost). As for the post-1978 contributions, a work for hire by a nonemployee must fit into one of the nine categories specified in the 1976 Act and be accompanied by a "written instrument" declaring that the work is a "work made for hire."[60] Here, the *Sabrina* work was "specially ordered or commissioned" as part of a "collective work"[61] (i.e., a comic book), and there were two agreements signed with *ACP* in 1988 and again in 1996 that expressly stated that DeCarlo's contributions were work for hire.

Why is this case important? As part of the creative team behind a comic book, you may or may not have rights in your contributions—the difference can be a matter of three words scrawled on the back of a check: *work for hire*. This case is a good reminder that just because you are not an employee, that does not guarantee that you own your work. And if you can, try to do a better job than Mr. DeCarlo at record-keeping—it can make all the difference.

--------CASE STUDY--------

SPAWNING A LAWSUIT

Gaiman v. McFarlane, 360 F.3d 644, 650 (7th Cir. 2004)

Facts: Todd McFarlane and Neil Gaiman are both "celebrated figures in the world of comic books,"[62] accomplished in their respective fields of illustration and writing. In 1992, McFarlane began publishing a comic book called *Spawn*, about a dead man who makes a Faustian pact with a demon and is returned to the world as a vengeful hell spawn. The first issues were praised for McFarlane's artwork but savaged by the critics for the poor quality of his writing. So, McFarlane invited Gaiman to take over the scriptwriting responsibilities. Their big mistake was that they never had a written contract, just an oral promise to pay Gaiman "better than the big guys."[63] The "big guys," *Marvel* and *DC*, usually hired writers on a "work made for hire" basis, where they owned all the rights to the work created, so it wasn't immediately obvious whether this is what McFarlane had intended.

Gaiman's hugely successful first issue of *Spawn* introduced three new characters: Medieval Spawn, Count Nicholas Cogliostro, and Angela, who eventually had her own series. Gaiman was well paid for his contributions and was even paid royalties on the sale of *Spawn* action figures. Eventually, Gaiman decided he needed to protect himself with a written contract but after many "desultory negotiations," McFarlane rescinded any offers on the table and denied Gaiman's copyright interest in the characters he had helped create.[64] And thus a lawsuit was spawned. At trial, Gaiman successfully asserted that he was a joint owner of the copyrights, and McFarlane appealed.

What did the court say? Under the Copyright Act of 1976, Gaiman's work could not be characterized as "work made for hire" because Gaiman was not an employee, and there was no written instrument stating that his work "shall be considered a work for hire."[65] That said, even if Gaiman wasn't a "formal" employee, he might still be a "de facto" employee, but the court saw no evidence of that, and furthermore, there was no written assignment of Gaiman's copyrights to McFarlane (or any written agreements at all, for that matter). McFarlane argued that his copyright notices and registration of the comic books and later paperbacks started the three-year statute of limitations clock because they gave Gaiman notice that his copyright had been repudiated. If true, then Gaiman had brought his case too late. But McFarlane's registration of the comic book as a compilation would not necessarily undermine a joint ownership claim to the work—so that doesn't count as repudiation—and neither does the copyright registration in the paperbacks because there was no evidence Gaiman had actual notice of the registration.

McFarlane's other ground for reversal was that two of the characters, Medieval Spawn and Cogliostro, were not "copyrightable."[66] The court conceded that ideas, without some original expression, are not protected by copyright and that the general rule is that the contribution of each co-author of a work must be "independently copyrightable."[67] But the requirement that the contribution "stand alone" doesn't necessarily apply to "the particular creative process" essential to comic book collaborations—in other words, you can imagine a comic book jointly created by a writer, penciller, inker, and colorist where "none of the separate contributions" are copyrightable, but the comic book and its characters are.[68] McFarlane's other argument was that Cogliostro was just a stock character, "so rudimentary, commonplace, standard, or unavoidable"[69] that it could not be copyrighted, but, once again, the court concluded that even if Gaiman's contribution "may not have been copyrightable by itself," it was copyrightable in combination with McFarlane's drawing, as a joint work.[70] As for Medieval Spawn, there was enough expressive content, and he was sufficiently distinguishable from Spawn (i.e., he said Medieval-esque things like "Good day, sweet maiden."[71]) that he was clearly copyrightable. The result of all this is that Gaiman was declared the joint owner of the copyrights, and McFarlane was instructed to hand over Gaiman's share of the profits (something McFarlane was still trying to avoid even as recently as 2012!).[72]

Why is this case important? When creative people collaborate to create new work without a well-drafted work-for-hire or collaboration agreement, then all that may be left is a Faustian bargain where no one knows exactly who owns what, and, as this case reveals, things can go "south" pretty fast. In the act of cleaning up the mess, the Seventh Circuit Court of Appeals confirmed that the "particular" process involved in creating comic books means that a comic contributor can still have a copyright in a joint work even if his/her specific contribution isn't copyrightable by itself.

Important note: Several other circuits disagree with the 7th Circuit, requiring copyrightability for each joint author's contributions. As you can see, *where* a lawsuit is brought matters tremendously.

---------CASE STUDY---------

THE MARVEL MENAGERIE

Marvel Worldwide v. Kirby, 777 F. Supp. 2d 720 (S.D.N.Y. 2011)

(Judgment Affirmed in Part, Vacated in Part by *Marvel Characters, Inc. v. Kirby*, 2nd Cir.(N.Y.), August 8, 2013)

Facts: The dream team of the silver age of comics, Jack Kirby and Stan Lee, can take credit for some of the most iconic and successful comic books of all time, including *The Fantastic Four*, *The Incredible Hulk*, *The Mighty Thor*,

The Avengers, *Iron Man*, and *The X–Men*. In 1972, Kirby assigned all his rights in these works to *Marvel Comics* and died in 1994, leaving his heirs without an interest in the copyright to these characters and properties. Lucky for the heirs, Congress included Section 304 in the Copyright Act of 1976, which gave an author and his/her heirs the power to terminate a transfer or license of copyrights even for works that pre-dated the 1978 effective date of the Act.[73] Unlucky for the heirs, Section 304 made an exception for "work[s] made for hire," which, for pre-1978 works,[74] meant that the copyright belonged "to the person at whose 'instance and expense' the work was created."[75] Even though Kirby was a freelancer, not an employee, if the court found that *Marvel* "induce[d] the creation" of the work and had "the right to direct and supervise the manner in which the work [was] carried out," then *Marvel* owned the copyrights, Kirby had nothing to assign, and the heirs had nothing to terminate.[76]

What did the court say? The District Court decided that the 1972 agreement was speaking "out of both sides of its mouth" (in other words, it was about as much use as Thor without Mjolnir) and looked instead to the facts surrounding the creation of the comic books.[77] Stan Lee, famous for his cameos, played the lead role in the case, and, arguably, it was his testimony that doomed the Kirby heirs. As it turned out, Lee ran the show, assigned the work, and retained all the power to "accept, reject, or modify" anything Kirby produced.[78] And it was *Marvel* that bore all the risks, not Kirby. For the court, the heirs failed to make "so much as a dent in the 'almost irrebuttable' presumption that the Kirby Works were works for hire," which meant that their termination notices were "of no force and effect" (in other words, they were about as much use as Tony Stark in a tin foil suit).[79]

On appeal,[80] part of this judgment was reversed on procedural grounds with respect to two of the plaintiffs; the 2d Circuit largely upheld the portions of the case that involved its work-for-hire analysis.

Why is this case important? The court insists that this case was not about whether Kirby and other freelance artists were "treated 'fairly' by companies that grew rich off the fruit of their labor."[81] But whether you believe that or not may not matter a whole lot when you find yourself in court squaring off against some corporate comic super-villain. The 1976 Act is definitely more freelancer-friendly than its predecessor, but even still, cases like this demonstrate how powerful a few words like "work for hire" can be and how very important it is to have clear working relationships—for you and your heirs.

---------CASE STUDY---------

THE SUPERMAN SAGA

Siegel v. Warner Bros. Entertainment 542 F.Supp. 2d 1098 (C.D. Cal. 2008)

Facts: In 1933, two teenagers, Jerome Siegel and Joseph Shuster, created the first and greatest superhero the world has ever known: a villainous bald, mad-man, mind-reader called Superman! Well, even comic visionaries need some time to iron out the creative wrinkles. And they did, five years later, when they unveiled their new and improved Superman (modern-day Hercules, part-time newsman, tight-fitting leotard, etc...) in *Action Comics*, Vol 1.

In exchange for all the rights to this intellectual property goldmine, *DC* paid Siegel and Shuster the princely sum of $130. During their lifetimes, Siegel and Shuster tried without success to get "their fair share of profits generated from the exploitation of their Superman creation."[82] By 1975, the *N.Y. Times* reported that the two men were living in "near destitute condition"[83] and, perhaps in response to this bad publicity, *DC* and its corporate affiliates agreed to provide modest annual payments to the two men and, later, to Siegel's surviving spouse, Joanne. It looked like this particular super-saga was at an end, but then Section 304 of the 1976 Copyright Act[84] came along and completely "changed the legal landscape."[85]

Section 304 provides artists and their heirs with "the ability to terminate any prior grants of the rights to their creations that were executed before January 1, 1978, regardless of the terms contained in such assignments."[86] When the statutory window of opportunity opened, the Siegel heirs wasted no time in serving *DC* with notices of termination. After attempting to reach a settlement in 2001 and 2002, negotiations broke down, resulting in this epic, labyrinthine decision from the California District Court. The court had three fundamental questions to resolve (and ten sub-questions!): (1) Were the termination notices valid and enforceable? (2) Did the parties' settlement negotiations result in an enforceable agreement? and (3) If the termination notices were enforceable, was there a limit to the scope of rights that could be recaptured?

What did the court say? The court recognized that the intricate statutory termination requirements were legal Kryptonite, creating "unexpected pitfalls that thwart or blunt the effort of the terminating party."[87] Just figuring out the effective date of a notice can require a historian and a calculator, and, in this case, *DC* had unearthed a Superman ad that pre-dated the debut in *Action Comics* by just 11 days, enough to be outside the "temporal reach" of the termination notices.[88] Luckily for the heirs, the "copyrightable elements" in the ad were not that extensive, so that still left plenty of rights to terminate.[89] *DC* countered that some of the work was "work made for hire" (which would mean *DC* owned the copyright from the outset), but this argument was "precluded as a matter of collateral estoppel"[90] (a fancy way of saying they had already lost that argument in a different court). *DC* tried at least four more ways to challenge the termination notices, but the court, after extensive legal and factual deliberations, was not persuaded. As for the settlement negotiations, the court did not believe the parties had ever reached an "agreement on all material terms," so there was no contract with which to resolve their dispute.[91] As the court put it, "[t]he devil, as it often is, was in the details."[92] The Siegel heirs had succeeded in recapturing many of the rights to Superman, but not all the profits: copyright terminations only apply domestically, so *DC* kept its foreign rights and, more importantly, all its foreign profits. *DC* also retained some profits from the use of Superman trademarks and from "unaltered pre-termination derivative works."[93]

The super-saga continues: In January 2013, the Ninth Circuit Court of Appeals reconsidered the question of whether the parties had created a binding settlement agreement during their negotiations in 2001 and 2002. The court concluded that a letter written on October 19, 2001, by the heirs' lawyer that said that *DC's* offer had been "accepted" was sufficient to create a binding contract despite the fact that some other important issues had yet to be resolved.[94] On remand, the District Court confirmed that the October 19 "agreement" was binding, which meant that *DC* owned all the transferred *Superman* rights.[95] But it doesn't end there...

On April 18, 2013, the California District Court tackled the last issue still on the table: whether the validated 2001 settlement agreement also covers the rights to *Superboy* as well as the ads that pre-dated *Superman's* debut in *Action Comics No. 1*. The heirs had originally filed their termination notices in 1997, but in 1998 Congress passed the Sonny Bono Copyright Term Extension Act ("CTEA")[96] which, among other things, extended the termination window for pre-1978 copyright grants and allowed the heirs to serve new termination notices for the *Superboy* and *Superman* ad works. *DC* argued that their settlement agreement effectively revoked the old copyright grant and then re-granted all the rights back to them, wrenching the works out of CTEA protection. The remaining question was whether the settlement was an "agreement to the contrary" under §304(c)(5) of the 1976 Copyright Act and thus ineffective against the heirs' termination notices. Citing a case involving the rights to A.A. Milne's *Winnie the Pooh*, the court concluded that the purpose of the statutory termination rights was to permit "an author's heirs to use the increased bargaining power conferred by the imminent threat of statutory termination to enter into new, more advantageous grants."[97] In the court's view, the heirs entered negotiations with *DC* with full knowledge of their new CTEA termination rights, used them to their advantage, and the resulting settlement agreement was exactly the "kind of renegotiation... intended by Congress."[98]

In the end, pretty much everything the California District Court gave the heirs in 2008 was taken away five years later. But keep in mind, under the 2001 settlement agreement, the heirs still get a $2 million advance, a $1 million bonus, $500,000 per year for ten years, and a 6% royalty share of gross revenues—that's quite a consolation prize.

Why is this case important? A successful termination of a copyright assignment can be a perilous and technically confounding process. That said, for many comic creators who make bad deals they come to regret, that second bite of the apple can be very sweet indeed.

Notes

1 Special thanks to Matt Tynan, Esq. for his hard work on this section, and to Sheafe B. Walker, Esq. for his work on early drafts of these summaries.
2 *Detective Comics v. Bruns Publications*, 111 F.2d 432, 433 (2nd Cir. 1940).
3 *Detective Comics v. Bruns Publications*, 111 F.2d 432, 433 (2nd Cir. 1940)
4 *Detective Comics v. Bruns Publications*, 111 F.2d 432, 433 (2nd Cir. 1940) ("Perhaps the periodicals of the complainant are foolish rather than comic... ").
5 *Detective Comics v. Bruns Publications*, 111 F.2d 432, 433 (2nd Cir. 1940) ("Perhaps the periodicals of the complainant are foolish rather than comic... ").
6 *Detective Comics v. Bruns Publications*, 111 F.2d 432, 433 (2nd Cir. 1940) ("Perhaps the periodicals of the complainant are foolish rather than comic... ").
7 *National Comics Publications v. Fawcett Publications, 93 F. Supp. 349, 355* (S.D.N.Y. 1950).
8 *National Comics Publications v. Fawcett Publications, 93 F. Supp. 349, 355* (S.D.N.Y. 1950).
9 *National Comics Publications v. Fawcett Publications, 93 F. Supp. 349, 355* (S.D.N.Y. 1950) at 359.
10 *National Comics Publications v. Fawcett Publications*, 191 F.2d 594, 597 (2d Cir. 1951).
11 *National Comics Publications v. Fawcett Publications*, 191 F.2d 594, 597 (2d Cir. 1951) at 601.
12 *National Comics Publications v. Fawcett Publications*, 191 F.2d 594, 597 (2d Cir. 1951) at 603.
13 *Netzer v. Continuity Graphic Associates, Inc.*, 963 F.Supp. 1308, 1313 (S.D.N.Y. 1997).
14 *Netzer v. Continuity Graphic Associates, Inc.*, 963 F.Supp. 1308, 1313 (S.D.N.Y. 1997).
15 17 USC §507(b).
16 *Netzer v. Continuity Graphic Associates, Inc.*, 963 F.Supp. at 1318 (citing *Cada v. Baxter Healthcare Corp.*, 920 F.2d 446, 451 (7th Cir.1990)).
17 *Netzer v. Continuity Graphic Associates, Inc.*, 963 F.Supp. at 1318 (citing *Cada v. Baxter Healthcare Corp.*, 920 F.2d 446, 451 (7th Cir.1990)).
18 *Netzer v. Continuity Graphic Associates, Inc.*, 963 F.Supp. at 1318 (citing *Cada v. Baxter Healthcare Corp.*, 920 F.2d 446, 451 (7th Cir.1990)) at 1323.
19 *Netzer v. Continuity Graphic Associates, Inc.*, 963 F.Supp. at 1318 (citing *Cada v. Baxter Healthcare Corp.*, 920 F.2d 446, 451 (7th Cir.1990)) at 1325.
20 *Netzer v. Continuity Graphic Associates, Inc.*, 963 F.Supp. at 1318 (citing *Cada v. Baxter Healthcare Corp.*, 920 F.2d 446, 451 (7th Cir.1990)) at 1324 (citing *Fairley v. Peekskill Star Corp.*, 83 A.D.2d 294, 296 (2d Dept.1981) for the proposition that under New York law, a statement is only defamatory if it "tend[s] to expose one to public hatred, shame, obloquy, contumely, odium, contempt, ridicule, aversion, ostracism, degradation or disgrace, or to induce an evil opinion of one in the minds of right-thinking persons, and to deprive one of their confidence and friendly intercourse in society.").
21 *Netzer v. Continuity Graphic Associates, Inc.*, 963 F.Supp. at 1318 (citing *Cada v. Baxter Healthcare Corp.*, 920 F.2d 446, 451 (7th Cir.1990)) at 1326.
22 *Netzer v. Continuity Graphic Associates, Inc.*, 963 F.Supp. at 1318 (citing *Cada v. Baxter Healthcare Corp.*, 920 F.2d 446, 451 (7th Cir.1990)) at 1327.
23 *Hogan v. DC Comics*, 48 F.Supp.2d 298, 308 (S.D.N.Y. 1999).
24 *Hogan v. DC Comics*, 48 F.Supp.2d 298, 308 (S.D.N.Y. 1999).

25 *Hogan v. DC Comics*, 48 F.Supp.2d 298, 308 (S.D.N.Y. 1999) at 309.

26 *Hogan v. DC Comics*, 48 F.Supp.2d 298, 308 (S.D.N.Y. 1999) at 310–311.

27 *Hogan v. DC Comics*, 48 F.Supp.2d 298, 308 (S.D.N.Y. 1999) at 310.

28 *Hogan v. DC Comics*, 48 F.Supp.2d 298, 308 (S.D.N.Y. 1999) at 311–312.

29 *Hogan v. DC Comics*, 48 F.Supp. 2d 298, 311 (S.D.N.Y. 1999), citing to *CK Co. v. Burger King Corp.*, 92 Civ. 1488, 1994 WL 533253, at *8 (S.D.N.Y. Sept. 30, 1994).

30 *Hogan v. DC Comics*, 48 F.Supp. 2d 298, 311 (S.D.N.Y. 1999), citing to *CK Co. v. Burger King Corp.*, 92 Civ. 1488, 1994 WL 533253, at *8 (S.D.N.Y. Sept. 30, 1994) at 314.

31 *Charles Atlas, Ltd. v. DC Comics*, 112 F.Supp. 2d 330, 331 (S.D.N.Y. 2000).

32 *Charles Atlas, Ltd. v. DC Comics*, 112 F.Supp. 2d 330, 331 (S.D.N.Y. 2000) at 333.

33 *Charles Atlas, Ltd. v. DC Comics*, 112 F.Supp. 2d 330, 331 (S.D.N.Y. 2000) at 332–333.

34 15 USC §1125(a), (c).

35 *Charles Atlas*, 112 F.Supp. 2d at 336.

36 *Charles Atlas*, 112 F.Supp. 2d at 336 at 337 (citing Cliffs Notes, Inc. v. Bantam Doubleday Dell Publishing Group, Inc., 886 F.2d 490, 494 (2d Cir.1989)).

37 *Charles Atlas*, 112 F.Supp. 2d at 336 at 338.

38 *Charles Atlas*, 112 F.Supp. 2d at 336 at 338.

39 This New York District Court used the eight-factor *Polaroid* test from *Polaroid Corp. v. Polarad Electronics Corp.*, 287 F.2d 492, 495 (2d Cir.1961). The 9th Circuit courts prefer the very similar *Sleekcraft* test from *AMF Inc. v. Sleekcraft Boats*, 599 F.2d 341 (9th Cir. 1979).

40 *Charles Atlas*, 112 F. Supp.2d at 339–340.

41 *Marvel Characters, Inc. v. Simon*, 310 F.3d 280, 283 (2nd Cir. 2002).

42 17 USC §304(c).

43 *Marvel Characters, Inc. v. Simon*, 310 F.3d at 285.

44 17 USC §304(c), 304(c)(5).

45 *Marvel Characters, Inc. v. Simon*, 310 F.3d at 290.

46 *Marvel Characters, Inc. v. Simon*, 310 F.3d at 290 at 291.

47 Cal. Civ. Code §3344.

48 *Watts v. Frito-Lay, Inc.*, 978 F.2d 1093, 1098 (9th Cir. 1992).

49 *Winter v. DC Comics*, 30 Cal.4th 881, 886 (2003).

50 *Winter v. DC Comics*, 30 Cal.4th 881, 886 (2003) at 885.

51 *Winter v. DC Comics*, 30 Cal.4th 881, 886 (2003) at 885

52 *Winter v. DC Comics*, 30 Cal.4th 881, 886 (2003) at 888.

53 *Winter v. DC Comics*, 30 Cal.4th 881, 886 (2003) at 890.

54 *Winter v. DC Comics*, 30 Cal.4th 881, 886 (2003) at 889.

55 *Winter v. DC Comics*, 30 Cal.4th 881, 886 (2003) at 892.

56 In one famous example cited by the court, the owner of the rights to *The Three Stooges* successfully sued an artist who had sold T-shirts with literal depictions of the comedy trio. *Comedy III Productions, Inc. v. Gary Saderup, Inc.* 25 Cal.4th 387, 396, (2001).

57 "Legal Claws Bared Over a Pussycat"—the N.Y. Times used this memorable description of one of DeCarlo's suits. Leslie Eaton, *Legal Claws Bared Over a Pussycat; Josie's Artist Claims Ownership in Suit Against Archie Comics*, N.Y. Times (Feb. 19, 2001).

58 *Archie Comic Publications, Inc. v. DeCarlo*, 258 F.Supp. 2d 315, 328 (S.D.N.Y. 2003).
59 *Archie Comic Publications, Inc. v. DeCarlo*, 258 F.Supp. 2d 315, 328 (S.D.N.Y. 2003).
60 17 USC §101(2).
61 17 USC §101(2).
62 *Gaiman v. McFarlane*, 360 F.3d 644, 649 (7th Cir. 2004).
63 *Gaiman v. McFarlane*, 360 F.3d 644, 649 (7th Cir. 2004) at 650.
64 *Gaiman v. McFarlane*, 360 F.3d 644, 649 (7th Cir. 2004) at 651.
65 17 USC §101.
66 *Gaiman v. McFarlane*, 360 F.3d at 657.
67 *Gaiman v. McFarlane*, 360 F.3d at 658.
68 *Gaiman v. McFarlane*, 360 F.3d at 659.
69 *Gaiman v. McFarlane*, 360 F.3d at 659.
70 *Gaiman v. McFarlane*, 360 F.3d at 661.
71 *Gaiman v. McFarlane*, 360 F.3d at 657.
72 See *Gaiman v. McFarlane*, 2010 WL 897364 (W.D.Wis. March 12, 2010).
73 17 USC §304(c)(1).
74 17 USC §304(c)(1).
75 *Marvel Worldwide, Inc. v. Kirby*, 777 F.Supp. 2d 720, 738 (S.D.N.Y. 2011) (citing the Second Circuit test first adopted in *Brattleboro Publishing Co. v. Winmill Publishing Corp.*, 369 F.2d 565, 567–68 (2d Cir.1966)).
76 *Marvel Worldwide, Inc. v. Kirby*, 777 F.Supp. 2d 720, 738 (S.D.N.Y. 2011) (citing *Martha Graham Sch. and Dance Found., Inc. v. Martha Graham Ctr. of Contemporary Dance, Inc.*, 380 F.3d 624, 634–35 (2d Cir.2004)).
77 *Marvel Worldwide, Inc. v. Kirby*, 777 F.Supp. 2d 720, 738 (S.D.N.Y. 2011) at 737.
78 *Marvel Worldwide, Inc. v. Kirby*, 777 F.Supp. 2d 720, 738 (S.D.N.Y. 2011) at 739.
79 *Marvel Worldwide, Inc. v. Kirby*, 777 F.Supp. 2d 720, 738 (S.D.N.Y. 2011) at 750.
80 *Marvel Characters, Inc. v. Kirby*, 11–3333-CV, 2013 WL 4016875 (2d Cir. Aug. 8, 2013).
81 *Marvel Characters, Inc. v. Kirby*, 11–3333-CV, 2013 WL 4016875 (2d Cir. Aug. 8, 2013) at 725.
82 *Siegel v. Warner Bros. Entertainment Inc.*, 542 F.Supp. 2d 1098, 1112 (C.D. Cal. 2008).
83 *Siegel v. Warner Bros. Entertainment Inc.*, 542 F.Supp. 2d 1098, 1112 (C.D. Cal. 2008) at 1112 (citing Mary Breasted, *Superman's Creators, Nearly Destitute, Invoke His Spirit*, N.Y. Times, Nov. 22, 1975, at 62).
84 17 USC §304.
85 *Siegel v. Warner Bros. Entertainment Inc.*, 542 F. Supp. 2d at 1113.
86 *Siegel v. Warner Bros. Entertainment Inc.*, 542 F. Supp. 2d at 1113. The general purpose of the termination right was to give authors a "second bite of the apple" based on the understanding that "an author's ability to realize the true value of his or her work was often not apparent at its creation." *Siegel v. Warner Bros. Entertainment Inc.*, 542 F. Supp. 2d at 1113 at 1139.
87 *Siegel v. Warner Bros. Entertainment Inc.*, 542 F. Supp. 2d at 1113 at 1117.
88 *Siegel v. Warner Bros. Entertainment Inc.*, 542 F. Supp. 2d at 1113 at 1120.
89 *Siegel v. Warner Bros. Entertainment Inc.*, 542 F. Supp. 2d at 1113 at 1126.
90 *Siegel v. Warner Bros. Entertainment Inc.*, 542 F. Supp. 2d at 1113 at 1127.
91 *Siegel v. Warner Bros. Entertainment Inc.*, 542 F. Supp. 2d at 1113 at 1138.

92 *Siegel v. Warner Bros. Entertainment Inc.*, 542 F. Supp. 2d at 1113 at 1137.
93 *Siegel v. Warner Bros. Entertainment Inc.*, 542 F. Supp. 2d at 1113 at 1142–1143.
94 *Larson v. Warner Bros. Entertainment, Inc.*, 2012 WL 6822241 (9th Cir. Jan. 10, 2013).
95 *Larson v. Warner Bros. Entertainment, Inc.*, 2013 WL 1164434 (C.D. Cal. March 20, 2013).
96 17 USC §§108, 203, 301–304.
97 *Milne ex. rel. Coyne v. Stephen Slesinger, Inc.*, 430 F.3d 1036, 1046 (9th Cir. 2005).
98 *Larson v. Warner Bros. Entertainment, Inc.*, 2013 WL 1164434 at *5.

Bibliography and Suggested Reading

Battersby, G. J., & Grimes, C. W. (n.d.). *Licensing Royalty Rates*. Aspen Publishers.

Blaylock, J. (2006). *How to Self-Publish Comics*. Devil's Due Publishing.

Buck, T. C. (2003). *Business and Legal Forms for Graphic Designers*. Allworth Press & The Graphic Artists Guild.

Chisum, D. S. et al. (1996). *Understanding Intellectual Property Law*. Matthew Bender Publishing.

Corbin, A. L. (1952). *Corbin on Contracts—One Volume Edition*. West Publishing Co.

Crowell, T. A. (2011). *The Pocket Lawyer for Filmmaker* (3rd ed.). Focal Press.

Daily, J. E., & Davidson, R. M. (2012). *The Law of Superheroes*. Gotham Books.

Dunlavey, F. V. (2012). *The Comic Book History of Comics*. IDW.

Eastland, T. (Ed.) (2000). *Freedom of Expression in the Supreme Court: The Defining Cases*. Rowman and Littlefield.

Eisner, W. (1990 (Expanded Edition). *Comics & Sequential Art*. Poorhouse Press.

Elias, S. et al. (2001). *Patent, Copyright & Trademark*. Nolo Press.

Emerson, R. W. et al. (1997). *Business Law*. Barren's Educational Series, Inc.

Fishman, S. (2006). *The Public Domain: How to Find & Use Copyright-Free Writings, Music, Art & More*. Nolo Press.

Fox, C. M. (2002). *Working with Contracts: What Law School Doesn't Teach You*. PLI Press.

Gallaher, D., & Ellis, S. (2009). *High Moon*. Zuda Comics.

Graphic Artists Guild (U.S.). (2021). *Graphic Artists Guild handbook: Pricing & Ethical Guidelines* (16th ed.). Graphic Artists Guild.

Greenburger, S. L. (2011). *Stan Lee's How to Write Comics*. Watson Guptill.

Hemnes, T. M. S. (Ed.) (2000). *Intellectual Property World Desk Reference: A Guide to Practice by Country, State, and Province*. Kluwer Law and Taxation Publishers.

Hennessy, G. (2020). *The Business of Independent Comic Book Publishing*. Nightlife Publishing.

Hennessy, G. (2022). *The Business of Freelance Comic Book Publishing*. Nightlife Publishing.

Hernandez, E. A. (2013). *Set the Action*. Focal Press.

Joyce, C. et al. (2000). *Copyright Law*. Lexis Publishing.

Joyce, C., Ochoa, T. T., & Carroll, M. (2020). *Copyright Law* (11th ed.). Carolina Academic Press.

Keller, B. P. et al. (2005). *Copyright Law: A Practitioner's Guide*. PLI Press.

Leaffer, M. (1999). *Understanding Copyright Law*. Lexis Publishing.

Lieber, N. G. (2009). *The Complete Idiot's Guide to Creating a Graphic Novel* (2nd ed.). Alpha Books.
Lieto, A. (2021). *Cognitive Design for Artificial Minds*. Routledge.
Lutzker, A. P. (2003). *Content Rights for Creative Professionals*. Focal Press.
Madden, J. A. (2008). *Drawing Words and Writing Pictures*. First Second.
Madden, J. A. (2012). *Mastering Comics*. First Second.
Mancuso, A. (2002a). *Form Your Own Limited Liability Company*. Nolo Press.
Mancuso, A. (2002b). *Your Limited Liability Company, an Operating Manual*. Nolo Press.
McCarthy, T. J. (2006). *The Rights of Publicity and Privacy* (2nd ed.). Thomson West.
McCloud, S. (2005). *Making Comics*. Harper.
Neuwirth, R. J. (2023). *The EU Artificial Intelligence Act: Regulating Subliminal AI Systems*. Routledge.
Nimmer, M. B. et al. (2006). *Nimmer on Copyright*. Matthew Bender.
Nordling, L. (1995). *Your Career in the Comics*. Andrews and McMeel.
Ochoa, T. T., Ghosh, S., & LaFrance, M. (2020). *Understanding Intellectual Property Law* (4th ed.). Carolina Academic Press.
Scalera, B. (2011). *Creating Comics from Start to Finish*. Impact.
Sedge, M. (2000). *Successful Syndication*. Allworth Press.
Sergi, J. (2015). *The Law for Comic Book Creators: Essential Concepts and Applications*. McFarland.
Steingold, F. S. (2005). *The Employer's Legal Handbook*. Nolo Press.
Stiller, S. P. (2001). *Employment Law in New York*. West Group.
Stim, R. (2000a). *Copyright Law*. West Legal Studies.
Stim, R. (2000b). *Getting Permission: How to License and Clear Copyrighted Materials Online and Off*. Nolo Press.
Stim, R. et al. (2001). *Nondisclosure Agreements*. Nolo Press.
Thakur, K., Barker, H. G., & Pathan, A. K. (2024). *Artificial Intelligence and Large Language Models*. CRC Press.
Tipton, C. R. (2009). *Comic Books 101*. Impact Books.
Top, I. B. (2008). *The Designer's Guide to Marketing and Pricing*. Impact Books.
Walker, K. S. (2002). *New York Limited Liability Companies and Partnerships*. West Group.

About the Author

THOMAS A. CROWELL, ESQ.

Thomas is an attorney and law professor who counsels clients on intellectual property, and a wide range of legal issues, in media practice areas that range from publishing, film and television to merchandizing, licensing, music, video games, manufacturing, and the graphic arts. A seasoned negotiator, Thomas spearheads deals for client programming appearing on Nickelodeon, Discovery, Starz, DIY Network, TLC, SyFy, WE, Smithsonian Channel, and others. He represents several popular comic book publishing companies and many of the comic book industry's most recognized artists and writers.

He is a co-creator and the former Director from Practice of The Indie Film Clinic at the Benjamin N. Cardozo School of Law, and the Executive Director, emeritus, of the New Jersey Volunteer Lawyers for the Arts. Since 2015, Thomas has taught continuing legal education courses on comic book legal practice at NY Comic Con and other "comic cons" across the country. Thomas also teaches law school courses on copyright, intellectual property, and media law professor in New York.

An avid writer, Thomas is the series editor of the "Pocket Lawyer for…" series of legal guides for artists and the author of both *The Pocket Lawyer for Filmmakers* (Focal Press, 3 ed. 2024) and the first dedicated legal guide to the comic book industry, *The Pocket Lawyer for Comic Book Creators*. Thomas is also a contributing author to Lexis/Nexus in its entertainment law product division.

Prior to becoming an attorney, Thomas was a television reporter, producer, and production executive, and most recently, the Director of Business and Program Development for The Science Technology Network. He has written comics for Waxwork Comics, and created the 1990's kids TV show, Professor Potto's Videolabs (Awarded the National Parenting Center Seal of Approval). For more on Thomas's lectures and publications, please see his personal website at www.thomascrowell.com, or his law firm's website: www.keylightlegal.com.

EDUCATION

Benjamin N. Cardozo School of Law, J.D., *Order of the Coif*

New York University, B.F.A., Film/TV Production

More about Thomas here:

- www.thomascrowell.com
- www.keylightlegal.com
- https://tinyurl.com/tcSTAGE32
- http://tinyurl.com/mr3j9ac
- https://tinyurl.com/PL-FILMMAKERS

Index

Note: **Bold** page numbers refer to agreements.

For Product Safety Concerns and Information please contact our EU representative GPSR@taylorandfrancis.com
Taylor & Francis Verlag GmbH, Kaufingerstraße 24, 80331 München, Germany

www.ingramcontent.com/pod-product-compliance
Ingram Content Group UK Ltd.
Pitfield, Milton Keynes, MK11 3LW, UK
UKHW022113190926
475702UK00013B/1418
9781032763446